Murder, Mayhem, and Madness

A Psychological Anthropology Perspective on Forensic and Criminal Investigation

First Edition

Written and edited by Sharon K. Moses, Ph.D.
Northern Arizona University

cognella
SAN DIEGO

Bassim Hamadeh, CEO and Publisher
Peaches diPierro, Acquisitions Editor
Danielle Gradisher, Project Editor
Jessica Delia, Graphic Designer
Laura Duncan, Licensing Coordinator
Stephanie Adams, Senior Marketing Program Manager
Natalie Piccotti, Director of Marketing
Kassie Graves, Senior Vice President, Editorial
Jamie Giganti, Director of Academic Publishing

Cover image copyright © 2014 iStockphoto LP/GeorgePeters.

Printed in the United States of America.

320 South Cedros Ave., Ste. 400, Solana Beach, CA 92075

Contents

Foreword

T HIS TEXTBOOK IS NOT INTENDED AS an introductory manual for those interested in the progression of lab analyses in traditional forensic sciences or its applications. There are many introductory books in forensic studies available for students and other individuals seeking those fundamentals. This book can more accurately be described as a psychological anthropology perspective on forensic science and crime scene methodologies within the context of culture, history, and society's values as they influence the shaping of personality and identity.

The importance of this approach is in identifying the influence of culture and historical context on individuals' criminal behaviors and personalities and how these contexts also influence societies' acceptance or rejection of forensic development and/or misuse it. In understanding these contexts, we may have a more enlightened discussion on how forensic science and methodology can be improved. Investigative procedures and some high-profile cases are used to illustrate comparisons that are vital to an anthropological understanding of cultural differences and dynamics.

Psychological anthropology seeks to understand the interplay of psychological issues and social/environmental pressures *through an anthropological lens*, meaning a comparative analysis of a range of identity development factors as well as behaviors impacted by culture and history, which differentiates it from a purely psychological approach. Further, psychological anthropology aims to gain a better understanding of the social constructs of a society linked to psychological issues within its populations. Psychological anthropology is interdisciplinary, with many overlaps in other fields of study besides psychology, and in this textbook criminology also figures largely. The goal and scope of anthropology, however, is holistic in nature and is oriented toward understanding humankind in its varied iterations. Thus, though there are similarities, psychological anthropology diverges from other fields as it examines how issues of age, gender dynamics, cultural conformity, intelligence, and mental illness, just to name a few, influence personality and behavior. There are many different avenues and topics regarding the human experience one can pursue in psychological anthropology, but for the purposes of this textbook the focus will be on criminality and decisions informing forensic development and application.

Most police academies are quick to impress upon new recruits that the job of the police officer is to secure the crime scene, not to touch anything, and to leave the forensic work to the specialists! However, individuals in law enforcement and the justice system sometimes hone their careers toward criminal investigation or forensic technologies and other specialty skill sets. It is beneficial to individuals on those career paths to have more background in varied perspectives and behavioral differences than the purely enforcement-centered training most are exposed to and to be more aware of their own behavioral influences as well.

Most often, when the public hears the phrase "forensic science," the image of a scientist in a lab coat looking through a microscope at unidentified goo in a petri dish comes to mind. Coupled with this is the assumption that forensic sciences are all "pure" sciences and that only natural and physical sciences count because they are irrefutable and absolute. The recent unprecedented and impressive resolution to decades-long unsolved crimes, such as the identification of the Golden State Killer, Joseph James DeAngelo Jr., through familial genetics and DNA genealogy databases, has contributed to this impression and made it the latest forensic darling. This book does not challenge those forensic sciences or the fact that they are rooted in scientific truths and are highly successful in their use, but neither does it mean they are inviolate. In actuality, forensic science is inherently multidisciplinary, drawing from a vast array of sciences both social and natural, and involves specialized skills that can contribute meaningfully to solving crime.

Studies indicate that approximately 24 percent of wrongful convictions are based upon so-called forensic evidence. How is it that a forensic science meant to produce more accuracy and objectivity can lead to such an egregious result? There is a need to address the general misconception that forensic science is infallible. For those going into law enforcement or who wish to contribute to the criminal justice system, this is perhaps a neglected area of study. From 1989 to 2020, the Innocence Project has *fully exonerated 375 wrongful convictions* of individuals who were convicted based upon forensic evidence—of those, 21 individuals were on death row awaiting execution ("DNA Exonerations," 2020)!

It is undeniable that human beings and their personal experiences and views are influential in the decision-making and process of applying forensic science to evidence. Yes, there is training to counteract against obvious biases and stereotyping among those of us who work on forensic applications and crime scene investigations. But there are also more subtle underpinnings not necessarily perceived or defined as bias that motivate our decision-making and actions of which we are not always consciously aware. Each of us is the sum of our lived experiences, based upon our backgrounds, identities, and communities. Unawareness of how and why we "tick" the way we do is perhaps the most difficult obstacle to overcome.

Unfortunately, the human aspect of forensic study has too often been ignored, dismissed, or overshadowed by the myth of forensic incontrovertibility. The public expects perfection or the "CSI effect," as some refer to it, and clings to truth-bending (usually very inaccurate or nonexistent) notions and romanticization of forensic science presented by popular entertainment. The truth of the matter is, most crimes are solved by the good old-fashioned hard work of law enforcement and investigators who spend hours, weeks, or even years interviewing, researching, and collecting evidence, then putting it all together, *based upon both their individual decisions and forensic methodologies*.

Forensic science plays a role, when possible, but there are limits even in the best of circumstances due to the nature of the evidence, the cost, and the applicability. Compromised crime scenes due to contamination, missed evidence, lost evidence, failure to follow protocols, and lax documentation are the nightmare of all law enforcement and subsequently of the district attorney who must ultimately decide whether to bring a case to trial based upon the likelihood of a successful prosecution. The average cost of homicide cases in America easily falls into the $50,000 and up range. Costs can escalate further into the tens of millions for the more complex cases with all the judicial and legal services and fees included (DiBiase, 2015; Hunt, 2016; Lowrey, 2010). High-profile trials of serial killers are a category unto themselves, and the American taxpayer can look forward to providing double- and triple-digit millions to prosecute them and bring out all the forensic evidence to make the case ironclad (Lowrey, 2010).

The Innocence Project, a national organization that seeks to overturn wrongful convictions of the innocent through use of DNA and other evidentiary material, has found that an average of 52 percent of the cases they take on had utilized evidence that was subjected to false or questionable forensic applications, misleading or incorrect interpretations, or a failure to adequately communicate to the jury the limitations of the forensic science utilized ("Overturning Wrongful Convictions," n.d.). Hair analysis, comparative bullet lead analysis, arson versus accidental fire analysis (*Chicago Tribune*, 2006), and bloodstain pattern analysis (Criminal Legal News, 2022)—all once thought to be indisputable in the world of forensics—are now challenged by the National Academy of Sciences (2004) and found unreliable under certain circumstances, and which can be subjectively driven.

"Subjectively driven" is another way of saying that human beings influence the selection process, applications chosen or dismissed, and finally the analysis and interpretation of forensic sciences and crime scene investigation practices. To truly understand the role of forensic science in our criminal justice system, we must first acknowledge that, *while the science itself may be objective, there is no such thing as a completely impartial scientific application or interpretation*. Forensic science in the traditional sense is based upon natural and physical laws about our world that dictate what can and can't be proven materially. However, human influence cannot be disregarded when the facts do not reconcile contradictions that are present, particularly when forensic evidence has been incorrectly used or misrepresented to convict 24 percent of the time. We must be willing to recognize the role human beings play even in our scientific endeavors. It is imperative that individuals who have set their sights on going into forensic and crime scene investigation–oriented careers understand the depth of responsibility they are undertaking and have the foresight to understand that social sciences cannot be artificially and completely removed from a very human system.

An analogy may help to clarify this concept. Think of the world of statistics. No one would question statistics is based upon hard values (numbers) that represent variables in a pattern search. Yet *how* we choose to define the variables also establishes the trajectory of the outcomes. *What* we choose to examine for patterns is also based upon personal preference, past experiences of success, and so on. Human beings are creatures of habit and practice, but there are times when circumstances and contexts do not easily align with fact-finding methods (protocols) that have been established. And yet, the evidence may be subjected to certain methods anyway, resulting in a skewed outcome. Human beings and their potential vagaries are present all along the path of forensic work. Understanding how we got here improves awareness and a more realistic sense of what forensic science can do as well as its limitations.

There are many fields that contribute to forensic work that do not rely solely upon lab analysis and yet are effective as aids to law enforcement. They are helpful in fleshing out the context of a crime through understanding motivations, utilizing technical skills such as mapping and documentation of crime scene and movement patterns, GPS, LiDAR, and multiple ways of pursuing identification of victims and offenders. Examples include forensic psychology, forensic archaeology and anthropology, geographic and environmental profiling, forensic digital and computer technology, challenged documents analysis, forensic accounting, forensic art and reconstructions, and analysis of social media platforms. These and other aspects of forensic work are not part of natural or physical science analyses, but some may be hybrid forms that combine hard science with social science. Not all are considered admissible in court as stand-alone evidence because they employ varied levels of subjectivity. Yet, these methods are unquestionably useful in the apprehension and identification of individuals involved in a criminal case. And lest we forget, "subjectively driven" theories about crimes are a factor even in the best of circumstances, because human beings also rely on their own judgment and intuitive understanding of what they see, rightly or wrongly. Skill sets often draw from both hard sciences and social sciences before any material even reaches a lab. To artificially exclude all things social science–oriented would be to deny the human side of the forensic equation in putting together a contextual understanding of a criminal case.

I hope this book will help illuminate some of the subtleties less often explored and raise awareness about the trajectory of forensic science and human foibles along the way for a better-informed population, particularly among those going into criminal justice, forensic, or anthropological work and their related fields.

Chapter Themes

Chapter 1 ("I'm Not Crazy, My Mother Had Me Tested") introduces psychological anthropology and examines the shared foundations between psychology and anthropology as social science fields with beginnings in academia and the health sciences. While psychological anthropology utilizes some of the same concepts as psychology, it is more focused on the formation of identity and personality within the social norms of a given historical and social context, and a cross-cultural perspective of how human beings deviate from the "norm." Both of these factors as they apply to criminality and violent behavior are the focus of this textbook. Chapter 1 explores the arguments surrounding the insanity defense and irresistible impulses, cognitive deficits, and the spectrum of mental illnesses that qualify (or exclude) a defendant from an insanity defense. The chapter also explores personality inventory tests, "junk science," and changing evidentiary standards about crime scene evidence and mental health. Neuropsychology examines the role of forensic neuropsychologists and how certain brain conditions intersect with criminal behavior, particularly with regard to serial killers and acts of repetitive violence.

Chapter 2 ("Cadavers, Relics, and the Devil Made Me Do It") examines the historical attitudes toward violent crime in literary treatments using the 1888 Jack the Ripper case with 19th-century contemporary writers Émile Zola (1890, *La Bête humaine*—or *The Beast Within*), Bram Stoker, and Robert Louis Stevenson to name a few, as well as 19th-century German psychiatrist Richard von Krafft-Ebing among others in the medical community. Their perspectives are compared to contemporary writer Jane Caputi's "Age of Sex Crime" and 20th-century views. This chapter demonstrates changing values about the human body, violence, and seemingly "motiveless" criminal behavior. The concept of power as embedded within the body and its parts are also examined, as these attitudes played a significant role in delaying scientific and medical research involving human remains. Alternately, this chapter will also examine society's historical acceptance of public torture, execution, and the idea that witnessing, experiencing, and celebrating pain was necessary to maintain a sense of identity with society.

Chapter 3 ("Cherubic Faces and Murderous Hearts: Nature Versus Nurture") revisits the conundrum of *nature versus nurture* to find the root of criminality in cases where children are the offenders in violent homicides. Social issues, culture, mental health, modern technology—all influence mental and emotional perceptions of the development of individual personality, and in some cases underly deviance. Contemporary efforts to intercede with troubled children may not offer the solution sought, but in some cases exacerbate the problem.

Chapter 4 ("Forensic Methods for the Who, What, and Where") pulls together different perspectives in social and forensic sciences and investigative techniques to identify offenders and their victims. This chapter first examines the history of evidence collection and use in aiding homicide crime scene interpretation and investigation. Social sciences play an important role in understanding offenders, as well as ascertaining their likely locations or their movements across landscapes in the commission of crime through the use of crime pattern theories such as geographic profiling and other spatial analyses. Identification of unknown human remains are also a major goal in forensic science and rely on hard sciences (biological and anatomical knowledge), but also require technical and social science skills to select meaningful ways to interpret the data and create a likeness that captures age, ethnicity, and unique facial nuances (think Elvis Presley's lopsided smile) that can aid law enforcement or help with identification.

Chapter 5 (**"A Woman's Touch: When Women Kill"**) examines the social and cultural backgrounds and interpersonal relationships of women who have committed homicide, whether as single homicide events or in a serial murder context with partner(s). There are similarities and notable differences between males and females who commit homicide. Cultural constructs of gender and expectations of behavior assigned to those constructs impact female identity and development of personality. What factors can alter behaviors toward extreme violence in women who have no prior breach of law and social norms? What factors enhance the shift toward extreme behavior, and how do they differ in women than men? Understanding that difference provides valuable insight on approaches to crime scene investigation.

Chapter 6 (**"Will the Real Serial Killer Please Stand Up? Popular Culture, Murderabilia, and Commercialization of Homicidal Violence"**) explores how contemporary popular culture influences public perceptions of homicide and violent crime and may also contribute to an offender's view of themselves and their criminal behavior in the construction of their own identity. Commercialization and ethical arguments are presented because they also impact policy making and work to maintain a cultural line dividing what is acceptable from what is not.

Chapter 1

I'm Not Crazy, My Mother Had Me Tested

FIGURE 1.1 Photo of James Parsons (Sheldon of the *Big Bang Theory* TV sitcom)

INTRODUCTION TO CHAPTER 1

Psychological anthropology shares its roots with the field of psychology, but with certain differences. Cross-cultural understanding of the development of personality and identity as influenced by historical context and culture is the main aspect that differentiates psychological anthropology from a purely psychological approach. However, both social sciences focus on understanding humanity, and so aspects of both fields overlap. The article by Eller (2019) points out this shared foundation between psychology and anthropology. He emphasizes how the hybrid field of psychological anthropology contributes significantly our understanding of human behavior in different contexts by not separating the cultural from the biological aspects of human behavior.

The concept of *mental competence* is important in our justice system and has roots in Britain's seminal nineteenth-century case of Daniel McNaghten. The McNaghten case helped to define the mental competency of an offender and acknowledged the difference between those aware of their actions and consequences and those who were not, prescribing a more equitable punishment or a treatment plan based upon that understanding. But in the aftermath of implementing the McNaghten Rule, we also see nineteenth-century issues of inconsistent application despite best intentions. The article by Bradstreet and Hill (2011) demonstrates this effectively with two different outcomes of two very similar cases wherein mental competency was an issue. They illustrate the inconsistency with which the concept was perceived and applied and discuss the resultant sentencing disparity for the offenders. The article goes further to explore why this occurred. Meanwhile, the public perception of the insanity defense as an overused legal loophole that sets criminals free to society's detriment persists even today.

Sweet et al.'s (2018) discussion of neuropsychology provides a general understanding of how injury and trauma are significant in the evaluation of competency and general standards, an established process by which evidence can be presented in court. As the criminal justice system evolved with the advent of twentieth-century forensic technology, defining an "expert" and the standards for accepting expert testimony also evolved, with a focus on weeding out "junk" or pseudosciences that had previously been accepted but were no longer perceived as acceptable due to changing cultural expectations.

It is important to remember that while there were strides forward in updating standards for evidence acceptability, cultural and social conformity to old, ingrained ideas about responsibility did not completely disappear overnight. Ingrained beliefs about "common sense" and right and wrong remained obstacles in the face of certain forensic and scientific developments in the early twentieth century, such as paternity tests. Essentially, by the 1920s, blood tests (DNA did not arrive on the scene until 1988) could eliminate men of certain blood types that did not match the children for whom they were being sued for child support (Williams, 2019). Even if the blood test itself could not yet prove who the biological father was, it could certainly prove who was *not*. And yet, juries often chose to ignore the science and declare a male as the father anyway under the early twentieth-century mindset that a woman "knew best" who the father of her child was and should be taken at her word. This was also further codified by laws stating that one did not actually have to be a biological father to be held accountable for a child's support. One only needed to have had a familial relationship with the mother or the child at some point—a very vague definition by any standard, used to legitimize this nonscientific and not-always-fair assessment.

Finally, serial killers have long been a topic of public interest for their often gruesome and sensationalist crimes. Strangers as victims of choice add to the mystery of why serial killers do what they do and defy most people's understanding of homicidal motivations. Studies indicate that the majority opinion among the public is that serial killers must be "insane," since their motivations are inexplicable and heinous. The truth of the matter is that they are not, by legal definition, insane.

Even though serial killers only account for 1 percent of homicides per year in the United States, their crimes frequently get more media coverage and discussion among crime and forensic science enthusiasts. For that reason, this textbook will recount some serial killer cases to help illuminate some of the socio-psychological and environmental impacts on their behaviors and over the centuries, as well as how they are perceived by different cultures.

Reading 1.1

Psychology in the Formation of Anthropology

By Jack David Eller

Key figures:
Edward Burnett (E. B.) Tylor (1832–1917)
Sigmund Freud (1856–1939)
Lucien Lévy-Bruhl (1857–1939)
Franz Boas (1858–1942)
William Halse Rivers (W. H. R.) Rivers (1864–1922)

Key texts:
Primitive Culture (1871)
How Natives Think (originally published as *Les fonctiones mentales dans les sociétés inférieures*, 1910)
The Mind of Primitive Man (1911)
Totem and Taboo (1913)
Sex and Repression in Savage Society (1927)

T HE EMINENT TWENTIETH-CENTURY ANTHROPOLOGIST CLAUDE LÉVI-STRAUSS wrote that anthropology, more specifically ethnology or the description and analysis of humankind's diverse cultures, "is first of all psychology" (1966: 131). We hope that he is wrong as this would make anthropology redundant or reduce it to a branch of another discipline, and indeed, he is wrong as anthropology has a different mission and different methods than psychology. Yet anthropology and psychology have been close companions since the 1800s, when both fields began to coalesce into their modern forms. Many of the early contributors to anthropology were professional psychologists, and many early professional anthropologists asked explicitly psychological questions while borrowing psychological theories and tools, like intelligence tests and Rorschach inkblots.

Jack David Eller, "Psychology in the Formation of Anthropology," *Psychological Anthropology for the 21st Century*, pp. 7–28, 235–258. Copyright © 2019 by Taylor & Francis Group. Reprinted with permission.

Especially in the United States but also in France and Germany, psychological concerns have pervaded anthropology and continue to do so; in fact, they may do so more today than at any time since the 1970s. American cultural anthropology in particular has actually spawned a number of specializations and subdisciplines, from psychoanalytic anthropology to culture-and-personality to ethnoscience or componential analysis to cognitive anthropology and neuroanthropology. The heyday of psychologically oriented anthropology was probably the 1960s and 1970s, when Francis Hsu (1972b: 6) proposed a new and more inclusive name for the subdiscipline—*psychological anthropology.*

Over the past century, anthropology has constructed, critiqued, transcended, and sometimes strenuously rejected this sequence of psychologically focused schools or theories, but psychological anthropology is not just the story of one failed and discarded paradigm after another. First, psychological anthropology from its inception offered an alternative to other dominant approaches, such as functionalism and structural functionalism. Second, even in its failures or excesses, each wave or generation of psychological anthropological thought can claim its accomplishments and insights, and has left its mark on the discipline. Third and ultimately, psychological anthropology speaks to the deepest issues of human culture and of the human individual, recognizing the essential connection or interpenetration of the two. In this way, it seeks to fulfill the promise of anthropology to be a true science of humanity and not mere antiquarianism or the collection of cultural oddities.

Setting the Question

Everyone (well, almost everyone) can agree that culture and the individual are intimately linked: culture shapes individual thought, feeling, and behavior, while individual action produces and reproduces cultural ideas, norms, relations, and institutions. It is of course possible to investigate cultural and social phenomena without appeal to psychology—just as it is possible to study, say, mathematics without referring to brain processes, although to be sure, doing math requires brain processes—and most ethnographic research makes no specific mention of it. However, culture only exists because of certain evolved human mental capacities and tendencies and, as psychologists have also discovered, human psychological processes are not independent of culture—are not "precultural"—but are reciprocally influenced by social experience.

What then is psychological anthropology? Hsu gave a very broad answer, asserting that it includes any work

> by an anthropologist who has a good knowledge of psychological concepts or by
> a member of another discipline who has a good knowledge of anthropological

concepts [By this definition, psychologists or neuroscientists doing cross-cultural research are in effect psychological anthropologists.]

Any work that deals with the individual as the locus of culture

Any work that gives serious recognition to culture as an independent or a dependent variable associated with personality [that is, culture may be explored as cause or effect of personality factors]

Any work by an anthropologist which uses psychological concepts or techniques or by a scholar in a psychological discipline which provides directly pertinent data in forms which are useable by anthropologists.

(1972b: 2)

Among the most persistent topics in psychological anthropology, particularly in its early to mid-twentieth-century manifestation, have been

(a) the relation of social structure and values to modal patterns of child rearing, (b) the relation of modal patterns of child rearing to modal personality structure as expressed in behavior, (c) the relation of modal personality structure to the role system and projective aspects of culture [i.e. art, myth, religion, etc.], and (d) the relation of all of the foregoing variables to deviant behavior patterns which vary from one group to another,

(2–3)

including mental illness and altered states of consciousness, like dreams and trance.

Finally, acknowledging that anthropologists are not the only scholars interested in social influences on thought or in cross-cultural differences in cognition, Hsu contrasted psychological anthropology with social psychology in the following ways:

1. Psychological anthropology is cross-cultural in approach from its inception while social psychology has traditionally drawn its data from Western societies
2. Social psychology is quantitative and even, to a certain extent, experimental in orientation, while psychological anthropology has paid little attention to research designs and only lately awakened to the need for rigor in the matter of hypothesis formation and of verification
3. Psychological anthropology deals not only with the effect of society and culture on psychic characteristics of individuals (a basic concern of social psychology) but also with the role of personality characteristics in the maintenance, development, and change of culture and society.

(12–13)

Admittedly, these distinctions are not as sharp today as they were half a century ago: some psychological research is truly cross-cultural, even ethnographic, while some anthropological research is quantitative and methodologically rigorous.

Defining "Culture" and "Personality"

In the noble and ambitious calling of psychological anthropology, a major obstacle has been deciding on and defining key terms for identifying and differentiating the collective and the individual, the external and the internal, the social and the mental, variables of behavior. The initial decades of the twentieth century, as we will soon see, leaned heavily on the concepts of "culture" and "personality," although especially in regard to the latter, many rival, overlapping but not synonymous, terms vied and still vie for a place in the discourse, including "mentality," "mind," "character," "self," "person," "cognition," and so forth. Neither anthropologists nor psychologists are entirely unanimous on the meaning of these terms nor, therefore, on their interrelation.

Beginning with culture, anthropologists recognize Edward Burnett (E. B.) Tylor as probably the first scholar to give an anthropological definition of culture in his 1871 *Primitive Culture*, where the opening sentence of the book reads, "Culture or Civilization, taken in its wide ethnographic sense, is that complex whole which includes knowledge, belief, art, morals, law, custom, and any other capabilities and habits acquired by man as a member of society" (1958: 1). The noteworthy features of this definition are its reference to mental content like knowledge and belief, its emphasis on acquisition or learning, and its appreciation of social membership—and thus, potentially, the differences in knowledge, belief, and learning in different societies.

Others have defined culture in similar but varying ways. In his 1963 *Culture and Personality*, Victor Barnouw characterized it as

> the way of life of a group of people, the configuration of all of the more or less stereotyped patterns of learned behavior which are handed down from one generation to the next through the means of language and imitation.
>
> (1973: 6)

Ralph Linton, one of the champions of culture-and-personality analysis at mid-century, characterized culture as "the configuration of behavior and results of behavior whose component elements are shared and transmitted by the members of a particular society" (1945: 32), reflecting a Tylorian view; emphasizing the place of the individual in culture, Linton went on to state that "real culture" is the sum of the behavioral configurations of all the members of a society (in other words, add up all the individuals, and you have "culture"), while the "culture construct" is a creation of the anthropologist who intuits (if not invents) "the mode of the finite series of variations which are included within each of the real culture patterns and then uss this mode as a symbol for the real culture pattern" (45). In a later summary of the field, Anthony Wallace rephrased his definition of culture to designate "those ways of behavior or techniques of solving problems which, being more frequently and more closely approximated than other ways, can be said to have a high probability of use by individual members of society" (1964: 6).

Assuredly, there are many other definitions of culture, some stressing thought and others stressing action, some including material objects and others not. If anything, the situation is even more fraught when it comes to the subject of personality—for which one might substitute (and many have substituted) mind, character, or other words. Barnouw considered personality to be "a more or less enduring organization of forces within the individual associated with a complex of fairly consistent attitudes, values, and modes of perception which account, in part, for the individual's consistency of behavior" (1963: 10). Wallace defined the term simply to mean "those ways of behavior or techniques of solving problems which have a high probability of use by one individual" (1964: 7), but Linton expanded considerably on the concept; for him, personality referred to

> the organized aggregate of psychological processes and states pertaining to the individual. This definition includes the common element in most of the definitions now current. At the same time it excludes many orders of phenomena which have been included in one or another of these definitions. Thus, it rules out the overt behavior resulting from the operations of these processes and states, although it is only from such behavior that their nature and even existence can be deduced. It also excludes from consideration the effects of this behavior upon the individual's environment, even that part of it which consists of other individuals. Lastly, it excludes from the personality concept the physical structure of the individual and his physiological processes. This final limitation will appear too drastic to many students of personality, but it has a pragmatic, if not a logical, justification. We know so little about the physiological accompaniments of psychological phenomena that attempts to deal with the latter in physiological terms still lead to more confusion than clarification.
>
> (1945: 84)

For his part, Robert LeVine made an effort to unpack the term a bit, asserting that personality "is the organization in the individual of those processes that intervene between environmental conditions and behavioral responses," adding that it consists of many variables, such as "perception, cognition, memory, learning, and the activation of emotional reactions—as they are organized and regulated in the individual organism" (1973: 5). Articulating the concept further, he distinguished between "observable behavioral consistencies" which he called "personality indicators"; the underlying psychological complex of "motivational, affective, and cognitive components and multiple forms of expression" which he called "personality dispositions"; and the structured "personality organization" in which those dispositions are embedded (9).

The Relationship(s) between Culture and Personality

Given the imprecision of its two fundamental terms, it is little wonder that anthropologists (and others) disagree about the actual relationship between culture (or shared, public processes and content) and personality (or individual, internal processes and content). British social anthropologist S. F. Nadel, for instance, was quick to insist that scientists

> may take it for granted that there is some connection between the make-up of a culture and the particular personality (or personalities) of its human carriers. Yet in taking this connection to be a simple and obvious one, so simple and obvious that one can be inferred from the other, we run the risk of arguing in a circle
>
> (1951: 405)

—in fact, probably two inverse circles: one in which culture causes personality and the other in which personality causes culture.

LeVine hypothesized that observers had advocated at least five different positions on the question of the relationship between culture and personality or, more generally and less argumentatively, between culture and the individual. First were those positions that were frankly disinterested in, if not hostile to, the issue of personality/individual altogether. Among these are Alfred Kroeber's view of the "superorganic" nature of culture—that is, that culture has its own level of reality *apart from and above* the individual—and the "culturology" of Leslie White, who believed expressly that anthropology should be the study of culture and not of the individual. Alongside Kroeber and White, LeVine counted the symbolic interactionists who explained behavior in terms of meanings and situations, both external to the individual; we might add the behaviorists, who considered personality as at best a "black box" of unknown and unknowable factors and at worst an academic fiction, and at least some Marxists, who viewed individuals as less relevant than—even as mere instantiations of—class and economic relations.

Second, LeVine posited the "psychological reductionists" for whom culture could and should be explained (away?) simply in terms of personality: in the reverse of anti-personality theories, psychological processes and forces are real, and "culture" is a mere epiphenomenon of that internal world. LeVine indicted Freudian psychology as the "major contemporary reductionism" (1973: 48) for claiming to find the root of sophisticated cultural matters like art and religion in child-rearing practices and, even more reductively, in psychological (or biological) drives and mental structures like the id, ego, and superego.

Ironically, this psychological reductionism was influential in anthropological studies of culture and personality, many of which took the form of LeVine's third position, which he dubbed the "personality-is-culture" view. He claimed that prominent practitioners of culture-and-personality anthropology, like Margaret Mead and Ruth Benedict, "rejected the conceptual distinction between culture and personality" (53); in an anthropological cliché, culture for them was nothing more than "personality writ large."

For a fourth contingent, including anthropologically informed psychologists and psychiatrists like Abram Kardiner, personality was intermediate between the so-called primary institutions of culture (like the family) and the secondary or more abstract cultural institutions of politics, religion, and so on. Finally, LeVine maintained that there was a fifth camp of theorists who took a "two systems" approach to culture and personality, seeing "personality and sociocultural institutions as two systems interacting with each other":

> Each system is comprised of interdependent parts and has requirements for its maintenance. Both sets of requirements make demands of individual behavior, the personality system for socially valued performance in the roles that are institutionalized in the social structure. Stability in the interaction of the two systems is attained only when their respective requirements are functionally integrated by standards of role performance that permit the individual to satisfy his psychological needs and meet sociocultural demands at the same time.
>
> (58)

Anthropologists Melford Spiro and A. Irving Hallowell are associated with this view.

In the end, LeVine represented the five models with simple equations stipulating the avowed relationship between culture (C) and personality (P):

Anti-personality	$C \rightarrow P$ (or in extreme cases, just C without any P)
Psychological reductionism	$P \rightarrow C$
Personality-is-culture	$P = C$
Personality-as-mediation	$C_1 \rightarrow P \rightarrow C_2$
Two systems	$P \rightarrow C$

(59)

While American cultural anthropology has had an abiding interest in psychological matters, British social anthropology was traditionally relatively disinterested. Strongly and overtly influenced by Émile Durkheim's sociology, British social anthropology was much more committed to "social facts" than its American counterpart. In fact, social anthropologists like Alfred Reginald (A. R.) Radcliffe-Brown doubted the utility, if not the very possibility, of studying either personality *or* culture. He asserted that one

> cannot have a science of culture. You can study culture only as a characteristic of a social system. ... If you study culture, you are always studying the acts of behavior of a specific set of persons who are linked in a social structure,
>
> (1957: 106)

rendering the mental realm irrelevant.

Physiological Psychology: Body, Race, and Mind

It is an underappreciated fact that psychology and anthropology both emerged around the same time (in the mid-to-late 1800s) and often shared practitioners but that both originally had their roots in biological and even medical sciences. Psychology, or what Gustav Fechner in 1860 deigned to call "psychophysics," initially grew out of investigations of the nervous system; other founders of the science, like Hermann von Helmholtz and Paul Broca, were also researchers in nerve and brain physiology and function, and Wilhelm Wundt (1832–1920), who founded the first psychology laboratory, attempted to measure sensory perception and thought itself (with his so-called "thought-meter") and penned a volume titled *Principles of Physiological Psychology*. The second source of early psychological exploration was mental illness, as in the work of Jean-Martin Charcot, who directed the French hospital of La Salpêtrière, where he studied not only spinal cord injuries, multiple sclerosis, and Parkinson's disease but also hypnosis and hysteria. Sigmund Freud began his career in neurology before going on to clinical psychology and ultimately his theories of mind and culture.

Anthropology was likewise conceived as a "natural science of man" before it became a cultural science. In his 1863 *Introduction to Anthropology*, Theodore Waitz asserted that the field "aspires to be the science of man in general; or, in precise terms, the science of the nature of man" (1863: 3), which should "study man by the same method which is applied to the investigation of all other natural objects" (5). Armand de Quatrefages, a nineteenth-century lecturer, explained that this meant that the anthropologist should study mankind "as a zoologist studying an animal would understand it" (quoted in Topinard 1890: 2). Paul Topinard summed up late nineteenth-century thinking when he declared that anthropology was "the branch of natural history which treats of man and the races of man" (1890: 3). Thus, anthropology was the name of the more inclusive science, including but not restricted to a branch of *ethnology* that examines the world's diverse human populations to describe their "manners, customs, religion, language, physical traits, and origins" (8–9).

More than a century previously, Carolus Linnaeus (1707–78) had inaugurated the natural-science study of humanity. In his 1740 *Systema Naturae*, he divided the human species into four subtypes, which were eventually labeled Homo europeaus, Homo afer, Homo americanus, and Homo asiaticus. Each category—or what we would today call "race"—was characterized by skin color but also by (alleged) behavioral habits and personality tendencies, often in shockingly insulting ways.

Box 1.1.2   Linnaeus's Races of Mankind

Linnaeus described his four types of humanity as:

> Homo europaeus (European/Caucasian): "white, sanguine, muscular. Hair flowing, long. Eyes blue. Gentle, acute, inventive. Covered with close vestments. Governed by laws."
>
> Homo afer (African): "black, phlegmatic, relaxed. Hair black, frizzled. Skin silky. Nose flat. Lips tumid. Women without shame. Mammae lactate profusely. Crafty, indolent, negligent. Anoints himself with grease. Governed by caprice."
>
> Homo americanus (Native American): "reddish, choleric, erect. Hair black, straight, thick; nostrils wide; face harsh; beard scanty. Obstinate, merry, free. Paints himself with fine red lines. Regulated by customs."
>
> Homo asiaticus (Asian): "sallow, melancholy, stiff. Hair black. Eyes dark. Severe, haughty, avaricious. Covered with loose garments. Ruled by opinions."
>
> (quoted in Slotkin 1965: 177–8)

For good measure, he added two purely imaginary species: Homo ferus (a hairy and mute being that walked on all fours) and Homo monstrosus (a monstrous race of nocturnal cave dwellers).

Others, writing before the dawn of modern anthropology, proposed other biological/racial schemes, like Johann Friedrich Blumenbach. In his 1770 *On the Natural Variety of Mankind*, he also announced four races—African, American, Asian, and "Caucasian," a term he introduced, later adding Malayan as a fifth entry. These races were, unsurprisingly, not only different but unequal: he judged Caucasians as both the original or "primeval" form of humanity and the most beautiful, and non-Caucasian strains were explained as a product of "degeneration" from this primary and ideal type.

The typologies or racial classifications of humans that appeared before modern anthropology and that were inherited by the discipline were purportedly based on real, empirical physical differences. Accordingly, much of nineteenth- (and even early twentieth-) century science was directed toward documenting these differences. One of the main methods of what has been called "scientific racism" was *anthropometry*, literally "man-measure." Anthropometry was and is a practice of measuring the bodies of human beings for the purpose of describing individual and collective physical characteristics—and, more importantly for many of its practitioners, of discovering the biological basis for supposed psychological differences between the races in terms of intelligence, temperament, morality, and so forth.

Many physical features were measured and cataloged, but of central importance were the ones that presumably indicated "primitiveness" or mental inferiority. For example, "facial angle" reflected the protrusion of the lower face and jaw on the assumption that more "primitive" races had more protruding faces (like dogs or monkeys), while higher races enjoyed flatter faces. Longer arms and legs also signaled primitiveness. No doubt the most important measurements were brain volume and cephalic index, the latter a ratio of the width and depth of the head. Surely, these scientists reckoned, larger brains with a higher index indicated greater intelligence and rationality. Physical traits, especially those of the head and face, were even seen as evidence of more complex and specific personality or psychological failings, such as immorality, criminality, or insanity. An entire parallel science of eugenics developed beside scientific racism, with the project to improve the intelligence and morality of the species (Figure 1.1.1).

It should not be difficult to see that this brand of physiological psychology was more (and less) than science but also what Eric Wolf (1994) pinpointed and critiqued as a "bio-moral" project, that is, a system to *justify* social inequalities—like slavery or colonial conquest—on the basis of putative biological and psychological differences and inadequacies. Social policies followed suit, from prohibiting interracial marriage to the selective sterilization

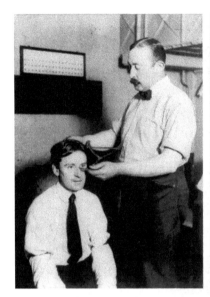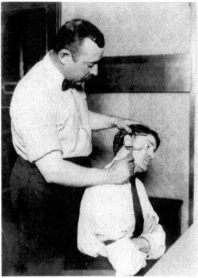

FIGURE 1.1.1   Nineteenth-century anthropometry measured human physical traits to establish differences between types (especially races) of humans; *Library of Congress*.

Box 1.1.3   Cesare Lombroso: Anthropological Criminology

Cesare Lombroso (1835–1909), a medical doctor and criminologist, devised a theory of "anthropological criminology" (or what we might call "racial profiling" today) on the basis of physical characteristics or defects that he claimed were diagnostic of deviant personality and behavior. In his learned view, criminals were throwbacks to a more primitive kind of humanity, a phenomenon that he termed "criminal atavism." Certain bodily traits were common to criminals, "primitive" humans, and prehistoric mankind, including long arms, sloping foreheads, misshapen faces and heads, and protruding faces. Such physical deformities were the visible evidence of personality or character deformities, like stupidity, immorality, impulsiveness, egotism, and cruelty. Ideally then, a criminal or other social inferior could be detected by sight and perhaps even at birth.

---

of "inferior types" to rejections of attempts to educate or uplift disadvantaged races since apparently, they were congenitally incapable of higher intellectual and moral functioning.

One example of this reasoning can be found in the work of Stanley Porteus (1883–1972), an Australian psychologist and inventor of the Porteus Maze Test of intelligence. He conducted intelligence and personality tests on "delinquent" and "feeble-minded" boys in

1915, determining that most of the boys were several years behind in their mental and moral development. He then applied his research to remote Australian Aboriginals, which he reported in a series of papers and in his 1931 book *The Psychology of a Primitive People*. Although he accepted that many of the aspects of traditional Aboriginal culture were clever adaptations to a harsh natural environment, he concluded that traditional life had left a deleterious brand on the Aboriginal mind. Mental development in Aboriginal children was normal, even rapid, early in life but was then followed by "a marked slowing-down mental development ... characteristic of the Australian race" (1933: 32). Further, they suffered from poor rote memory from listening and a lack of abstract intelligence matched only "by the abilities of the feeble-minded of our race" (34), not to mention "the common racial characteristics of indolence, shiftlessness, and lack of foresight" (1917: 38). Consequently, he predicted "the improbability of marked advancement in civilization of the Australian race" (1933: 34) since it is "very difficult indeed to educate them beyond about the fourth grade" (1917: 38).

Folk Psychology and the Question of the Primitive Mind

Although modern-day psychology is usually associated with the individual and internal/mental processes, while anthropology is assumed to concentrate on collective and public/social ones, we have seen already that this division is by no means absolute today nor was it true of the disciplines in their formative years. Not only were and are anthropologists interested in psychological questions, but psychologists were and are interested in cultural ones.

As far back as the late 1700s, historian Johann Herder (1744–1803) had suggested that each *Volk* (German for folk, people, or nation) had its own unique qualities, genius, or even soul or spirit. Herder used such phrases as *Nationalgeist* (national spirit), *Seele des Volks* (soul of the people), *Geist der Nation* (spirit of the nation), and *Geist des Volks* (spirits of the people) to capture this collective peculiarity which was, to him, inexpressible and invaluable. The spirit of a people was to be found in its art, its literature, its philosophy, its folklore, etc., depending on the particular society. This emphasis on, even obsession with, a nation's identity and cultural patrimony led directly to an interest in national or group beliefs, behaviors, and accomplishments, that is, to " culture" in the anthropological sense. This, in turn, led to an attempt to identify the group/collective processes which gave rise to national cultures, that is, a *Völkerpsychologie*, a "folk psychology" or "psychology of a people," in contrast to an "individual psychology" (Diriwachter 2004: 87–8):

> That is, the study of psychology was also to include the products of collective mental processes of peoples identified as a unified body (e.g. the Germans),

distinctly separate from others (e.g. the French). Individual psychology was limited to the focus of the capabilities of one person.

(88–9)

One of the great early psychologists became one of the great proponents of *Völkerpsychologie*: namely, Wilhelm Wundt, mentioned earlier. In an 1888 article, he defended research into national psychology:

> Just like it's the objective of psychology to describe the actuality of individual consciousness, thereby putting its elements and developmental stages in an explicatory relationship, so too is there a need to make as the object of psychological investigation the analogous genetical and causal investigations of those actualities which pertain to the products of higher developmental relationships of human society, namely the folk-communities (*Völkergemeinschaft*).
>
> (quoted 96)

However, in the case of *Völkerpsychologie*, standard (especially experimental) psychological methods would not suffice; rather, it was necessary to employ a comparative method, to do "historical comparisons," to examine the products of these collectivities and collective minds. For Wundt, then, *Völkerpsychologie* was not a strictly psychological enterprise but "in essence a social-developmental discipline: social because it predominantly moves within societal dimensions; and developmental because it also needs to examine the different steps of mental development in humans (true psychogenesis), from underdeveloped to higher cultures" (97). He even attempted to construct an outline of this historical-developmental process from "primitive man" to "the totemic era" to "the ages of heroes and gods" to "the development of humanity":

> Each stage has its own unique characteristics that mark the achievements of the group under examination. For example, while primitive man is said to be closest to nature, comparable to wild animals, the man of the totemic era is already distinguished by a realization of the possession of a soul. In fact, the totem itself is the manifestation of a soul, either the soul of an ancestor or the soul of a protective being, often in the shape of an animal.
>
> (98)

In the late 1800s and early 1900s, many scholars went beyond the notion of unique "national minds" to ponder whether all humans of all nationalities, races, and societies shared the same thought processes and mental abilities. Did "primitive peoples," in a word, think like "modern" (read: "Western") people, or did they have a decisively different (and inferior) mind? What were Western travelers and intellectuals to make of the fact that native peoples around the world seemed to believe and do things that were, to "civilized" eyes, strange, irrational, and often demonstrably false?

On one side of the debate were those who defended the *psychic unity of humankind*, that is, the position that humans everywhere had similar psychology, even if their minds produced diverging or contradictory results. One of the earliest to stake this claim was Adolf Bastian (1826–1905). After traveling around the world and spending four years in Southeast Asia in the 1850s and 1860s, he concluded that the innate and universal processes of mind generated "elementary ideas" or *Elementarkgedanken* (what Carl G. Jung, a follower of Freud, might later call "archetypes") that were found in all places and times. However, because of local historical and environmental/geographical forces, these universal ideas might be expressed differently in different populations as "ethnic" or "folk" ideas or *Völkergedanken*. For Bastian, as for Herder and Wundt, a group's folk ideas could be discovered in its folklore, art, mythology, and so on, but underneath this variation were recurring themes. One crucial implication from this perspective was the importance of conducting "investigations of the most isolated and simple societies," that is, doing what anthropologists would come to endorse as fieldwork and ethnography. Bastian was committed to the view that the ideas of "primitive" or "natural" humans "grow according to the same laws" as those of Westerners but that their "growth and decline are easier to observe, since we are looking at a limited field of observation which could be compared to an experiment in laboratory" (quoted in Penny 2002: 23).

Around the same time, an even more seminal figure was advancing a similar conclusion. In his aforementioned 1871 *Primitive Culture*, E. B. Tylor began by enunciating that "the condition of culture among various societies of mankind ... is a subject apt for the study of laws of human thought and action" (1958: 1). Surveying such disparate topics as emotion, language (including proverbs, riddles, and nursery rhymes), counting, and religion (myth, ritual, and, most famously, his concept of "animism"), he argued for the continuity of human thought, even if different groups were at different levels of development of their knowledge and understanding. For instance, Tylor reasoned that "the language of civilized men is but the language of savages, more or less improved in structure, a good deal extended in vocabulary, made more precise in the dictionary definition of words"; however, "development of language between its savage and cultured stages has been made in its details, scarcely in its principle" (445–6). Religion too, from the most rudimentary myths and ceremonies to the glories of European Christianity, revealed consistent thought processes operating below the surface. Further, refuting the scientific racism of his day, Tylor saw no reason to introduce race into the analysis of mind and action: everywhere he looked, he encountered "similarity and consistency" of "character and habit" (6), making it "both possible and desirable to eliminate considerations of hereditary varieties or races of man, and to treat mankind as homogeneous in nature, though placed in different grades of civilization" (7).

Box 1.1.4   E. B. Tylor: Psychological Origin of Religion

For Tylor, religion itself had a psychological origin. The most basic form or expression of religion in his view was belief in spiritual beings, and this idea arose as a reaction to certain mental experiences, such as dreams, visions, hallucinations, and trance or out-of-body experiences. Prehistoric individuals naturally speculated that the source of these uncanny occurrences, Tylor reasoned, was that some part of a person was separate from—even detachable from—their body, so that dreams, visions, etc. were authentic experiences by this immaterial part, perhaps of other people's immaterial parts. This disembodied component of a human being (and maybe some or all other beings) is "spirit," the first religious idea and the foundation of all subsequent religious ideas.

One other early supporter of the psychic unity position was James George Frazer (1854–1941), a student of comparative mythology and the author of *The Golden Bough*. Frazer opined that the religious beliefs and stories of all societies demonstrated common motifs (including half-human, half-divine beings and dying gods) and that those motifs were often related to cultural practices, like agriculture, or to natural phenomena, like the solstices. More, he judged that religion and magic were not so irrational after all but evinced rational if erroneous thinking; primitive (and religious) people use the same processes of thought, but they merely start from false premises and thus reach false conclusions. Later psychological anthropologist Richard Shweder put it this way: "All people are applied scientists. 'Primitives' are just not very good at it. That, in a nutshell, is Tylor's and Frazer's view of the relationship between the 'primitive' mind and the 'modern' mind" (1980: 70).

On the opposing side of the debate over diversity in human thought processes were the advocates of a distinct (if not defective) "primitive mentality," of which Lucien Lévy-Bruhl (1857–1939) is the arch-representative. In his 1910 *Les functions mentales dans les societes inferieures* (literally, "Mental Functions in Lower/Inferior Societies" but published in English under the inoffensive title *How Natives Think*), Lévy-Bruhl laid out an elaborate case for the incommensurability of the primitive and the modern mind.

Contrary to Bastian, Tylor, Frazer, and Rivers, Lévy-Bruhl bluntly asserted that "primitives perceive nothing in the same way as we do. ... Primitives see with eyes like ours, but

Box 1.1.5   Haddon and Cort: Early Study of "Primitive" Cognition and Perception

One of the assumptions, if not stereotypes, of "primitive" cognition was that native peoples, although deficient in logic, were advanced in sensory perception. It was frequently claimed that indigenous people (sadly, probably like animals) possessed highly developed senses of sight, hearing, and smell. Indeed, one of the first formal ethnographic expeditions had the express psychological mission of testing "primitive" perception. The Torres Straits Expedition of 1898 was led by Alfred Cort (A. C.) Haddon, a trained biologist and zoologist, to study the inhabitants of the islands between Australia and Indonesia. He recruited three medical doctors plus an experimental psychologist and neurologist, William Halse Rivers (W. H. R.) Rivers (1864–1922). The team collected all sorts of data during their comparatively brief sojourn in the islands, but Rivers, who had investigated color vision, optical illusions, and other aspects of perception in his psychology lab at Cambridge, seized the occasion to study the natives in regard to

> visual acuity, color vision, color blindness, after-images, contrast, visual illusions, auditory acuity, rhythm, smell and taste, tactile acuity, weight discrimination, reaction times to visual and auditory stimuli, estimates of time intervals, memory, muscular power, motor accuracy, and a number of similar topics.
>
> (Berry et al. 2002: 197)

He disproved that Torres Strait Islanders had extraordinary vision, but he did notice one tantalizing difference in visual perception. Rivers administered the Müller-Lyer illusion (see the following) to natives of Murray Island (and later to Todas of India) and found that they were less susceptible to the illusion than Westerners, that is, they judged the length of lines more accurately. Years later, although Rivers turned increasingly to anthropology and ethnographic fieldwork, he affirmed that "the ultimate aim of all studies of mankind ... is to reach explanation in terms of psychology ... by which the conduct of man, both individual and collective, is determined ... by the social structure of which every person ... finds himself a member" (1924b: 1). Indeed, today, Rivers is more celebrated in the annals of cross-cultural psychology than in anthropology.

The Müller-Lyer illusion: Westerners tend to misjudge the length of lines depending on the direction of the arrows on the lines (Figure 1.1.2).

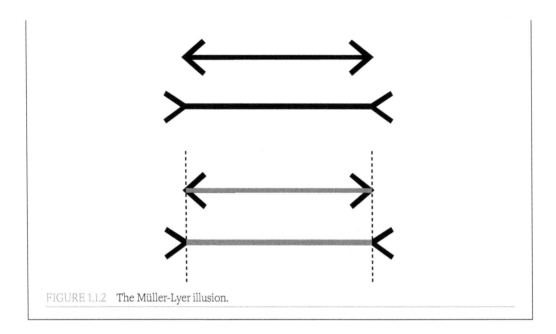

FIGURE 1.1.2   The Müller-Lyer illusion.

they do not perceive with the same minds" (1966: 30–1). He also rejected the Frazerian claim that natives were just bad scientists: myth and magic, for instance, "do not appear to originate in the desire for a rational explanation; they are the primitives' response to collective needs and sentiments which are profound and mighty and of compulsive force" (14–15). So, primitives were slaves to traditional and collective thoughts and feelings, unlike Western freethinkers. But more, those traditional and collective "representations" (as he called them, probably following Durkheim's use of the term) had certain deep flaws:

> The collective representations of primitives, therefore, differ very profoundly from our ideas or concepts, nor are they their equivalent either. On the one hand ... they have not their logical character. On the other hand, not being genuine representations, in the strict sense of the term, they express, or rather imply, not only that the primitive actually has an image of the object in his mind, and thinks it real, but also that he has some hope or fear connected with it, that some definite influence emanates from it, or is exercised upon it. ... I should say that this mental activity was a *mystic* one.
>
> (24–5)

This takes us to the essence of Lévy-Bruhl's characterization of "primitive mentality." Reality for the primitive mind, he posited, is itself mystical. Not a single being or object or natural phenomenon in their collective representations is what it appears to be to our minds. Almost everything that we perceive therein either escapes their attention or is a matter of indifference to them. On the other hand, they see many things there of which we are unconscious.

(25)

—by which he meant, indubitably, that they do not exist. Rocks, trees, and other natural objects "readily assume a sacred character in virtue of their supposed mystic power" (27), which the rational mind denies. In a word, the primitive mind was, he said explicitly, a *prelogical* mind, one that did not make all the distinctions that a logical mind can and must make. The prelogical, primitive mind, to start, is incapable of cause-and-effect thinking, sometimes failing to recognize the causal relationship between events and sometimes assuming a noncausal, magical relationship. It cannot think abstractly, and it is indifferent to contradiction. Most profoundly and problematically, it functions according to a principle that he called the "law of participation." At bottom, this means that the primitive mentality does not sufficiently distinguish between self and not-self, between one object and another object, or even between different kinds of objects or phenomena. A natural object like a tree, or a cultural object like an Australian Aboriginal *tjurunga* (a sacred board or stone, with or without incised markings), may be part of a human person—or a person in its own right. Or a physical object may have or be a spirit at the same time; as logicians say, the law of participation violates the "law of exclusion" that X cannot be not-X at the same time. Finally, the law of participation grants a kind of transmission or "communication of qualities (through transference, contact, projection, contamination, defilement, possession, in short, through a number of varied operations) which, either instantaneously or in the course of time, bring a person or a thing into participation with a given faculty" (83). Frazer had noted something similar in what he dubbed "sympathetic" and "contagious" magic: in the former case, resemblance (say, between a voodoo doll and an intended human victim) could cause an effective connection, and in the latter case, contact between two objects (say, a person and a bit of their hair or fingernail) could have the same effect. But whereas Frazer explained this as clever but faulty reasoning, Lévy-Bruhl interpreted it as a fundamental inability to comprehend how the world works.

Later in life, Lévy-Bruhl retracted his most extreme assertions about primitive mentality, acknowledging, among other things, that modern Western individuals sometimes make associations based on resemblance or contagion (e.g. talking to photographs or holding onto possessions of a departed loved one) and accepting the dual quality of certain objects (e.g. that a wafer could be a wafer and the body of Christ simultaneously). But such analysis continued on despite his retraction, as in the work of renowned psychologist Lev Vygotsky. In a collection of essays ominously titled *Ape, Primitive, Man, and Child* (Luria and Vygotsky 1992), first published in 1930, he reiterated that "primitives" suffered from lack of abstraction and metaphor in their language and thought. For that reason, they were burdened with concreteness and detail, which prevented them from reaching higher levels of literacy, numeracy, and logic. And Vygotsky made these accusations with abundant references to Lévy-Bruhl's work.

Franz Boas, Psychological Anthropologist

"One of the chief aims of anthropology is the study of the mind of man under the varying conditions of race and environment" (1901: 1), wrote Franz Boas in the opening sentence of his article "The Mind of Primitive Man." Widely regarded as the father of American cultural anthropology, Boas studied psychology (or "psychophysics") and geography before becoming a protégé of Bastian and turning to anthropology in the waning years of the nineteenth century. He was also a tireless critic of racial explanations of cultural and psychological differences, especially in three publications between 1901 and 1911—the essay cited earlier, a book by the same title, and an article conspicuously called "Psychological Problems in Anthropology" (Boas 1910).

In the earliest of these writings, Boas weighed the two competing options—that possibly "the minds of different races show differences in organization; that is to say, the laws of mental activity may not be the same for all minds" or that

> the organization of mind is practically identical among all races of man; that mental activity follows the same laws everywhere, but that its manifestations depend upon the character of individual experience that is subjected to the action of these laws

> (1901: 2)

before coming down solidly on the experiential side. Forcefully, he declared that "there can be no doubt that in the main the mental characteristics of man are the same all over the world" (3). Granting that there might be differences in brain size between the races, he still maintained repeatedly in the article that the "functions of the human mind are common to the whole of humanity" (5), even if "the degree of development of these functions may differ somewhat among different types of man" (6). But where there are differences between "primitive" minds and "civilized" ones, his position was firmly that any dissimilarity "in the mode of thought of primitive man and of civilized man seems to consist largely in the difference of *character of the tradition material with which the new perception associates itself*" (7, emphasis added). In other words, it is *culture*, the shared and transmitted *content* of thought—or, in simple terms, experience—rather than the underlying *processes* of thought that separate various populations of humans. For a cautious anthropologist,

> the development of *culture* must not be confounded with the development of *mind*. Culture is an expression of the achievements of the mind, and shows the cumulative effects of the activities of many minds. But it is not an expression of the organization of the minds constituting the community, which may in no way differ from the minds of a community occupying a much more advanced stage of culture.
>
> (11, emphasis in original)

Boas reiterated these points in his 1910 essay, stipulating first that anthropology "deals with the biological and mental manifestations of human life as they appear in different races and in different societies" (1910: 371). The three questions of the science, consequently, concerned the origin of "human types" (the eventual province of physical or biological anthropology), the historical development of culture (the realm of cultural anthropology), and "the psychological laws which control the mind of man everywhere, and that may differ in various racial and social groups" (371). Indeed, he charged what he called "anthropological psychology" with the duty "of looking for the common psychological features, not in the outward similarities of ethnic phenomena, but in the similarity of psychological processes so far as these can be observed or inferred" (375–6). He did not discount all deviations between "primitive" and "civilized" mentality: for instance, he allowed that ideas and concepts are separated or combined in a "peculiar manner" in the mind of "primitives" (376) and that for them, concepts and categories "have never risen into consciousness, and that consequently their origin must be sought not in rational, but in entirely unconscious processes of the mind" (377)—a foreshadowing of the influence of Freud in anthropology (see the following and later chapters). Ultimately, Boas pronounced, the "primary object of these researches would be the determination of the fundamental categories under which phenomena are classified by man in various stages of culture" (377).

Boas's position is most fully articulated in his 1911 book *The Mind of Primitive Man*, a significant portion of which is dedicated to the speciousness of race. Recognizing that "in many quarters the popular view still prevails that all psychological tests reveal an organically determined mentality," or more specifically, "a biological oriented psychology" (1938: 30) and most odiously, a race-based psychology, he set about to dismantle this claim completely. "Ethnological material," he said, "does not favor the view that different human types have distinct personalities," refuting the contention that "the habits of life and cultural activities are to any considerable extent determined by racial descent" (129). Simply put,

> personality so far as it is possible to speak of the personality of a culture will *depend upon outer conditions that sway the fate of the people*, upon its history, upon powerful individuals that arise from time to time, upon foreign influences.
>
> (129–30, emphasis added)

Boas went so far as to address particular planks in the "primitive mentality" platform (mentioning Lévy-Bruhl by name), such as lack of impulse control, inability to concentrate, and prelogical thought. On the subject of impulse control, Boas insisted that taboos, gender segregation, and other cultural restrictions were proof of curbs on impulsiveness, while allegedly weak concentration could be dismissed as boredom with the artificial situations and incessant questions posed by fieldworkers. As for the prelogical quality of "primitive" thought, Boas wrote,

> This conclusion is reached not from a study of individual behavior, but from the traditional beliefs and customs of primitive people. It is believed to explain the identification of man and animal, the principles of magic and the beliefs in the efficacy of ceremonies. It would seem that if we disregard the thinking of the individual in our society and pay attention only to current beliefs that *we should reach the conclusion that the same attitudes prevail among ourselves that are characteristic of primitive man.*
>
> (135, emphasis added)

This did not mean that no psychological or cognitive differences between human groups exist at all but that such differences as we can verify empirically are to be attributed to "individuals and family lines" (138) and, in the final analysis, to experiential (including cultural) influences and not to the mind or brain.

Sigmund Freud, Anthropological Psychologist

> It is largely due to Sigmund Freud that we understand the importance of these forgotten incidents which remain a living force throughout life the more potent, the more thoroughly they are forgotten. Owing to their lasting influences many of the habits of thought and traits of personality which we are all too ready to interpret as due to heredity are acquired under the influence of

the environment in which the child spends the first few years of its life. All observations on the force of habit and the intensity of resistance to changes of habit are in favor of this theory.

(Boas 1938: 143)

So stated Boas in 1911, when Freudian theory was still relatively new and, frankly, unfinished. Sigmund Freud (1856–1939) had published his first major book, *The Interpretation of Dreams*, only in 1900, and most of his major theoretical statements were yet to come. Nevertheless, his impact was clearly already felt in anthropology, and this impact would persist for decades—for many anthropologists and other social scientists, to this very day.

Freud's thinking unfolded gradually over the course of more than four decades, so it is difficult if not incorrect to assert what *the* psychoanalytic theory was. He began his career, like many other psychologists in the late 1880s, in neurology and medicine, doing experimental/ surgical, clinical, and academic work. In 1885, he apprenticed under Charcot in France (see earlier), where Freud learned of the therapeutic value of hypnosis. He incorporated the technique into his treatment of patients in Vienna, developing what one of his patients called a "talking cure," during which they would discuss their symptoms and feelings while hypnotized. Soon abandoning hypnosis in favor of what he named "free association" or speaking freely about whatever was on their minds, he came to the determination that their psychological complaints seemed to be tied to thoughts of which they were unconscious or to experiences that they had actively forgotten (referred to as "repression").

By the first years of the twentieth century, Freud had arrived at what he called psychoanalysis, which he regarded as effective for treating neurosis and especially "hysteria," which could often be explained and cured as a translation of psychological or emotional trauma into physical symptoms like paralysis or blindness. The unknown, forgotten, or repressed mental content could also express itself in dreams (and later, he found, in jokes, slips of the tongue [hence, "Freudian slips"], and all the little and innocent behaviors that he called in a 1901 book "the psychopathology of everyday life"), leading to his landmark 1900 study of dreams.

It was in *The Interpretation of Dreams* that many of Freud's bedrock concepts were enunciated. A preliminary structure of the mind was proposed, featuring a conscious, preconscious, and unconscious component. He also identified two distinct mental processes operating in all people, primitive and civilized alike. The first was the *primary process*, functioning on the basis of wish fulfillment, pleasure-seeking and pain-avoidance, and "magical thinking," that is, the mind believing that merely thinking or wishing makes it so. The primary process is the principle of the unconscious and therefore of children (and, he and others would go on to say, of "primitives" and neurotics). The *secondary process*, a more mature way of thinking, works on what Freud would eventually call the *reality principle*, understanding cause and effect, and adapting itself to the (sometimes painful) realities of life. Finally, as he had opined in writings for several years, most overtly his 1898 "Sexuality in the Aetiology of Neuroses," at the foundation of much psychopathology, if not of most ordinary life, was sexuality—including childhood sexuality, a rather shocking declaration at the time.

Hence, Freud summarized his analysis of dreams by announcing that the "interpretation of dreams is the royal road to a knowledge of the unconscious activities of mind" (1965: 647). This was about all that was known of Freudian theory at the time of Boas's essays and book on mind. It would not be until 1915 that Freud would offer his further thoughts on instincts; he would only transcend his ideas about the pleasure principle, suggesting a "death" or disintegration principle, in 1920, and his now-familiar mental structure of ego, id, and superego would not be formulated until 1923. Before those books, though, Freud would show another dimension of his psychological curiosity and of the potential of psychoanalysis by applying his models to cultural phenomena, such as art, religion, and the very origins of society.

Specifically, his *Totem and Taboo*, subtitled "Some Resemblances/Points of Agreement between the Mental Lives of Savages and Neurotics" and released in 1913, would reverberate through anthropology and the social sciences. On the first page of that epochal book, Freud surmised that in contemporary "primitive" or "savage" peoples, we see "a well-preserved picture of an early stage of our own development," and if so,

> a comparison between the psychology of primitive peoples, as it is taught by social anthropology, and the psychology of neurotics, as it has been revealed by psycho-analysis, will be bound to show numerous points of agreement and will throw new light upon familiar facts in both sciences.
>
> (2001: 1–2)

For this purpose, as his title indicates, he chose two characteristic notions from "primitive" societies—totems and taboos—and naturally and necessarily, he borrowed data from anthropologists, such as James Frazer's 1910 *Totemism and Exogamy*; Andrew Lang's 1905 *The Secret of the Totem*; and, most notably, Baldwin Spencer and F. J. Gillen's 1899 *The Native Tribes of Central Australia*, the latter of which would also be crucial for Durkheim's contemporaneous sociological theory of religion.

Of all primitive taboos, the one most interesting to Freud was the incest taboo, which he seized upon to imagine the very origin of human society itself. Evaluating and rejecting sociological and competing psychological theories for the existence of totemism (that is, the association of individuals and groups with a particular plant and animal species, which is frequently subjected then to taboos against killing or eating that species), Freud advanced a view based on the rule of exogamy (i.e. marrying outside one's own family or group), which is nothing more than an elaboration of the incest taboo. But why there should be such a deep and universal "horror of incest" (2001: 144) remained to be explained. The only possible answer for Freud was something equally if not more deep and universal, namely, the Oedipus complex. Named after a character in ancient Greek literature, Freud's Oepidus complex maintains that every male child secretly desires his mother and would if he could kill and replace his father; at the same time, the boy fears that his father will kill or at least castrate him (the equally infamous "castration anxiety").

Freud reasoned that the Oedipus complex is not only at the root of individual (male) psychology but at the root of human sociality itself. By a circuitous route, he concluded that the totem animal is a substitute for a prehistoric father and that all of society stems from an original Oedipal drama. In the beginning, before there was orderly society,

> there is a violent and jealous father who keeps all the females for himself and drives away his sons as they grow up. ... One day the brothers who had been driven out came together, killed and devoured their father and so made an end of the patriarchal horde. United, they had the courage to do and succeeded in doing what would have been impossible for them individually. (Some cultural advance, perhaps command over some new weapon, had given them a sense of superior strength.) Cannibal savages as they were, it goes without saying that they devoured their victim as well as killing him. The violent primal father had doubtless been the feared and envied model of each one of the company of brothers: and in the act of devouring him they accomplished their identification with him, and each one of them acquired a portion of his strength. The totem meal, which is perhaps mankind's earliest festival, would thus be a repetition and a commemoration of this memorable and criminal deed, which was the beginning of so many things—of social organization, of moral restrictions and of religion.

(164–5)

After the great crime that lies at the foundation of all society, the men vowed never to kill a father again, sacrificing in his place the symbolic totem animal. Further, and to the point of Freud's opening question, they agreed not to hoard their daughters and sisters among themselves but to marry them out to other families in exchange for wives from those families—establishing the first incest taboo, exogamy, marriage exchanges, and hence regulated society.

Anthropologists would exploit psychoanalytic thinking extensively, becoming more, not less, reliant on it over the next several decades. Many anthropologists applied psychoanalysis in their research, and some actually became trained psychoanalysts; at the same time, some psychoanalysts conducted anthropological fieldwork of their own, like Géza Róheim and his 1925 *Australian Totemism: A Psycho-analytic Study in Anthropology*. In sum, we can say that among the specific—and largely positive—effects of Freudian theory on the discipline are:

- attention to the ways in which social experience shapes individual character, that is, a fundamentally developmental or constructionist perspective on personality
- focus on childhood, child-rearing practices, and family relations
- awareness of the central importance of sexuality specifically and embodied experience in general
- search for clues to personality and mind in cultural evidence, such as dream content, art, and myths
- cross-cultural testing, in the field, of supposedly universal psychological phenomena, including but not limited to the Oedipus complex.

Box 1.1.6   Bronislaw Malinowski: Testing Freud in the Field

Bronislaw Malinowski (1884–1942) is generally seen as the equivalent of Boas in British social anthropology and not as a central figure in psychological anthropology. However, more so than the structural functionalists who succeeded him (like Radcliffe-Brown, mentioned earlier), he did emphasize the role of the individual in his own brand of functionalist theory. Generally, he believed that culture functioned to fill the needs of individual members of society, which was true even or especially for religion. In analyzing the religion of the Trobriand Islanders, he noticed that when navigating the ocean out of view of shore, the natives tended to indulge in religious behavior, but when sailing near land, they did not. He reckoned that open-water travel was much more dangerous, and therefore, religion served the human psychological need for safety and a sense of control over circumstances. Emphasing not safety but control, Malinowski explored the subject of religion and magic in relation to gardening in his major ethnographic study of Trobriand culture, his 1922 *Argonauts of the Western Pacific,* and in his 1935 *Coral Gardens and Their Magic,* supporting Tylor and Frazer's view that natives were practical-minded and rational, even when they engaged in "irrational" acts like magic. Trobriand gardening, indeed all of Trobriand life, was shot through with magical incantations and rituals, but Malinowski fully appreciated that magic alone, without realistic knowledge and practice of planting, weeding, and sowing, would leave people starving to death. (We might also consider this a case of Freud's primary process [magic] coexisting with secondary process [rational action in response to reality].) Malinowski wrote, for instance, that along with garden magic,

> soil, rain, proper work, are given their full due. None the less, no one would dream of making a garden without the full magical performance being done over it. Garden magic is thought to make just this difference, which a man hopes for from 'chance,' or 'good luck'. ... So we see that, in all these cases, magical influence runs parallel to and independently of the effects of human work and natural conditions. It produces these differences and those unexpected results, which cannot be explained by any of the other factors.
>
> (1984: 421)

More importantly for present purposes, Malinowski was one of the first, if not the first, to engage Freud and *to test Freudian theory in the field*. In 1929, he produced a study of Trobriand sexuality, clearly beholden to Freud's accent on sex in the formation of culture and character; in the preface to the book, sex researcher Havelock Ellis wrote,

> the genius of Freud ... has given an impetus to the study of the sexual impulse and to its possible manifestations even in the myths and customs of savages. To these developments Dr. Malinowski is fully alive. He was even prepared at one time to be much more nearly a Freudian than we can now describe him. Today he is neither Freudian nor anti-Freudian; he recognizes the fertilizing value of Freud's ideas, and he is prepared to utilize them whenever they seem helpful in elucidating the phenomena under investigation.
>
> (1929: xi)

But he was also prepared to submit Freud's ideas to the court of ethnographic fact and to criticize or reject them if necessary.

Hence, Malinowski's 1927 *Sex and Repression in Savage Society*. Granting that psychoanalysis "has given to the study of mental processes a concrete turn," one that "had led us to concentrate on child psychology and the history of the individual" as well as "the unofficial and unacknowledged sides of human life" (1927: viii), he nevertheless revealed that he found himself "less and less inclined to accept in a wholesale manner the conclusions of Freud" (ix). The case in point was his core concept of the Oedipus complex, which for the psychologist was universal and inevitable. Malinowski discovered a defect in Freud's thinking on the matter: rather than universal—but oddly consistent with broader psycho-analytic theory—the conventional Oedipus complex might be conceived as a particular intersection of psychological processes and socially determined childhood experience. First, Malinowski asserted that psychoanalysis

> is essentially a theory of the influence of family life on the human mind. We are shown how the passions, stresses and conflicts of the child in relation to its father, mother, brother and sister result in the formation of certain permanent mental attitudes or sentiments towards them, sentiments which, partly living in memory, partly embedded in the unconscious, influence the later life of the individual in his relations to society.
>
> (2)

This is a fair assessment of the psychoanalytic project. But when we introduce the anthropological fact "that *the family* is not the same in all human societies" (3), it suddenly becomes possible that the standard Oedipus complex is *one possible psychosocial outcome but not the necessary or only one*. Malinowski proceeded to demonstrate this point by comparing Trobriand family and society to Western family and society. The crucial difference is matrilineal kinship or "mother-right" in the Trobriands. In matrilineal kinship systems, the child belongs to the mother's kin group; the father is a less central male figure in the child's life, that role being played by the mother's brother. In places like the Trobriand Islands, the father "is thus a beloved, benevolent friend, but not a recognized kinsman of the children. He is a stranger, having authority through his personal relations to the child, but not through his sociological position in the lineage" (10). In short, the father is not the threatening, frightening character that he is in patrilineal and patriarchal societies. Chronicling the psychosexual development of the Trobriand child, in the context of a freer sexual culture where there is "nothing suppressed, nothing negative, no frustrated desire forms a part of" feelings toward parents (75), it becomes incumbent "not to assume the universal existence of the Oedipus complex, but in studying every type of civilization *to establish the special complex which pertains to it*" (82, emphasis added). In other words—and this is the very hallmark of anthropology—what Freud described may not be a universal psychological force but a *culturally specific one*, and anthropologists may uncover other different culturally specific complexes when (universal) psychology confronts (particularistic) culture.

Interestingly—and frustratingly to some anthropologists—Malinowski did not thereby jettison Freudian theory. Of the psychohistorical drama of the first father-murder and the invention of the incest taboo, Malinowski insisted that it "has in itself nothing objectionable to the anthropologist" (159), still placing great value on psychoanalytic ideas about sexuality, instincts, and the unconscious. All the same, he offered his own discussion of how presumably innate and universal psychological drives and instincts are groomed by culture in specific ways. In the final analysis, if there are universal instincts or emotions, they "can be trained, adjusted, and organized into complex and plastic systems" (236), yielding variations of personality and mentality depending on social experience.

Summary: Achievements and Shortcomings

Psychology and anthropology were born at virtually the same moment in history. They share many of the same ancestors, and as siblings, they regularly collaborated and continue to collaborate. In the first generations of psychological anthropology (roughly mid-1800s to approximately 1927), the discipline had some notable accomplishments:

- It recognized a vital interconnection between society/culture and personality/mind.
- It began and largely completed the detachment of psychological questions from race, bitterly critiquing assumptions about racial mental inequalities.
- It established without much doubt the psychic unity of humanity.
- It commenced the project of collecting quantitative cross-cultural data on cognition and perception.
- It proved that, whatever aspects of psychology may be innate and universal, individual and group character is shaped by social experience (in the family and beyond) and cultural content (specific beliefs, values, institutions, etc. of societies).

This early version of psychological anthropology still suffered from a number of limitations, including:

- It lacked a sophisticated theory of personality and learning.
- It was not yet quantitative; in fact, little research was yet conducted specifically on early-life experiences and personality qualities for the purposes of demonstrating any link between the two.

- It was too preoccupied with racial questions; it also still talked in terms of "primitive" or "savage" personality or mind.

- It was too beholden to one psychological model (Freudian psychoanalysis).

Bibliography

Barnouw, Victor. 1973 [1963]. *Culture and Personality*. Homewood, IL: The Dorsey Press.

Berry, John W., Ype H. Poortings, Marshall H. Segall, and Pierre R. Dasen. 2002. *Cross-Cultural Psychology: Research and Applications*, 2nd ed. Cambridge and New York: Cambridge University Press.

Boas, Franz. 1901. "The Mind of Primitive Man." *The Journal of American Folklore* 14 (52): 1–11.

———. 1910. "Psychological Problems in Anthropology." *The American Journal of Psychology* 21 (3): 371–84.

———. 1938 [1911]. *The Mind of Primitive Man*. New York: The Macmillan Company.

Diriwachter, Rainer. 2004. "*Völkerpsychologie*: The Synthesis that Never Was." *Culture Psychology* 10 (1): 85–109.

Freud, Sigmund. 2001 [1913]. *Totem and Taboo: Some Points of Agreement between the Mental Lives of Savages* Hsu, Francis L. K.

———. 1972b [1961]. *Psychological Anthropology*. Cambridge, MA: Schenkman Publishing Company.

Lévi-Strauss, Claude. 1966 [1962]. *The Savage Mind*. George Weidenfeld, trans. Chicago: The University of Chicago Press.

LeVine, Robert A. 1973. *Culture, Behavior, and Personality: An Introduction to the Comparative Study of Psychosocial Adaptation*. Chicago: Aldine Publishing Company.

Linton, Ralph. 1945. *The Cultural Background of Personality*. New York: Appleton-Century Crofts.

Luria, Alexander R. and Lev S. Vygotsky. 1992 [1930]. *Ape, Primitive, Man, and Child: Essays in the History of Behavior*. Evelyn Rossiter, trans. New York: Harvester Wheatsheaf.

Malinowski, Bronislaw. 1927. *Sex and Repression in Savage Society*. Chicago: The University of Chicago Press.

———. 1984 [1922]. *Argonauts of the Western Pacific*. Long Grove, IL: Waveland Press.

Nadel, Siegfried F. 1951. *The Foundations of Social Anthropology*. Glencoe, IL: The Free Press.

Penny, H. Glenn. 2002. *Objects of Culture: Ethnology and Ethnographic Museums in Imperial Germany*. Chapel Hill: University of North Carolina Press.

Porteus, Stanley D. 1917. "Mental Tests with Delinquents and Australian Aboriginal Children." *Psychological Review* 24 (1): 32–42.

———. 1931. *The Psychology of a Primitive People*. London: Arnold & Co., London; New York: Longmans Green.

———. 1933. "Mentality of Australian Aboriginals." *Oceania* 4 (1): 30–6.

Radcliffe-Brown, Alfred R. 1957. *A Natural Science of Society*. Glencoe, IL: The Free Press.

Rivers, William H. R. 1924b. *Social Organization*. London: Kegan Paul, Trench, and Trübner.

Slotkin, James S., ed. 1965. *Readings in Early Anthropology*. London: Methuen & Co. Ltd.

Topinard, Paul. 1890 [1876]. *Anthropology*. London: Chapman and Hall.

Tylor, Edward B. 1958 [1871]. *Primitive Culture*. New York: Harper Torchbooks.

Waitz, Theodor. 1863. *Introduction to Anthropology*. London: Longman, Green, Longman, and Roberts.

———. 1964 [1961]. *Culture and Personality*. New York: Random House.

Wolf, Eric. 1994. "Perilous Ideas: Race, Culture, People." *Current Anthropology* 35 (1): 1–12.

Reading 1.2

Forensic Mental Health: Criminal Justice's Second Revolving Door

By Georgette A. Bradstreet and Cheryl A. Hill

I N A SMALL APPALACHIAN STATE, a disheveled man named Joe walks up to a woman and robs her because he is hearing voices telling him that the money she has is his. Police officers quickly catch up with Joe, who, believing the officers are there to kill him, attacks one of the officers. Joe is subdued, arrested and taken to jail, a place Joe has been many times for a variety of offenses. Unfortunately for Joe, he is facing aggravated robbery and multiple felonious assault charges, and this time he is in real trouble. Joe has family, but they will not have anything to do with him. He has been diagnosed with schizophrenia, refuses to take his medications and often behaves erratically because of his condition. After multiple failed attempts to get Joe committed to various psychiatric hospitals, they gave up. Joe's family is unaware of the fact that there has been a 90 percent reduction in available psychiatric beds in the United States since the 1970s and that a person with mental illness is up to 10 times more likely to be in the criminal justice system than in a hospital.[1]

On the other side of the state, Gary is homeless, having been recently kicked out of a group home for refusing to take his psychiatric medication. He too is schizophrenic and was hearing voices when he robbed a woman. Like Joe, he fights with a police officer and ends up in jail facing charges of aggregated robbery and multiple felonious assault charges. Gary has been in and out of psychiatric hospitals for many years. He has a long criminal history, has been in jail numerous times and served time in prison twice. Gary has frequently been among the more than 22 to 24 percent of offenders with severe mental illness in jails and 16 percent in prisons throughout the U.S.[2]

Six months later, Gary is sitting in prison, having been sentenced to not less than 10 years for first-degree robbery and an additional three to 15 years for assault. Joe is in the state psychiatric hospital, having been found not guilty by reason of insanity (NGRI) for both assault and first-degree robbery, and he will be under the jurisdiction of the court for 35 years. What is the difference—why is one in a psychiatric hospital and the other in prison? They are both mentally ill and both have a long history of incarceration due to criminal behavior. The answers are two legal concepts: competency and NGRI.

Georgette A. Bradstreet and Cheryl A. Hill, "Forensic Mental Health: Criminal Justice's Second Revolving Door," *Corrections Today*, vol. 73, no. 5, pp. 42–44. Copyright © 2011 by American Correctional Association. Reprinted with permission. Provided by ProQuest LLC. All rights reserved.

Neither Joe nor Gary could afford an attorney, so they are represented by public defenders. Gary's attorney recommended that he plead guilty because of the amount of evidence against him. He enters a plea and is sentenced to prison. Joe's attorney had just been to a training course on mental illness and the criminal justice system. He is concerned about Joe's mental illness and wants to ensure Joe understands his legal charges and the court system, so he recommends a defense strategy of NGRI.

Competence to Stand Trial

In the U.S., the due process clause of the Constitution requires that defendants be competent to stand trial. A defendant is assumed to be competent unless a reason to question it is raised. The issue may be raised by anyone involved in the legal proceedings. The standard for competency to stand trial is based on the Supreme Court decision *Dusky v. United States* (1960). The court ruled that to be competent, a defendant must have "sufficient present ability to consult with his lawyer with a reasonable degree of rational understanding" and a "rational and factual understanding of the proceedings against him."

In our theoretical example, if Joe's attorney had raised the question of competency to stand trial, the court would have ordered an evaluation to be conducted by a psychologist or psychiatrist. This assessment would help the court determine if Joe was competent. If the court deems a defendant incompetent, in accordance with the state's legislative code, a period of time is set in which an attempt is made to restore the defendant to competency. In 38 states, the maximum time for restoration is one year.[3] Primarily, competency restoration includes commitment to a state psychiatric hospital, stabilization of symptoms of mental illness, and education about the legal system and criminal proceedings. Those defendants who are restored to competency then proceed to trial. The greatest predictors of being found incompetent are psychosis, unemployment and previous psychiatric hospitalization.[4]

Defendants who are deemed unrestorable by the court, meaning no matter how long they are hospitalized in all likelihood they will never meet the Dusky standard of competency, are usually recommitted to a psychiatric facility. Up until the 1970s, this could have meant a life sentence even for a minor crime. In *Jackson v. Indiana* (1972), the U.S. Supreme Court addressed this issue and held that "A defendant cannot be held more than the reasonable period of time necessary to determine whether there is a substantial probability that he will attain competency in the foreseeable future. If it is determined that he will not, the State must either institute civil proceedings applicable to the commitment of those not charged with a crime, or release the defendant."

Most state legislators have set standards for oversight of the unrestorable defendant. For example, in West Virginia the statute requires that an unrestorable defendant shall

"... remain under the court's jurisdiction until the expiration of the maximum sentence unless the defendant attains competency to stand trial and the criminal charges reach resolution or the court dismisses the indictment or charge."[5] In the case of Joe, if he were found to be incompetent and unrestorable, he might be facing the possibility of 35 years in a psychiatric hospital.

Not Guilty by Reason of Insanity

NGRI is an affirmative criminal defense in which the defense argues that the defendant should not be held accountable for a criminal act committed while he or she was insane. The legal definition of insanity differs from a psychiatric diagnosis of mental illness. Courts have wrestled with this definition, which has changed over time and has been substantially influenced by public opinion. Many of the legal standards have their basis in English common law.

The pivotal case in defining legal insanity was the M'Naghten case of 1843. Daniel M'Naghten was mentally ill (most likely paranoid schizophrenic) and believed that he was being persecuted by the British government. He planned to assassinate the British prime minister, Robert Peel, but mistakenly shot and killed his secretary, Edward Drummond. M'Naghten was found NGRI. The public disapproved of this verdict, and Queen Victoria was incensed. She ordered the House of Lords to look into this case and they ultimately came up with the M'Naghten rules, which are now a formal definition of NGRI. The M'Naghten rules state that a defendant should not be held responsible for his actions only if, due to his mental disease or defect, he did not know that his act would be wrong or did not understand the nature and quality of his actions.[6]

The M'Naghten rules has been criticized because it is only a cognitive standard and does not have a volitional arm. In other words, it does not take into consideration a mentally ill defendant who knew his actions were wrong, but because of his mental illness was unable to control his behavior and committed the crime anyway. This led to the concept of the "irresistible impulse," which absolves a defendant who can distinguish right and wrong, but is nonetheless unable to stop himself from committing an act he knows to be wrong.

In 1962, the American Law Institute published the Model Penal Code, which combined the strictly cognitive M'Naghten rules and the irresistible impulse test. The Model Penal Code states that the defendant is not responsible for criminal conduct if at the time of the offense his actions are the result of mental disease or defect, and the perpetrator lacks substantial capacity either to appreciate the criminality of his conduct or to conform his conduct to the requirements of the law.[7]

In the U.S., the NGRI or insanity defense came into question after an assassination attempt by John Hinckley on President Ronald Reagan on March 30, 1981. Hinckley was obsessed with actress Jodie Foster, believing if he became famous he would be her equal. In 1982, he was found NGRI, a verdict that outraged the American public. This surge of public opinion about the insanity defense led to several changes, including the U.S. Insanity Defense Reform Act of 1984. Montana, Utah and Idaho abolished the insanity defense altogether; other states adopted the more stringent M'Naghten rules over the Model Penal Code definition of insanity; several states shifted the burden of proof from the prosecution to the defense; and 14 states offered an alternative to NGRI, which is the guilty but mentally ill verdict.[8]

Once again, the insanity defense came under scrutiny as a result of the Andrea Yates verdict. Yates was found to be NGRI for the drowning deaths of her five children in 2001. Public opinion is influenced by several myths or misconceptions about this defense. These myths include that the defense is used frequently, mostly for heinous crimes; that those found NGRI "get off easy;" and further, that the acquitted are released from custody even though they are dangerous.

The reality is that the insanity defense is only raised in about one percent of all felonies and it is successful in only one out of every four cases.[9] While 35 percent of the cases are murder cases, the success rate is the same for all other felonies.[10] Most NGRI acquittees are not released from custody, but are committed to a psychiatric facility until such time as they are no longer a danger and/or no longer mentally ill.[11]

Data comparing the length of confinement between NGRI acquittees and defendants convicted of similar crimes is variable. In Georgia and Ohio, NGRI acquittees spend less time confined than convicted defendants; in New Jersey, Washington and Wisconsin, they spend about the same time; and in California, Connecticut, Colorado and the District of Columbia, they spend more time.[12] If released, similar to convicted offenders, most NGRI acquittees are released on conditional release and remain under the court's jurisdiction for a period of time equal to the maximum amount of time they would have served if found to be guilty. Finally, the recidivism rate of NGRI acquittees is similar to that of convicted defendants.[13]

In fiscal year 2010–2011, West Virginia had 538 court ordered forensic evaluations conducted, in which either competency or NGRI were assessed. Only 15 percent of the defendants were found to be incompetent, and 93 percent of those were successfully restored and returned to stand trial. Additionally, only five percent of the assessed defendants were deemed to be NGRI. In the case of defendants charged with murder, competency and/or NGRI were assessed in 35 cases and none of the defendants were found to be either incompetent and/or criminally responsible.[14]

Disposition of Mentally Ill Defendants

In the theoretical examples of Joe and Gary, both have a mental illness and both committed a similar violent crime, but they have very different dispositions, Gary is in prison—a system focused on incarceration and security and not well-equipped to treat mental illness. Joe is in a psychiatric hospital—a system focused on relatively short-term treatment of mental illness and not well-equipped to deal with long-term incarceration. Both systems are overburdened.

It is time for society to consider alternatives to the revolving door. Some states have created forensic assertive community treatment for offenders with severe and chronic mental illness released on parole. These programs focus on working with people in their homes and community with the goals of improving compliance with psychiatric treatment, decreasing inpatient psychiatric hospitalizations and decreasing the likelihood of criminal behavior. There is a great deal of similarity between the mentally ill offender in prison and forensic patient in a state psychiatric hospital, and both tend to cross back and forth between the systems. Perhaps there may be a future when the conditionally released forensic patient and the mentally ill parolee may be treated and monitored by one group consisting of staff from both systems. After all, Gary and Joe have more in common than not.

Endnotes

1. Torrey, E.F. 2008. *The insanity offense: How America's failure to treat the seriously mentally ill endangers its citizens.* New York: Norton.

2. Steadman, H., F. Osher, P. Rohbins, B. Case and S. Samual. 2009. Prevalence of serious mental illness among jail inmates. *Psychiatric Services*, 60(6):761–765.

3. Bureau of Justice Statistics. 2006. *Mental health problems of prison and jail inmates.* Washington, D.C.: U.S. Government Printing Office.

4. Wolber, G. 2008. The unrestorable incompetent defendant: Length of attempted restoration and factors contributing to decision of unrestorable. *American Journal of Forensic Psychology*, 26(3):63–77.

5. Preli, G., W. Gottdiener and P, Zapf. 2011. A meta-analysis review of competency to stand trial research. *Public Policy and Law*, 17:1–53.

6. West Virginia Legislative Code, Chapter 27-6A-3(h).

7. M'Naghten Case, 8 End. Rep. 718. 1843.

8. American Law Institutes. 1985. *Model Penal Code and Commentaries.* Philadelphia, Pa.: The Institute.

9. Melville, J. and D. Nairnark. 2002. Punishing the insane: The verdict of guilty but mentally ill. *American Academy of Psychiatry and Law*, 30(4):553–555.

10. Perlin, M., P. Champine, H. Dlugacz and M. Connell. 2008. *Competence and the law: From legal theory to clinical application.* Hoboken, N.J.: Wiley.

11. Melton, G., J. Petrila, J. N. Polythress and C. Slobogin. 2007. *Psychological evaluations for the courts: A handbook for mental health professionals and lawyers*, 3rd Ed. New York: Guilford.

12. Thomas, J. and P. Herbert. 2005. Commitment pursuant to insanity acquittal: Clear and convincing burden of proof on an insanity acquittal hearing. *Journal for the American Academy of Psychiatry and Law*, 33(4):558–561.

13. Miller, R. 2003. Forensic evaluations and treatment in the criminal justice system. In *Principles and Practices in Forensic Psychiatry* 2nd Ed, ed. Richard Rosner, 181–246. London, U.K.: Hodder Arnold; distributed in the USA by Oxford University Press Inc.

14. Silver, E. 1995. Punishment or Treatment: Comparing the length of confinement of successful and unsuccessful insanity defendants. *Law and Human Behavior*, 19(4): 375–389.

15. West Virginia Department of Health and Human Resources. 2011. *A review of forensic evaluations: study in process.*

Reading 1.3

Selection from Forensic Neuropsychology: An Overview of Issues, Admissibility and Directions

By Jerry J. Sweet, Paul M. Kaufmann, Erick Ecklund-Johnson, and Aaron C. Malina

Introduction

Professional surveys show that involvement in forensic activities has become a common part of professional practice for clinical neuropsychologists (e.g., Sweet, Peck, Abramowitz, & Etzweiler, 2003). For example, a survey by Sweet, Moberg, and Suchy (2000) found that attorneys are the number one referral source for private practice neuropsychologists, who now represent the majority of the field. As a specialty practice of psychology, clinical neuropsychology applies unique methods and legally protected test materials (Kaufmann, 2009) in conjunction with the brain-behavior knowledge base to evaluate, diagnose, and treat individuals with known or suspected neurological disease and/or injury (Kaufmann, 2012). Lawyers increasingly seek consultation with neuropsychologist experts on an expanding set of legal issues, in part, because neuropsychologists apply scientific approaches that meet judicial standards for expert testimony (Larrabee, 2012).

Forensic neuropsychology has also become prominent within the neuropsychological literature and at relevant professional meetings. More specifically, examination of publication content within the most important clinical neuropsychology journals from 1990 through 2000 has demonstrated that forensic neuropsychology is a common topic within journal articles and at professional meetings (Sweet, King, Malina, Bergman, & Simmons, 2002), accounting for up to 16% of journal content and 11% of conference presentations. Thus, because of its increasing prominence, presumably associated with increasing influence, it is appropriate within this comprehensive handbook on the practice of clinical neuropsychology to consider important issues and directions of forensic neuropsychology. The present chapter will describe the historical background, major activities, key issues, admissibility challenges, and future directions of forensic neuropsychology.

For the purposes of the present chapter, we will consider *forensic neuropsychology* to include all neuropsychological practice in which a clinician provides evaluation or consultative services to an individual involved in a proceeding that is potentially *adversarial* in nature. Adversarial proceedings are those that involve two or more interested parties who must reach a resolution of a common concern or disagreement from potentially antagonistic positions. Adversarial proceedings may be either *formal*, often taking place in a courtroom and involving criminal, civil (including personal injury and medical malpractice), or family (including divorce and child custody) law, or *informal*, often involving administrative matters, such as disability determination, fitness for duty, and due process educational hearings. Greiffenstein and Kaufmann (2012) note the criminal, civil, administrative, probate, and alternative dispute resolution settings in which neuropsychologists are commonly asked to consult. In all these proceedings, the offering of specialty knowledge by the clinical neuropsychologist is to inform a "trier of fact" or a less-formal process regarding an individual who is designated a *litigant*, if involved in formal court proceedings, or as a *claimant*, if involved in less formal proceedings (e.g., seeking disability status or seeking special considerations in an educational system). As such, a forensic opinion occurs within a context that can be distinguished from the normal clinical routine in which a health care service is provided to a "patient" who is seeking treatment for a malady. Stated differently, forensic services are viewed as outside routine health care, which explains why these services are not reimbursed under health insurance benefits.

Historical Background

As noted earlier, there is strong evidence from professional surveys that involvement in forensic neuropsychology has increased substantially over time, such that it is a common part of practice for most clinical neuropsychologists and a major portion of practice for some. The growth of forensic consulting in neuropsychology is well documented (Sweet et al., 2002; Heilbronner, 2004; Kaufmann, 2009), including pediatric populations (Sherman & Brooks, 2012). Braun et al. (2011) noted a 6% average rate of annual growth in Lexis cases referencing neuropsychology from 2005 to 2009, and an unprecedented 20% increase in 2010. Kaufmann has closely tracked these trends for the past decade, most recently showing how neuropsychology is outpacing every related area of brain-behavior expertise (Kaufmann & Greiffenstein, 2013). Recently, Kaufmann (2016) noted a 97% increase in time devoted to forensic consulting over the past decade when comparing professional practice survey data from Sweet and his colleagues (2006, 2011, and 2015). Figure 1.3.1 shows a steady upward trend in forensic consulting for neuropsychologists.

It is likely that these historical data pertaining to formal litigation proceedings are paralleled by equally impressive growth in separate informal adversarial proceedings, such as disability determination and due process educational hearings.

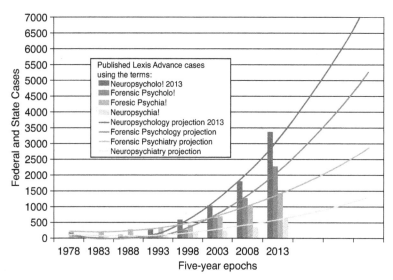

FIGURE 1.3.1 Number of U.S. federal and state cases using the root terms *Neuropsycholo!*, *Forensic Psycholo!*, *Forensic Psychia!*, and *Neuropsychia!* in five-year epochs for the past 35 years, used as a basis for polynomial regression projections for the next 15 years. These frequency counts represent the "tip of the iceberg" because the Lexis Advance database includes only appellate cases and narrowly selected trials introducing novel legal concepts. The interested reader may review the first references to these disciplines in published legal cases. See *Smith v. Metropolitan Life Ins., Co.* (1943) for neuropsychology, *Hovey v. Hobson* (1867) for forensic psychology, *State v. Knight* (1901) for forensic psychiatry, and *Hines v. Welch* (1928) for neuropsychiatry.

An interesting question is, what caused this impressive practice growth? In the sections immediately following, we explore possible causative factors.

Health Care Advances and Resulting Societal Change

In discussing reasons for the growth of forensic neuropsychology, Taylor (1999) offered five factors that were deemed significant in explaining the emergence of neuropsychologists as litigation experts. These factors were (a) an increasing traumatic brain injury (TBI) population, (b) development of advocacy organizations, (c) advent of *neurolaw* (Taylor's approach to proceedings involving neurological injury), (d) increasing supply of neuropsychologists, and (e) response of the legal system. In Taylor's view, increased TBI survival rates stem directly from medical advances, which in turn impact society and result in items (a) through (c). Common causes of TBI include vehicular accidents and accidents in the workplace, which are often associated with subsequent litigation. Whereas if TBI results in death, neuropsychologists are an unlikely expert witness, TBI survivors can have cognitive, emotional, and behavioral changes that are best assessed by neuropsychologists, who therefore become key witnesses in resulting litigation. Thus, a sizeable TBI survivor cohort leads to development of advocacy groups, such as the Brain Injury Association of America, which in turn leads to

greater consciousness raising among the general public and politicians, and greater alloca-
tion of societal resources, such as resources for rehabilitation and residential living. Lawyers
develop greater interest in the unique aspects of brain injury as pertains to litigation and
increasingly need relevant expert witnesses. Demand for clinical neuropsychologists arises
then out of both the clinical need and the litigation need to deal expertly with TBI survivors. These factors influence one another in a positive and synergistic fashion. As clinical
neuropsychologists played a greater clinical role in dealing with TBI survivors, such that
physicians and other health care providers relied upon them to assist in evaluating and treating TBI patients, ultimately, the court system acknowledged their role in the courtroom by
promulgating common law (i.e., the rulings of judges) and statutory law that facilitate their
involvement. As Taylor (1999) notes, "the law encourages that which it permits" (p. 424).

Health Care Market Forces

In the same interval of time in which forensic neuropsychology has grown substantially,
health care reimbursement models changed meaningfully. The era of *managed care* in U.S.
health care greatly changed the means and amounts of reimbursements for routine clinical
services, including those of clinical neuropsychologists. Instead of indemnity insurance,
managed care became a dominant force in U.S. health care. In a 2000 national survey of
clinical neuropsychologists, managed care was identified as the number one reimbursement
source for clinical services (Sweet et al., 2003). In response to the increased paperwork and
reduced reimbursement associated with managed care, many U.S. clinicians, including
neuropsychologists, pursued *self-pay* opportunities. Self-pay refers to non-insurance-based
reimbursement, which of course includes forensic activities, which, as unrelated to health
services, do not rely upon insurance. At this point, although varying greatly from one individual to another, forensic activities constitute a sizeable source of income to the field in
general (cf. Sweet et al., 2000, 2003), to the point that some private practices are entirely
based on forensic consultations.

Scientist-Practitioner Model

Based on the previous discussion of factors that may explain the growth of forensic neuropsychology, it already seems likely that multiple factors are involved. Sweet (1999a) has argued
that a predominant factor in this growth is the scientist-practitioner conceptual foundation
of the field. This viewpoint suggests that the well-recognized scientist-practitioner model
(cf. Barlow, Hayes, & Nelson, 1984), which was originally developed to conceptualize the
training of clinical psychologists and their subsequent idealized clinical practice methods,
has resulted in neuropsychologist subspecialists being attractive and valuable experts for
adversarial proceedings. Specifically, Sweet opines that among the "relevant by-products of

a scientist-practitioner approach are: familiarity with disciplined scrutiny (i.e., peer review), clinical procedures emphasizing data-based decision-making (i.e., accountability), and comfort with hypothesis-testing (i.e., objective differential diagnosis)" (Sweet, 1999a, p. xviii).

As Lees-Haley and Cohen (1999) have noted, the fundamental contributions of experts, including neuropsychologists, to forensic adversarial proceedings are embodied in being a *scientific expert*. The empirical foundation, ability to entertain reasonable alternative hypotheses, ability to acknowledge limitations of method and research literature, and also to be open to reasoned criticism, among other characteristics, are the hallmarks of both a good scientist and a good expert witness. That clinical neuropsychology is rooted in science appears salient in making practitioners in the field attractive to triers-of-fact. It may well be that this scientific foundation in describing cognition, behavior, and emotion provides the essential attractive feature to attorneys, which when coupled with societal and health care changes that provided motivation for individual practitioners, explain the growth of forensic neuropsychology in the last two decades.

Judicial Standards for Admissibility

Although forensic consulting in neuropsychology began in the 1970s, Figure 1.3.1 shows that the rapid growth in preference for neuropsychologist experts did not appear in published legal cases until the early 1990s. Coincidentally, the U.S. Supreme Court handed down its landmark ruling in *Daubert v. Merrell Dow Pharm., Inc.* (1993) that changed the admissibility standards for expert witnesses. Even as some feared that *Daubert* might be used to exclude psychologist experts, the nonexclusive factors suggested by the Court have been favorable for neuropsychologist experts and likely contributed to increased utilization. Psychologists evaluate clinical impressions from an interview, behavioral observations, and informal assessment, with the added benefit of comparing the individual's test performance to norms. Indeed, it is the integration of divergent sources of information with test findings that draws upon the unique skills of professional psychologists. The competent practice of modern neuropsychology requires current understanding and reasonable fluency in the behavioral and cognitive neurosciences. This brain-behavior knowledge base from the neurosciences, used in conjunction with standardized psychometric tests, neuroimaging results, neurodiagnostic findings, neurologic history, interviewing, behavioral observations, and informal assessment means that neuropsychological formulations and expert opinions are scientifically informed and refined by objective test results. These techniques easily fulfill state and federal legal standards for scientific methodology because psychological tests and neurodiagnostic techniques are widely accepted and, more importantly, experimentally verified. Kaufmann (2005) argued this practice distinguishes clinical neuropsychology in forensic settings, such that it has little or no redundancy with other health care disciplines or mental health expertise. Neuropsychologist experts who conduct evaluations using standardized, reliable, valid, and norm-referenced psychological tests with technical manuals easily fulfill *Daubert's* nonexclusive evidentiary standards.

Assessment of Response Bias, Effort, and Malingering

The publication of Faust and Ziskin's (1988: 33) blistering critique that experts in psychology and psychiatry "will most likely move the jury further from the truth, not closer to it," highlighted the questionable methods used by mental health experts and set off alarm bells among consulting neuropsychologists. There were predictable rebuttals offered to the methods skeptics (Matarazzo, 1990; Barth, Ryan, & Hawk, 1991) and obligatory surrebuttals (Faust, 1991; Faust, Ziskin, & Hiers, 1991; Matarazzo, 1991). However, when methods skeptics suggested that "MMPI indices for malingering may sometimes aid the court" (Faust & Ziskin, 1988: 34) neuropsychologists took the criticisms seriously and began devising new methods to improve the relevance and reliability of expert options. Shortly thereafter, the Minnesota Multiphasic Personality Inventory (MMPI) "fake bad" scale was introduced (Lees-Haley, English, & Glenn, 1991). The last two decades have witnessed an unprecedented effort by the neuropsychology community to develop and implement symptom validity and performance validity techniques to detect response bias, suboptimal effort, and malingering (Slick, Sherman, & Iverson, 1999; Bianchini, Greve, & Glynn, 2005), culminating in the American Academy of Clinical Neuropsychology (AACN) Consensus Conference statement (Heilbronner et al., 2009). In the 1980s, neuropsychologists were trained to give mild TBI patients the benefit of the doubt; but now they apply symptom and performance validity techniques, and work to reduce doubt. The increasingly successful neuropsychological methods for detecting malingering have captured the attention of the judiciary and contributed substantially to the preference for forensic neuropsychologist consultants in court.

Key Issues in Forensic Neuropsychology

There are a number of important issues that relate to the practice of clinical neuropsychology within a forensic context. Many of these issues relate to the interface between the field of neuropsychology and the legal profession. Differences exist between the two disciplines in their underlying philosophies and expectations, and it is important that neuropsychologists understand how these differences are likely to affect their interactions with the legal system.

Empirical Bases for Conclusions Based on Neuropsychological Tests

Although empirically grounded practice is important for all neuropsychological activities, issues regarding the scientific bases for conclusions take on particular importance within the forensic context. This is largely because of standards for admissibility of evidence that have been developed to protect the legal system from the influence of "junk science" (i.e., pseudoscientific theories derived from unreliable methods; see Huber, 1991). While clinical neuropsychology enjoys a firm grounding in empirical research, issues remain with respect to the validity of our methods for forensic purposes.

Evidentiary Standards

For many years, the Frye standard (*Frye v. United States*, 1923), which stated that evidence provided by experts must be "generally accepted" within the particular field from which it was derived, was the prevailing standard governing the admissibility of expert testimony (Laing & Fisher, 1997). More recently, several U.S. Supreme Court rulings have addressed the issue of admissibility of expert evidence, beginning with *Daubert v. Merrell Dow Pharm., Inc.* (1993).

Under federal rules, courts must examine expert qualifications to determine the relevance of the expert opinions to the issue in dispute and the reliability of the bases for those opinions, before those opinions are admitted into evidence and heard by a jury. Judges must decide whether special experience is required to develop expert opinions that will assist the jury in resolving an issue in the case at bar.[1] Therefore, consulting neuropsychologists should understand the court standards for evaluating expert qualifications and the admissibility of testimony as addressed in Fed. R. Evid. 104 Preliminary Questions and Fed. R. Evid. 403 Relevance. Then, experts should understand how jurisdictions use *Frye*, *Daubert* and its progeny, and Fed. R. Evid. 702 Testimony of Experts to make final determinations.

Although state Rules of Evidence vary somewhat, the legal basis for judicial review of expert methodology and testimony begins with Fed. R. Evid. 104 (a) Preliminary Questions of Admissibility, and (b) Relevancy Conditioned on Fact, as follows:

a. The court must decide any preliminary question about whether a witness is qualified, a privilege exists, or evidence is admissible. In so deciding, the court is not bound by evidence rules, except those on privilege.

b. "When the relevance of evidence depends on whether a fact exists, proof must be introduced sufficient to support a finding that the fact does exist. The court may admit the proposed evidence on the condition that the proof be introduced later."

Some courts refer generically to Rule 104 hearings when hearing *Daubert* or *Frye* challenges to expert testimony. Rule 104(b) refers to Fed. R. Evid. 403, as follows:

> Although relevant, evidence may be excluded if its probative value is substantially outweighed by the danger of unfair prejudice, confusion of the issues,

or misleading the jury, or by considerations of undue delay, waste of time, or needless presentation of cumulative evidence.

(Fed. R. Evid. 403)

These federal rules (and state equivalents) set the stage for challenging expert testimony. However, not all state courts have adopted the *Daubert* framework, and a few still rely on *Frye*.[2]

The second-degree murder conviction in *Frye* was appealed, claiming the trial court erred when it excluded expert testimony on a "systolic blood pressure deception test" (*Frye v. United States*, 1923: 1013). Defense efforts to conduct the test in the court and admit expert opinions were denied. The *Frye* court affirmed the trial judge and created the following rule by quoting from the government's brief:

> when the question involved does not lie within the range of common experience or common knowledge, but requires special experience or special knowledge, then the opinions of witnesses skilled in that particular science, art, or trade to which the question relates are admissible in evidence.
>
> (*Frye v. United States*, 1923: 1014)

In a two-page unanimous opinion, the appellate court found that the deception test did not have "standing and scientific recognition among physiological and psychological authorities as would justify the courts in admitting expert testimony" (*Frye v. United States*, 1923: 1014). Essentially, the test was not admitted because it was not *generally accepted* in the relevant scientific community. *Frye* was the law governing experts for the next 70 years, and it is still used today to exclude evidence that is not generally accepted in the scientific community (e.g., restricting behavioral genetics evidence in federal and *habeas corpus* review; *Cullen v. Pinholster*, 2011).

In *Daubert v. Merrell Dow Pharm., Inc.* (1989), infants and guardians sued to recover for limb reduction birth defects caused by ingestion of the anti-nausea "morning sickness" drug Bendectin during pregnancy. Merrell Dow won on summary judgment[3] under *Frye* with the trial judge noting the "prevailing school of thought" (*Daubert v. Merrell Dow Pharm., Inc.*, 1989: 572) about Bendectin and legal authority that epidemiological studies are the most reliable causation evidence in this field of study. The plaintiffs failed to present "statistically significant epidemiological proof that Bendectin causes limb reduction defects" because their expert relied, in part, on in vitro animal and chemical studies (*Daubert v. Merrell Dow Pharm., Inc.*, 1989: 575). The plaintiffs appealed, arguing the trial court erred when excluding the scientific studies and reanalysis of the epidemiological data by their experts. The three-judge Ninth Circuit Appellate Court unanimously affirmed the trial court, *Daubert v. Merrell Dow Pharm., Inc.* (1992), citing *Frye* and following the precedent, referencing

> a well-founded skepticism of the scientific value of the reanalysis methodology employed by plaintiffs' experts; they recognize that "[t]he best test of certainty we have is good science—the science of publication, replication, and verification, the science of consensus and peer review." P. Huber, Galileo's Revenge: Junk Science in the Courtroom 228 (1991).
>
> *(Daubert v. Merrell Dow Pharm., Inc.,* 1989: 1131)

The Ninth Circuit suggested in vitro studies were junk science, affirming the trial court decision to ignore this new scientific evidence because it failed *Frye's* general acceptance test. The plaintiffs appealed and the U.S. Supreme Court granted *Certiorari*.[4]

In a landmark decision regarding expert testimony, the U.S. Supreme Court held that Fed. R. Evid. 702 superseded *Frye's* general acceptance test, thereby requiring all federal courts to admit any "scientific, technical, or other specialized knowledge" that assists the trier of fact to understand the evidence (*Daubert v. Merrell Dow Pharm., Inc.,* 1989: 580). "General acceptance" was no longer required to admit scientific evidence in federal court. A 7–2 majority also found that District Court judges (gatekeepers) must evaluate the admissibility of expert testimony, although Honorable Chief Justice William Rehnquist disagreed on the trial judge's role, writing

> I do not doubt that Rule 702 confides to the judge some gatekeeping responsibility in deciding questions of the admissibility of proffered expert testimony. But I do not think it imposes on them either the obligation or the authority to become amateur scientists in order to perform that role.
>
> *(Daubert v. Merrell Dow Pharm., Inc.,* 1989: 600–601)

Chief Justice Rehnquist was "at a loss" in understanding what "falsifiability" meant when applied to a scientific theory and he predicted other federal judges would too. Nevertheless, the Ninth Circuit decision was reversed and remanded for further proceedings.

For efficient justice, the Ninth Circuit conducted the "brave new world" of *Daubert* analysis of Fed. R. Evid. 702, framing the question as follows: "How do we figure out whether scientists have derived their findings through the scientific method or whether their testimony is based on scientifically valid principles?" (*Daubert v. Merrell Dow Pharm., Inc.,* 1989: 1316). A unanimous Ninth Circuit affirmed the original summary judgment under Rule 702 and *Daubert* because the plaintiff presented only experts' qualifications, their conclusions, and their assurances of reliability. *Daubert* plaintiff s received due process, equal protection, and justice, but no compensation, because the expert scientific evidence failed to show, with a preponderance of the evidence, that Bendectin caused the birth defects.

Two subsequent U.S. Supreme Court cases, *General Electric Co. v. Joiner* (1997) and *Kumho Tire Co. v. Carmichael* (1999), refined *Daubert* and extended its holding. In *Joiner*, a city electrician with lung cancer brought suit against the manufacturer of polychlorinated biphenyls (PCBs) and the manufacturers of electrical transformers and dielectric fluid, alleging his exposure to these materials caused his cancer. Joiner relied on an expert to prove his case. The District Court judge excluded the expert testimony, finding it "subjective belief or unsupported speculation" (*General Electric Co. v. Joiner*, 1997: 140) and Joiner appealed. Under a stringent standard of review, the 11th Circuit Appellate Court reversed the trial court, finding the judge erred in excluding the expert testimony. The U.S. Supreme Court reversed the 11th Circuit, thereby affirming and strengthening the gatekeeping function of the trial court, and directing appellate courts not to review admissibility of expert opinions unless the trial judge committed a clear abuse of discretion. Basically, appellate courts were ordered to show great deference to the gatekeeping judges in District Courts and to not disturb the decisions of the trial judge regarding the admissibility of expert testimony absent gross error.

In *Kumho Tire*, a vehicle overturned when a right rear tire blew out, killing one passenger and injuring others. The plaintiffs sought to admit a tire analyst's visual and tactile tire inspection testimony, under the theory that the absence of at least two of four specific physical indicators meant a tire defect caused failure. The defendant moved to exclude the tire analyst testimony, claiming the methodology failed Fed. R. Evid. 702 requirements. The trial court applied *Daubert* and the judge excluded the tire analyst after finding the methodology employed was insufficiently reliable. Carmichael appealed. The 11th Circuit held that the trial court erred in applying *Daubert*, believing that it only applied to scientific testimony. The U.S. Supreme Court reversed the 11th Circuit and clarified that *Daubert* factors apply to the testimony of engineers and other experts who are not scientists. Experts may also be evaluated and admitted to testify based on skill, experience, and other specialized knowledge, not only scientific knowledge. Even after broadening the criteria, the tire expert opinion was excluded.

In 2002, the U.S. Supreme Court holdings from the *Daubert* "trilogy" were codified into an amendment to Rule 702 governing expert testimony. Rule 702 reads as follows:

> If scientific, technical, or other specialized knowledge will assist the trier of fact to understand the evidence or to determine a fact in issue, a witness qualified as an expert by knowledge, skill, experience, training, or education, may testify thereto in the form of an opinion or otherwise, if (1) the testimony is

based upon sufficient facts or data, (2) the testimony is the product of reliable principles and methods, and (3) the witness has applied the principles and methods reliably to the facts of the case.

(Fed. R. Evid. 702)

In summary, *Daubert* incorporated the *Frye* "general acceptance" test and added other factors that federal court gatekeepers may consider when evaluating expert testimony. After general acceptance within the relevant scientific community, *Daubert* also encouraged judges to consider whether the methodology employed by the expert was subject to peer review, testable (falsifiable), and had a known error rate. Generally, psychologist experts have fared well under *Daubert* because standardized methods supported by data in a technical manual are favored. However, these factors are neither exhaustive nor exclusive, and subsequent federal courts have departed from the original *Daubert* list to consider more factors, such as

- Whether experts are proposing to testify about matters growing naturally and directly out of research they have conducted independent of the litigation, or whether they have developed their opinions expressly for purposes of testifying. *Daubert v. Merrell Dow Pharm., Inc.* (1995).

- Whether the expert has unjustifiably extrapolated from an accepted premise to an unfounded conclusion. *General Elec. Co. v. Joiner* (1997).

- Whether the expert has adequately accounted for obvious alternative explanations. *Claar v. Burlington N.R.R.* (1994).

- Whether the expert "is being as careful as he would be in his regular professional work outside his paid litigation consulting." *Sheehan v. Daily Racing Form, Inc.* (1997).

- Whether the field of expertise claimed by the expert is known to reach reliable results for the type of opinion the expert would give. *Kumho Tire Co. v. Carmichael* (1999).

Daubert clearly provides the court greater flexibility in its analysis of new science and although it offers courts greater protection against junk science, it also places a greater burden on trial court judges. Chief Justice Rehnquist described that burden when noting the "amateur scientist" role implicit in the gatekeeping function. Nevertheless, *Daubert* flexibility is considered to have liberated courts to seek relevant and reliable expert opinions to assist the trier of fact. With each passing year, more jurisdictions adopt its basic framework, while restricting or completely abandoning *Frye*.

Early legal experts believed that *Daubert* would tighten the evidentiary standards for admissibility (Dixon & Gill, 2002; Grove & Barden, 1999), and there has been some empirical evidence to suggest that it has had or is beginning to have the desired effect (Dixon & Gill, 2002; Johnson, Krafka, & Cecil, 2000; Krafka, Dunn, Treadway Johnson, Cecil, & Miletich, 2002). For instance, Dixon and Gill (2002) found that the proportion of cases in which the reliability of expert evidence from various types of experts was challenged, including health care/medicine and social/behavioral science, appears to have increased significantly since the *Daubert* ruling to 62% and 84%, respectively during the most recent period examined, which was July 1997 to June 1999, as compared to 23% and 56% during the period immediately prior to *Daubert*, which was July 1989 to June 1993. Furthermore, Dixon and Gill (2002) found that the proportion of *successful* challenges to social and behavioral science evidence also increased significantly during the same time period, from 8% of cases challenged between July 1989 and June 1993 to 47% between July 1997 and June 1999 (although the period of July 1989 to June 1993 appears to be somewhat of a statistical outlier, as 43% of challenges were successful during the decade of the 1980s). Interestingly, the proportion and success rate of challenges to physical science evidence were highest relative to all other types of evidence (health care/medicine, engineering/technology, social/behavioral science, and business/law/public administration) during most of the time periods examined by Dixon and Gill (2002). In spite of these apparent changes, it appears that the *Daubert* standard may not be applied consistently to behavioral science evidence (Shuman & Sales, 1999; Tenopyr, 1999), and that judges in many jurisdictions may continue to rely primarily on the *Frye* standard (Krafka et al., 2002). Furthermore, individual judges and attorneys vary considerably in their level of sophistication in dealing with issues of admissibility and their knowledge of scientific methods. These issues highlight what might appear to be a confusing state of affairs confronting the neuropsychological expert witness. A table of admissibility decisions that pertain to *Daubert* and related federal and state standards involving neuropsychological testimony, taken from the Daubert Tracker online database (MDEX Online, 2017), have been included, and provide some idea of the challenges facing neuropsychologists who serve as expert witnesses.

The *Daubert* decision and other similar rulings have caused some concern among neuropsychologists that such standards might lead to the exclusion of neuropsychological tests and expert witnesses. However, ... this is not the case, as neuropsychologists do not appear to have fared worse than other experts. It is important to recognize that decisions involving evidentiary standards are case-specific and are influenced by the individual expert, the procedures he or she uses, and the underlying scientific evidence in a particular case. Thus, it is quite possible that a particular expert's testimony might be accepted in one instance and denied in another, depending on whether his or her assertions in each specific case are judged to have a valid scientific basis. Mainstream scientist-practitioner neuropsychologists have never been threatened by the need to provide empirical justification for their work, and should applaud such standards, as they target witnesses from fields without a firm grounding in science.

Since publication of the first edition, two civil cases heard by state supreme courts illustrate the nature of admissibility challenges confronting expert neuropsychologists under *Daubert*. The first case showed how neuropsychologist opinions may be wrongfully excluded (*Baxter v. Temple*, 2008); the second suggested that expert opinions about brain-behavior relations may be wrongfully admitted (*Bennett v. Richmond*, 2012).

In *Baxter v. Temple* (2005), the defense filed a motion *in limine*[5] to exclude the testimony of Barbara Bruno-Golden, Ed.D. as insufficiently reliable under *Daubert*. During the evidentiary hearing Bruno-Golden described the Boston Process Approach (BPA) she employed in the neuropsychological evaluation of a child exposed allegedly to lead poisoning. The defendants argued successfully that her testimony should be excluded because her BPA methodology is not generally accepted in the appropriate scientific literature, has not been subject to peer review and publication, and has no known or potential error rate. Hearing testimony reveals how a trial judge used *Daubert* factors to exclude expert neuropsychological evidence and how such outcomes may be avoided (Desmond, 2007).

All three neuropsychologists, Bruno-Golden, Sandra Shaheen, and David Faust, testified that the BPA methodology employed was untested (*Baxter v. Temple*, 2005, p. 8). Bruno-Golden added that the BPA she used in this evaluation, "has never been … and *cannot be* tested, because it varies from practitioner to practitioner" (p. 9) [*emphasis added*]. In fact, Bruno-Golden testified that she "could not recall if she had ever administered the same test battery" (p. 9) on the thousands of other patients she evaluated during her career. The trial judge ruled that Bruno-Golden's BPA cannot be and was not tested in this case.

The neuropsychologist experts also agreed that the BPA methodology employed was not subjected to peer review, nor described in published articles. Although Bruno-Golden offered a professional position paper supporting the BPA, Faust noted it was not in a peer-reviewed publication. Shaheen noted learned treatises on BPA general acceptance in clinical neuropsychology practice, yet admitted that Bruno-Golden's specific methodology had not been subject to peer review or described in published articles. Finally, Bruno-Golden admitted she had not previously used the methodology employed and it was likely that no other clinician had either. Therefore, the trial judge found the BPA as employed in this case had not been subject to peer review and publication.

The BPA error rate was essentially unknowable and no evidence was offered. Bruno-Golden testified that she disregarded standardized time constraints in order to "test the limits" of the child's performance on selected tests. No experts offered any evidence on the reliability of testing the limits. Faust noted that variations in the standardized instructions interfere with test interpretation and destroy the normative comparisons of the child's performance to like-aged peers, making it impossible to determine an error rate. Faust testified that when Bruno-Golden modified the BPA she created an "idiosyncratic combination, if not hodge-podge of multiple influences" (p. 11). The court detailed some departures from standardized techniques. Faust concluded, the methodology employed was "not scientifically validated … founded on guesswork, speculation, and conjecture, which sometimes flies directly in the face of scientific literature" (p. 11). Hence, the judge ruled the methodology employed by Bruno-Golden did not have a known or potential error rate.

The *Baxter* trial court concluded its analysis by distinguishing between appropriate scientific literature for clinical assessment and "a 'forensic' approach to assessing children with lead poisoning" (p. 13). Faust explained how a clinical or forensic referral changes the expert neuropsychologist role. This important distinction between the clinical provider and forensic examiner has been described often (Greenberg & Shuman, 1997; Heilbrun, 2001). Although most authorities agree that clinical and forensic roles are irreconcilable and every effort should be made to avoid conflicts of interest (Greenberg & Shuman, 2007), others' approaches are more situational (Woody, 2009), and a minority even suggest that the roles are potentially compatible (Heltzel, 2007). In the end, neuropsychologists in forensic practice must employ objective methods that allow them to be unbiased truth seekers.

Upon reviewing the *Daubert* hearing testimony, the *Baxter* trial court seemingly had overwhelming undisputed evidence that Bruno-Golden's methodology was not sufficiently reliable for forensic analysis (Desmond, 2007). The trial court judge found her methodology failed to meet any *Daubert* factors. Therefore, the motion *in limine* was granted, Bruno-Golden's testimony was excluded, and the jury never heard her opinions in the case. The plaintiff appealed and the New Hampshire Supreme Court certified three questions for judicial review, asking whether the trial court erred when excluding: (a) the neuropsychologist's testimony based on the BPA, (b) the IQ test testimony, and (c) the pediatrician's testimony that reasonably relied upon the neuropsychologist's report.

In a unanimous decision that includes a thorough analysis of neuropsychological test administration errors, the New Hampshire Supreme Court reversed the trial court on the first question and vacated the subsequent questions as moot. The *Baxter* court reasoned, "the *Daubert* test does not stand for the proposition that scientific knowledge must be absolute or irrefutable" (citing *State v. Dahood*, 2002). Referring to the trial court's conclusion, it

> focused upon the plaintiff's failure to demonstrate that the specific battery—
> the entire series of tests viewed as a whole—employed by Dr. Bruno-Golden
> in this case was, or could not be, tested, was subject to peer review and publication, or has a known or potential error rate.
>
> (*Baxter*, p. 174)

The high court cited *Kumho Tire* language that *Daubert* factors "do not constitute a definitive checklist or test," but even if they did, "the BPA meets three of four *Daubert* factors." (p. 184). The *Baxter* court expressly rejected the battery as a whole argument, finding "that the individual tests he or she administered as part of the battery, not the battery as a whole, have been tested, have been subject to peer review and publication, and have a known or potential error rate" (p. 184). The *Baxter* court wrote, "we reject the defendant's assertion that Dr. Bruno-Golden's methodology, the BPA as a flexible battery approach, is not a sufficiently reliable methodology to assist the fact finder in understanding the plaintiff's neuropsychological status" (p. 187). The case was remanded back to the trial court with the instruction to admit Dr. Bruno-Golden's opinions based on the BPA.

The *Baxter* court relied, in part, on an Amicus Brief from the AACN. Justices referred to the AACN brief during oral arguments, raising questions about the standard of care for clinical neuropsychology. AACN drew an analogy between the specialty practices of clinical neuropsychology and neurology, arguing that neurologists do not "conduct either an invariant exam procedure or order an invariant set of diagnostic tests for each and every patient" (p. 9). AACN asserted "that administering the same set of tests to all patients and litigants, regardless of the known or suspected condition is uninformed and inappropriate practice" (p. 9). Further, AACN noted "a standardized battery runs counter to an acceptable standard of care in neurology" and "we know of no area of specialty or subspecialty in clinical medicine in which a routine, invariant battery of tests across all medical conditions being evaluated would be acceptable practice" (p. 9). Although not explicitly written, AACN was seemingly advocating for a flexible battery standard of care for clinical neuropsychology. For most referral questions, a flexible battery approach is the predominant form of practice, even as the fixed battery method remains a respectable minority practice in clinical neuropsychology. In what is probably the best example of the application of *Daubert* factors to neuropsychological methodology, *Baxter* illustrates how federal courts and most state courts would address admissibility based on battery selection. *Baxter* also illustrates how neuropsychology is approaching early questions about standards of care for the profession.

Although *Baxter* resolved admissibility questions of flexible batteries in forensic practice for New Hampshire, Dr. Bruno-Golden withdrew and her testimony was never heard, in what was the oldest pending case in New Hampshire (McCrystal, September 23, 2012). Indeed, *Baxter* was a plaintiff in a second lawsuit alleging that state budget cuts resulted in an unconstitutional delay of justice (*Baxter et al. v. State*, 2010). The second lawsuit was promptly dismissed and a retrial took place in September 2012. In the end, the Temples were negligent landlords in not providing notice of lead paint to the Baxters, but no money damages were awarded to Shelby Baxter or her parents. Despite elevated lead levels as an infant, the jury found that the negligence identified did not cause any damages. This case was the first lead case in New Hampshire that went to trial.

On May 24, 2004, John Richmond was sitting in his van, stopped for a school bus, when it was rear-ended by Henry Bennett, who was driving a 42,000-pound roll-off container truck for his employer. Upon collision, Richmond's one-ton van was propelled 300 feet from a stopped position. Richmond sustained head and neck injuries. In December 2004, Richmond sustained a back injury in the course of employment that exacerbated injuries incurred during the May 2004 accident. Apparently, he was a self-employed builder-contractor. In December 2005, Richmond and his wife sued Bennett and his employer for injuries Richmond sustained to his neck and back in the collision. Upon referral by his attorney, Richmond underwent a neuropsychological evaluation with Dr. Sheridan McCabe in October, 2006.

McCabe obtained a M.A. degree in General Psychology in 1956 and a PhD in Counseling Psychology in 1958. McCabe testified that Counseling Psychology was an applied field "working with people who were not psychiatric patients, but rather kind of regular people who had some sort of problem and counseling dealt with that," and that it involved "the assessment of a patient's psychological well-being." (Appellant's App., p. 235). He attended continuing education workshops specializing in forensic applications of psychology that "touched on subjects that relate to evaluation of traumatic brain injuries" (p. 69). McCabe reported that two neurologists referred cases to him for "specific aspects of brain behavior relationship questions" (p. 70), and other general practitioners referred cases to him for insight into the "relationship between the presenting psychological problems and ... underlying medical issues" (p. 70). McCabe's route to clinical neuropsychology practice reflects a bygone era of exclusive reliance upon workshop training that does not meet modern standards for neuropsychology training (Hannay et al., 1998).

The defense hired a board-certified clinical neuropsychologist, David Kareken, PhD, ABPP, to conduct an independent neuropsychological evaluation of Richmond. Kareken's evaluation used modern approaches to forensic neuropsychology (e.g., using symptom validity techniques), which disputed McCabe's findings. Both parties filed motions to exclude the opposing experts. The trial court denied both motions. However, Kareken did not testify as an expert witness, presumably because the defense decided to challenge whether a psychologist could render an opinion about the cause of brain damage. If the defense strategy was to argue that psychologists cannot render causation opinions, then it would not make sense to call a psychologist expert to rebut such opinions.

The court denied defense motions to exclude McCabe's opinion before and during the trial. McCabe testified that Richmond suffered a TBI in the accident and the jury returned a $200,000 judgment in his favor. Bennett appealed the judgment, claiming the trial court abused its discretion by permitting a psychologist to testify as to the cause of a brain injury.

In a unanimous opinion, the appellate court agreed with Bennett, and reversed and remanded for a new trial (*Bennett v. Richmond*, 2010). The court added,

> no medical doctor or other qualified practitioner diagnosed Richmond with a brain injury. Rather, based upon neuropsychological testing given more than two years after the accident, Dr. McCabe opined that Richmond had sustained a brain injury as a result of the accident. The trial court should have exercised its discretion as gatekeeper prior to trial to exclude Dr. McCabe's proffered causation testimony based upon his lack of qualifications to give such testimony.
>
> And the evidence regarding Richmond's damages other than the alleged brain injury is not sufficient to support the $200,000 jury verdict.
>
> (*Bennet v. Richmond*, 2010: 712)

The defense strategy worked, then Richmond appealed.

In a stunning reversal, a unanimous Indiana Supreme Court vacated the appellate court opinion and affirmed the trial court's determination that McCabe's opinion testimony was admissible. That is, it was not an abuse of discretion for the trial court to admit, as sufficiently reliable, a psychologist's opinion that the rear-end collision caused the motorist to suffer TBI. (*Bennett v. Richmond*, 2012). Such dramatic swings in judicial opinion warrant further consideration of McCabe's credentials, methodology, and bases for his expert opinions.

Dr. McCabe denied being a neuropsychologist, yet clearly asserted his expertise regarding TBI. He reviewed medical records before and after the accident, including a radiologist's impressions of a December 13, 2007 brain magnetic resonance imaging (MRI) report, as follows:

> The MRI report indicates small chronic lacunar infarction in the head of the left caudate nucleus. While this type of finding is more indicative of ischemic episodes, it does not rule out the possibility of other causes such as the closed head injury that I suggested in my report. ... [T]his MRI finding is consistent with the sort of brain damage that could produce memory problems.
>
> (Appellant's App., p. 255)

Despite these equivocal impressions, McCabe concluded that the MRI results "were consistent with *his* findings of brain injury." [emphasis added] (Appellant's App., p. 252.). However, other brain structures, such as the frontal/temporal poles or the corpus callosum, are more commonly vulnerable to damage following closed head injury than the head of one caudate nucleus. McCabe selectively misconstrued the radiologist's opinion.

What was the basis for McCabe's findings of brain injury? McCabe administered, scored, and interpreted a battery of neuropsychological tests. However, his opinion also relied upon clinical and collateral interviews, that is, the self-report of interested parties. Specifically, the trial court heard McCabe's impressions based on clinical interviews, but also testimony provided by Richmond's wife, Jennifer, and Richmond's brother, Andrew. Richmond also relied on the testimony of a treating chiropractor, Gary McLeod. All of these witnesses testified about injuries sustained in the accident and problems that evolved after the accident. For example, Richmond called his wife Jennifer from the accident scene and she reported he "sounded shaken-up and was slurring at the time and sounded like he was hesitating on what he was trying to say" (Appellee's App., p. 120; Tr. 447). After the accident, Jennifer also noticed that her husband "was always forgetting things and leaving sticky notes all over the place to remind him of things" (Appellee's App., p. 122; Tr. 449). Richmond also complained of persistent headache.

McCabe administered the Wechsler Adult Intelligence Scale, Third Edition (WAIS-III), the Wechsler Memory Scale, Third Edition (WMS-III), and the Halstead-Reitan Neuropsychological Test Battery (HRB). His brain injury findings were inferred from discrepancies noted among subtest scores on the WAIS-III and the WMS-III that he characterized as "cognitive inefficiency" and "some sort of interference with [Richmond's] cognitive process" (Appellant's App., pp. 89–90; Tr. 331/24–25; 332/1–5). Dr. McCabe also found a mild to moderate impairment on the HRB with special emphasis on category test performance, noting "the first test … is a test of problem-solving thinking ability, very sensitive to brain damage" (Appellant's Appendix, p. 91; Tr. 333/1–10). From these findings, McCabe inferred that Richmond

> sustained a diffuse axonal injury [in the course of the rearend accident in which he was involved]: that is to say, that kind of motion to the head caused damage to the connections between the cells of the brain through the axons. They were sufficiently messed up to provide him with these processing problems that he has manifested—by the time I saw him two years later.
>
> (Appellant's App., p. 92; Tr. 334/6–13)

However, McCabe also agreed that depression and/or anxiety could have caused the cognitive inefficiency noted in his evaluation (Appellant's App., p. 154; Tr. 396).

McCabe testified that Richmond sustained a diffuse axonal injury, which he offered, "as a kind of explanation of the damage [Richmond] sustained" (Appellant's App., p. 145; Tr. 387). However, when asked what he meant by diffuse brain damage, McCabe responded, in part, that the pattern of functioning revealed by the tests is that the damage that underlies it is of a diffuse character. That is, its across various areas of the brain. ... I would infer, not assert, but suggest that the damage is in the axonal connections in the frontal lobe between the cortex and the lower brain centers, providing this kind of inefficiency: not localized to the visual cortex or the auditory cortex or so on.

(Appellant's App., p. 145; Tr. 387)

McCabe expressly refused to testify to a reasonable degree of medical certainty. Similarly, when asked whether he could testify to a reasonable degree of psychological certainty, McCabe responded, "No. I am asserting it upon the pattern of functioning." (Appellant's App., pp. 146–147; Tr. 388–389).

When asked to further explain his opinion that Richmond sustained a diffuse axonal injury, McCabe said that it was an inference he drew from "the pattern of what I call 'cognitive inefficiency' that I saw in the test results" (Appellants App., p. 172; Tr. 414). In commenting on the physician's impression about a "small chronic lacunar infarction in the head of the left caudate nucleus" on the MRI, McCabe agreed that such a finding was more often indicative of ischemic episodes and not a closed head injury. However, McCabe maintained that the MRI results did not rule out the possibility of other causes, such as the closed head injury he suggested (Appellant's App., pp. 254–255).

McCabe did not testify about symptom or performance validity. There was no reference to EMT records from the accident scene and there was no description of Richmond's acute neurologic status following the collision. Again, as a counseling psychologist, McCabe's evaluation and inferences about brain damage causation reflected a bygone era of neuropsychological test interpretation. His conclusions were not consistent with those of a board certified clinical neuropsychologist who had conducted an evaluation that defense counsel elected not to file. Ultimately, defense counsel made two strategic errors. First, the defense failed to call for a *Daubert* hearing to challenge the reliability and relevance of McCabe's credentials, methodology, and basis for his expert opinions. Second, the defense should have called a board certified neuropsychologist to dispute McCabe's testimony at trial.

Baxter and *Richmond* are not easily harmonized, in part, because the defense strategies were so different. In *Baxter*, the defense aggressively attacked the plaintiff expert by retaining an opposing expert to testify at a pretrial *Daubert* hearing about the inadequacies of her methodology. This strategy was initially successful in excluding the plaintiff expert. Even though the trial court erred in excluding Bruno-Golden, in the final analysis, she withdrew and never testified. Even though the defendant landlord was found negligent, this was a defense verdict because the insurance company was not required to pay any damages.

Defense counsel in *Richmond* took a very different approach. Rather than attack the specific methodology of the plaintiff expert in a *Daubert* hearing, the defense elected to pursue a failed attack on the profession of psychology as a whole on appeal. Initially, that strategy was successful and the defense may have felt they simply needed to shore up a win. Basically, the defense argued that psychologists and neuropsychologists are not qualified to render expert opinions about the causes of brain damage. No *Daubert* hearing was conducted and no opposing neuropsychologist testified, even though a defense neuropsychological evaluation consistent with modern practice was performed and readily available. By failing to call an opposing board certified neuropsychologist at trial to detail the inadequacies in McCabe's methods, the *Richmond* defense missed an opportunity to distinguish the outdated methods of a counseling psychologist using a fixed battery from the modern methods of a board-certified neuropsychologist using a flexible battery with symptom validity techniques. Moreover, there was no record developed by the defense to show the plaintiff's acute neurologic status immediately after the collision. Appeals can only review facts presented at trial.

The heterogeneity that exists in the application of evidentiary standards makes it difficult to draw general conclusions about admissibility of neuropsychological evidence. However, it is clearly in the best interest of neuropsychologists who engage in forensic activities to have solid empirical support for their opinions and to resist the temptation to speculate beyond what is apparent and can reasonably be inferred from the data. As clinical neuropsychologists, we often take great pride in the scientist-practitioner tradition embodied in our field, but there are a number of challenges related to the validity of our methodology that must continue to be addressed through research and continued refinement of methods, including the quality and applicability of available norms for many neuropsychological instruments, inferences about changes in cognitive functioning, and current limitations of neuropsychological tests in predicting functional outcome.

Quality and Applicability of Norms

Normative studies provide empirical reference points for comparisons of patient performances, and are thus crucial to our ability to understand the meaning of test scores. Given the important role of norms for clinical (and forensic) decision making, it is perhaps surprising that relatively few neuropsychological tests have had large-scale normative studies performed on them (Mitrushina, Boone, & D'Elia, 1999). With the exception of a few very-well-researched measures, neuropsychologists are often forced to rely on converging evidence from multiple less well-normed instruments, as well as patient history and behavioral observations. Even when relatively large normative studies are available, the validity of conclusions based on test performance may be attenuated if individuals tested are dissimilar to the normative sample in some way (e.g., in terms of age, education, racial/ethnic background), which can limit the conclusions that can be made based on test scores (Joint Committee on Standards for Educational and Psychological Testing, 1999). Furthermore, it is important to remember that no test is a pure measure of a particular neuropsychological function or neurological disorder, and most tests encompass a number of different functions (Rankin & Adams, 1999). For example, a low score on the learning trials of a verbal list-learning task could reflect poor encoding of information, poor attention span, language disturbance, or poor effort, among other possibilities. Thus, it is incumbent upon the forensic neuropsychologist to demonstrate that his or her conclusions fit the data better than plausible alternative explanations (Kay, 1999). This is best achieved through rational interpretation based on careful integration of various test results and other available data (e.g., behavioral, historical, collateral). ...

Endnotes

1. Meaning the current case being heard by the court.
2. Jurisdictions relying on a *Frye* standard include California, the District of Columbia, Florida, Illinois, Kansas, Maryland, Minnesota, New Jersey, New York, Pennsylvania, and Washington. Most recently, Arizona, Alabama, and Wisconsin abandoned *Frye*. California is likely next; see *Sargon Enters., Inc. v. Univ. of S. Cal.* (2012).
3. There is no genuine issue of material fact upon which the plaintiff could prevail as a matter of law. The trial judge rendered a verdict for Merrell Dow based on briefs without a trial.
4. The most common mechanism used by the U.S. Supreme Court chooses to hear a case by order directing a lower court to deliver the case record.
5. A motion to limit or exclude allegedly prejudicial evidence presented to the judge or during a trial.

References

Barlow, D. H., Hayes, S. C., & Nelson, R. O. (1984). *The Scientist Practitioner: Research and Accountability in Clinical and Educational Settings.* New York: Pergamon.

Barth, J. T., Ryan, T. V., & Hawk, G. L. (1991). Forensic neuropsychology: A reply to the method skeptics. *Neuropsychology Review, 2* (3), 251–266.

Baxter et al. v. State, No. 217-2010—CV—00683 (N.H. Sup. Ct., October 29, 2010) (order dismissing claim alleging unconstitutional delay of justice).

Baxter v. Temple, No.01—C—0567 (N.H. Sup. Ct. Aug. 8, 2005) (order granting motion *in limine*).

Baxter v. Temple, 949 A.2d 167 (N.H., 2008).

Bennett v. Richmond, 932 N.E.2nd 704 (Ind. Ct. Ap., 2010).

Bennett v. Richmond, 960 N.E.2nd 782 (Ind., 2012).

Bianchini, K. J., Greve, K. W., & Glynn, G. (2005). On the diagnosis of malingered pain-related disability: Lessons from cognitive malingering research. *The Spine Journal, 5* (4), 404–417.

Braun, M., Tupper, D., Kaufmann, P., McCrea, M., Postal, K., Westerveld, M., ... Deer, T. (2011). Neuropsychological assessment: A valuable tool in the diagnosis and management of neurological, neurodevelopmental, medical, and psychiatric disorders. *Cognitive and Behavioral Neurology, 24* (3), 107–114.

Claar v. Burlington N.R.R., 29 F.3d 499 (9th Cir. 1994).

Cullen v. Pinholster, 131 S. Ct. 1388 (U.S. 2011).

Daubert v. Merrell Dow Pharm., Inc., 43 F.3d 1311 (9th Cir., 1995).

Daubert v. Merrell Dow Pharm., Inc., 509 U.S. 579 (U.S. 1993).

Daubert v. Merrell Dow Pharm., Inc., 727 F. Supp. 570, 575 (S.D. Cal. 1989).

Daubert v. Merrell Dow Pharm., Inc., 951 F.2d 1128 (9th Cir. 1992).

Desmond, J. M. (Winter, 2007). Admissibility of neuropsychological evidence in New Hampshire. *New Hampshire Bar Journal, 47* (4), 12–17, [Online]. Retrieved from www.nhbar.org/publications/display-journal-issue.asp?id=347 (last visited November 30, 2013).

Dixon, L., & Gill, B. (2002). Changes in the standards for admitting expert evidence in federal civil cases since the *Daubert* decision. *Psychology, Public Policy, and Law, 8* (3), 251–308.

Faust, D. (1991). Forensic neuropsychology: The art of practicing a science that does not yet exist. *Neuropsychology Review, 2* (3), 205–231.

Faust, D., & Ziskin, J. (1988). The expert witness in psychology and psychiatry. *Science, 241,* 31–35.

Faust, D., Ziskin, J., & Hiers, J. (1991). *Brain Damage Claims: Coping With Neuropsychological Evidence.* Los Angeles: Law and Psychology Press.

Frye v. United States, 293 F. 1013 (D.C. Cir. 1923).

General Electric Co. v. Joiner, 522 U.S. 136 (1997).

Greenberg, S. A., & Shuman, D. W. (1997). Irreconcilable conflict between therapeutic and forensic roles. *Professional Psychology: Research and Practice, 28,* 50–57.

Greenberg, S. A., & Shuman, D. W. (2007). When worlds collide: Therapeutic and forensic roles. *Professional Psychology: Research and Practice, 38* (2), 129–132.

Grove, W. M., & Barden, R. C. (1999). Protecting the integrity of the legal system: The admissibility of testimony from mental health experts under *Daubert/Kumho* analyses. *Psychology, Public Policy, and Law, 5* (1), 224–242.

Hannay, H. J., Bieliauskas, L. A., Crosson, B. A., Hammeke, T. A., Hamsher, K. deS., & Koffler, S. P. (1998). Proceedings of the Houston conference on specialty education and training in clinical neuropsychology. *Archives of Clinical Neuropsychology, Special Issue, 13* (2), 157–250.

Heilbronner, R. L. (2004). A status report on the practice of forensic neuropsychology. *The Clinical Neuropsychologist, 18*, 312–326.

Heilbronner, R. L., Sweet, J. J., Morgan, J. E., Larrabee, G. J., Millis, S. R., & Conference Participants. (2009). American academy of clinical neuropsychology consensus conference statement on the neuropsychological assessment of effort, response bias, and malingering. *The Clinical Neuropsychologist, 23* (7), 1093–1129.

Heilbrun, K. (2001). *Principles of Forensic Mental Health Assessment.* New York: Kluwer Academic/ Plenum.

Heltzel, T. (2007). Compatibility of therapeutic and forensic roles. *Professional Psychology: Research and Practice, 38* (2), 122–128.

Hines v. Welch, 23 F.2d 979 (D.C. Cir. 1928).

Hovey v. Hobson, 55 Me. 256 (Me. 1867).

Huber, P. W. (1991). *Galileo's Revenge: Junk Science in the Courtroom.* New York: Basic Books.

Johnson, M. T., Krafka, C., & Cecil, J. S. (2000). *Expert Testimony in Federal Civil Trials: A Preliminary Analysis.* Washington, DC: Federal Judicial Center.

Joint Committee on Standards for Educational and Psychological Testing. (1999). *Standards for Educational and Psychological Testing.* Washington DC: American Educational Resource Association.

Kaufmann, P. M. (2009). Protecting raw data and psychological tests from wrongful disclosure: A primer on the law and other persuasive strategies. *The Clinical Neuropsychologist, 23*(7), 1130–1159.

Kaufmann, P. M. (2012). Admissibility of expert opinions based on neuropsychological evidence. In G. Larrabee (Ed.), *Forensic Neuropsychology: A Scientific Approach* (2nd ed., pp. 70–100). New York: Oxford University Press.

Kaufmann, P. M., & Greiffenstein, M. F. (2013). Forensic neuropsychology: Training, scope of practice, and quality control. *NAN Bulletin, 27* (1), 11–15.

Kaufmann, P. M. (2016). Neuropsychologist experts and civil capacity evaluations: Representative cases. *Archives of Clinical Neuropsychology, 31* (6), 487–494.

Kay, T. (1999). Interpreting apparent neuropsychological deficits: What is really wrong? In J. J. Sweet (Ed.), *Forensic Neuropsychology: Fundamentals and Practice* (pp. 145–183). Lisse, Netherlands: Swets & Zeitlinger.

Krafka, C., Dunn, M. A., Treadway Johnson, M., Cecil, J. S., & Miletich, D. (2002). Judge and attorney experiences, practices, and concerns regarding expert testimony in federal civil trials. *Psychology, Public Policy, and Law, 8* (3), 309–332.

Kumho Tire Co. v. Carmichael, 526 U.S. 137 (1999).

Laing, L. C., & Fisher, J. M. (1997). Neuropsychology in civil proceedings. In R. J. McCaffrey, A. D. Williams, J. M. Fisher, & L. C. Laing (Eds.), *The Practice of Forensic Neuropsychology: Meeting Challenges in the Courtroom* (pp. 117–133). New York: Plenum Press.

Larrabee, G. J. (2012). *Forensic Neuropsychology: A Scientific Approach* (2nd ed.). New York: Oxford University Press.

Lees-Haley, P. R., & Cohen, L. (1999). The neuropsychologist as expert witness: Toward credible science in the courtroom. In J. Sweet (Ed.), *Forensic Neuropsychology: Fundamentals and Practice* (pp. 443–468). Lisse, Netherlands: Swets & Zeitlinger.

Lees-Haley, P. R., English, L. T., & Glenn, W. J. (1991). A fake bad scale on the MMPI-2 for personal injury claimants. *Psychological Reports, 68* (1), 203–210.

Matarazzo, J. D. (1990). Psychological assessment versus psychological testing: Validation from Binet to the school, clinic, and courtroom. *American Psychologist, 45* (9), 999–1017.

Matarazzo, J. D. (1991). Psychological assessment is reliable and valid: Reply to Ziskin and Faust. *American Psychologist, 46*(8), 882–884.

McCrystal, L. (2012, September 23). Concord/Wakefield 11 years on, verdict in lead case. *Concord Monitor.* Retrieved November 30, 2013 from www.concordmonitor.com/news/

MDEX Online. (2017). *Daubert Tracker* [website]. Retrieved from www.dauberttracker.com.

Melton, G. B., Petrila, J., Poythress, N. G., & Slobogin, C. (1997). *Psychological Evaluations for the Courts: A Handbook for Mental Health Professionals and Lawyers* (2nd ed.). New York: Guilford Press.

Mitrushina, M. N., Boone, K. B., & D'Elia, L. F. (1999). *Handbook of Normative Data for Neuropsychological Assessment.* New York: Oxford University Press.

Rankin, E. J., & Adams, R. L. (1999). The neuropsychological evaluation: Clinical and scientific foundations. In J. J. Sweet (Ed.), *Forensic Neuropsychology: Fundamentals and Practice* (pp. 83–119). Lisse, Netherlands: Swets & Zeitlinger.

Sheehan v. Daily Racing Form, Inc., 104 F.3d 940, 942 (7th Cir. 1997).

Sherman, E. S., & Brooks, B. L. (2012). *Pediatric Forensic Neuropsychology.* New York: Oxford University Press.

Shuman, D. W., & Sales, B. D. (1999). The impact of *Daubert* and its progeny on the admissibility of behavioral and social science evidence. *Psychology, Public Policy, and Law, 5* (1), 3–15.

Slick, D. J., Sherman, E.M.S., & Iverson, G. L. (1999). Diagnostic criteria for malingered neurocognitive dysfunction: Proposed standards for clinical practice and research. *The Clinical Neuropsychologist, 13* (4), 545–561.

Smith v. Metropolitan Life Insurance Company, 317 Ill. App. 624 (Ill. App. Ct. 1943).

State v. Dahood, 814 A.2d 159 (N.H., 2002).

State v. Knight, 95 Me. 467, (Me. 1901).

Sweet, J. J. (Ed.). (1999a). *Forensic Neuropsychology: Fundamentals and Practice.* Lisse, Netherlands: Swets & Zeitlinger.

Sweet, J. J., Benson, L. M., Nelson, N. W., & Moberg, P. J. (2015). The American Academy of Clinical Neuropsychology, National Academy of Neuropsychology, and Society for Neuropsychology (APA

Division 40) 2015 TCN Professional Practice and "Salary Survey": Professional Practices, Beliefs, and Incomes of U.S. Neuropsychologists. *The Clinical Neuropsychologist, 29* (8), 1069–1162.

Sweet, J. J., King, J. H., Malina, A., Bergman, M., & Simmons, A. (2002). Documenting the prominence of forensic neuropsychology at national meetings and in relevant professional journals from 1990–2000. *The Clinical Neuropsychologist, 16,* 481–494.

Sweet, J. J., Meyer, D. G., Nelson, N. W., & Moberg, P. J. (2011). The TCN/AACN 2010 "Salary Survey": Professional Practices, Beliefs, and Incomes of U.S. Neuropsychologists. *The Clinical Neuropsychologist, 25* (1), 12–61.

Sweet, J. J., Moberg, P., & Suchy, Y. (2000). Ten-year follow-up survey of clinical neuropsychologists: Part II: Private practice and economics. *The Clinical Neuropsychologist, 14,* 479–495.

Sweet, J. J., Peck, E., Abramowitz, C., & Etzweiler, S. (2003). National Academy of Neuropsychology/ Division 40 (American Psychological Association) Practice Survey of Clinical Neuropsychology in the United States, Part II: Reimbursement experiences, practice economics, billing practices, and incomes. *Archives of Clinical Neuropsychology, 18* (6), 557–582.

Taylor, J. S. (1999). The legal environment pertaining to clinical neuropsychology. In J. Sweet (Ed.), *Forensic Neuropsychology: Fundamentals and Practice* (pp. 419–442). Lisse, Netherlands: Swets & Zeitlinger.

Tenopyr, M. L. (1999). A scientist-practitioner's viewpoint on the admissibility of behavioral and social scientific information. *Psychology, Public Policy, and Law, 5* (1), 194–202.

Woody, R. H. (2009). Ethical considerations of multiple roles in Forensic Services. *Ethics and Behavior, 19* (1), 79–87.

As you read through the articles in this chapter, be prepared to discuss the following topics:

1. How and why would a personality inventory test, a tool typically used to discover the suitability of different career paths, be helpful in assessing personality disorders related to criminality?
2. How might understanding personality disorders be helpful in interpreting a crime scene?
3. What is the difference between the Frye standard and the Daubert standard of evidence for the acceptability of expert testimony?
4. Why is forensic neuropsychology an important consideration in criminal cases?
5. What are some psychosocial statistics about serial killers, and what do they imply about the societies in which they are present?
6. Why are serial killers not considered legally insane?
7. How does intelligence influence the condition of a crime scene?
8. How and why would environmental factors impact the development of a psychopathic personality?

Image Credits

Fig. 1.1: Copyright © by MelodyJSandoval (CC by 2.0) at https://commons.wikimedia.org/wiki/File:Jim_Parsons_(The_Big_Bang_Theory)_3781567513.jpg.

Fig. 1.1.1a: Source: https://www.loc.gov/item/2006677371/.

Fig. 1.1.1b: Source: https://www.loc.gov/item/2006677370/.

Chapter 2

Cadavers, Relics, and the Devil Made Me Do It

FINDING THE MUTILATED BODY IN MITRE SQARE

FIGURE 2.1   1888 illustration of Jack the Ripper in a local newspaper.

INTRODUCTION TO CHAPTER 2

There is an often-repeated quote attributed to Jack the Ripper that he "gave birth to the twenti-eth century." This is not true, of course, since history has documented a long line of serial killers that equal or surpass the Ripper in body count and/or viciousness. Over a century later we still do not know who Jack the Ripper was and there is no evidence that he ever uttered this state-ment. But this fictional quote suggests that the creation of a serial killer is rooted in a failing society (in this case, during the transition from the nineteenth to the twentieth century) as London was perceived by some to be in a state of social and moral decline and reflected a general disregard for human life. The Whitechapel District was an infamous slum area of East London where the poor and socially disenfranchised lived, worked, and died, often in squalor. It was hardly unique, as metropolitan centers around the globe can point to their own neglected neighborhoods where violence and crime are part of a daily struggle. It was the combination of a more literate society and access to mass-produced newspapers that turned the Jack the Ripper case into a spotlight on one of those neighborhoods.

As Downing's article points out, Western media about serial killers and their heinous crimes often paint them as individuals of unusual or exceptional abilities that change society. The "evil genius" narrative often predominates, and although there are some individuals who are found to possess high intelligence, they are by no means common any more than exceptionally high intelligence is common among the general populace. Furthermore, these killers often blend into society, are considered unremarkable in appearance and demeanor by neighbors and colleagues, and only come to light when law enforcement discovers their connection to a crime. Media aligns the killer as a symbol of society, an embodiment of social ills, such as the Whitechapel slums producing a serial killer capable of incredibly heinous acts. We need to reassess the reality of the "common" serial killer, how most of them successfully blended into normal society. Many have serious personality disorders that create social obstacles for them and yet, or in spite of, occasionally "odd" interactions with others, most go about the business of being nondescript while leading a double life.

According to police and archival records, the Whitechapel District was home to over 1,200 prostitutes by the late nineteenth century (Rumbelow, 2013). By 1888, Jack the Ripper made his appearance and literally carved out his place in history on human flesh. Increasing savagery and mutilation of his victims reached a crescendo on the night of September 30, 1888, when the Ripper was credited with committing two murders within the space of a single hour. It is speculated (and challenged) that his first murder was interrupted, robbing him of time with his victim, and so he found a second victim in Mitre Square upon which to complete this pattern with Catherine Eddowes. (See Figure 2.1.) There is a general misconception that the Ripper was the first true serial killer in history—a killer whose actions are not grounded in the usual motivations of greed, vengeance, or jealousy that most of us can understand as precursors to committing homicide. The Ripper's murders were grounded in something else—something so unfathomable and incomprehensible as to add to the fear and mystique that there existed seemingly "motiveless" crimes. This concept entered a nascent stage of development in criminal theory. The field of forensic psychology was in its infancy in the late nineteenth century. It began the journey set in motion by Wilhelm Wundt that would prove invaluable to understanding criminal behavior and decision-making.

As we study criminal behaviors and personalities in different historical and cultural contexts, we find this assumption about the Ripper as our first serial killer to be woefully incorrect. But the Ripper's case teaches us the ways in which serial killers take full advantage of the limits and idiosyncrasies particular to their historical period and the societies in which they live in order to commit their crimes and elude capture. However, both a criminal's behavior and personality are also uniquely a product of their times and molded by them, despite the traits they may share with other serial killers across history.

Studies in violence today build upon modern concepts about crime and violence and underlying social issues. We seek ways to intervene and prevent unnecessary suffering and crime. Yet in contradiction, pain and suffering were historically regarded as necessary rather than something that could be or even should be eliminated, and so, expectations about and the acceptability of violence were quite different and impacted the psychological development of individuals differently. We cannot judge the tolerance and use of violence in the past by today's standards as they simply do not apply. The article by Impara (2016) illuminates our need to put violence in contextual perspective to understand individuals who engage with violence and pain in a different way.

Western society's perception of the human body and mind has evolved over time. The body has been perceived as a locus of spiritual and supernatural power, depending upon one's cultural and religious context. Tarlow's article (2016) looks at the relationships between the dead and the living in terms of a perception of ongoing power wielded by the body and its disarticulated parts. Concepts of spiritual pollution, possession, or otherworldly interference (such as demons) as causes for inexplicable murder are constant themes throughout human history. Those views have proven resistant to scientific explanation at times.

Medieval regard for human remains dictated restraint in dealing with the dead, both as a point of respect and in fear of spiritual contamination. These views presented obstacles to scientific study of the human body and delayed understanding of internal systems for centuries. Ironically, the waves of plague, or the Black Death as it was known, that began in the early fourteenth century and claimed the lives of 30–60 percent of the population across the European continent resulted in an obsession with death in art and literature. Death had become an entity, and he was to be courted and appeased, negotiated with, and sometimes depicted in playful (if deadly) repose with his human counterparts.

The articles in this chapter are intended to open discussions and raise awareness about different social and cultural views that impacted forensic development and scientific study throughout history. Delays and prohibitions of scientific experimentation paved the way for attitudes that remained even after science gained a foothold in our approach to crime.

The Beast in the Man: Jack and the Rippers Who Came After

By Lisa Downing

Man is the hunter; woman is his game.
The sleek and shining creature of the chase,
We hunt them for the beauty of their skins;
They love us for it and we ride them down.

—(Alfred Lord Tennyson, "The Princess," 1847)

I'm not a butcher
I'm not a Yid,
Nor yet a foreign skipper,
But I'm your own light-hearted friend,
Yours truly, Jack the Ripper.

—(Included in one of many letters allegedly sent by the Whitechapel murderer, 1888)

Wild beasts remain wild beasts, and all attempts to invent better disguises will be in vain: there will still be wild beasts underneath.

—(Zola, *La Bête humaine*, 1890)[1]

THE ACTIVITIES OF JACK THE RIPPER, the still unidentified killer who terrorized London's impoverished Whitechapel in 1888, killing and dismembering at least five, and possibly several more, women in the most violent and bloodthirsty ways,[2] were disseminated and discussed avidly throughout both Europe and America. While "Jack" may not technically have been the first serial murderer,[3] he nevertheless stood at "the gateway of the modern age,"[4] inaugurating what Caputi calls the age of sex crime. The simultaneity of the Ripper killings and such modern cultural phenomena as a literary taste for the Gothic and detective fiction, the explosion of the pulp press, and the rise of sexual and criminological science suggests a complex network of discursive and social trends that interrelated to produce an event that would resonate beyond its immediate moment and shape the figure of the murderer in the cultural imaginary for centuries to come and across geographical boundaries. The anonymous Ripper became the archetype for that subject of modernity, the serial sex murderer. In Mark Seltzer's words: Jack the Ripper was "from the start a projective surface for all sorts of stories."[5]

The stories projected onto the figure of Jack include, of course, speculative stories about his identity, framed in discourses that are both of their time and recognizable. He was sometimes cast as the aesthetekiller, reminiscent of Lacenaire, as seen in the speculations of "Ripperologists," both at the time of the killings and in recent years, that the murderer may have been a poet, actor, or artist, "a gentleman of leisure … seeking after luxurious cruelties which could stimulate his jaded sensibilities."[6] Decadent poet Algernon Charles Swinburne and American actor Richard Mansfield, who portrayed Stevenson's Dr. Jekyll and Mr. Hyde with extraordinary skill at the Lyceum, were both contemporary suspects. And crime writer Patricia Cornwell has recently produced what she considers definitive proof that minor artist Walter Sickert was the killer.[7] Other theories have suggested that the killer was an aristocrat—even a minor royal (the Duke of Clarence). Given the extensive "gynecological"[8] mutilation of the victims' bodies, the theory that the Ripper was a doctor or butcher has also held sway.

The Ripper case also served as a hook on which to hang a story central to nineteenth-century criminological and sexological thinking: the narrative of civilization's decline, as dramatized by degeneration theory. The "degenerate criminal" suggested by the anonymous Ripper's crimes is an atavistic throwback, a "beast." The elitist aspect of degeneration theory is seen in the fact that this threat of destructive atavism was felt to issue primarily from the proletarian "masses," from socialists, and from nonwhite, non-Christian ethnicities and religions. The counterpoint to theories of the Ripper as artist or aristocratic gentleman was the idea that he was a member of the London East End's Eastern European Jewish community. While some theories cast him as an American, a more pervasive, if rather vague, description of the Ripper that circulated was of a man of "foreign appearance"[9] (implying, presumably, dark skin). This led to increased hostility toward Jewish immigrants, exacerbated by the allusion to an alleged Talmudic injunction that a Jewish man who had sex with a Christian woman should subsequently kill her.[10] The tendency of Western Christian culture to project misogyny onto non-Christian religions is a long-standing patriarchal strategy for distracting attention from more local examples thereof. The fact that the location of the Ripper murders was the cosmopolitan, largely Jewish, and extremely poor milieu of Whitechapel served to reinforce (despite the various contradictory conjectures that the criminal may have been an artist, doctor, or aristocrat) the belief that the socially deprived and the ethnic other posed an ineffable threat to the middle classes.

The East End of London was also, of course, the locus of prostitution, from which the Ripper profited in choosing his victims. It is of note that the prostitute was contemporaneously seen as a degenerate female and bearer of disease. One fanciful theory that circulated regarding the possibility of the killer being a doctor or medical student held that this man may have contracted a sexually transmitted disease, probably syphilis, from a prostitute and was "down on whores" and "ripping them"[11] as a form of revenge. Sander Gilman has argued brilliantly that the whore, the Jew, and the lust murderer are seen as the differently gendered embodiments of end-of-century diseased culture, such that, whereas police and physicians were powerless to remove prostitutes from the streets, "Jack could kill the 'source of infection' because he too was fatally diseased";[12] he became "the sign of deviant human sexuality destroying life, the parallel to the destructive prostitute."[13] The victim-blaming of murdered prostitutes implicit in this view of the Ripper murders is, as Cameron and Frazer have painstakingly shown, a phenomenon that the Jack the Ripper case bequeathed to subsequent sex murder cases, notably, but not solely, that of the English prostitute-killer, Peter Sutcliffe, in the 1970s and 1980s.

Jack thus became the archetype of a "new" murdering subject—the lust murderer—produced in the 1880s and 1890s in Europe. This figure of a sexually destructive male emerged as the seamy alter ego of the rational subject of progressive modernity. Bearing the mark of sexual excess, it provoked a fear of "uncivilized" animality. In the predominantly German science of sexology, the sexological type of the *Lustmörder*—proponent of what Foucault has rather fancifully called the "insane dialogue of love and death"[14]—found his place among the perverts carefully classified and catalogued by Richard von Krafft-Ebing and his sexological brethren. Although the Ripper crimes did not begin until two years after the first edition of *Psychopathia Sexualis*, in the numerous editions that followed, "Jack" provided Krafft-Ebing with exemplary illustrative material for his theory that in sadistic and murderous sexual perversion, the instinct to reproduce has been replaced with a desire to destroy. He writes of Jack: "He does not seem to have had sexual intercourse with his victims, but ... the murderous act and subsequent mutilation of the corpse were equivalents for the sexual act."[15] This definition of the lust murderer, which persists beyond the epoch of German sexology, largely ensured that this figure would be male, as the idea that "sex" *is* penetration is a particularly masculine conception, a product of a patriarchal imaginary. While, as we will see, Krafft-Ebing's sexology reveals a definite suspicion of male sexuality as potentially dangerous (and therefore of men as a moral and social threat), it remains heavily conservative and misogynistic in gender political terms, since it assumes aggressivity as a "natural" quality of masculinity/maleness (and passivity as a "natural" quality of femininity/femaleness).

This chapter analyzes some modern assumptions about sexuality, gender, class, race, and civilization that led to the production of the subject of the "lust murderer" or "sex killer," of which Jack is the exemplum, in a series of discursive fields. The ways in which nineteenth-century European medicine and sexual science figured male and female sexuality, and "specified as an individual" the murdering sexual pervert, will be analyzed in the first part. The second will consider in detail a near contemporary French response to the Ripper case and to Krafft-Ebing's *Psychopathia Sexualis*, Zola's novel *La Bête humaine* (1890), a work that functions as a fictional version of sexological and criminological discourse. In crafting the figure of Jacques Lantier, the innate criminal with an inherited compulsion to lust murder, it draws for inspiration on the aberrant pathological masculine typology described in sexology by Richard von Krafft-Ebing and in criminological accounts by Cesare Lombroso. It adheres rigidly to a model of predetermination and the belief in inherited moral, criminal, and sexual traits, while taking artistic license with some elements of the gendered portraits drawn. In a third section, I will examine how Jack the Ripper—in part owing to his continued anonymity, and therefore his qualities as a tabula rasa—provided the template for representing other sex-motivated multiple killers of both men and women that came after him, such as the "Düsseldorf Vampire" (Peter Kürten), the "Yorkshire Ripper" (Peter Sutcliffe), and "Son of Sam" (David Berkowitz). It explores how these later sex killers were culturally represented—and how they actively self-represented—using the very discursive means made available by the nineteenth-century phenomenon of Jack the Ripper and the language of the "beast" that issued from both science and the popular press.

Medical Models

In the first chapter of his encyclopedic work of sexual classification, *Psychopathia Sexualis* (1886), Krafft-Ebing makes the following claim: "The propagation of the human species is not committed to accident or to the caprice of the individual, but made secure in a natural instinct, which, with all-conquering force and might, demands fulfilment."[16] Krafft-Ebing starts, then, from the assumption of a biological imperative: that the survival of the species guides the individual toward reproductive activity. The strength of conviction here may strike us as a case of protesting too much, given that Krafft-Ebing then goes on to devote some 500 pages to cataloguing the many instances of sexuality's determined *resistance* to acts that would lead to reproduction, in the form of the sexual perversions. Perhaps in recognition of this contradiction, Krafft-Ebing then appeals to the necessity for moral restraint on the part of men to prevent the natural instinct from going awry. Men are instructed to apply reason and moral sagacity in their sexual lives, as their natural predisposition toward a higher sex drive than women makes them particularly vulnerable. Krafft-Ebing tells us— in terms that abundantly confuse nature and class-bound culture—that "if [a woman] is normally developed mentally and well bred, her sexual desire is small. If this were not so the whole world would become a brothel and marriage and a family impossible."[17] Whereas "from the fact that man by nature plays the aggressive *rôle* in sexual life, he is in danger of overstepping the limits which morality and law have set."[18] This normative description of the "natural" predispositions of men and women leaves in no doubt the danger that is perceived to issue from the female prostitute and the male sexual sadist, the very players in the Jack the Ripper drama.[19]

Two belief systems operate side by side and in tension with each other in Krafft-Ebing's sexology. On the one hand, degeneration is innate and inevitable: a degenerate pervert cannot be cured and, if he or she should reproduce, the taint will be passed down the line. On the other hand, corruption and contagion are consistently warned against and such pursuits as masturbation, that would be recognized today as harmless, could be sufficient to provide the foundation of ruin in a formerly "healthy" subject. The logic of sexual weakness in the *Psychopathia Sexualis*, then, is much the same as that of the alienists earlier in the century with their diagnosis of monomania, a single-minded compulsion that gripped the afflicted subject and robbed him of reason and free will. Sexual continence, like reason, is precarious. The biggest threat to the (male) individual and his society is loss of self-control, understood in sexology as giving in to sexual excess. But at the same time, men must retain just enough sexual aggressiveness to remain properly masculine. Krafft-Ebing states:

> The *rôle* which the retention of sexual functions plays in the case of a man, both in originating and retaining his feeling of self-respect, is remarkable. In the deterioration of manliness and self-confidence which the onanist, in his weakened nervous state, and the man that has become impotent, present, may be estimated the significance of this factor.[20]

Concerns over semen conservation and the potential of masturbation to lead to weakness, neurasthenia, and disease, as posited by Swiss physician Samuel-Auguste Tissot as early as 1760, raise their head here. Sexual excess risks not only undermining the masculine imperative to build society and propagate the next generation, but also weakening the nervous and moral system of the individual and laying him open to worse consequences. In a system haunted by the logic of corruption and contagion, masturbation could lead to depleted moral faculties, which could lead to more "serious" perversions such as sadism, necrophilia, and eventually, perhaps, to lust murder.

Lust murder is diagnosed by Krafft-Ebing, as we have seen, in cases where the act of killing can be said to have taken the place of the act of intercourse, as seen in Lombroso's patient Vincent Verzeni who, in 1783, made the following confession: "I had an unspeakable delight in strangling women, experiencing during that act erections and real sexual pleasure … much greater than that which I experienced while masturbating."[21] Krafft-Ebing further refines his definition, adding an element of mutilation to the consideration of the phenomenological killing/sex equivalence:

> The presumption of a murder out of lust is always given when injuries of the genitals are found, the character and extent of which are not such as could be explained by merely a brutal attempt at coitus; and still more when the body has been opened and parts (intestines, genitals) torn out and wanting.[22]

This conforms, of course, with the case of Jack the Ripper, who provides "an outline, a repository, a *type*"[23] for the diagnosis, even though he is far from being the earliest case of a lust murderer that Krafft-Ebing discusses:

> It is probable that he first cut the throats of his victims, then ripped open the abdomen and groped among the intestines. In some instances he cut off the genitals and carried them away; in others he only tore them to pieces and left them behind.[24]

It is in discussing lust murder that Krafft-Ebing deploys most freely a language of uncontrolled animal instinct. So, "a certain Grassi," who stabbed to death a female relative, is described as engaging in "acts of bestiality."[25] And the subjects in this category are referred to en masse as "psycho-sexual monsters."[26] It is perhaps not surprising that repulsion for such extreme violence should lead the doctor to use such emotive terms to describe the behavior in question. However, one cannot read this animal and teratological vocabulary as referring *only* to the specific and extreme acts and subjects it purports to be describing. The language of instinct leading to bestiality echoes Krafft-Ebing's words of warning regarding the citizen's socio-sexual duty to avoid "the lustful impulse to satisfy" the instinct of "sensuous love" (whether by adultery, masturbation, or other harmless acts, as well as by sadism and lust murder). For in doing any of this, he tells us, "man stands on a level with the animal."[27]

It was a Frenchman, Bénédict Augustin Morel (1809–1873), who in 1857 was the first to define degeneration as the source and cause of the rise of crime, in his *Traité de dégénérescences physiques, intellectuelles et morales de l'espèce humaine* (Treatise on the physical, intellectual and moral degeneration of the human species). This idea was expanded upon by Lombroso's criminal science in Italy and by Max Nordau in Germany. While, as Daniel Pick has pointed out in his study of this "European disorder," degeneration took varying forms in the distinct national cultures, it nonetheless shared common concerns, precepts, and obsessions.[28] Degeneration theorists pursued the logic that nonreproductive sexuality contributed to the moral, physiological, and mental deterioration they perceived to afflict the European population at the turn of the century. About sexual excess, that is, perversion, Nordau wrote that it renders the whole society, as well as the individuals in it, "too worn out and flaccid to perform great tasks."[29] This worn-out and flaccid population risked regressing from its position of evolved reason to an atavistic condition: "It is a descent from the height of human perfection to the low level of the mollusc."[30] Rather than being civilized men, the modern population risked becoming "anti-social vermin."[31] The regressive beast of degeneration, then, is described by Nordau in the same terms as the unreasoned sexual excess in Krafft-Ebing that devitalizes the population and turns its mind to destruction rather than procreation: from will and reason to animal instinct. Sexual perversions, writes Nordau, "run directly contrary to the purpose of the instinct, i.e., the preservation of the species."[32]

Sexual science, then, sets up the ideal of masculine agency, the "naturalness" of male aggression in sex, and the force of male sex drive. It warns, on the one hand, against weakening good virile male aggression by means of masturbation or effeminacy and, on the other, against the excessive pursuit of satisfaction of the sexual appetite, for this leads to an animalistic exacerbation of the instinct that could result in sadism and lust murder. It demonstrates a belief both in heredity (in the inherited predisposition toward mental and physiological dysfunctions) and in the corrupting or contagious power of exposure to sex. This is demonstrated by the fact that Krafft-Ebing rendered the most obscene details of his case studies in Latin, so that the uninitiated could not be corrupted into imitative behavior if their eyes should fall upon an open copy of his book. Effectively, then, the ideal of masculine behavior presented leaves little room for maneuver for those aspiring to it; the nineteenth-century male is trapped in a series of tautologies and logical double binds. The discourse of sexual science has high expectations of masculinity as the fantasized embodiment of reason, but also a fatal suspicion of male weakness. It only barely manages to disguise this latter by means of its misogynistic projection of passivity and low sex drive onto women, seen in Krafft-Ebing's comment on the high number of male sadists and lust killers as compared to female ones. Since sadism is, for Krafft-Ebing, "a pathological intensification of the masculine sexual character," it is inevitable in his system that "the obstacles which oppose the expression of this monstrous impulse are ... much greater for a woman than for a man."[33] The perverse intensification of the natural "feminine" sexual character would be sexual masochism.[34] Indeed, Krafft-Ebing points out that so natural is the instinct of submission to the heterosexual female that feminine masochism is more or less the norm rather than a perversion: "ideas of subjection" are the "tone-quality of feminine feeling"[35] and "the male 'sadistic force' is developed ... by the natural shyness and modesty of women."[36] Krafft-Ebing comes perilously close to suggesting that women's "natural" sexual passivity *causes* male sexuality to take an aggressive, violent form—effectively blaming the victim for the crime. Furthermore, dressing the absence of female sex murderers as a matter of natural submissiveness neatly obviates the need to consider the factor of male social domination of women, via such institutions as church and medicine, which inculcated in women a very *cultural* passivity from their youngest age. Neither does this explanation address the idea that the lust murderer is constructed a priori as a masculine subject by dint of the shared investment of this individual *and his culture* in a myth of male agency, potency, and aggression, in which penetrating and killing can be intelligibly interchangeable.

The figure of the lust murderer described by nineteenth-century scientists actualizes in the public sphere the destructive and disruptive potential of male sexuality gone awry that the onanist risks only in the confines of his bedchamber. This figure haunted the scientific and literary discourses of degeneration in the form of Robert Louis Stevenson's Mr. Hyde, the underside of "rational" man embodied by Dr. Jekyll; in the form of Bram Stoker's Dracula, a predator from an Eastern European land preying on Western women and infecting them with a voracious sexuality; and, of course, in the figure of the anonymous Whitechapel murderer striking after dark in the East End of London. The lust killer, to some extent, became the poster child of conservative medical and social discourses, then, for it would have been hard to convince the reader that foot fetishism or erotomania so directly threatened the survival of civilization. But there is no question that for Krafft-Ebing, these nonprocreative sexual activities lie on a continuum of masculinity. The hybrid figure of the lust murderer, uniting hypermasculinity and evirated masculinity, became an appropriate specter of beastly horror—and of fascination—for the culture that gave birth to him.

Strikingly and counterintuitively, then, the radical feminist analysis of the meaning of lust murder expounded by Caputi and by Cameron and Frazer, which holds that it is "a distinctly male crime"[37] and "male violence taken to its logical extreme,"[38] is already the unspoken subtext of the very authority discourse that produces the lust murderer as a subject (even if this is not the political *intention* of this discourse). To clarify: both nineteenth-century sexologists and twentieth-century feminist scholars perceive male murderous sexuality as a real threat, but, crucially, where Krafft-Ebing sees it as a symbolic threat to civilized (patriarchal) social order, feminist writers see it as a very real threat to female lives, safety, and subjectivity; where Krafft-Ebing sees male destructivity as rooted in biology, in essence, feminists see this rhetoric as the strategy of a culture invested in justifying and maintaining its constructed system of domination, in which men are dominant and women submissive.

Zola's Beast

Naturalism was the literary school that, in the words of Daniel Pick, dreamed both of "mastering disorder" and of providing a "master narrative of disorder,"[39] by trying to make literary craft approximate scientific method. It is widely acknowledged that *La Bête humaine* constitutes an attempt to construct, in literary form, a case history of the sexual criminal subject in conformity with the scientific theorization of the day. Work by Geoff Woollen,[40] Daniel Pick,[41] and Pauline McLynn[42] has demonstrated various filiations between Zola's text and the ideas of Krafft-Ebing, Lombroso, Morel, and Nordau. The response of the scientists in question to Zola's project differed considerably. Delighted to have a novelist popularizing his theories, Lombroso wrote approvingly of the physiognomical characterization of Zola's dramatis personae. Noting that Zola's lust murderer is described as a "handsome fellow with a round face and regular features, but spoiled by a too prominent jawline,"[43] he remarked that "this Jacques Lantier definitely has some characteristics of the inborn criminal."[44] However, he also argued that Zola's portrayal was not consistently psychologically accurate as the "real" murderer with a hereditary predisposition toward lust killing would never be able to enjoy sexual intercourse with a woman without feeling the need to kill her, as Jacques is shown doing in his early encounters with Séverine. For Nordau, on the other hand, Naturalist literature was a symptom and cause of degeneration, not a means of enlightening the population about it, and Zola's novels were among those that he condemned most forcefully. Nordau strongly believed that degenerate art, such as he termed Naturalism, was rooted in the "sexual psychopathology" of its creator. In the context of a system in which artists and writers were seen to bear strong resemblances to the mentally ill, Nordau was able to write of novelists that "all persons of unbalanced minds ... have the keenest scent for perversions of a sexual kind."[45] However, the ambivalence of degeneration theory comes in its concession that the genius as well as the mad man or the criminal is a "degenerate." In its adherence to the very idea of genius, and in approximating genius to criminality, degeneration theory bears no doubt unintended comparisons and parallels with the discourse of Romanticism. The focus on the unique, singular, better-than-normal individual persists, albeit with a different ideological bias.

As well as borrowing theories from scientific contemporaries, Zola drew, like them, on the popular press for case material. Sketches for a novel about a man with an overwhelming desire to kill women—"un homme qui a besoin de tuer"[46]—first occur in Zola's notebooks as early as 1874. However, Jacques Lantier owes both his name and certain characteristics to the sensationalist press coverage of the murders of Jack the Ripper (whom the French called *Jacques l'éventreur*—the verb éventrer meaning "to eviscerate"). And true to form, the narrative of Zola's text parallels Krafft-Ebing's statement that murder replaces penetrative sex for the inborn lust murderer (despite the episode criticized by Lombroso, in which Jacques is able to perform "normally"). When the reader is first made aware of Jacques's unorthodox desire, it is in the following terms: "Kill a woman, kill a woman! This rang in his ears, from the days of his youth, with the growing, maddening, fever of desire. As others, at the dawn of puberty, dream of possessing a woman, he was obsessed with the idea of killing one."[47] Jacques's murderous desire first occurs at puberty, suggesting an unhealthy parallel to "normal" development, the supplanting of sex with death-lust. Yet the choice of verb to describe "healthy" sex with a woman is telling: it is *posséder*, "to possess." Zola draws attention to the aggressive masculinity that is the "natural" sexual response to "the weaker sex" (and suggests, to a reader aware of gender politics, the domination paradigm on which heterosexuality is discursively founded). This passage about Jacques's youth is designed to read like the confessions included in the studies of individual patients in contemporaneous sexological manuals. And it succeeds in so doing; the following, taken from the confessions of the "Vampire of Montparnasse," the necrophile soldier Sergent Bertrand, tried in 1849, bears resemblances to the description of Jacques's adolescent desires:

> At thirteen or fourteen I knew no limits. I masturbated up to seven or eight times a day; the mere sight of women's clothing excited me. While masturbating, I was transported in my fantasy to a room where women were at my disposal. There, after having sated my passion on them, and having amused myself by torturing them in every manner, I imagined them dead and exerted upon their cadavers all sorts of profanations.[48]

Both fictional and medical accounts of the pervert's and the lust murderer's experience are collated in the course of the nineteenth century, such that they eventually constitute a cultural repository of ideas about the phenomenon.

Geoff Woollen[49] and Philippe Hamon[50] have pointed out the probable influence on Zola of a short story by the little known Belgian Naturalist Camille Lemonnier, "L'Homme qui tuait les femmes" ("The man who killed women"), which appeared in *Gil Blas* on 2 November 1888, and which was also inspired by the Whitechapel killings. Lemonnier's treatment of the subject matter is, however, rather different from Zola's. The narrative is voiced in the first person by the murderer, who speaks of himself in the third person at one point, stating: "I bequeath to science ... the perverse and complex being who, to me, will always remain an unfathomable problem."[51] In the change of person from first to third, Lemonnier's hero expresses a dissociation from the unknowable part of himself that feels the need to kill, whereas Jacques Lantier asks endless questions about the cause of his condition expressed via free indirect style, a narrative technique beloved of French Realist and Naturalist novelists of the nineteenth century. Musing on the origins of his sexual inclination, Jacques wonders: "Did it come from a distant time, from the evil that woman had done to his race, from the accumulated spite felt by male after male since the first deception?"[52] What is very visible in Jacques's speculation is the victim-blaming tendency that runs through discourses of sex killing—scientific, journalistic, and those produced by (fictional and real) lust murderers themselves. Here, the familiar projection of male aggression onto women is accorded ancient origins. The "first deception" reminds us of an atavistic, primal, perceived wrong wrought by a female: we may think of Pandora, of Lilith, of Eve. Too, Jacques's self-interrogation is consistent with the ideology of heredity and degeneration, since the more local explanation of the "first deception" is understandable in terms of the fact that Jacques comes of a degenerate line, that of the Rougon-Macquarts, whose taint of sickness originated with the mentally deficient middle-class Adelaide Fouque, Jacques's grandmother, who had three illegitimate children with a low-class smuggler, Macquart. The descendants of this coupling all bear degenerate traits: alcoholism for Jacques's mother, Gervaise, of *L'Assomoir*; prostitution for his sister, the eponymous Nana; and lust murder for Jacques, showing again how the nineteenth century imagined gendered complementarity between the "perversions" of whoredom and lust murder.

Vernon Rosario has argued that it is, in fact, the trace of the feminine that is feared and despised in the figure of the beast in man in a culture in which weakness and lack of reason are associated with the feminine: "La bête humaine crouching in the dark recesses of the individual and collective psyche was the primitive, pathological, deadly erotic imagination, and its sex was female."[53] As we have seen, weakness and a proximity to nature and the instinctual were codified as feminine in nineteenth-century philosophy and sexual science, while the mastery of reason connoted masculinity. However, as the following extract from *Psychopathia Sexualis* reveals, the supposed greater capacity of the male for sexual lust rendered him in danger of "feminine" weakness precisely at the moment that he was apparently most masculine: "Undoubtedly man has a much more intense sexual appetite than woman. ... In accordance with the nature of this powerful impulse, he is aggressive and violent in his wooing."[54] Yet "the weakness of men in comparison with women lies in the great intensity of their sexual desires." The more desirous he is, "the weaker and more sensual he becomes."[55] Here Krafft-Ebing is describing the condition of the so-called normal, healthy male. Jacques's fantasy of destructive revenge on the female ancestor who provoked his weakness is thus understandable as an exaggeration of a "normal" masculine attitude. We see, then, that Zola's lust murderer, Jacques Lantier, and the sexologist Krafft-Ebing employ the same logic in relation to the female: the "weakness" that desire suggests for the male is projected onto the object of his lust, from whom the weakness is erroneously perceived to emit. The fantasy of sexual and moral weakness with which femininity was associated and the fantasy of a monstrous, exaggerated destructive masculinity both come to rest in the same site: the figure of the "lust murderer."

A fascinating feature of *La Bête humaine* is that it seems to suggest at moments that the representation of Jacques's desire to kill women may not (only) be the result of the perversion of the instinct of conservation peculiar to the exceptional perverted male, or the fatal trait inherited from a degenerate family line, but rather a logical consequence of the ways in which heteronormative culture dreams the asymmetrical distinction between the sexes—a collective fantasy. Yet this is never *explicitly* given, and Jacques's status in the text is ambiguous, swinging between the two perspectives. If sometimes it is made abundantly clear that Lantier is intended to do no more than fulfill the criteria for a case study of the lust murderer, at other points in the novel, Jacques's proclivities suggest a paradigm of a more general model of (nonexceptional) masculinity in which sex and killing lie on an imaginary continuum, exactly as argued by Caputi and by Cameron and Frazer, and as fearfully posited by nineteenth-century sexology. It is by drawing the reader close to the perspective of Jacques that he is permitted to shift, sometimes, from the aberrant subject matter of a case study, to an agentic subject. Rhetorical questions such as the following draw the reader in, creating collusion with the character, and forcing us to question too: "possessing, killing; were the two equivalent?"[56] It is because of Zola's manipulation of the narrative point of view in *La Bête humaine* that our understanding of Jacques's perspective is allowed to slip from one of exceptional aberration to one of universality. Caputi has described the way in which the reader/viewer is commonly aligned with the point of view of the killer, rather than the victim, in most spectacles and narratives of lust murder, and this is certainly the case here.

The terms in which the murder of Séverine is framed are particularly revealing in this respect: "She inclined her submissive face and, with a supplicating tenderness, revealed her bare neck. ... And he, seeing this white flesh, as in a burst of flames, lifted his fist which held the knife."[57] The strategy is one of dramatic irony. The reader, possessed of the knowledge of the secret of Jacques's desire, can anticipate the radical misreading of Séverine's signals that will occur. Intending to tempt her lover to have sex with her, Séverine fatally mismanages the other's desire and hastens her own murder—in another example of implied victim-blaming. It is, then, because the reader's attention is aligned throughout much of the narrative with Jacques's point of view—and crucially never with Séverine's—that the dramatic irony of this episode can function. We know that Jacques's desire is to "throw her onto her back, dead, like some prey that one has grabbed from the others."[58] The passage cited above, describing the moment, before Séverine's murder, shows how the woman's motivation is construed from the masculine viewpoint. The figure of Jacques fluctuates in the course of the novel between personifying the pathologized figure of the sexological object of inquiry and the universal masculine subject of the culture. At the moment when he should so clearly be the former, distanced from the reader as horrifically "other," the narrative point of view, which suggests irresistible collusion with him, forces the reader to relate to him as the latter.

The gender bias of the viewpoint of *La Bête humaine* is brought into even sharper relief if we compare the passage I have just quoted with an extract from a minor female-authored Naturalist text, treating similar subject matter, which places the female perspective into the foreground. Rachel Mesch has brought recent critical attention to Lucie Delarue-Mardrus's *Marie, fille-mère* ("Marie, child-mother") (1908), contending that this novel constitutes a spirited feminist response to Zola's famous novelistic account of masculine beastliness.[59] In one passage of *Marie, fille-mère*, we are given the following account of heterosexuality:

> She didn't know that desire is a hunter without pity. She had never asked herself why all female animals, more intelligent than girls, start to flee from males after having called them, because a sort of fear grips them in the face of the deathliness of sex. ... She didn't know that there is struggle within love and murder in possession, that there is from one side attack and from the other defense, and that man, more cruel than any other beast, is stirred during his youth by the deaf desire to lay a woman out as he would a weaker adversary.[60]

Here, the language of murderous attack is used to describe romantic love. Drawing on the lexicon of the animal world: man as beast, and woman as prey, Delarue-Mardrus both cites and inverts Zola's formula. Using the figure of the lust murderer, Zola literalizes and puts at the surface the destructive misogyny and the paranoia regarding male sexual incontinence that run through nineteenth-century scientific accounts of heterosexual desire. The female novelist, on the other hand, dresses the socially prescribed act of sexual intercourse as a *metaphorical* murder. The difference is that our close collusion with Jacques's point of view at its most extreme naturalizes misogyny and makes lust murder appear inevitable, while our proximity to Marie's perspective here, invites us to question, in the terms of the scientific discourse itself, the inevitability of masculine destructivity and, crucially, the obligation of female collusion with it. This restores female subjectivity to what, in Zola's account, is only a victim-position.

Yet the figure of desire-as-destructivity that is at the center of Zola's conception paradoxically allows him, via the characterization of female protagonist Flore, to separate masculinity (which is aligned with destructivity) from biological maleness. As Hannah Thompson rightly points out, Philippe Hamon's division of Zola's dramatis personae into "personnages féminins" or "personnages masculins"[61] is too simplistic.[62] It conforms with the elision of the distinction between sexed bodies and cultural codes of gender that the French language presupposes. That is, it collapses masculinity unproblematically onto maleness and femininity onto femaleness, as if they are naturally linked rather than forced together by cultural constraints. This supposition is certainly the common belief of the time. However, the treatment of desire and identity in *La Bête humaine* is not quite consistent with this supposition. The character of Flore is presented to us in terms that are strikingly similar to the presentation of Jacques. Like him, she is troubled by a blood lust: "She had a fascination with accidents."[63] Unlike Séverine, defined as rape victim, abused wife, and finally murder victim—that is, archly feminine and heterosexual—Flore is described as impenetrable: "virgin and warrior; disdainful of men."[64] While Sévérine is an unwilling and traumatized accomplice in the murder of her former guardian and abuser, Grandmorin, Flore's single-minded jealous passion gives birth to devastation, when her attempt to kill Jacques and Sévérine leads to the derailment of a train and the death of many of its passengers. And, significantly, Zola has her die of her own volition after the mass murder, walking into the path of the oncoming train, like a warrior walking into battle: "She needed to walk right to the end, to die upright, guided by the instinct of a virgin warrior."[65]

The supposition of binary sex and gender difference determines the position one occupies in regard to desire in the master-slave paradigm of heterosexuality. In *La Bête humaine*, however, the binary difference in question is no longer simply the division and assumed complementarity between (aggressive) male and (passive) female, but that between destructive agency and passive victimhood. The fact that these are, in social reality, most often—and programmatically—mapped directly onto masculinity and femininity, and thence onto maleness and femaleness, is undeniable, but the text allows for a moment of doubt about the inevitability of this. The logic of desire in *La Bête humaine*, in which active sexual desire equates with the desire for death, results in an elaborate analogy of same- and hetero-desire, where the desired quality in the other is not sex or gender but a position around destruction or victimhood: being "doer" or "done-to." Flore's desire for Jacques, who like herself is an agent of death, suggests a model of desire analogous to homosexuality, but—crucially—from which the privileged term of sex/gender is removed. (She does not desire another woman, but another murderer like herself.) Jacques, in preferring, ultimately, the tempting victimhood of Sévérine as complement to his murderous assertiveness, metaphorizes the heterosexual choice.

This game with agency and passivity is not quite proto-queer, as it still retains a binary logic and a domination-subordination paradigm that run parallel to heterosexuality. Writing of homosexuality in a letter to Dr. Laupts, Zola recapitulates the notion of homosexuality as the soul of one sex in the body of another that was popularized by Karl Ulrichs (1825–1895). By formulating homosexuality as understood according to heterosexual principles, Zola gives in to regressive stereotypes: "the effeminate, delicate, cowardly man; the masculine, violent, hard-hearted woman."[66] Using the masculine-encoded desire for destruction, rather than biological sex, as the crucial identity category in the case of Flore and Jacques frees up gender attributes from biological sex (whether "appropriately" or "inappropriately" assigned), making a more complex picture of Zolian desire than Hamon allows for, and making the human beast a matter of *masculine identification* rather than *male biology*. The effect of this is that it emphasizes its cultural constructedness, rather than its naturally occurring status, and therefore suggests that male murderousness is culturally produced (and avoidable?) rather than eternally and essentially inevitable.

What Zola's novel does, by dint of its novelistic, and more specifically its Naturalist qualities (since Naturalist novels sought to depict objectively the whole of human life in its minutiae), is to make the perspective of pathological marginalized masculinity into a universal of masculinity. The value of the literary narrative is that it allows us to see where the subject and object of theorization touch. Zola's theory of homicidal masculinity echoes the alienists' language of the "perversion of the instinct" and delineates the degenerate, pathological individual described by Krafft-Ebing for whom murder replaces penetration. Yet it also echoes the anxious voice of the scientists musing on the potential weakness and destructivity of *all* male sexuality if moral restraint cannot hold men in check. That is, it crisscrosses continuously between the individual and the social, the apparently aberrant exception and the apparently universal, demonstrating how the one segues irresistibly into the other, and thereby allowing for a reading against the grain that shows up the fictitiousness of the division.

The Invention of the Twentieth-Century Serial Sex Killer: The Rippers Who Came After

If the high-profile case of Jack the Ripper consolidated Krafft-Ebing's construction of the lust murderer and inspired Zola to create his "human beast" in the nineteenth century, the specter of the Ripper did not disappear as one century turned into another. Rather, he has remained a cultural figure of folklore through which the contemporary serial sex killer can be read and understood. As Caputi puts it: "Succeeding sex killers are not only incessantly compared and even identified with Jack the Ripper, but now as then, fictional constructs are superimposed upon the events of modern serial murder."[67]

The "fictionalization" of real killers is of key relevance to the concerns of this book, as it is by identifying with archetypes and antecedents that subjectification occurs in the case of murderers (both for the public and for the murderer). One way in which this happens is through the process of naming. Serial killers are often attributed a colorful moniker while at large, in the tradition of "Jack the Ripper" (who is again paradigmatic here as he remained perpetually at large, such that his nickname and all it conveyed trumped any revelation of identity). While some of these names are creations of the press, such as the derivative "Yorkshire Ripper" or "Boston Strangler," others are produced by the killer himself and included in letters written to the news or the police—as was the case with the founding father, "Jack." It has even been argued that, were it not for the catchy name and the wide press he received, the White chapel murderer might have been forgotten after his crime spree came to an end.[68]

The trope of the killer who writes witty or taunting letters to the press is often assumed to originate with the Ripper, even though a precedent is found in the case of Lacenaire, whose open letters were printed in the Paris press (though these came after, not prior to, arrest). The common critical tendency to assume Jack was the first murderer to write to the press is, perhaps, a symptom of the Anglophone-centrism of much writing on murder. That said, the Ripper correspondence is intriguing in that, although its authenticity remains in question (an issue hotly debated among "Ripperologists"), this does not in any way diminish the effect or influence it has undoubtedly had. Moreover, the whole question of authenticity of authorship is relatively unimportant here, since our focus is on the way in which myths of subjectivity are built. What is of especial interest, however, is that, given that some 128 pieces of Ripper correspondence were received by press and police, it is reasonable to assume that at least some of them were written by "ordinary" people who identified, aspirationally, with Jack the Ripper. The line between the killer and the "ordinary" citizen is again blurred here, since the desire to occupy the subject position of killer suggests the very potency and availability of that role in the cultural imaginary. The following, most commonly quoted letter, sent to the Central News Agency, on 18 September 1888, was the first to use the name "Jack the Ripper":

> Dear Boss,
> I keep on hearing the police have caught me but they wont fix me just yet. I have laughed when they look so clever and talk about being on the right track. The joke about Leather Apron gave me real fits.
> I am down on whores and I shan't quit ripping them until I do get buckled. Grand work, the last job was. I gave the lady no time to squeal. How can they catch me now? I love my work and want to start again. You will soon hear of me and my funny little games.
> I saved some of the proper red stuff in a ginger beer bottle over the last job, to write with, but it went thick like glue and I can't use it. Red ink is fit enough I hope. Ha! Ha!
> The next job I do I shall clip the lady's ears off and send to the police, just for jolly, wouldn't you? Keep this letter back till I do a bit more work, then give it out straight. My knife's so nice and sharp, I want to get to work right away if I get a chance. Good Luck.
>
> > Yours truly
> > Jack the Ripper
>
> Don't mind me giving the trade name. Wasn't good enough to post this before I got all the red ink off my hands; curse it. No luck yet. They say I'm a doctor now. Ha! Ha![69]

The letter gives a sense of the "personality" that the public would go on to associate with the killer: brash, dry, teasing; in short, "a stylish, likeable rogue,"[70] obscuring the horror and misogyny of his crimes. Moreover, the direct appeal to the readership to identify with the intention to clip off the ears of the next victim—"wouldn't you?"—implicates the (implicitly male) reader in the "funny little games," suggesting that "Jack" is the active representative in the field of murder on behalf of all those armchair enthusiasts who support, desire, and approve of his actions, but don't dare do likewise.

That the phenomenon of the Ripper letters inaugurated a tradition among murderers and their public is beyond question. In 1977, in New York City, David Berkowitz shot a number of young women walking in the street or seated in parked cars. Berkowitz styled himself the "Son of Sam" ("Sam" being a paranoid projection of the devil who was allegedly ordering him to kill) in letters to both police and newspapers. Like the Ripper in the letter cited above, Berkowitz uses his correspondence to announce more crimes to come: "Don't think that because you haven't heard from me for a while that I went to sleep. No, rather, I am still here, like a spirit roaming the night. Thirsty, hungry, seldom stopping to rest. Anxious to please Sam."[71] Extracts of Berkowitz's letters were published in the *Daily News*, resulting in record sales. Then mayor of New York, Abraham Beame, commented:

> Son of Sam. I even liked the name and that in itself was terrifying. I knew it
> would stick ... would become his trademark. There had been six attacks, all laid
> at the feet of a single individual, and you could see it all building.[72]

The power of a name—of the assertion of identity—is certainly conveyed by these examples.

In the case of the Yorkshire Ripper, active in the 1970s and '80s in England, a cassette tape sent to the police, allegedly from the killer, was found to be a hoax, produced not by Peter Sutcliffe, but by a wishful pretender who called himself "Jack" after the press's naming of Sutcliffe as a "Ripper." The tape announced, much in the style of the original Jack and of Berkowitz: "I'm Jack. I see you are still having no chance catching me. ... I'm not sure when I will strike again, but it will definitely be some time this year, maybe September or October—even sooner if I get the chance."[73] Three letters claiming to be from the Yorkshire Ripper were also received. The police took the decision to have the tape played on air in regular news broadcasts, and made a recording of it permanently available by calling a telephone number. It is estimated that 40,000 people per day called the number to listen to the "Ripper's" voice.[74] Samples of the letter-writer's handwriting were also published in the newspapers, with requests that readers should inform the authorities if they recognized the voice or hand. The confusion to which this led considerably delayed the progress of the police investigation, but it also had the effect, as Caputi has described it, of insinuating the Ripper "into every atmosphere,"[75] facilitating "fantasy identification with a Ripper."[76]

Perhaps most disturbingly, and offering the most persuasive corroboration of those theories that hold that a murderer-worshipping culture is a misogynistic one, is the following anecdote told by Cameron and Frazer: "In Leeds, football crowds adopted 'Jack' [the still-at-large Yorkshire Ripper] as a folk hero and chanted at one stage 'Ripper eleven, police nil.'"[77] This demonstrates persuasively that those dis-identifying with—seeing as worthless—the (female, mainly prostitute) victims of crime, and identifying instead with the masculine killer, cannot simply be dismissed as a rare few who could be properly termed "outsiders," eccentrics, the exception to, rather than the rule of, the cultural norm. Rather, such phenomena lend weight to Caputi's argument that "the myth of the Ripper—from its very beginnings—was a *collective* male invention,"[78] a myth of exceptional individuality with which all could identify. Furthermore, with regard to the Ripper case, it is striking that the lionization of the killer and disregard felt for the victims expressed by the Leeds football crowd finds an echo in a statement made by West Yorkshire's acting chief constable, Jim Hobson, writing of the fact that Sutcliffe's latest victim, 16-year-old Jayne McDonald, was not, like his earlier targets, a prostitute:

> He has made it clear that he continues to hate prostitutes. Many people do. We, as a police force will continue to arrest prostitutes. But the Ripper is now killing innocent girls. That indicates your mental state and that you are in urgent need of medical attention. You have made your point. Give yourself up before another innocent woman dies.[79]

In stating that it is normal and acceptable to "hate prostitutes," in implying that the public and police themselves share the killer's view in this regard, we see another disturbing, misogynistic echo of the case that gave Sutcliffe his pseudonym. Just as Jack the Ripper (and his culture) were "down on whores," so, for Peter Sutcliffe, the self-styled "Streetcleaner" (and his culture): "the women I killed were filth, bastard prostitutes who were just standing round littering the streets. I was just cleaning the place up a bit."[80]

The flip side of the lionization of the sex killer as a folk hero is, of course, the hypocritically moralistic tendency in the media to dub him a "monster" or "beast," discourses that persist since the nineteenth-century application of them to Jack, likening him to the vampires and other Gothic horrors that titillated the Victorian imagination, and which also appear, as we have seen, in the scientific writings of Nordau and Krafft-Ebing. This delineation of the killer as beast is not dissimilar in function to the naming of him as a hero. It serves, again, to mark him as different from other men, as an exception not a symptom, and to deliver the mawkish disapproval that is the flip side of titillation. "Sex-beast" is a staple of the Anglophone tabloid lexicon and the public readily adopts such othering, mythologizing discourses. Jayne McDonald's mother announced to Sutcliffe on television: "I think you are the devil himself. You are a coward. You are not a man. You are a beast."[81] And, in turn, Sutcliffe himself, assuming subjectification as a killer in the terms of available discourse, said of the voices in his head: "They are all in my brain, reminding me of the beast I am. Just thinking of them all reminds me of what a monster I am."[82] The language for making the killer other than human—a beast, a monster—belongs to, saturates, shapes, and has meaning for the culture as a whole, including murderers themselves.

Another way in which the influence of the Jack the Ripper case contributes to the discursive construction of later murderers is in their explicit familiarity—and identification—with the archetypal figure and the minutiae of his crimes. Peter Kürten, the "Düsseldorf Vampire," who killed at least 9 and possibly as many as 60 people of all ages and sexes, between 1913 and 1929, was one of a disproportionately large number of sex murderers active in Weimar Germany.[83] He produced extensive confessions which were written up by Dr. Karl Berg in 1931. Kürten was a sadist who, like Vincent Verzeni cited earlier, found strangling a victim to be a great source of sexual pleasure in itself (and sometimes stopped short of outright killing if he achieved sexual satisfaction before the victim was fatally asphyxiated). He also, like Zola's fictional "Flore," enjoyed witnessing train crashes and derailments, and bloody accidents of all kinds. Kürten has made the following statement: "I did myself a great deal of damage through reading blood-and-thunder stories. For example, I read the tale of Jack the Ripper several times."[84] While we might be cautious about assuming the straightforwardly imitative nature of Kürten's crimes (the theory of moral contagion), what is suggestively hinted at here is that his identification with the Ripper gave Kürten a way of understanding his subjectivity as a lust murderer. This identification then led to active self-stylization: Kürten, like "Jack," wrote letters to the press, acting knowingly in the style of his hero and, in his confessions to his therapist, was able to acknowledge consciously the influence "Jack" had had on him.

Ordinary, Decent Men?

My gender-aware readings of discourses of the figure of the lust murderer exemplified by Jack the Ripper in this chapter are influenced largely by Cameron and Frazer's conclusion that misogyny alone does not account for sexual murder, rather than by Caputi's more radical view that all sex murder is "gynocide." As Cameron and Frazer point out, men kill boys and men for sexual kicks too. Rather than focusing on women as the sole victims of sex killers, it is helpful to focus on the gender of the murderer and recognize that "the common denominator [in lust murders] is a shared construction of masculine sexuality, or even more broadly, masculinity,"[85] which accounts, perhaps, for the fact that it is overwhelmingly men who kill in this particular way. For it is men, not women, who are commonly culturally encouraged to identify as transcendental, agentic subjects, and to find heroism in an idea of freedom enacted at the expense of an "other" (often a female other). In the rare cases in which a sadistic sex killer has been revealed to be female, English murderers Myra Hindley and Rosemary West (both of whom acted in tandem with a male partner) being the two obvious examples, public condemnation wholly replaces the jokey, hero-worshipping discourses provoked by cases of male Rippers who kill women. And, even more than the unadulterated hostility that accrued to Hindley and West as women involved in the killing of children and young women, American serial killer Aileen Wuornos, whose victims were solely men, was so vilified as to have rendered her execution an imperative.

In the first section of this chapter, it was noted that foundational sexological discourse tends to exaggerate the stereotypical characteristics of "ordinary" masculinity and femininity, and to insist that these are "naturally" present in biological males and females. Also noted was the tendency to make women both the gatekeepers of male sexuality within marriage (as their supposed weaker sexual desire fits them to such a role) and the agents of their own destruction, in Krafft-Ebing's extraordinary statement that women are too naturally shy to lust murder and that their passivity therefore spurs men on to do it to them instead. (This is an idea encapsulated in the memorable episode in *La Bête humaine* in which Séverine submissively bares her throat to her lover—who just happens to be an inborn lust murderer.) It becomes clear that the creation of the categories of, for example, nymphomania or masochism in the female and sadism and lust murder in the male reveal more about the gender ideologies of the culture that produces the subjects diagnosed with them than about the so-called conditions themselves. Equally, however, it is less often noted that analyzing the ideology behind taxonomies of perversion, which locate antisocial acts and desires in an exceptional aberration, can contribute in turn to our understanding of the cultural ideologies governing expectations of "ordinary" masculinity and femininity.

We have seen how destructivity is related to sexual instinct and to maleness in the scientific discourses of the mid- to late nineteenth century. Sexual murder is understood as the reproductive instinct gone awry, the desire for intercourse replaced by the desire to kill, and is attributed to the pathological figure of the lust murderer, a subject who, in the personage of Jack the Ripper, came to center stage at the moment of burgeoning modernity. The popularity of Jack the Ripper—his capacity to give rise to fictional "sons," such as Jacques Lantier, and to influence the understanding of murderers who came after him, such as Kürten, Berkowitz, and Sutcliffe—can be understood as having had a paradoxical, at once sensationalizing and normalizing, effect on the understanding of lust murder. As Caputi has relentlessly catalogued, sex crime is everywhere. It is the titillating subject matter of crime fiction, television, film, men's magazines; naturalized and banalized in our culture as "entertainment." Yet owing to the persistence of traces of Jack's extravagant, Gothic persona that continues to accrue to representations of actual sex killers with their fanciful nomenclatures and media celebrity personae, these subjects are rendered exotic, exceptional, and different from "ordinary" men. Such mechanisms serve to obscure a clear assessment of the contemporary condition of masculinity and to prevent the understanding that casual cultural misogyny and sadistic male violence are not radically separate, but lie on a continuum: that, to recycle Cameron and Frazer's pun, the assumption of an absolute qualitative difference between "Jack the Ripper" and "Jack the Lad" is an ideological sleight of hand.[86]

Endnotes

1. "Les bêtes sauvages restent des bêtes sauvages, et on aura beau inventer des mécaniques meilleures encore, il y aura quand même des bêtes sauvages dessous."

2. The Ripper's "known" victims (the "canonical five") were Mary Ann "Polly" Nichols, Annie Chapman, Elizabeth Stride, Catherine Eddowes, and Mary Jane Kelly. Other possible victims include Emma Smith, Martha Tabram, Rose Mylett, Alice McKenzie, and Frances Coles.

3. Masters and Lea, in their historical account of sex murder, chronicle the existence of an "infestation" of Rippers between 1885 and 1895, including Vacher, the French Ripper; a Moscow Ripper in 1885; a Texas Ripper who killed black prostitutes; and a Nicaraguan Ripper in 1889. Masters and Lea, *Sex Crimes in History*, pp. 79, 93–94.

4. Alexandra Warwick and Martin Willis, "Introduction," in *Jack the Ripper: Media, Culture, History* (Manchester, UK: Manchester University Press, 2007), p. 2.

5. Seltzer, *Serial Killers*, p. 48.

6. Christopher Frayling, "The House That Jack Built," in *Jack the Ripper*, ed. Warwick and Willis, p. 13.

7. Patricia Cornwell, *Portrait of a Killer: Jack the Ripper—Case Closed* (New York: Penguin Putnam, 2002).

8. See: Caputi, *Age of Sex Crimes*, pp. 124–133.

9. See: Frayling, "The House That Jack Built," p. 18.

10. See: Cameron and Frazer, *Lust to Kill*, p. 124.

11. Jack the Ripper's letter to the Central News Agency, 18 September 1888, cited in Sander Gilman, " 'Who Kills Whores?' 'I Do,' Says Jack: Race and Gender in Victorian London," in *Jack the Ripper*, ed. Warwick and Willis, p. 215.

12. Gilman, " 'Who Kills Whores?,' " p. 215.

13. Ibid., p. 216.
14. Foucault, *Madness and Civilization*, p. 210.
15. Krafft-Ebing, *Psychopathia Sexualis: The Case Histories* (London: Velvet, 1997), p. 32. Hereafter cited as Krafft-Ebing, *Case Histories*. References to Krafft-Ebing, *Psychopathia Sexualis* refer to Krafft-Ebing, *Psychopathia Sexualis with Especial Reference to Contrary Sexual Instinct*, cited in the introduction.
16. Krafft-Ebing, *Psychopathia Sexualis*, p. 1.
17. Ibid., p. 13.
18. Ibid., p. 14.
19. What is striking is that the social gender politics and power structure of patriarchy are taken wholly for granted in Krafft-Ebing's imagined dystopia here. Excessively concupiscent women would become *prostitutes*, not simply women who seek their own sexual gratification. It is a strange sort of "uncontrollable," natural sexual instinct indeed that has a commercial imperative and can adapt itself to servicing a paying client.
20. Krafft-Ebing, *Psychopathia Sexualis*, p. 12.
21. Ibid., p. 67.
22. Ibid., p. 398.
23. Caputi, *Age of Sex Crime*, p. 14.
24. Krafft-Ebing, *Case Histories*, p. 32.
25. Krafft-Ebing, *Psychopathia Sexualis*, p. 62.
26. Ibid., p. 64.
27. Ibid., p. 1.
28. Pick, *Faces of Degeneration*, p. 106.
29. Max Nordau, *Degeneration*, p. 557.
30. Ibid., pp. 141–142.
31. Ibid., p. 557.
32. Ibid., p. 260.
33. Krafft-Ebing, *Psychopathia Sexualis*, p. 87.
34. Ibid., pp. 138, 140.
35. Ibid., p. 137.
36. Ibid., p. 148.
37. Cameron and Frazer, *Lust to Kill*, p. 25.
38. Ibid., p. 164.
39. Pick, *Faces of Degeneration*, p. 74.
40. Geoff Woollen, "Zola: La machine en tous ses effets," *Romantisme*, 41, 1983, and "Des brutes humaines dans *La Bête humaine*," in *Zola: La Bête humaine: Colloque du centenaire à Glasgow*, ed. Geoff Woollen (Glasgow: Glasgow University Press, 1990).

41. Pick, *Faces of Degeneration*, pp. 84–85.

42. Pauline McLynn, "Human Beasts? Criminal Perspectives in *La Bête humaine*," in *Zola: La Bête humaine: Colloque du centenaire à Glasgow*, ed. Geoff Woollen (Glasgow: Glasgow University Press, 1995).

43. "beau garçon au visage rond et régulier, mais que gâtaient des mâchoires trop fortes." Emile Zola, *La Bête humaine* [1890], in *Œuvres complètes*, vol. 6 (Paris: Cercle du livre précieux, 1967), 11–310, p. 48.

44. "le Jacques Lantier a bien quelques caractéristiques anatomiques du criminel né." Cesare Lombroso, "*La Bête humaine* et l'anthropologie criminelle," *La Revue des Revues*, 4–5, 1892, p. 261.

45. Nordau, *Degeneration*, p. 451.

46. See: McLynn, "Human Beasts?," p. 126.

47. "Tuer une femme, tuer une femme! Cela sonnait à ses oreilles, du fond de sa jeunesse, avec la fièvre grandissante, affolante du désir. Comme les autres, sous l'éveil de la puberté, rêvent d'en posséder une, lui s'était enragé à l'idée d'en tuer une." Zola, *La Bête humaine*, p. 61.

48. Cited in Vernon Rosario, *The Erotic Imagination: French Histories of Perversity* (Oxford: Oxford University Press, 1997), pp. 69–70.

49. Geoff Woollen, "Une nouvelle de Camille Lemonnier: De Jack l'Eventreur à *La Bête humaine*," *Les Cahiers naturalistes*, Paris, 1995.

50. Philippe Hamon, *La Bête humaine d'Emile Zola* (Paris: Gallimard, 1994).

51. "Je lègue à la science … l'être pervers et compliqué qui pour moi demeura un insondable problème." Cited in ibid., p. 135.

52. "Cela venait-il donc de si loin, du mal que les femmes avaient fait à sa race, de la rancune amassée de male en male depuis la première tromperie?" Zola, *La Bête humaine*, p. 62.

53. Rosario, *Erotic Imagination*, p. 163.

54. Krafft-Ebing, *Psychopathia Sexualis*, p. 13.

55. Ibid., p. 14.

56. "posséder, tuer, cela s'équivalait-il?" Zola, *La Bête humaine*, p. 153.

57. Elle renversa son visage soumis, d'une tendresse suppliante, découvrait son cou nu. … Et lui, voyant cette chair blanche, comme dans un éclat d'incendie, leva le poing armé du couteau." Ibid., p. 269.

58. "la jeter sur son dos, morte, ainsi qu'une proie qu'on arrache aux autres." Ibid., p. 151.

59. Rachel Mesch, "The Sex of Science: Medicine, Naturalism and Feminism in Lucie Delarue-Mardrus's *Marie, fille-mère*," *Nineteenth-Century French Studies*, 31, 3&4, 2003, 324–340, p. 327.

60. "Elle ignorait que le désir est un chasseur sans pitié. Elle ne s'était jamais demandé pourquoi toutes les femelles animales, plus intelligentes que les filles, commencent par fuir les males après les avoir appelés à cause qu'une sorte de peur les talonne devant la fatalité de l'amour. ... Elle ne savait pas qu'il y a de la lutte dans l'amour et de l'assassinat dans la possession, qu'il y a d'un coté l'attaque, et de l'autre la defense, et que l'homme, plus cruel que tout autre bête, est agité dans sa jeunesse par la sourde envie de terrasser la femme comme un adversaire plus faible." Lucie Delarue-Mardrus, *Marie, fille-mère* (Paris: Eugène Fasquelle, 1908), p. 20.
61. Philippe Hamon, *Le Personnel du roman: Le système des personnages dans les "Rougon-Macquart" d'Emile Zola* (Paris: Droz, 1983).
62. Hannah Thompson, *Naturalism Redressed: Identity and Clothing in the Novels of Emile Zola* (Oxford: European Humanities Research Centre, 2004), p. 97.
63. "Elle avait la curiosité des accidents." Zola, *La Bête humaine*, p. 68.
64. "vierge et guerrière; dédaigneuse du mâle." Ibid., p. 58.
65. "Elle avait le besoin de marcher jusqu'au bout, de mourir toute droite, par un instinct de vierge et de guerrière." Ibid., p. 250.
66. l'homme efféminé, délicat, lâche; la femme masculine, violente, sans tendresse." Zola, "Préface au Roman d'un inverti-né," in *Nos ancêtres les pervers: La vie des homosexuels au dix-neuvième siècle*, ed. Pierre Hahn (Paris: Olivier Orban, 1979), 231–235, p. 234.
67. Caputi, *Age of Sex Crime*, p. 5.
68. Donald McCormick, *The Identity of Jack the Ripper* (London: Arrow Books, 1970).
69. Cited in Tom A. Cullen, *When London Walked in Terror* (Boston: Houghton Mifflin, 1965), p. 105.
70. Caputi, *Age of Sex Crime*, p. 21.
71. Cited in Lawrence D. Klausner, *Son of Sam: Based on the Authorized Transcription of the Tapes, Official Documents and Diaries of David Berkowitz* (New York: McGraw-Hill, 1980), p. 168.
72. Cited in ibid., p. 146.
73. Cited in Carol Kennedy, "Striking Again," *Time*, 17 September 1979, p. 49.
74. Joseph Collins, "A New Jack the Ripper Is Terrorizing England," *Us*, October 1979, p. 31. Cited in Caputi, *Age of Sex Crime*, p. 45.
75. Caputi, *Age of Sex Crime*, p. 43.
76. Ibid., p. 45.
77. Cameron and Frazer, *Lust to Kill*, p. 33.
78. Caputi, *Age of Sex Crime*, p. 22.
79. Cited in ibid., pp. 93–94.

80. Cited in John Beattie, *The Yorkshire Ripper Story* (London: Quartet Books, 1981), p. 133.

81. Cited in Cameron and Frazer, *Lust to Kill*, p. 128.

82. Ibid.

83. This is a phenomenon discussed at length by Maria Tatar in *Lustmord*.

84. Cited in Donald Rumbelow, *The Complete Jack the Ripper* (Boston: New York Graphic Society), p. 204.

85. Cameron and Frazer, *Lust to Kill*, p. 166.

86. Ibid., p. 44.

Reading 2.2

Medieval Violence and Criminology: Using the Middle Ages to Understand Contemporary Motiveless Crime

By Elise Impara

IN MEDIEVAL EUROPE, TORTURE WAS NOT just a form of punishment or a deterrent for serious crimes like treason, sexual violence, homicide and arson, but also a sanguinary, collective experience: ordinary people would gather together in order to witness the torments inflicted upon the criminal. The delinquent's abdomen could be sawed when s/he was still alive, the body could be dismembered, eyes excavated, the agonizing body stabbed with incandescent pokers. A thrilled public would take part to this physical and psychological humiliation by insulting the condemned or cheering at the violence ... a form of attraction for a society whose social life was based on mainly feudal and religious duties and where entertainment mainly occurred during restricted periods (e.g. festivals). In contemporary Europe, physical violence is no longer a form of 'lawful' control: oppression, segregation or social cleansing have all replaced violence, giving rise, at times, to violent forms of resistance. Society attempts to find motivations for that type of brutal crime that does not emerge as a consequence of unemployment, social inequality, political extremism or poverty; these are, in fact, not only regarded as the cardinal pillars of criminological discussions, but also the main crime explanations that Power finds it easy to engage with. Crime for crime's sake is dismissed as 'motiveless'. Is this really so? The aim of this essay is to explore how an investigation of violence in the Middle Ages can inform our understanding of 'motiveless' violence today. Has society moved away from the bi-dimensional relationship between deviance and entertainment?

Using a hermeneutic interpretation framework (Gadamer, 2011, Betti, 1955), this essay will explore descriptions of medieval brutality (in both primary and secondary sources, and art), along with contemporary accounts of seemingly 'motiveless' crime. Arguing the importance of language as a mediated means to understand our historical culture, and ourselves, Gadamer (2011) suggested that it is not possible to assess how contemporaries understood a particular historical work. Decades and centuries of interpretation give us a more complex vision of history. This is, however, an opportunity rather than a deficiency: Gardamer claimed this allows us to develop what he defined as truth of self-understanding. Betti (1955) argued that texts are objectified representations of human intentions and to interpret them is to give them life. As interpreters, we may overcome our personal views so that we can ensure our understanding of the text. Finally, this work has considered Lorde's concept of biomythography (Lorde, 1982) in its interpretation of sources: our accounts and interpretations are not simply factual, but are rather shaped by our emotions, culture and imagination. In other words, they are subject to what Du Bose Brunner (1998) calls human resignification, an inevitable reinterpretation of events.

Theoretically, the work will attempt to establish a bridge between medievalism and cultural criminology by discussing the elements of spectacle/carnival, pain and excitement. These elements (as my examples will emphasize) are common features of both medieval and contemporary violence. The essay will raise the question of whether these elements can help us decode the seemingly 'motivelessness' of some contemporary crimes.

Contributions to the study of criminology have emphasized the need to move away from a static administrative approach to the study of crime (Presdee, 2004) to an approach that sets humankind and human emotions at the center of a criminological discourse. Cultural criminology evolved as a response to this need: it looks at criminal behavior and the bodies involved with the criminal justice system in terms of culture. Ferrell (1999) discussed the processes by which crime becomes a form of culture and culture becomes criminalized. Questions about whether graffiti art is 'proper' art or a simple criminal activity are an example of the processes discussed by Ferrell. The birth of cultural criminology has also encouraged scholars to engage with scholarly work on excitement and transgression: in *The Seductions of Crime,* Katz (1988) explored the sensuality of criminal behavior, arguing that emotions (thrills, excitement) constitute the reason for youth crime. Presdee (2000) in *Cultural Criminology and the Carnival of Crime* associated the excitement of transgression with the dynamics of chaos historically underpinning the carnival. In 2003, Young attempted to give a structural context to the notion of transgression as understood by criminology (Young, 2003). In his discussion, however, Young remained within the domains of sociology of deviance and criminology without really attempting to explore the idea of transgression from a more philosophical or historical perspective. Picart (2007) suggested that society's on-going infatuation with evil and blood-lust and the growing popularity of crime favors the emergence of a Gothic criminology.

There is something missing in all this. It is a deep understanding of where these ideas of transgression and excitement come from. Criminology has based its investigation of the reasons for criminal behavior on fairly recent contributions: these come from the field of sociology of deviance or psychology or from statistical analysis. The need to investigate violence in medieval times emerges from the fact that human nature has always embraced aggressive behavior: today we may enjoy scenes of extreme violence in films, but we struggle to understand when individuals actively engage with criminal behaviors that we cannot associate with a rational motivation. Medieval history tells us that nailing a cat to a post was a form of entertainment at the time, as was being a spectator of a capital punishment display. Today, reports of sadistic behavior, such as cruelty to animals, understandably shock us, mainly because we cannot make sense of them. From a criminological perspective, this inability to discuss violence for violence's sake constitutes the starting point of my discussion. Georges Bataille's work on Eroticism (1957/2002), Julia Kristeva's notion of abjection (1980/1982) and Roger Caillois' idea of the festival (1959/2001) all attempt to define the euphoric experience of transgression; they tell us how its fascination has always been part of our social landscape. They argued that historically humankind has always had a tendency to be fascinated by transgressive acts: these provoke both revulsion and curiosity. The need to transgress is almost 'healthy': society, through the institution of (religious) festivals, has always allowed people to have periods where order and regulations were suspended (eg. carnival before lent). This was done because after the excesses of transgression, people felt the need to go back to law and order. "Moderation is a fatal thing. Nothing works like excess" (Wilde, 1892/1996): law and order were reinforced by the period of excessive debauchery. Whereas the contrast between "despair and distracted joy, between cruelty and pious tenderness" (Huizinga, 1979: 10) seem acceptable in medieval times, they are no so easily digestible today. Discussing violence in terms of excitement and spectacle is problematic for various reasons: unlike torture in the Middle Ages, the horrors of the holocaust in War World II have been immortalized in videos and pictures; images of mass graves in various parts of the globe bounce from one continent to another. Violence in medieval times is nowadays romanticized and fantasized (the popularity of TV shows like Game of Thrones prove this point), whereas the images we witness daily remind us of its veracity and brutality. In our visual society, maintaining a desensitized approach to violence is a hard challenge. Not only this: also discussing it (even within the intellectual, 'scientific' ring of academia) can represent a problem. In this respect analyzing the links between violence, excitement and spectacle from a historical perspective can provide a valuable tool: we no longer look at the processes by which contemporary motiveless violence occurs, but we explore the same dynamics in a distant past.

A Criminologist's Attraction To Medieval Studies

Torture as a form of control is not confined to medieval history and, in fact, at the time, torture was less widespread than we may think (Mills, 2005): my choice of establishing a parallelism between the Middle Ages and contemporary society is, however, not a random one: Roman times also witnessed a high level of violence, but, as Larissa Tracy (2012) suggests, accounts of torture and brutality in the Middle Ages bring to the surface not just a lust for blood (as popular culture induces us to believe), but also satire, cultural anxieties and dissent. That analysis of the 'emotions'/experiences attached to medieval torture can encourage and feed a broader criminological discourse on crime and violence as cultural criminology is also pushing for an analysis that explores the satire, the cultural anxiety and the ideological dissent present in crime.

Describing the modes of vision in medieval gothic art and in particular of the way the martyrdom of saints is depicted, Michael Camille suggests how in the Middle Ages people were receptive to the idea of the body "as a theater of torment, a site of incredible horror" (Camille, 1996: 159). He affirms "images of death were produced in a culture ravaged by constant war and quite used to the public spectacle of corporal punishment meted out to miscreants in the public squares of towns. While the naked sexual body was consigned to the margins, the naked, sadistically tormented body, whether of Christ or the saints, was given center stage" (Ibid, p.60). Analogies could be made between medieval visual arts and some of the images we are exposed to in the media:

1. At the Victoria and Albert Museum in London, the Scene of the Martyrdom of Saint George (c. 1400) by Andrés Marçal de Sax explored what we would today define as the objectification and the commodification of violence. Presdee (2000) gives numerous examples of evidence of the consumer's need for privately consumed violence, humiliation and cruelty. The notion of the grotesque comes to play an important role in the way violence, crime, and pain are consumed. The grotesque refers to the use of the bizarre, the absurd, irony, laughter and excess, dealing with the dichotomy of life and death. Looking at the Martyrdom of Saint George and the grinning of one of the executioners, we are reminded of the fascination we have today (as perhaps in Medieval times) for the grotesque and for the modus operandi of violent suffering. In the grotesque executioners of Saint George, we can see, for instance, the spectacle of death produced by the contemporary exhibition *Body Worlds* by pathologist Gunter von Hagens. This exhibition displays real human bodies and body parts preserved using a plastination method. Attended by millions of visitors around the world, the exhibition triggered various controversies regarding the use of cadavers and their display as art artifacts.

2. The 'transi' tomb of Cardinal de la Grange at the Petit Palais, Avignon visualizes the decomposition of the dead body of the Bishop. We know from some drawings held at the Vatican library that four heads in different stages of putrefactions were located above the main body of the piece. The inscription starts with the word 'spectaculum', indicating, according to Camille (1996), that this decomposition of the body was certainly a spectacle to be seen. Analogously, contemporary news images tell us stories

of death and decay in parts of Africa and the Middle East afflicted by war. The death of 26-year-old Lt. Muath Al-Kaseasbeth is an unfortunate example of this: burnt to death by Islamic State militants, his torture was recorded on video (Hendawi, 2015).

Medieval art had various functions: it was a celebration of Christ and the Bible, a way for the artist to be closer to God through his/her art; it was also a way to study the body and its functions. Medieval artists insisted on painting the dying Christ or the dying saints and made sure the decomposing body was exaggeratedly represented; it had a pedagogical valence, both in terms of helping illiterate people visualize the passages of the Bible or in terms of visually describing what would happen to a potential criminal. Merback (1999: 104) emphasizes how in medieval times, perceptions and feelings aroused by devotional art were channeled and expressed through the various elements of *iustitia*: the spectacle of pain, penance, expiation and redemption.

The combination of disgust, horror and attraction is a constant throughout our social history. The martyrized body, sacred or profane, sickens us, yet makes us curious. Merback (1999: 113), again suggests "with a macabre curiosity unmatched in history of art, numerous late medieval painters applied their illusionistic skills to the problem of creating wounds whose severity and gruesomeness could expose the perviousness of the body and [...] attract the spectator's gaze like powerful magnets". Caroll (1992: 85) believes that our fundamental pleasure with respect to horror fiction is a matter of fascination with the transgressive: we are attracted to what is horrific in virtue of this specific horrific value. Horror for horror's sake.

The Journal d'un Bourgeois de Paris, 1405–1449, is a valuable source for, I believe, historians and criminologists alike. The text, in fact, contains descriptions of events happening in Paris in the first half of the 15th century. The manuscript is full of descriptions of spectacular punishments and execution rituals:

1. On the 7th October 1409, Jehan de Montagu, *grant maistre d'oste du roy* de France, was executed for treachery. Two trumpeters escorted him to Les Halles, the market area, before he was beheaded and his torso exposed. Huizinga (1979) highlights how executions were astutely staged so that people were not left without the effect of assisting at a theatrical spectacle.

2. On the 12th June 1418, Bernard D'Armagnac, *le connestable de France*, in the course of a popular insurrection, ended up in a despicable death: his body was exposed to the violence of the population for three days, dragged around the streets of Paris, and left to rest in the middle of manure. Whereas this behavior would be dismissed as something belonging to a distant past where people did not have the same level of empathy as we do, contemporary accounts of prolonged violence are explained in terms of mental impairment (the perpetrator must be mad to engage in those actions). This could be true in some incidents, but could this always be the case? Almost 600 years after the execution of Bernard D'Armagnac, another example of prolonged

spectacular violence (again performed by 'authority') raise similar points: the acts of systematic, sadistic torture and abuse performed by American soldiers on the Iraqi inmates of Abu Ghraib prison in Iraq in 2003 (Hersh, 2004) could be interpreted as either the actions of an unstable mind or the product of thrill/excitement.

The graphic description or *mise en scene* of the martyrdom of Saints or the punishment of offenders represents a further useful tile in the historical discussion of the relationship between pain and spectacle in contemporary crime. According to Enders (1999: 172), medieval religious drama renegotiates the spectacle of brutality as something joyful, cathartic and even musical. In a way, it is possible to argue that we witness an 'inversion' of values, where what is deemed 'sadistic', 'cruel' or 'abominable' becomes metabolized or even celebrated. For example, the story of St Alban and St Amphibal in the *Legenda Aurea*, a collection of hagiographies written by Jacobus de Voragine in 1483, describes the cruel calvary endured by St Amphibal: his brutal torture serves as a means to reach something holy (martyrdom). This inversion of values (where perpetrators of a crime regard their actions as 'positive'/purposive) can also be noticed in contemporary cases, like ritualistic killings (see the murders of a mother and two sons in Florida in July 2015[1]).

According to Nerbano (1997), we can talk of a gothic naturalism in relation to the morbid insistence in which macabre details of the death of Christ are displayed in drama. Nudity and torture contribute to sketch an exhibitionist sanguinary realism. It seems that medieval theatre, painting and contemporary crime have in common a curiosity for violent, gory details. Enders (1999), again, goes back to the idea that medieval drama gives violence a positive value. From a criminological perspective, this is an important aspect, a point of reference for contemporary crime. For the medieval man and woman, violence was positive because through violence Christ died for humanity or through violence justice was preserved: it had a pedagogical, yet amusing, valence. However, violence was still consumed and enjoyed, even though fear was not completely excluded from this process: criminology does not digest well this notion of 'positive value', which can be interpreted as willing engagement in a contemporary carnival of brutality. The London riots in 2011, for instance, moved beyond their sense of protest to become a frenzy of violence: some participants relished in looting, destroying and 'doing' violence. If we accept to consider this aspect, we may look at cases of seemingly 'motiveless' crime from a new angle. The medieval man and woman allowed themselves to engage with brutality as a form of entertainment. If we apply the notion of entertainment to crime, we no longer need to fit crime into a specific rational and opportunistic box: the burning of the Jordan pilot by the Islamic State in early 2015 is no longer just a brutal political message, but it also brings to surface a crafted spectacle of pain.

Old French Fabliaux (12th–13th century) are another good example that can be employed when drawing a parallel between medieval times and contemporary times. The use of a sexual and obscene violence makes the audience laugh: they laugh at the sight of castration, at the nudity, at the torture and the punishments. All this is constructed in the form of spectacle. Pain adopts a humoristic valence, in spite of its legal side. Today TV shows like *Game of Thrones*, 'real TV' programs showing people laughing at others' injuries and accidents and video games have replaced the fabliaux. Violence still displays a level of humor and entertainment, but its educative side is no longer there. When the element of humor is displayed in crime, criminological discourses do not take it into consideration: frequently explanations are sought in more traditional sociological approaches.

Medieval literature demonstrates a voyeuristic attitude towards violence. The value of this violence has, however, an entertainment nature. The links among pain, spectacle and laughter are well established in historical and philosophical literature. Plato argued that comedy amalgamates pleasure and pain. The 'comical' is malicious: it induces a mental pain where the man who feels it is pleased by his neighbor's misfortune (Plato, td Frede, D. 1993). Bakhtin (1984) suggests that laughter was extremely important in the medieval carnivals, as it would pull together various elements of the festive imagery: the banquet, the market, the grotesque and the body. Georges Bataille (1985) in his sociological essays described the fundamental role of laughter in transforming repulsive forces into attractive ones. Tracy (2012: 191) emphasizes how "medieval comedy is often the refuge for gratuitous violence where pain is [inflicted] without any consequences, where an audience can laugh at the discomfort". Comedy is the channel through which violent voyeurism can be articulated: the 'spectacle' allows us to watch and consume pain and repulsion. The medieval theater has today become the virtual theater of YouTube, where we can consume the grotesque spectacle of the body being subject to distress in an anonymous manner (e.g. videos of beheading of civilians by the Islamic State have been widely watched). This attractive repulsion can be a fundamental element in our understanding of seemingly 'motiveless' violence as well. Witnessing the infliction of physical pain was accepted and understood in medieval times, but our contemporary uneasiness with the practice prevents us from publicly understanding this in relation to crime. It is not just out of respect for the victims of these crimes, but also because assessing this approach in a neutral methodical manner is very challenging. In this respect, looking at humanity's past can help cast light on our present. After all, our ancestors probably shared our fears and our fascinations.

Violence For Violence's Sake: A Selected Overview From 5th Century To Present Time

Based on the principle that we probably share similar sentiments to our medieval ancestors, I will now outline a series of seemingly 'motiveless' criminal cases in both medieval and contemporary times. The common denominators are the sense of excitement, pain and spectacle–they are all examples of 'thrill killing'.

The idea of spectacle of pain not only brings to the surface the infringement of rules, but it also highlights those inner factors that lead to illegal activities. According to Bataille (2002), as previously pointed out, it is exciting to infringe the limit, we feel pleasure and we are fulfilled. Humankind has a natural tendency not to conform to rules and rebel against the social order and in doing so experiences enjoyment. This is what Bataille (2002) defined as *la fête*, the release of tension, a liberation from order, and what Kristeva (1982) defines as the discharge of the pollution of identity. This "liberation" is exciting. The following stories all seem to fit into this theoretical background.

Zu Shenatir

Frequently considered the first serial killer in the history of humanity (Newton, 2006), Zu Shenatir lived in 5th century Yemen, where, according to accounts, he attracted young boys to his home with the promise of money and food. He sodomized them and then killed them by throwing them out of the window.

Peeter Stubbe, the Werewolf of Bedburg

A 15th century German farmer, Peeter Stubbe was accused of incest, cannibalism and the murder of children and pregnant women. He claimed he drank blood and ate foetuses and scattered limbs of children and women around the fields of nearby villages (Orenstein, 2002).

Peter Niers

In 1581 a notorious Bavarian criminal, Peter Niers was subjected to a particularly gruesome three day execution, following his cannibalistic and murderous acts. He killed and/or helped to kill approximately 75 people, including pregnant women, whose foetuses would be ripped from their bodies (Wiltenburg, 2012).

Richard Ramirez aka The Night Stalker

A self professed Satan worshipper, Richard Ramirez was sentenced to death for murder, sexual assault and child molestation in 1989. AC/DC's song 'Night Prowler' became his personal anthem (Newton, 2006: 219), which allowed media to reinforce the connection between his actions and metal music.

The Eliza Jane Murder

In 2006, two teenage girls were accused of murdering their friend Eliza Jane in Western Australia; in the course of the trial, it emerged that the two girls were interested in emo music and forensic science. They did not display any sense of remorse for their action, but stated they simply wanted to experience what killing would feel like (Fleming, 2007).

Dexter-mördaren (The Dexter Killer)

In 2010 a 21-year-old Swedish girl stabbed her father to death. After her arrest, she stated that she had a passion for the American TV series Dexter. From her diary it emerged she felt a desire to experience killing somebody (The Local, 2011).

James Holmes

Obsessed with Batman, James Holmes admitted he identified himself with the Joker following his theatrical spree killing during the screening of the last Batman film in Colorado in 2012. Prior to the events, he told a classmate he would like to kill people (The Associated Press, 2013). He also had questions about how Batman would select and kill his victims (was it random or did it follow a 'logic'?).

By looking at cases of murder and how they are portrayed in the media, one notices how problematic it is to find a way that is neutral and non moralistic to report and discuss killings that do not fit into traditional sociological and criminological parameters: there is no apparent motive for each crime, and the crime seems emotionless. Perpetrators lack remorse. Emphasis is drawn to the subcultural or theatrical element. While this can be identified as 'thrill killing' by psychology, other social sciences do not necessarily find this discourse easy to implement.

In order to discuss this typology of crime, we should employ a narrative that emphasizes the philosophical and historical element of excitement, rather than a sociological narrative of deviance. Historical accounts of violence inform us of its diverting nature. Attiring our cases with traditional sociological elements does not increase our comprehension of these acts. Perpetrators do not hold an opportunistic motivation to commit crime, but they seem to indicate they are fascinated by the implementation of violence and death.

Autopsies on bodies of victims of extreme violence, for instance, reveal that the way the bodies are tortured to death indicates an escalation of aggression: the attacker clearly does not plan the attack and progressively "gets into it", almost as if s/he gets excited by doing it. There is something in here that indicates a tendency to perform atavistic violence and to enjoy it. Where is this coming from? Is there something imprinted in our "historical genes"[2] that can help theorize and understand violence for violence's sake? In 14th century Paris, the students of the Norman nation[3] of the University asked their members if they should launch an attack against members of another university nation: one clerk ended up being wounded and another one died (Muchembled, 2012): a youth rivalry served as excuse to engage with a violent conflict. In the course of the medieval Festival of the Boy Bishop, young clerics would celebrate eclectic parodist rites in church and, then, would go out beating up any women they met in order to ensure the fertility of both women and fields. Rites of violence seemed to be infrequent, but, at the same time, not outside the norm. A discussion on the elements that underpin medieval violence, such as its rituality, its grotesqueness, its recreational function, especially in the forms of carnival, festivals, comic songs and stories, can help to decode some elements of contemporary crimes: the transgressive cultural necessity of carnival in everyday life (Presdee, 2000). Through the exploration of medieval violence we can metabolize the ceremonial interplay between order and disorder, transgression and excess. In order words, we can understand some individuals' lust for blood and violence.

Conclusive Reflections

Rational choice theories of crime taught us that transgressive behavior is the product of rationality. Nonetheless, when we are faced with particularly cruel crimes, examples of which have been listed further above, a rational approach does not necessarily explain crime motivations. Consequently, I proposed in this essay to look at our medieval past in order to employ medieval violence as an interpretative tool to encourage a discussion around the issues of 'motivelessnes' and crime spectacularization. In so doing, I attempted to identify the sentiments behind the consumption of brutality and what we would define as irrationality. In particular, I explored the elements of excitement, pain and spectacle, which can be associated to seemingly 'motiveless' crimes.

In the course of this work, I referred to some examples, but many more could have been chosen: a shooting by a man in Brazil in April 2011 killed 12 children aged between 10 and 13; in April 2011 a gunman murdered 6 people before killing himself in the Netherlands; July 2011 saw a man bombing the government buildings in Oslo and then killing 69 young people in Utøya Island, Norway. Anders Breivik, the perpetrator, was part of a neo-medieval paramilitary group called Knights Templar; in December 2012, 26 people, adults and children, were killed in an elementary school in Connecticut by Adam Lanza; We witnessed protests ending up in riots in London in 2010 and 2011 and, recently, riots in Syria, Turkey, Greece and Brazil; violence employed by Islamic State militants (e.g. use of decapitation) seems to be chosen more to satisfy television standards, rather than solely military strategies.

Examination of medieval violence and crime today can be connected to what Bakhtin (1984) called the 'second life of people'. In this second life, transgressions are articulated and come out. This second life is where our irrationality resides. Criminology should acknowledge that the world of irrationality is also the world of crime. We seem to accept violence as a form of entertainment when it comes to cinema, music or literature, but we do not see this element when it comes to real cases. Tracy (2012: 192) suggests, "Satire and parody are common motifs of medieval comic literature, as common people get one over on their 'betters' and social structures are subverted and inverted as means of either comic relief or social commentary". As in seemingly motiveless crimes (where the transgressive experience is turned upside down) evil, crime and violence are regarded by the perpetrators as positive experiences and justifications for their actions, whereas order, limits and regulations are perceived as intoxicating forces.[4] Enders (1999: 171) talks about an "enactment of the cathartic pleasures of pain". As medieval society recognized a potential entertainment value in the pedagogy of physical punishment and pain, so we need to acknowledge that some individuals may see a potential recreational nature in crime. This ludic side of criminal behavior also constitutes a criminal motivation.

In the course of this work I also referred to the experience of festivals, carnivals and theater in connection to criminal rationales. Bakhtin (1984) saw the carnival as something that went beyond a simple festivity. The carnival would suspend any social dynamics: no status, no power, no prestige, everybody is equal. The carnival reverses the make-up of society norms. It was an important part of existence where the scattered fragments of rationality could be subverted in the name of the celebration of the incomprehensible. In different époques and locations, visual arts seem to have embraced this approach: Bruegel's painting *The Fight between Carnival and Lent* (1559), John Bock's performance *Lütte mit Rucola* (2006) or the film *The Purge* (2013) are just some examples of this inversion. Understanding the central role these festivities played in the past can help us appreciate some individuals' thirst for the grotesque, for the transgressive and the irrational.

Like us, medieval people experienced both revulsion and disgust over violence, which contain(ed) an element of excitement; these could be represented or actual. However, the association between physical punishment and entertainment was neither unfamiliar nor shocking to them. In line with the expression of historical genes I mentioned earlier, it seems that proximity to violence re-enacts this 'inherited' trait: for medieval people this proximity was physical, 'pedagogical' (legal) and holy (the passion of Christ). For us, this violence is more virtual: when some individuals engage with it, on one side we 'consume' it, on the other side, we seek to understand it without resorting to thrill/excitement.

This allows me to advance the idea of carnival of crime[5] elaborated by Presdee (2000) by integrating it with a discussion on medieval spectacles of pain in order to create a criminological discourse that considers how historically violence has been represented and experienced and how we can apply this knowledge to analyze contemporary cases. In more simple words, I advocate the use of the ideas of thrill/excitement for criminological purposes.

Talking about a transhistorical Middle Ages, Mills (2005) believes that the middle ages possess elements of continuity with the present. A medieval criminological approach would make our analyses less static because a look into history would offer us the ability to explore crime without the scaffolding imposed by traditional criminology and sociology.

Endnotes

1. A 77-year-old Florida woman and her two sons were killed in their house. The crime has been defined as 'ritualistic' and linked to the blue moon in July 2015 (Associated Press, Thursday 6th August 2016).
2. The use of the word 'genes' should not be understood in biological terms, but in a figurative manner.
3. During the Middle Ages, university nations were corporations of students, similar to university societies (UK) or fraternities (US). Usually, students coming from similar backgrounds chose the same nation (e.g. the Norman nation for Norman-born students). All main medieval universities, like Bologna, Oxford or Padua had some. The university of Paris had initially four nations: Norman, English, French and Picards. Violent confrontations or rivalries among nations were quite common.
4. De Sade was of the same opinion. In Justine, he puts forward the argument that the real good is doing crime and order is violence against the self.
5. The process by which contemporary society engages with violence, both consumed or performed.

References

Anonymous, (1990) *Journal d'un Bourgeois de Paris, 1405–1449*. Le Livre de Poche.

De Voragine, J. (2000) *Legenda Aurea*. Le Lettere Editore. Td by. Levasti, A.

Secondary Sources

Associated Press (2015) 'Ritualistic killing of Florida family may be linked to blue moon, occult—police'. *The Guardian, 6th August 2015*. Posted at: http://www.theguardian.com/us-news/2015/aug/06/ritualistic-killing-of-florida-familymay-be-linked-to-blue-moon-occult-police

Bakhtin, M. (1984) *Rabelais and his world*. Td by Iswolsky, H. Bloomington, Ind.: Indiana University Press.

Bataille, G. (1985) *Visions of Excess: Selected Writings, 1927–1939*. Td by Allan Stoekl, Minneapolis: University of Minnesota Press.

Bataille, G. (2002) *Eroticism*. London: Penguin.

Betti, E. (1955) *Teoria Generale dell'Interpretazione. Vol. 1*. Giuffré.

Caillois, R. (1959) *Man and the Sacred*. Glencoe: Free Press of Glencoe.

Caroll, N. (1992) 'Disgust or fascination: a response to Susan Feagin'. *Philosophical Studies, 65*: 85–90.

Du Bose Brunner, D. (1998) *Between the Masks: Resisting the Politics of Essentialism*. Rowman and Littlefield Publishers Inc.

Enders, J. (1999) *The medieval theater of cruelty: rhetoric, memory, violence*. London: Cornell University Press, 1999.

Ferrell, J. (1999) 'Cultural Criminology'. *Annual Review of Sociology*, Vol 25, 395–418.

Fleming, K. (2007) *'Teens felt like killing friend'*. Accessed: 25th August 2007. See: bulletin.ninemsn.com.au

Gadamer, H. (2011) *Wahrheit und Methode*. Walter De Gruyter Inc.

Hendawi, H. (2015) 'Outrage Boils in Middle East Over Purported Video of IS Burning Jordanian Pilot to Death'. Accessed: 7th February 2015. See: 24news.ca

Hersh, S.M. (2004) 'Torture at Abu Ghraib'. *The New Yorker*. 10th May, 2004 issue.

Huizinga, J. (1979) *The Waning of the Middle Ages*. Penguin Books.

Katz, J. (1988) *Seduction of Crime: Moral and Sensual Attractions in Doing Evil*. New York: Basic Books.

Kristeva, J. (1982) *The Powers of Horror: an Essay on Abjection*. New York: Columbia University Press.

Lorde, A. (1982) *Zami: a new spelling of my name—A biomythopgraphy*. The Crossing Press.

Merback, M.B. (1999) *The thief, the cross and the wheel: pain and the spectacle of punishment in medieval and renaissance Europe*. London: Reaktion Books.

Mills, R. (2005) *Suspended animation: pain, pleasure and punishment in medieval culture*. London: Reaktion Books.

Muchembled, R. (2012). *A history of violence: from the end of the Middle Ages to the present*. Td by Birrell, J. Cambridge, UK: Polity Press.

Nerbano, M. (1997) 'Cultura materiale nel teatro delle confraternite umbre'. *Teatro e Storia*, Annali 4, XII.

Newton, M. (2006) *The Encyclopedia of Serial Killers*. VB Hermitage.

Orenstein, C. (2002) *Little Red Riding Hood Uncloaked*. Basic Books.

Picart, C.J. (2007) *Monsters in and Among Us: Toward a Gothic Criminology*. Fairleigh Dickinson University Press.

Plato, (1993) *Philebus*. Td Frede, D. Hackett Pub Co.

Presdee, M. (2000) *Cultural Criminology and the carnival of crime*. London: Routledge.

Presdee, M. (2004) 'The Long and Winding Road'. *Theoretical Criminology*. 8(3): 275–285.

The Associated Press (2013) *'Why did James Holmes Do It? One Year Later accused Dark Knight Killer Remains a Mystery'*. Accessed: 13th December 2014. See: nydailynews.com

The Local (2010) *'Woman Charged for Dexter Killing in Sweden'*. Accessed 13th April 2015. See: thelocal.se

Tracy, L. (2012) *Torture and Brutality in Medieval Literature: Negotiations of National Identity*. D.S. Brewer.

Wilde, O. (1996) *A Woman of No Importance*. Penguin Classics.

Wittenburg, J. (2012) *Crime and Culture in early Modern Germany*. University of Virginia Press.

Young, J. (2003) *'Merton with Energy, Katz with Structure: The Sociology of Vindictiveness and the Criminology of Transgression'*. 7; 388 Theoretical Criminology.

Reading 2.3

Selection from Curious Afterlives: The Enduring Appeal of the Criminal Corpse

By Sarah Tarlow

ABSTRACT *Not only did the criminal corpse have actual medicinal and magical power for Europeans, it also had social and cultural meaning as an object, a curio or secular relic. This paper considers the appeal of notorious bodies. From books bound in the skin of a criminal, to preserved and exhibited heads, from fragments of the hangman's rope to the exhibition of the skeleton, the story of the afterlife of criminal bodies and the material culture most immediately associated with them begins with the collection and exchange of bodies and moves into contemporary preoccupations with authenticity. This paper considers the bodies of three notorious criminals of the eighteenth century: Eugene Aram, William Burke and William Corder. It ends with some reflections on the glamour of the authentic body of a notorious or celebrated individual—using the response to the discovery of the body of Richard III as an example.*

KEYWORDS: criminal corpse; glamour; dead body; anatomy; phrenology

Becoming Really Dead

Thomas Laqueur noted recently that 'becoming really dead—even in the West where supposedly death is a precipitous event-takes time' (Laqueur, 2011, p. 802). This paper takes as its starting point the observation that death—even, or perhaps especially, the judicial execution of a criminal—is a process rather than a moment. Equally, biological life in the sense of a beating heart and an electrically active brain—is not always essential for the body to be a potent and meaningful locus in ongoing relationships with the living. The criminal body is powerful and dangerous, and biological death does not end that power or that danger.[1] A current interdisciplinary project based at the University of Leicester, UK, and funded by the Wellcome Trust, is following the journey of the condemned criminal's body from sentencing to execution and beyond. This article deals with the later stages of that process and in particular looks at those journeys that did not end in the grave. Numerous attempts to channel or harness the power of the newly executed man—such as the healing power of the hanged man's hand, and the curative or totemic power of body parts or of objects

Sarah Tarlow, Selection from "Curious Afterlives: The Enduring Appeal of the Criminal Corpse," *Mortality*, vol. 21, no. 3, pp. 210–217, 226–228. Copyright © 2016 by Taylor & Francis Group. Reprinted with permission.

contagiously associated with the execution (Matteoni this volume, Penfold-Mounce, 2010; Noble, 2011; Sugg, 2011)—attest to a belief that at some level the dead body of the criminal retained something of the living individual's force and character. This paper examines the way that the criminal's corpse was first indexical of the living man, and second that its body parts could be synecdochal of the whole criminal. Body parts were put to a variety of uses: scientific, practical, ritual and, most of all, as curios which emitted a kind of contagious glamour from the notorious criminal himself. Parts of an authentic and famous body were desirable commodities in the nineteenth century. The stories of three famous criminal bodies help to illustrate the uses to which body parts were put, and their changing post-mortem significance.

Case Study: Eugene Aram's Head

My first case study considers the fascinating life, death and afterlife of Eugene Aram (Dobson, 1952a; Scatcherd, 1838; *The Critical Review, or, Annals of Literature,* 1759). Almost forgotten

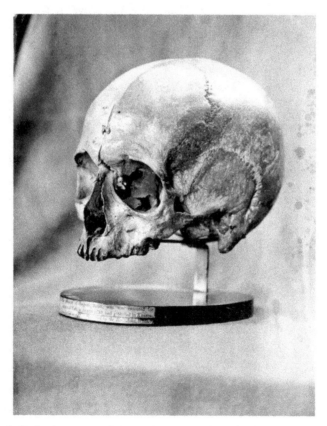

FIGURE 2.3.1   The skull of Eugene Aram. Photograph courtesy of King's Lynn Museums.

FIGURE 2.3.2   Mounted skeleton of William Burke, Anatomy Museum, University of Edinburgh (photograph by author).

today, Aram was the focus of enormous public interest from the time of his arrest, trial and execution in 1759 up until the early twentieth century. His life, crime and death formed the subject matter of a narrative poem by Thomas Hood and a hugely popular sentimental novel by Edward Bulwer Lytton, later adapted for the stage.

Eugene Aram was born in 1704 to a family of labourers in Yorkshire in the north of England. His unusual intellectual energy and quick mind enabled him to gain an education and to discover and develop a particular gift for languages, especially ancient ones. His works on the relationships between Celtic and classical languages were serious contributions to philology. After the disappearance of his associate Daniel Clark in 1744, Aram precipitously left his wife and teaching job in Knaresborough and entered a series of other positions, eventually ending up teaching at a school in King's Lynn, Norfolk. Thirteen years later, some bones were discovered in Knaresborough close to where Clark had last been seen. Suspicions were raised that the bones could be Clark's and within a couple of years, following some incriminating evidence given by a mutual friend of Clark and Aram, the sheriff's men traced Eugene Aram to his new home, arrested him and charged him with a murder committed 15 years earlier. Unwisely, Aram chose to conduct his own defence, and despite the slender evidence of the prosecution, he was found guilty and sentenced to be hanged and then gibbeted. According

FIGURE 2.3.3   William Corder display case, Moyses Hall Museum, Bury St. Edmunds. The display includes an account of Corder's crime and trial bound in his own skin, and a piece of his preserved skin (photograph by author).

to criminal defence attorney Rodney Noon, it is very unlikely that any contemporary court would convict on such evidence or that such a conviction would be safe enough to withstand any appeal (Noon, 2003). However, public feeling at the time required a conviction, and accordingly one was swiftly obtained.

Because the Murder Act (1752) had come into effect between the crime and the conviction Aram was, as a convicted murderer, subject to the Act's stipulation that his body could not be buried in consecrated ground after his execution but as a 'further mark of infamy' should be either dissected or gibbeted ('hung in chains'). The latter was to be Aram's fate and so, after his execution at York, his body was brought to Knaresborough. As was customary, his gibbet was erected close to the scene of crime, overlooking the river Nidd at Knaresborough, and his body remained there, gradually decomposing, for many years. There was no time limit on how long a body might hang in chains. Some gibbet cages remained in place for many decades until wind, weather, changing sensibilities or the exigencies of land development intervened (Tarlow & Dyndor, 2015). Aram's gibbet seems to have remained in place for at least 25–30 years. At some point, probably before the end of the eighteenth century, a doctor called Hutchinson, then practising in Knaresborough, decided to augment his private cabinet of curiosities with the skull of Eugene Aram, and managed to remove it from its gibbet cage. Writing in 1832, the pseudonymous correspondent of a literary journal imagines Hutchinson's attempt to extract the skull:

> on a dark and stormy night, agitated by conflicting feelings, like a bridegroom on the eve of marriage, the doctor sallied forth, from the town of Knaresborough, with a ladder on his shoulder, and with the firm purpose of mounting the gibbet and detaching from the iron hoop which bound it the skull of Eugene Aram. The gibbet clung to its own property with wonderful tenacity; but the ardour of the doctor became a furore, and he succeeded in extricating another neck, almost at risk of his own.[2] (Civis, 1832, p. 25)

Why was Hutchinson so keen to acquire Aram's skull? It is probable that he simply wanted it as a curiosity because of its association with a significant local event—and one which had attracted national attention. However, it is evidence for the new 'science' of phrenology that Aram's skull became best known. If the correspondent of the *Phrenological Journal* of 1839 is right that Norrison Scratcherd had seen the skull in Hutchinson's possession forty years earlier (Simpson, 1839, p. 67) then it is unlikely that phrenological study was a motivation for its original acquisition, as phrenology only became popular following the publications of Gall and Spurzheimer in the early nineteenth century. Indeed, Simpson claims that Hutchinson was only 'desirous of possessing the skull of so noted a person as Eugene Aram'

(1839, p. 67). However, within a few decades the skull was important not only as a phrenological specimen, but also as a test case, on the interpretation of which turned the credibility of phrenology as a whole.

On Hutchinson's death the skull passed to his successor Dr Richardson. When in 1837 the young Dr James Inglis took up a post as physician at the public dispensary in neighbouring Ripon, burning with phrenological zeal, it is probable that he found out about Aram's skull from Richardson, as a fellow medical man working in a neighbouring town (Wilson, 1973). It was Inglis who presented the skull to the Newcastle meeting of the British Association for the Advancement of Science in 1838. At that stage phrenology was not universally accepted as a science, and indeed it was always treated with suspicion and scepticism by many, or indeed most, of the British scientific establishment. Accounts of the 1838 meeting are mostly unsympathetic, like, for example, this one from the Literary Gazette:

> the Doctors had a dose of phrenology foisted into their section; and hardly has that science made a more absurd appearance since Tony Lumpkin practised it upon Crackskull Common.

The skull was acquired, said Inglis in his presentation to the Society, by Hutchinson, and was inherited by his widow's second husband, formerly Hutchinson's apprentice, Dr Richardson, who sent it to Johann Spurzheim, one of the founders of phrenology, for examination. Spurzheim concluded it was the head of a woman: 'this was unlucky'. Fortunately, more useful phrenological reports were soon obtained that cast doubt on Aram's having had a violent or greedy character. Dr Inglis went on at the 1838 meeting to review the evidence on which Aram was convicted, find it inadequate, and conclude that he was wrongly convicted on the basis of both historical evidence and, most compellingly for Inglis, on the grounds that his skull, said Inglis, showed him to be a gently, scholarly man, and not a murderer: 'we almost expected to hear a motion for the publication of [the jurors'] names, and their being branded to all posterity as persons so profoundly ignorant of phrenology as to have committed a most cruel legal murder'. (The British Association, 1838)

Aram was a celebrity criminal. Although convicted of a murder whose motivation appeared to have been purely monetary, his life and character did not fit the normal stereotype of a violent criminal. He had not lived the life of a thug but that of a scholar, a teacher and a man of apparently refined sensibilities, all of which both interested the public and occasioned later doubts about his guilt. Fictionalised retellings of his life, crime, flight from justice and eventual trial and execution were produced from the imagination of poet Thomas Hood and popular novelist Bulwer Lytton. Bulwer Lytton's book is ludicrously melodramatic and sentimental for modern tastes but nineteenth-century English speakers around the world lapped it up. Their narrative accounts of Aram were both best-sellers; the novel was adapted for the stage and was the inspiration for a series of prints by Gustav Doré. Aram thus remained the object of popular interest well into the twentieth century. PG Wodehouse even has Bertie Wooster quoting Hood's poem in proper Wooster style:

> All I can recall of the actual poetry is the bit that goes: Tum-tum, tum-tum, tum-tumty-tum, I slew him, tum-tum tum! (PG Wodehouse, *Jeeves Takes Charge*, 1916)

Aram's story continued to be the subject of cultural elaboration and the proliferation of narratives. But Aram's fame was not the only kind of 'afterlife' he enjoyed; his actual body continued to be a thing of powerful and changing meanings long after his final breath. Aram's skull was both a curiosity and a scientific exhibit, as we have seen, and continued its own journey through a gentleman's private museum, through a phrenologist's laboratory and onto the lectern of a scientific meeting. After the controversy of the 1838 meeting, the skull retired from public life for a while and did not reappear until it came into the possession of the museum of the Royal College of Surgeons in London. A letter from Hutchinson's grandson that was sent at the time of its donation to the College in 1869 suggests that it had been passed down through the family as an heirloom (Dobson, 1952a). However, by 1869 it had become something of a strange embarrassment to its owner, an Anglican minister, who therefore sought to place it in a museum. This event co-incides with the moment of change in Victorian sensibilities around 1870 identified by Crone (2012) when overtly gory and salacious entertainments give way to more sequestered and elliptical cultural discourses of death and crime. The skull was included in the Royal College catalogues compiled by Sir William Flower in 1879 (p. 49, entry 337) and 1907. In 1993 it was given to the Old Gaol House in King's Lynn where it remains to the present time (Figure 2.3.1).

William Burke: The Biter Bit

William Burke and his accomplice William Hare were among the most notorious criminals of the nineteenth century. Burke's name even entered the language in the verb 'burking', meaning to kill quietly by smothering, after their favoured method of obtaining a corpse for the surgeons without marking the body. In 1828 Burke and Hare murdered at least 16 people in Edinburgh, in order to sell their fresh bodies to the anatomist Robert Knox. Their victims were poor people, often without family and travelling away from home: people on the fringes of society who would not be much missed. When Burke and Hare were finally caught and the details of their crimes emerged, the grisly fate to which their victims were consigned both appalled and enthralled contemporary newspaper readers—not only in Edinburgh but around the world. William Hare turned King's evidence and thus managed to avoid execution, but Burke, who was generally accounted the brighter of the two and the main instigator of the murders, bore the full vengeful wrath of society. Under the provisions of the Murder Act of 1752 Burke's body would in any case probably be sent for anatomical dissection, but given the nature of his crime there was an especially pleasing symmetry to his post-mortem punishment. Passing sentence on Burke, the Lord Justice Clerk David Boyle decreed that not only would his body be subject to the same fate as those of his victims but also added 'I trust, that if it is ever customary to preserve skeletons, yours will be preserved, in order that posterity may keep in remembrance of your atrocious crimes' (Roughead, 1921).

William Burke was executed on 28 January 1829 in front of an Edinburgh crowd of up to 25,000 people, many of whom had waited for more than 24 h in the rain to secure a good view (MacGregor, 1884, p. 169–72). His body was then brought to the University for dissection, where there were riotous scenes as huge crowds surged in, hoping to see the process. Disgruntled medical students found themselves unable to get into their own teaching rooms. Eventually, after the dissection, his bones were indeed preserved, as were some other body parts, notably his skin (Figure 2.3.2).

The public outcry in the wake of the Burke and Hare case was decisive in the legislative change that culminated in the Anatomy Act of 1832 (Richardson 1989). After the passage of that act, the needs of anatomy students for fresh cadavers would be supplied by the bodies of paupers who died in the workhouse or in charitable institutions. This regulated the traffic in corpses and undermined the economic basis of grave-robbing or burking as an occupation profitable enough to outweigh the risks.

The Police Information Centre in Edinburgh holds a pocket book made from the skin of William Burke, and Surgeons' Hall holds other items also allegedly made from Burke's skin. The Anatomy museum in the same city still has Burke's skeleton, on which the post-mortem cut of a craniotomy can be clearly seen, and a cast of his head. How and why did these gruesome items come to be made, traded, collected and curated? And why are they still on public display? ...

Endnotes

1. This paper uses research gathered as part of the programme 'Harnessing the Power of the Criminal Corpse', funded by the Wellcome Trust. The author is indebted not only to the Trust, but also to colleagues on the project: Owen Davies, Zoe Dyndor, Elizabeth Hurren, Peter King, Francesca Matteoni, Shane McCorristine, Floris Tomasini and Richard Ward. She also thanks the University of Leicester for supporting her research,

and Melissa Schrift for inviting her to participate in a panel at the American Folklore Society annual meeting 2013 in Providence, RI, for which a version of this paper was originally written.

2. The florid style adopted by Civis is a deliberate reference to Bulwer Lytton's novel *Eugene Aram*, also published in 1832. It is, however, Bulwer Lytton's 1830 novel *Paul Clifford* that opens: 'It was a dark and stormy night …'.

3. It also allowed the members of the Criminal Corpse project to carry out an experiment in interdisciplinarity, in which each of us wrote an account of the Corder affair from the perspective of our own discipline. The results of this experiment include project member Shane McCorristine's monograph, William Corder and the Red Barn Murder (2014).

4. Letter from Spurzheim to Child, reproduced at http://www.stedmundsburychronicle.co.uk/rbexhib.htm.

5. Thanks to Anton Banchy for tracing this production.

6. Thanks to my colleague Elizabeth Hurren for her insights on this point.

References

ALBERTI, S. (2011). *Morbid curiosities: Medical museums in nineteenth-century Britain*. Oxford: Oxford University Press.

ARNOLD, K., & OLSEN, D. (2003). *Medicine man: The forgotten museum of Henry Wellcome*. London: British Museum.

BUCKLEY, R., MORRIS, M., APPLEBY, J., KING, T., O'SULLIVAN, D., & FOXHALL, L. (2013). 'The king in the car park': New light on the death and burial of Richard III in the Grey Friars church, Leicester, in 1485. *Antiquity, 87*, 519–538.

CARR, J. (1809). *Caledonian sketches; or a tour though Scotland in 1807*. London: James Humphreys.

CHERRYSON, A., CROSSLAND, Z., & TARLOW, S. (2012). *A fine and private place: The archaeology of death and burial in post-medieval Britain and Ireland* (*Leicester Archaeology Monograph 22*). Leicester: Leicester Archaeology Monographs.

CIVIS. (1832, January 14). Eugene Aram: Phrenology (letter to the editor). *Journal of the Belles Lettres/ The Literary Gazette 782*: 25.

CRONE, R. (2012). *Violent victorians: Popular entertainment in nineteenth-century*. London: Manchester University Press.

CUNNINGHAM, A. (2010). *The anatomist anatomis'd: An experimental discpline in Englightenment Europe*. Farnham: Ashgate.

DOBSON, J. (1952a, April). The college criminals 2: Eugene Aram. *Annals of the Royal College of Surgeons of England 10*: 267–275.

DOBSON, J. (1952b, October). The College Criminals 4: William Corder. *Annals of the Royal College of Surgeons of England* 11: 249–255.

EVELYN-WHITE, C. H. (1886). *The East Anglian; or, notes and queries on subjects connected with the counties of Suffolk, Cambridge, Essex and Norfolk* (Vol. 1). Norwich: Agas H. Goose.

GALL, F. J. (1808). *Discours d'ouverture, lu ... a` la premie`re se´ance de son cours public sur la physiologie du cerveau, le 15 janvier 1808.* Paris: F. Didot.

GALL, F. J. (1822–1825). *Sur les fonctions du cerveau et sur celles de chacune de ses parties. avec des observations sur la possibilite´ de reconnaitre les instincts, les penchans, les talens, ou les dispositions morales et intellectuelles des hommes et des animaux, par la configuration de leur cerveau et de leur te^te.* 6 Vols. Paris: J. B. Baillie`re.

GALL, F. J., & SPURZHEIM, G. (1809). *Recherches sur le syste`me nerveux en ge´ne´ral, et sur celui du cerveau en particulier; Me´moire pre´sente´ a` l'Institut de France, le 14 mars, 1808; suivi d'observations sur le Rapport qui en a` e´te´ fait a` cette compagnie par ses Commissaires.* Paris: F. Schoell.

GALL, F. J., & SPURZHEIM, G. (1810). *Anatomie et physiologie du syste`me nerveux en ge´ne´ral et anatomie du cerveau en particulier, avec des observations sur la possibilite´ de reconnoî^tre plusieurs dispositions intellectuelles et morales de l'homme et des animaux, par la configuration de leurs te^tes.* Paris, F. Schoell (q.v. Gall, F. J., and G. Spurzheim, vol 2, 1812; Gall, F. J., vol 3, 1818; Gall, F. J., vol 4, 1819).

GALL, F. J., & SPURZHEIM, G. (1811). *Des dispositions inne´es de l'a^me et de l'esprit: du mate´rialisme, du fatalisme et de la liberte´ morale, avec des re´flexions sur l'e´ducation et sur la le´gislation criminelle.* Paris: F. Schoell.

GATRELL, V. A. C. (1994). *The hanging tree: Execution and the English people 1770–1868.* Oxford: Oxford University Press.

GIBBS, D., & MALTBY, H. (1949). *The true story of Maria Marten.* Ipswich: East Anglian Magazine.

GORDON, R. M. (2009). *The infamous Burke and Hare: Serial killers and resurrectionists of nineteenth-century Edinburgh.* Jefferson, NC: McFarland.

HALLAM, E., & HOCKEY, J. (2001). *Death, memory and material culture.* New York, NY: Berg.

HARRISON, S. (2010). Bones in the rebel lady's boudoir: Ethnology, race and trophy-hunting in the American Civil War. *Journal of Material Culture, 15,* 385–401.

HOLTORF, C. (2013). On pastness: A reconsideration of materiality in archaeological object authenticity. *Anthropological Quarterly, 86,* 427–443.

HURREN, E. (2012). *Dying for victorian medicine: English anatomy and its trade in the dead poor, 1832 to 1930.* London: Palgrave.

HURREN, E. (2016). *Dissecting the criminal corpse: Staging post-execution punishment in early modern England.* London: Palgrave Macmillan.

JONES, S. (2010). Negotiating authentic objects and authentic selves: Beyond the deconstruction of authenticity. *Journal of Material Culture, 15,* 181–203.

LAQUEUR, T. W. (2011). The deep time of the dead. *Social Research, 78,* 799–820.

MACDONALD, H. (2005). *Human remains: dissection and its histories*. Newhaven, CT: Yale University Press.

MACGREGOR, G. (1884). *The history of Burke and Hare*. Glasgow: Thomas D. Morison.

MCCORRISTINE, S. (2014). *William Corder and the Red Barn Murder*. London: Palgrave Macmillan.

NOBLE, L. (2011). *Medicinal cannibalism in early modern english literature and culture*. London: Palgrave.

NOON, R. (2003). Should Eugene Aram have hanged? *Web Mystery Magazine*. Retrieved from http://lifeloom.com/Eugene_Aram.htm

PENFOLD-MOUNCE, R. (2010). Consuming criminal corpses: Fascination with the dead criminal body. *Mortality, 15,* 250–265.

PORTER, R. (2003). *Flesh in the age of reason: How the enlightenment transformed the way we see our bodies and soul*. London: Penguin.

RICHARDSON, R. (1987). *Death, dissection and the destitute*. London: Routledge and Kegan Paul.

ROUGHEAD, W. (1921). *Burke and Hare*. London: W. Hodge.

SAPPOL, M. (2002). *A traffic of dead bodies: Anatomy and embodied social identity in nineteenthcentury America*. Princeton, NJ: Princeton University Press.

SCATCHERD, N. (1838). *Memoirs of the celebrated Eugene Aram*. London: Simpkin, Marshall.

SIMPSON, J. (1839). On the supposed skull of Eugene Aram. *The Phrenological Journal, 12,* 66–76.

SOFAER, J. (2006). *The body as material culture*. Cambridge: Cambridge University Press.

SPURZHEIM, J. G. (1827). *Outlines of phrenology; being also a manual of reference for the marked busts*. London: Treuttel, Wurtz and Richter.

STONE, T. (1829). *Observations on the phrenological development of Burke, Hare and other atrocious murderers*. Edinburgh: Robert Buchanan.

STOREY, N. (2004). *A grim almanac of Suffolk*. Stroud: The History Press.

SUGG, R. (2011). *Mummies, cannibals and vampires: The history of corpse medicine from the Renaissance to the Victorians*. London: Routledge.

TARLOW, S., & DYNDOR, Z. (2015). The landscape of the gibbet. *Landscape History, 36,* 71–88.

THE BRITISH ASSOCIATION. (1838, July). The literary Gazette, and Journal of the Belles Lettres. Eighth meeting: Newcastle. Retrieved from https://books.google.co.uk/books?id= 5MNLAAAAYAAJ

THE CRITICAL REVIEW, OR, ANNALS OF LITERATURE. (1759 September). The genuine account of the life and trial of Eugene Aram. 8: 229–238.

WILSON, G. M. (1973, April 14). Early photography, goitre and James Inglis. *BMJ, 2,* 104–105.

VAN WYHE, J. (2004). *Phrenology and the origins of victorian scientific naturalism*. Farnham: Ashgate.

CHAPTER 2 QUESTIONS AND DISCUSSION TOPICS

1. Explain why human corpses and body parts were glamorized and celebrated in the past and how this may have contributed to prohibition of the study of human cadavers. Provide some examples of this phenomenon.
2. One theory about Jack the Ripper's homicides suggests that he may have contracted an incurable sexually transmitted disease, which may have been his motive for the killings. Explain how this reflects cultural attitudes toward the victims and women in general.
3. Why do you think the doctor in the Burke and Hare case was never charged with being complicit in their crimes, even though after the purchase of sixteen "fresh" bodies there was a high probability he knew something was wrong?
4. Explain what "religious drama" is, its role in medieval art, and how it might have negatively impacted attitudes of people living in that historical period, preventing them from developing scientific concepts about human bodies and death.
5. Explain how medieval culture justified and normalized torture, pain, and suffering and promoted the view that they were cause for celebration and reverence.
6. Who was actually regarded as the *first recorded serial killer* in history?
7. Victim-blaming is nothing new. Explain how the cultural norms of the nineteenth century perpetuated this attitude.
8. Explain how eighteenth- and nineteenth-century attitudes about morality and sex were linked to crime.

Image Credit

Fig. 2.1: Source: https://commons.wikimedia.org/wiki/File:Illustrated_Police_News_-_Jack_the_Ripper_2.png.

Chapter 3

Cherubic Faces and Murderous Hearts: Nature Versus Nurture

FIGURE 3.1   Still photo from the 1956 film *The Bad Seed*. Youthful murderess Rhoda, played by child actor Patty McCormack, and her mother, played by Nancy Kelly, shocked audiences with the innocence of a child masking a murderous personality.

INTRODUCTION TO CHAPTER 3

Among the most unsettling cases in the study of homicidal behavior are those that involve children as offenders. There are a number of high-profile cases involving children killing other children that reached international infamy. We know that children who kill tend to select victims who are younger than themselves or who are perceived as weaker, such as physically or perhaps mentally disabled individuals. Cherubic faces that mask a deep and unresolved rage unleashed by one child upon another catch society unprepared. Childhood is supposed to be a time when we are viewed through a lens of youthful innocence, and yet child killings committed by other children are no less heinous than homicides committed by adults.

There is ongoing debate over whether a killer is born (nature) due to biological factors or created (nurture) due to environmental factors, including poverty, abuse, and trauma. For most forensic psychologists, the answer lies somewhere in the middle. Joel Norris, a psychologist who specializes in criminology, makes an argument for the "nature" component early on in his book *Serial Killers*, published in 1989. Though some of his ideas are now considered out of date, others have borne fruit. While Norris does not advocate that a homicidal personality is fully formed at birth, his research about the innate inability to feel empathy, remorse, or other emotions (as opposed to someone conditioned to deny their feelings through trauma and other external influences) explores the psychopathic personality as at least partially organically defined. There are current studies that document psychopaths among those who have deficits in neurological connections of the prefrontal cortex of the brain, a condition that begins in utero, and that validate a number of Norris's hypotheses. Adverse environmental factors added to the life experience of people born with this condition can then trigger behaviors that cross the boundary into criminality.

Other social scientists consider criminality more a symptom of social ills left untreated, with most sufferers those who are marginalized and face an ongoing struggle for opportunities to thrive in society. They veer away from the idea of biological roots for criminal behavior, as historically there is a blemish of social Darwinism from the nineteenth century that blamed the poor for their poverty based upon their so-called biological inferiority. Social Darwinism also lent itself to arguments of criminality linked to ethnic identity and racial prejudices. So, it behooves the researcher to balance nature and nurture arguments through an awareness of this history.

The articles in this chapter examine some of the high-profile cases involving children and teenagers, the different trajectories of their punishments or treatments, and the outcomes. These are comparatively examined for the different approaches taken in the United States and the United Kingdom.

Mary Bell is the youngest female convicted of manslaughter (not first-degree murder) on record in the United Kingdom. The charge was downgraded from murder due to "diminished capacity" of a child to comprehend the enormity of her homicidal actions (Kotlowitz, 1999). She was a day short of her eleventh birthday when she killed the first of her two victims on May 25, 1968, four-year-old Martin Brown, whom she strangled and left in a derelict house. Again by strangulation, she killed her second victim, three-year-old Brian Howe, two months later on July 31, 1968, in an overgrown undeveloped lot known as the "Tin Lizzie" by the children in her Tyneside neighborhood in England. After the killing, she mutilated the body with a broken pair of scissors. Her friend Norma Bell, to whom she was not related but who shared the same last name, was present for part of the crime, but maintained she did not participate in the killing. Later, Norma was acquitted of charges in the killings (Sereny, 1999).

The youngest convicted offenders on record for abduction and murder were two ten-year-old boys, Jon Venables and Robert Thompson, who on February 12, 1993, led two-year-old James Bulger away from his mother in a shopping mall in Bootle, England, when she was distracted and looking away. They walked him two and half miles away to a railway track, where they tortured and beat him to death before mutilating his body and leaving it lying across the railroad tracks. Their child reasoning made them confident that once a train ran over the body, it would be believed that the toddler had wandered off and had been accidentally killed. Closed-circuit TV cameras at the mall made identification of the boys possible, and they were arrested within a week of the murder (Finnis, 2021).

In both cases the justice system in the United Kingdom ensured anonymity for the child defendants once they were released from incarceration. Bell was first placed in Red Bank (a juvenile institution) from 11 to 16 years of age and then transferred to the women's prison system and released at the age of 23. Venables and Thompson were held until they reached the age of majority (eighteen years old). All of them were provided new identities in accordance with the juvenile justice system to try to protect them from journalists and public harassment as they attempted to start new lives. Bell is now a grandmother, and though she voluntarily gave interviews to author Gitta Sereny, who wrote a book about her life, Bell still lives under a different identity and tries to live in anonymity wherever she goes. Thompson continues to live in anonymity, but Venables reoffended in 2017 and was convicted of child abuse and child pornography. He was denied parole in 2020 but will be up for consideration again every two years.

Conversely, in the United States, juvenile offenders are treated differently, and public and legal attitudes are very different from those in the United Kingdom. In the United States some juveniles are tried as adults for capital offenses such as homicide, while others manage to go to court under the juvenile justice system, resulting in time sentenced in juvenile detention facilities rather than adult prison. Juvenile detainees receive shorter sentences, usually ending when the offender reaches the age of majority, but there are no nationally accepted protocols in place to provide new identities to facilitate a more successful second chance at life. There are differences from state to state in how these cases are handled, allowing prosecutors to exercise personal judgment when considering the nature of the crime, resulting in inconsistent adjudication rather than following a clear-cut template for processing juvenile offenders.

Eric Smith from Savona, New York, was thirteen years old when he killed four-year-old Derrick Robie on August 2, 1993. He lured his victim into the woods as the child was walking to summer camp, beat him with rocks, and strangled him to death. Smith gave indications in 2004 of psychopathology in that he admitted he felt "good" strangling the victim; he went so far as to admit that if he hadn't been caught in 1993, he probably would have killed again (Teurfs, 2022). Smith was reportedly constantly bullied as a child, and the killing was emotionally cathartic for him, although he did not know his victim. He was repeatedly denied parole until February 2022. After serving twenty-eight years, Smith was released at forty-two years old.

The Columbine High School shooting on April 20, 1999, in Littleton, Colorado, resulted in fifteen dead, including the two teenaged shooters, and twenty-four injured. Columbine was perhaps the first case of its kind to receive nonstop and days-long coverage on the national news. Extended coverage included the families of the victims and the shooters, Eric Harris and Dylan Klebold, as well as their friends and neighbors. The 24/7 news cycle continued long after the event was over. Political and public safety issues were hotly debated, and the news became interactive, with general public participation in polls and on-camera interviews to fill out TV time slots.

It was initially reported that the reason for the murderous rage the shooters brought to campus that day was that they were brutally bullied social outcasts. Further, they were reportedly part of an outlier group called the "Trench Coat Mafia," because they wore long trench coats during the shootings, and were alienated loners with no friends who despised the "jock" population of popular athletes at the school. All of this mythology surrounding Eric Harris and Dylan Klebold has been proven partially or completely wrong in ensuing years, yet many of these misconceptions persist (Cullen, 2009). Deeper investigation reveals a much more complex relationship between the two shooters and their peers, the school, and in their attitude toward the rest of humanity.

In reality, Harris and Klebold were bullies as well as the bullied; Harris's writings show he had sadistic leanings and rather than looking to exact perceived revenge against specific peers whom he may have held grudges against, he was most interested in killing strangers. Additionally, there was some resignation in both Harris and Klebold that some of their "friends" might end up as casualties. Both boys belonged to extracurricular school and social activities and were considered to have their own group of friends. Both also had part-time jobs and access to their own money. In short, many of the allegations about Harris and Klebold are simply wrong or misunderstood, and unfortunately the mythology has been used as a basis for how best to identify future school shooters. Erroneous assumptions continue to mislead understandings about the how and why of Columbine and future Columbines.

As you read the articles included in this chapter by Soyer (2018) and Mar (2017), consider their topics and arguments and be prepared to discuss them.

Reading 3.1

The Making of Life-Course-Persistent Offenders

By Michaela Soyer

MANY INCIDENCES RECALLED BY THE YOUNG men during interviews went beyond ordinary childhood poverty and reached the level of traumatic experiences. The psychological impact that abuse and neglect have on young children is profound. Children who are either victimized or witness domestic violence tend to display higher levels of anger and depression (Turner, Finklehor, and Ormrod 2005). The "cycle of violence" (Spatz Widom 1989) that turns victims into victimizers manifests through a complex interaction of biological and social factors. Childhood trauma leaves a visible imprint on the young, still highly malleable brain. Chronically elevated cortisol levels, for example, may impact children's ability to adapt to stressful situations (Shonkoff et al. 2012). Experiencing childhood trauma also stunts the normal development of neural pathways and synaptic pruning—i.e., the elimination of unused synapses that takes place during early childhood and is said to continue until late adolescence. These processes determine cognitive development and may even be related to severe mental health problems such as schizophrenia that emerge during adolescence (Watt et al. 2017; Sekar et al. 2016; Selemon 2013; Feinberg 1982). The area most affected is the right brain hemisphere—the part of the brain responsible for regulating emotions and social interactions (Heide and Solomon 2006).

In this chapter I argue that childhood trauma significantly shaped the young men's criminal trajectories. Their traumatic experiences were closely related, if not caused by, their families' precarious existence. Traumas inflicted their full negative impact because the young men's families did not have easy access to nonpunitive mental health support. Thus, the absence of a social safety net not only allowed poverty to reach traumatic proportions, it also prevented diagnosis and intervention that could have mitigated destructive emotional and behavioral consequences.

Lenore Terr (1991: 11) defines trauma as an external event that leads to lasting internal changes, which can later manifest as mental illness. According to Terr's typology, Type I trauma is generated by a one-time external shock. Type II trauma results from repeated victimization and prolonged suffering. Terr uses examples from her clinical practice to illustrate the types of events she defines as traumatic; for example, death of a parent or sibling, or different types of sexual abuse and physical violence. Felitti et al.'s (1998) adverse childhood experience inventory more specifically distinguishes among psychological, physical, and sexual abuse, household dysfunction, and criminal behavior in the household.

Based on Terr's and Felitti et al.'s work, I have developed a cluster of traumatic events that recurred in the young men's narratives. I coded the interviews according to three main categories and ten subcategories: (1) Violence: being physically abused, being verbally abused, violence between parents, neighborhood violence; (2) Extreme Poverty: food scarcity, homelessness; (3) Breaking of Social Ties: death, incarceration, Department of Children and Families (DCF) involvement, other. DCF involvement indicates either that mothers voluntarily gave up custody or that the DCF intervened and placed children in care of a relative, in most cases the grandmother. The subcategory "other" subsumes cases in which mothers or fathers left their children in care of the other parent or a grandparent. In one case a mother abducted the respondent and his brother, who were in the care of their father at the time.

Eleven young men recall four or more traumatic events during their early childhood. Fourteen respondents remembered two or three traumatic experiences. Twenty respondents report that they lost a caregiver (death or incarceration were the most common reasons). Seven experienced food scarcity growing up, and three young men witnessed extreme neighborhood violence such as a friend or relative being gunned down. The most extreme cases, represented in Table 3.1.1, combined a Level 1 trauma, such as witnessing the death of a friend, with extended physical and emotional abuse and neglect.[1]

In addition to the sheer number of traumatic life events, the intersection between Level 1 and Level 2 trauma in this group of respondents is notable. Abject poverty, the "prolonged suffering" (Terr 1991) of the young men and their families, created the conditions under which Level 1 traumas are more prone to take place and are less likely to be managed therapeutically later on. Living in a poor urban neighborhood, for example, increases the likelihood that a child witnesses gun violence, especially in cases where family members are involved in gangs. These families likely also do not have the financial means to pay for effective, individualized therapeutic interventions in the aftermath of a traumatic event.

The narratives affirm that most respondents have been severely traumatized during their childhood. A great majority had not previously opened up about their experiences.[2] When I asked them why they never told anyone about their home life before, the answer usually was that they would not have felt comfortable sharing that information with a representative of the criminal or juvenile justice system—even if that person was a therapist or social worker. The young men's mental health problems remained below the surface, even though they participated in a variety of juvenile justice interventions. Consequently, the unaddressed trauma could fully unfold its negative impact on their decision-making skills, impulse control, and general emotional well-being.

TABLE 3.1.1 High Level of Childhood Trauma

Name	Race	Exposure to Violence				Extreme Poverty				Breaking Ties		
		Physical Abuse	Verbal Abuse	Domestic Violence between Parents	Death of a Friend	Neighborhood Violence	Food Scarcity	Housing insecurity	Death of Caregiver	Incarceration of Caregiver	DCF Involvement	Other
Bryan	Black	X		X			X				X	
Connor	Mixed	X		X				X	X			
Dylan	Black	X	X	X	X	X				X		
Gabriel	Black				X	X	X	X				
Henry	White	X	X	X					X			
Jesus	Latino	X		X	X	X						
Jordan	Black	X	X	X						X		
Joshua	Black	X		X			X				X	
Luke	White	X		X					X			
Miguel	Latino			X			X	X				X
Tyler	Black	X	X						X			

TABLE 3.1.2 Medium Level of Childhood Trauma

Name	Race	Exposure to Violence					Extreme Poverty		Breaking Ties			
		Physical Abuse	Verbal Abuse	Domestic Violence between Parents	Death of a Friend	Neighborhood Violence	Food Scarcity	Housing insecurity	Death of Caregiver	Incarceration of Caregiver	DCF Involvement	Other
Alexander	Latino	X					X		X			
Andrew	Mixed			X							X	
Blake	Black					X				X		X
Isaac	Black					X				X		
Jaxon	Black						X	X				
Jeremiah	Black			X							X	
Julian	White		X	X						X		
Kayden	Black					X						X
Marc	Black						X	X				X
Mateo	Latino			X								
Nate	Asian	X		X								
Robert	White			X					X			
William	White									X		X

TABLE 3.1.3 Low Level of Childhood Trauma

Name	Race	Exposure to Violence					Extreme Poverty			Breaking Ties		
		Physical Abuse	Verbal Abuse	Domestic Violence between Parents	Death of a Friend	Neighborhood Violence	Food Scarcity	Housing insecurity	Death of Caregiver	Incarceration of Caregiver	DCF Involvement	Other
Austin	Black		X									
Elijah	Black			X								
John	Mixed					X						
Josiah	Black											X
Oliver	White			X								
Samuel	Black											

Life-course-persistent Offenders

Terrie Moffitt's (1993) taxonomy of life-course-persistent versus adolescence-limited offenders offers further insight into the relationship between childhood adversity and persistent antisocial behavior. Moffitt argues that a majority of offenders will age out of crime some time after adolescence. Adolescence-limited offending is driven by a "maturity gap." Teenagers turn to deviance when their physical development has already reached maturity while they are still considered children socially. Life-course-persistent offenders, in contrast, begin to display antisocial behavior during early childhood and continue offending past adolescence.

According to Moffitt, life-course-persistent offending has its roots in an adverse early childhood environment. Maternal drug use and general poor prenatal care, for example, disrupt neural growth. When newborns are emotionally neglected, insufficiently stimulated, and lack access to nutritious food, they experience delays in executive functions and verbal abilities. As Moffitt points out, "the link between neuropsychological impairment and antisocial outcomes is one of the most robust effects in the study of antisocial behavior" (680). While the relationship between antisocial behavior and neuropsychological deficits operates independently of class, "children with cognitive and temperamental disadvantage are generally not born into supportive environments" (681). Parents, whose children suffer from neuropsychological impairment, tend to be cognitively challenged themselves. They have neither the economic nor social capital to advocate for their children. As a result, the families who need it most often lack access to the kind of interventions that would allow their children to catch up to their peers over time (ibid.).

A great majority of the young men in this study grew up in families unable to care for them adequately when they were infants or toddlers. The PADOC files offer several data points in support of the life-course-persistent offender paradigm. A majority of the respondents, for instance, had below-average IQ scores. PADOC reports IQ scores for twenty-one of thirty respondents. Those scores range between 75 and 120. Three respondents measure over 100 (the average IQ in the population), whereas ten score between 75 and 89, and five of those ten score less than 80, a threshold that conventionally indicates borderline intellectual functioning. Koenen et al. (2007) find that low IQ is a risk factor for developing PTSD, in that a low IQ might limit someone's ability to narrativize and work through traumatic experiences. The below-average IQ of most respondents therefore constitutes a disadvantage. Not only are the young men more likely to experience trauma, their low IQ scores may also predispose them to developing PTSD.

The young men's case summary files also testify to limited educational achievement and their early onset of violent offending. Both aspects are factored into the Pennsylvania Risk Screen Tool (RST) that is administered to every inmate held at a state correctional institution. RST scores range from 0 to 9 with a higher number indicating a higher risk of recidivism. The average RST score for this group was 5.8 and is slightly higher than the 5.4 average my colleagues and I calculated based on a full sample of PADOC prisoners (Soyer et al. 2017). Two-thirds of the respondents have RST scores of 6 or 7.[3]

Both IQ and RST scores are quantifiable indicators that the young men grew up in socially and economically deprived social environments. Beyond these standardized measurements, the PADOC files do not include any valuable information about the specific abuse and neglect the respondents experienced. To understand the level of adversity the young men lived through, it is necessary to delve deeper into the narrative data.

Childhood Poverty and Violence

According to his case summary file Joshua is nineteen years old, African American, and six feet tall. He has brown eyes and weighs 190 pounds. Joshua was seventeen when he was charged as an adult for robbery. His social history states that he denies "any form of childhood abuse." The file also notes that Joshua insists "his basic needs were met" when he was growing up. In the interviews Joshua and his mother offer a very different narrative. His mother, a former crack addict, readily admits to her parenting failures. She recalls that Joshua's father was abusive, beating her and controlling her social life. When she was pregnant with Joshua, she left her partner only to start dating another abusive man. "I been through hell and back and my kids [have] been there with me," she says.

Her parenting choices reflect the domestic violence that she herself endured. She remembers almost choking "the life out [of]" her son when Joshua was eight years old. It was her way of punishing him for stealing money from her. As I speak to her eleven years later, she expresses remorse about this incident. After she had gone for her son's throat, she called the police herself, telling the dispatcher: "I'm gonna need you to come get him before I kill him." When the police saw the red marks on Joshua's neck, he ended up in foster care. Joshua, however, wanted to stay with his mother. He ran away from different foster care placements, just to show up at her doorstep again. As she puts it: "So every day, Joshua would be here [with me]. No matter where they took Joshua, no matter what facility they took him, he brought his ass right back here."

Although Joshua loves his mother, he struggles to recover happy childhood memories. There were too many siblings and other relatives who needed to be taken care of and not enough resources for everybody. Access to nutritious food wasn't anything that he could take for granted. "Ramen noodles—that was lunch, dinner, and sometimes breakfast," he remembers. And occasionally there were not even ramen noodles to be had. On those days, he fought hunger pains: "You feel like your stomach is touching your back, your head hurt, and then, it would always be physically." When he was younger, Joshua used to be angry about the poverty and instability he confronted on a daily basis: "I wanted a normal [life], to be able to have a conversation with somebody else and we talk about family, you know, good memories, ... and have fun pictures from when you was younger. I didn't have none of that."

This intersection between poverty, drugs, and violence particularly impacted the young men who grew up in urban areas. Jesus, a twenty-year-old Latino man from Kensington, Philadelphia, describes the general despair he witnessed in his neighborhood:

> You see a lot of weird shit, like being around fiends all day. We called it the walking dead down there, 'cause all you see is fiends, doped out, cracked out, walking slow. Like, like they're dead. ... You might walk by and you see a fiend overdosing on their arm, or they already overdosed. ... Or you'd be chilling and somebody would be shooting at the block over 'cause they want their money or drugs. Or next block you might be around and somebody catch a stray bullet. Or over at basketball game, somebody get shot.

Gabriel, who spent some of his childhood in Pittsburgh, witnessed the murder of his friend on a playground next to the shelter where he was staying at the time with his mother and siblings:

> This is when I was in like fourth or fifth grade. ... Like you'd be so young, you'd be so not thinking, you just hear the noise. ... I remember he was by the slide, and then I came down by him on the slide and he was just lying there. I think it hit his chest or something like that. I went downstairs, and his mom's yelling, screaming, everybody's screaming and all that.

Jesus remembers a similar incident:

> My cousin got killed in front of me. And, we was all around. ... It all started over a fight. ... It was a summer day, everybody was around. And two bulls [physically strong males] came walking on the street, but they got hoodies on. We like, what the hell is going on? We thinking they were smokers, like fiends. Bull just walked up to my cousin, and just shoot him in his head. I'm like, what the hell? I see his body drop, and my grandmom scream, everybody screamed. Ahh, what's going on? Know what I'm saying? These two running off. Like oh shit, shit real. This was before I even really, really took the streets serious. I was like 10 or 11. I started having problems, like I was messed up. I went to [the] crazy hospital like a week after that. I wanted to kill my teacher. I was mad at everybody. ... I was pretty messed up for a little bit.

Even though Jesus recalls that he spent time in a psychiatric hospital, the violence he witnessed was quickly buried under the constant struggle that engulfed his childhood.

Like Jesus, Alexander grew up in an area where hearing gunshots was a daily occurrence. Amidst the general violence, Alexander also was an eyewitness to his aunt's murder:

> I was in the room with my aunt when this happened. I was in the room with my aunt, and they got into an argument. He shot her. Just pulled the gun out, they was arguing and I was watching them. He shot her and ran out the door. My uncles started chasing him. The cops caught him and killed him 'cause the cops surrounded him, and he started shooting at the cops. And then, the cops shot him.

At the time of our interview Alexander still recalls PTSD-like symptoms that started after he witnessed his aunt's violent death: "I'd wake up sweating all the time ... I always wake up and be all shakin' and stuff." He never saw a psychiatrist and initially believed that waking up shaking and sweating may be an aspect of hitting puberty. After a while getting shot at also became an occupational hazard of his gang involvement. Alexander lost two more friends to gun violence.

Most of the white respondents, who lived in rural or suburban areas, confronted less violence on the neighborhood level. Their life histories are nevertheless interspersed with personal tragedies and deprivation. Henry, for example, grew up in a small town close to Pittsburgh. He is over six feet tall with short-cropped, blond hair. His arms and neck are covered in tattoos. Henry's parents divorced soon after he was born. Each of them remarried and Henry moved back and forth between his father and mother. The brief social history in his file indicates "no substance abuse or domestic violence among his family members." In our interviews Henry remembers a much more volatile childhood. His father, who was an alcoholic, initially received custody because of his mother's drug addiction. Henry was placed in foster care when his father showed up at his school drunk and threatened to "punch his son in the face." Henry hated his foster care placement and went on the run shortly after he had arrived there.

Despite his father's alcoholism, he preferred to stay with him rather than with his mother and stepfather. Henry vividly remembers that his stepfather physically and emotionally abused him as a young child:

> I can remember, I might have been like five, it was like 1999 or early 2000. ... I'm down there and my mom she gave me two lollipops. And she said, here, you can have them after dinner, and she went to work. She worked until like

three in the morning. So after I get done with dinner, I go ... they're on top of the fridge, so I climb up there and get them. My stepdad gets mad because I didn't ask him. But my mom already told me I could have them. So he takes them and puts them back up there, I throw a little fit. He locks me in the bathroom, dark, and any time I turn the light on, he come in there and whoop my ass. [He] made me stay in the dark that whole night until about one in the morning before my mom came home.

Robert, another white participant, also grew up in a small town. His mother was an alcoholic and had been arrested for DUIs multiple times. Robert remembers drunken fights between his parents but can no longer recall the details. At seven years old, Robert lost his father to suicide. When his father shot himself at a gun range, his mother was serving twenty-three months in county jail for drunk driving. He remembers feeling like both of his parents had abandoned him. After his father's death, Robert lived with his grandmother, his father's mother. She was in her late sixties when I visited her. The small, crumbling house used to belong to her parents. She had lived in it all her life and it was the only property she had ever owned. A few years ago her daughter bought the house to avoid foreclosure.

The poverty of Robert and his family symbolizes the decline of the white, rural working class. Fifty years ago, when Robert's grandmother came of age, Robert's hometown was prosperous. His great-grandfather and his grandfather worked for Bethlehem Steel. Back then, his grandmother remembers, the rumbling from the train tracks by her house never stopped. Today the tracks are eerily quiet. According to Robert's grandmother, "everything went to the dogs" when the steel mills closed. By the time Robert was a teenager, those who could leave had left. The white, working-class part of the town that Robert and his family live in turned into a predominantly African American neighborhood. As Robert's family was struggling to hold on to the little they had, helping Robert to cope with the loss of his father was a low priority. As Robert's grandmother remembers, her daughter-in-law simply expected Robert to "get over it."

The Social Origin of Malformed Habits

The above narratives indicate that Level 1 and Level 2 traumas are intertwined in the young men's experience. The traumatic incidences that fall into the Level 1 category are framed by the abject poverty and generalized violence—the Level II trauma—that defined their lives. Middle-class children may also experience traumatic events; however, their trauma is more likely to be an isolated event rather than a constant experience of deprivation and violence.

Acknowledging that the young men in this book lived through a traumatic childhood is the first step toward humanizing inmates who have been stigmatized as incorrigible "super-predators." The neuropsychological lens is indispensable for understanding pathways into crime. On the other hand, framing criminality as a social problem of the uneducated, cognitively challenged underclass allows the majority to absolve themselves from any responsibility toward those who have shown to be "unfit" for living a middle-class lifestyle for generations.[4]

The social philosopher John Dewey offers an important perspective on the responsibility of society as a whole for individual criminal acts. Taking his view seriously, I believe, allows for an analysis of pathological behavior but without blaming the individual for his or her moral failings. Dewey's understanding of socialization and identity development argues that society—in this case American society, not just the immediate family or peer networks—bears responsibility for the criminal acts the young men committed.

In *Human Nature and Conduct* Dewey develops a theory of identity and habit formation that is fundamentally social in its approach. Dewey sees habits as a form of action and argues that they are acquired through interaction with the social environment. Habits, as he puts it, "involve the support of environing conditions" ([1922] 1988: 16). Any action we engage in is a shared endeavor. The response a specific conduct elicits from the surrounding environment invariably shapes an actor's future behavior. According to Dewey, it is therefore impossible to separate human conduct from the social environment in which the individual is embedded.[5]

Dewey's ideas are especially important for understanding the emergence of criminal behavior. Rejecting a metaphysical understanding of morality, Dewey proposes that good and bad behaviors are established through adaptation to the environment. "Punitive justice," he argues, fails to recognize the "social partnership in producing crime" (ibid., 17). Assuming a "social partnership," however, does not imply that human beings are pure products of their environment. The social environment and the individual are inseparable from each other and they both influence habit formation.

I refer to Dewey's work because, more than other theorists, he emphasizes the social nature of action. According to Dewey, similar habits develop because people react to the same set of circumstances in almost identical ways. Likewise, morals that guide individual behavior emerge out of the group. "Each person," Dewey argues, "is born an infant, and every infant is subject from the first breath he draws and the first cry he utters to the attention and demands of others" (ibid.).

Taking Dewey's perspective to its logical conclusion implies that criminal behavior is a form of social action for which both parties, the individual and society, bear responsibility. Individual behavior manifests itself as a reaction to values that go beyond the individual family unit, or even local institutions.

Following Dewey, the young men's criminal behavior should be understood as malformed habits. These habits are formed in relation to the different social structures in which they are embedded. Gabriel, the young man from Pittsburgh, spent his childhood moving between shelters in violent neighborhoods. He developed his habits in relation to this volatile environment. His mother, who was still a child herself when Gabriel was born, was also adapting to these challenging circumstances. While Gabriel and his mother were able to exercise agency, the choices in front of them were limited and more likely to lead down a criminal path (McLeod 2008).

Dewey's ideas seem to contradict the core American value of individualism. Yet even John Stuart Mill realizes that the vulnerable, not yet fully formed person deserves protection. Mill argues that the individual is sovereign "over his own body and mind." Yet he qualifies this statement by stating: "It is, perhaps, hardly necessary to say that this doctrine is meant to apply to human beings in the maturity of their faculties. We are not speaking of children or of young persons below the age which the law may fix as that of manhood or womanhood" ([1869] 1978: 9). Further he notes: "Those who are still in a state to require to be taken care of by others must be protected against their own actions as well as against external injury" (ibid.).

As children, the respondents needed protection from their own actions. By refusing to adequately support their families, American society has deprived them of their ability to live the kind of individualism American society holds dear. Mill emphasizes that "a true freedom does not attempt to deprive others of theirs or impede their efforts to obtain it" (ibid., 12). By letting poverty and trauma warp the life of these young men so fundamentally, American society is not only guilty of depriving them of freedom but also of teaching them self-destructive habits.

Focusing on the role of drug dealers in poor urban neighborhoods further exemplifies how negative habits emerge through social adaptation. While selling drugs to their mothers, several young men remember that dealers relieved their conscience by giving food and money to the children who were left uncared for. Even at a young age most of the young men understood that drug dealing is a crime. They witnessed the devastating effects that drug use had on their mothers and fathers. Nevertheless, the dealers supported them consistently in ways no other social institution did. Knowing that drug dealing is an illegal and violent trade was outweighed by the immediate gratification of having money in your pocket and by feeling a sense of belonging.

From Dewey's perspective, actors—in this case the young men—did not make a conscious choice to maximize their utility when they committed a crime. Rather, their social environment was structured such that it rewarded certain habits and discouraged others. The young men were not only desensitized to violence but also learned that neither their mothers nor the social institutions they were embedded in met their emotional and physical needs.

Acknowledging that our habits are a product of the social environment we live in does not mean absolving actors from their responsibility. Social processes are highly contingent, and human beings retain agency even under the most oppressive circumstances (Rhodes 2004). The respondents' life-course histories nevertheless raise the question of social responsibility and the need to redistribute wealth. With more comprehensive support for young single mothers, Joshua's mother may have felt empowered to leave her abusive spouses much earlier. Access to mental health services may have diagnosed Robert's father as suicidal in time for him to receive psychological help. Speculating about these potentialities reveals the extent to which American society has abandoned any concept of shared responsibility for the well-being of those who are—at least momentarily—unable to take care of themselves.

Conclusion

The young men I interviewed represent the tail end of the poverty and violence distribution—even in disadvantaged communities. They had long criminal histories and dealt with an unusual amount of trauma in their lives. These young men are "life-course-persistent offenders"—a small fraction of the population that is responsible for a large volume of criminal behavior (Moffitt 1993). Their long-term involvement in the criminal justice system has been costly, even without counting the lost human capital.

Given the clear connection between childhood trauma and criminal behavior, researchers have long advocated for systematic, better-suited mental health services in the juvenile justice system (Ford et al. 2012; Teplin et al. 2002). In 2012, Attorney General Eric Holder's National Task Force on Children Exposed to Violence elevated the prevalence of childhood trauma to an issue of national importance. The task force's executive summary argues that millions of American children experience or witness violence and abuse. Children in the juvenile justice system, the report maintains, have "almost always been exposed to several types of violence" (Listenbee et al. 2012: 171). Therefore, "integrating widely available and culturally adaptive interventions for traumatized children ... in the juvenile justice system" is an absolute necessity (180).

Despite this call for action, treatment of childhood trauma has not been systemically integrated in juvenile justice interventions. Most importantly, even the task force's critical accounting overlooks the crucial relationship between childhood trauma and abject poverty that is clearly visible in the data I have collected.

According to the National Center for Children in Poverty at Columbia University, in 2016, 23 percent of infants and toddlers under the age of three live in families that make less than the federal poverty threshold (Jian, Granja, and Koball 2017). So far, American society has not taken responsibility for the high level of childhood poverty in its midst. Extreme poverty creates the backdrop of a social environment in which children are victimized by overwhelmed caregivers and dysfunctional social institutions. By neglecting poverty as a catalyst for trauma, it is still possible to blame parents for failing to raise their children adequately.

John Dewey, on the other hand, describes criminal behavior as a shared social act. For him any action is social because the principles that guide our decision-making are inseparable from the society we live in. The trauma the young men lived through is rooted in their families' marginalized social position. Their choices are *not* just a reaction to specific pressures (Agnew 1992). Better coping skills or higher self-esteem could not have protected them from hunger pains. Their criminal behavior manifested in relation to a dysfunctional social structure that has brutally cast aside those unable to succeed in a globalized economy.

Over the last three decades the United States has progressively dismantled social welfare for its poorest citizens. The respondents had to cope with extreme poverty and violence that put them at an almost insurmountable disadvantage. Even under the best of circumstances the trauma they lived through can create irreparable psychological damage and behavioral problems. Poor families do not receive high-quality psychological support. In fact, nonpunitive treatment options are not easily accessible for most of them (Soyer 2016). As a result, the trauma that interrupted the respondents' childhood was never addressed and eventually forgotten amidst the daily struggle of making ends meet.

In the chapters that follow I focus on the specific ways childhood trauma, poverty, and crime are interwoven in the life-course histories of the young men. The respondents used criminal behavior to create the illusion of agency over an environment that was beyond their control. Many had become desensitized to violence, and they could barely imagine how their lives might have been if their childhood had not been defined by a lack of food, shelter, and clothing.

Endnotes

1. Despite this staggering level of self-reported trauma, the estimates I provide are likely conservative. Even in retrospective interviews child abuse is substantially underreported, while false positive reporting is considered to be highly unlikely (Hardt and Rutter 2004).

2. The methodological appendix contains a more detailed discussion of the interviews and the specific reasons why the respondents likely felt willing to share sensitive information with me.

3. For information on the RST, see Latessa et al. 2009.

4. This kind of argumentation became well known to broader audiences through the publication of the controversial *The Bell Curve: Intelligence and Class Structure in American Life* (Herrnstein and Murray 1994). For a critique see Fischer et al. (1996).
5. Dewey's work is a precursor to several modern sociological theories that have attempted to unpack the relationship between the individual agent and social structure. Defined as embodied history Pierre Bourdieu's habitus resonates with Dewey's concept of habit. In contrast to Dewey, Bourdieu focuses on the implications habitus has for social mobility. In "Distinction: A Social Critique of the Judgment of Taste," Bourdieu describes habitus as the mechanism that binds the individual, their taste, and aspirations to a particular class position. Similar to Dewey's "habit," Bourdieu's habitus represents a form of behavior subconsciously manifesting itself in relation to structure. In contrast to Bourdieu, Dewey is less concerned with social closure.

   Describing the formation of habit as a reflection of societal structures and the values attached to them, Dewey focuses explicitly on the responsibility of society for the individual's moral formation. Ann Swidler is another modern social theorist whose ideas closely resemble Dewey's theory of habit formation. In "Culture in Action," Swidler (1986) argues that disadvantaged and middle-class children share a similar set of values. She maintains that children growing up in poor neighborhoods do not act according to their actual values because they lack the "cultural tools" to develop adequate strategies for action. This inability to reconcile opportunities and goals leads to frustration that may be channeled into deviant behavior. Swidler develops a concept of culture that is action focused. Similar to Dewey, she implies that given the right tools—for example, educational opportunities—disadvantaged children can develop strategies of action that may allow them to reach their goal without resorting to criminal behavior. I am focusing on Dewey in this book because his work implies the moral obligation of society to ensure the formation of the habits that the collective deems desirable.

References

Agnew, Robert. 1992. "Foundation for a General Strain Theory of Crime and Delinquency." *Criminology* 30:47–87.

Dewey, John. 1988. *Human Nature and Conduct: The Middle Works of John Dewey* 1899–1924, edited by Ann J. Boydston. Carbondale: Southern Illinois University Press.

Feinberg, Irwin. 1982. "Schizophrenia: Caused by a Fault in Programmed Synaptic Elimination during Adolescence." *Journal of Psychiatric Research* 17(4): 319–34.

Felitti Vincent J., Robert F. Anda, Dale Nordenberg, et al. 1998. "Relationship of Childhood Abuse and Household Dysfunction to Many of the Leading Causes of Death in Adults: The Adverse Childhood Experiences (ACE) Study." *American Journal of Preventive Medicine* 14(4): 245–58.

Fischer, Claude S., et al. 1996. *Inequality by Design: Cracking the Bell Curve Myth*. Princeton, NJ: Princeton University Press.

Ford, Julian, John Chapman, Daniel F. Connor, and Keith R. Cruise. 2012. "Complex Trauma and Aggression in Secure Juvenile Justice Settings: Criminal Justice and Behavior." *Criminal Justice and Behavior* 39(6): 694–72.

Hardt, Jochen, and Michael Rutter. 2004. "Validity of Adult Retrospective Reports of Adverse Childhood Experiences: Review of the Evidence." *Journal of Child Psychology and Psychiatry* 45(2): 260–73.

Heide, Kathleen M., and Eldra P. Solomon. 2006. "Biology, Childhood Trauma and Murder: Rethinking Justice." *International Journal of Law and Psychiatry* 29: 220–33.

Herrnstein, Richard J., and Charles Murray. 1994. *The Bell Curve: Intelligence and Class Structure in American Life*. New York: Free Press.

Jiang, Yang, Maribel R. Granja, and Heather Koball. 2017. "Basic Facts about Low-Income Children: Children under 3 Years, 2015." National Center for Children in Poverty, Columbia University Mailman School of Public Health.

Latessa, Edward J., Paula Smith, Myrinda Schweitzer, and Lori Lovins. 2009. *Evaluation of Selected Institutional Offender Treatment Programs for the Pennsylvania Department of Corrections*. Washington, DC: Justice Research and Statistics Association.

Listenbee, Robert, Joe Torre, et al. 2012. *Report of the Attorney General's National Task Force on Children Exposed to Violence*, December 12. Office of Juvenile Justice and Delinquency Prevention, Office of Justice Programs, U. S. Department of Justice. Accessed October 3, 2017. www.justice.gov/defendingchildhood/cev-rpt-full.pdf.

Mill, John Stuart. [1869] 1978. *On Liberty*. Edited by Elizabeth Rappaport. Indianapolis and Cambridge: Hackett.

Moffitt, Terrie E. 1993. "Adolescence-Limited and Life-Course-Persistent Antisocial Behavior: A Developmental Taxonomy." *Psychological Review* 100(4): 674–701.

Sekwar, Aswin, Allison R. Bialas, Heather de Rivera, et al. 2016. "Schizophrenia Risk from Complex Variation of Complement Component 4." *Nature* 530: 177–83.

Selemon, Lynn D. 2013. "A Role for Synaptic Plasticity in the Adolescent Development of Executive Function." *Translational Psychiatry* 3(3): e238.

Shonkoff, Jack P., Andrew S. Garner, et al. 2012. "The Lifelong Effects of Early Childhood Adversity and Toxic Stress." *Pediatrics* 129(1): 2011–63.

Soyer, Michaela. 2016. *A Dream Denied: Incarceration, Recidivism and Young Minority Men*. Berkeley: University of California Press.

———, Susan McNeeley, Gary Zajac, and Kristofer Bucklen. 2017. "Measuring the Criminal Mind: The Relationship between Intelligence and CSS-M Results among a Sample of Pennsylvania Prison Inmates." *Criminal Justice and Behavior* 44(11): 1444–61.

Spatz Widom, Cathy. 1989. "The Cycle of Violence." *Science* 244(4901): 160–66.

Swidler, Ann. 1986. "Culture in Action: Symbols and Strategies." *American Sociological Review* 51(2): 273–86.

Teplin, Linda A., Karen M. Abram, Gary M. McClelland Gary, Mina K. Dulcan, and Amy A. Mericle. 2002. "Psychiatric Disorders in Youth in Juvenile Detention." *Archives of General Psychiatry* 59: 1133–43.

Terr, Lenore C. 1991. "Childhood Traumas: An Outline and Overview." *American Journal of Psychiatry* 148(1): 11–20.

Turner, Heather A., David Finkelhor, and Richard Ormrod. 2005. "The Effect of Lifetime Victimization on the Mental Health of Children and Adolescents." *Social Science and Medicine* 62: 13–27.

Watt, Michael J., Matthew A. Weber, Davies R. Shaydel, and Gina L. Foster. 2017. "Impact of Juvenile Chronic Stress on Adult Cortico-Accumbal Function: Implications for Cognition and Addiction." *Progress in Neuro-Psychopharmacology and Biological Psychiatry* 79(Part B): 136–54.

Reading 3.2

Out Came the Girls: Adolescent Girlhood, the Occult, and the Slenderman Phenomenon

By Alex Mar and Taylor Callery

Here is an image, picked from the notebooks of an eleven-year-old girl in a suburb of Milwaukee, Wisconsin: a head portrait, in pencil, of a man in a dark suit and tie. His long neck is white, and so is his face—bald and whited-out, with hollows where his eyes should be.

Here is another: an androgynous kid (a girl, like the artist?) in a sweatshirt and flared jeans leaping across the page. She has huge, glassy black eyes and dark, stringy hair; she reaches out with one hand and brandishes a dagger in the other. Filling the page around her, tiny rainbows and clouds and stars and hearts—all the signatures of the little girl the artist recently was—burst in a fireworks display.

There are cryptic messages, too: a page covered in Xs; another inscribed he still sees you. These notebooks are charged with the childlike paranoia of sleepovers after bingeing on horror movies, of Ouija boards and *Light as a feather, stiff as a board*. ...

What is *occult* is synonymous with what is hidden, orphic, veiled—but girls are familiar with that realm. We have the instinct. Girls create their own occult language; it may be one of the first signs of adolescence. This is a language of fantasy, of the desire for things we can't yet have (we're too young), of forces we can't control (loneliness, an unrequited crush, the actions of our family). This invention of a private language, both visual and verbal, shared with only a chosen few, gives shape to our first allegiances; it grants entry into a universe with its own rationale— the warped rationale of fairy tales. Its rules do not bleed over into the realm of the mundane, of parents and teachers and adult consequences.

But in May 2014, the occult universe of two young girls did spill over into the real. And within days of her twelfth birthday, all of Morgan Geyser's drawings and scribblings— evidence of the world she had built with her new best friend—were confiscated. More than three years later, they are counted among the state's exhibits in a case of first-degree intentional homicide.

On a Friday night in late spring of 2014, in the small, drab city of Waukesha, Wisconsin, a trio of sixth-grade girls gets together to celebrate Morgan's birthday. They skate for hours under the disco lights at the roller rink: tame, mousy-haired Bella Leutner; Anissa Weier, with her shaggy

brown mop top; and Morgan, the "best friend" they have in common, with her moon of a face, big glasses, and long blond hair. They are three not-so-popular girls at Horning Middle School, a little more childish than the others, a little more obsessed with fantasy and video games and making up scary stories. Morgan casts herself as a creative weirdo, and she relates to her new friend Anissa on this level, through science fiction—Anissa, who has almost no other friends and who moved down the block after her parents' recent divorce. When they get back to the birthday girl's house, they greet the cats, play games on their tablets, then head to Morgan's bedroom, where they finally fall asleep, all three together in a puppy pile in the twin-size loft bed.

In the morning, the girls make a game out of hurling clumps of Silly Putty up at the ceiling. They role-play for a while—as the android from *Star Trek* and a troll and a princess—then eat a breakfast of donuts and strawberries. Morgan gets her mother's permission to walk to the small park nearby.

As they head to the playground, Bella in the lead, Morgan lifts her plaid jacket to show Anissa what she has tucked into her waistband: a steak knife from the kitchen. Anissa is not surprised; they have talked about this moment for months.

After some time on the swings, Anissa suggests they play hide-and-seek in the suburban woods at the park's edge. There, just a few feet beyond the tree line, Morgan, on Anissa's cue, stabs Bella in the chest.

Then she stabs her again, and again, and again—in her arms, in her leg, near her heart. By the time Morgan stops, she has stabbed her nineteen times.

Bella, screaming, rises up—but she can't walk straight. Anissa braces her by the arm (both of them are small) and she and Morgan lead her deeper into the trees, farther away from the trail. They order Bella to lie down on the ground; they claim they will go get help. Lying on the dirt and leaves, the back of her shirt growing damp with blood, slowly bleeding out in the woods, Bella is left to die.

About five hours later and a few miles away, while resting in the grass alongside Interstate 94, Morgan and Anissa are picked up by a pair of sheriff's deputies. The deputies approach them carefully, aware that they are possible suspects in a stabbing but confused by their age. One of the men notices blood on Morgan's clothes as he handcuffs her. When he asks if she's been injured, she says no.

"Then where did the blood come from?"

"I was forced to stab my best friend."

Morgan and Anissa do not yet know that Bella, against all odds, has survived. After their arrests, over the course of nearly nine combined hours of interviews, they claim that they were compelled to kill her by a monster they had encountered online. When discovered, the girls were making their way to him, heading to Wisconsin's Nicolet National Forest on foot, nearly 200 miles north. They were convinced that, once there, if they pushed farther and farther into the nearly 700,000-acre forest, they would find the mansion in which their monster dwells and he would welcome them.

Morgan and Anissa packed for the trip—granola bars, water bottles, photos by which to remember their families. (As Anissa tells a detective, "We were probably going to be spending the rest of our lives there.") Though they were both a very young, Midwestern twelve, they had been chosen for a dark and unique destiny which none of their junior-high classmates could possibly understand, drawn into the forest in the service of a force much greater and more mysterious than anything in their suburban-American lives. What drew them out there has a name: Slender Man, faceless and pale and impossibly tall. His symbol is the letter X.

GIRLS LURED OUT INTO THE DARK WOODS—this is the stuff of folk tales from so many countries, a New World fear of the Puritans, an image at the heart of witchcraft and the occult, timeless. Some of our best-known folk tales were passed down by teenagers—specifically teenage girls.

When Wilhelm and Jacob Grimm published their first collection in 1812, they'd collected many of the stories from young women—from a handful of lower-class villages, but also from the far more sophisticated German cities of Kassel and Münster. At least one of the girls—Dortchen, a pharmacist's daughter Wilhelm would later marry—was as young as twelve. In their earliest published form, 125 years before the first Disney adaptation, these stories are closer to the voices of the original storytellers, less polished, blunt.

The common belief is that many of these tales, when told to children, serve as warnings for bad behavior, harsh lessons, morality plays. But on the flipside, they're remarkable for their easy violence and malleable moral logic, like that of a child. Even mothers are potential villains (converted to *step*mothers in later editions); even the youngest protagonists may kill or maim—as in Dortchen's story of Hansel and Gretel, who burn that evil old woman alive in her own oven. Punishments are meted out, but unevenly; one offending parent meets her death, while the other is forgiven for his sadistic deed—the smoothest path to a happy ending.

The sense that these stories, however peculiar or perverse, rose up from the heart of the culture, seemingly authorless, gives them a unique authority. It is part of why they endure. The same can be said of religious allegories and rituals, or, today, of the new legends that emerge from the internet with the barest of contexts and the illusion of timelessness; time-less elements, those that seem to transcend our moment, are essential to the spinning of myths. The characters are archetypes, blank, faceless—"the girl," "the boy," "the old woman"; the settings are those of epics—a faraway castle, a mountain few can summit, a dark forest.

Nearly a third of the original eighty-six tales of the Grimms' collection feature young people, many of them girls, making their way into the woods—lured out by a trickster, or the need to pass a life-or-death test. In these stories, to enter the forest is to exit everyday life, leaving its rules behind; to encounter magic, and sometimes evil; and finally, deep within the tangle of trees, to be initiated, transformed—maybe even to conquer death—in order to cross into the next phase of life. To enter the forest is to cross over into adolescence.

The woods are also (according to common knowledge) the natural domain of witchcraft, the site at which wayward women gather in the dead of night, naked, to conspire against their neighbors, to blight the crops, to make blood pacts with the devil. They travel out to the edge of town—out into the darkness, between the tops of trees, carried through the night air by demons. At least, this was the Puritan nightmare. In the first American settlements, simple houses stood close together, without streetlights to guide the way at night, and a dark wilderness stretched out just beyond the town limits. The settlers clung for comfort and stability to their vision of a harsh and unforgiving god—but the woods beyond were free from authority.

There are also the woods as they belong to the Pagans of today—those we usually mean when talking about present-day witchcraft in this country. For the Pagan movement, nature is the seat of the sacred, and the black trees the architecture of a natural temple. There the witches—Pagan priests, many of them women, some of them naked—gather for ritual. In that renegade space, they circle out under the moon, chanting, invoking their gods and goddesses.

Then there are the generations of adolescent girls who have experimented with witchcraft—whether some form of Paganism, or folk spells, or totally improvised rites and incantations. For them, the woods have been an occult "room of one's own," a site at which to assert that they are separate and unique, a place to be unseen and un-self-conscious. This is an impulse, untrained: As Emily Dickinson writes, "Witchcraft has not a pedigree,/'Tis early as our breath." Girls are drawn out from their homes, even in the cleanest of suburbs with their bright glass malls, drawn to seek out some kind of magic; to be surrounded by trees, wrapped in the dark, hidden; to become perfect, if only for an hour.

To be an adolescent girl is, for many, to view yourself as desperately set apart, powerfully misunderstood. A special alien, terrible and extraordinary. The flood of new hormones, shot from the glands into the bloodstream; the first charged touches, with a boy or a girl; the first years of bleeding in secret; the startling feeling that your body is suddenly hard to contain and, by extension, so are you. It's an age defined by a raw desire for experience; by the chaotic beginning of a girl's sexual self; by obsessive friendships, fast emotions, the birth and rebirth of hard grudges, an inner life that stands outside of logic. You have an undiluted desire for private knowledge, for a genius shared with a select few.

You bend reality regularly.

Add to this heightened state a singular intimacy with another girl who feels the same isolation—you've encountered the only other resident of your private planet—and the charge is exponentially increased.

THERE MAY ONLY BE one other crime, committed by girls, that closely evokes that of Morgan and Anissa. It took place sixty years earlier, in 1954, in New Zealand.

Pauline Parker and Juliet Hulme met at their conservative all-girls' school in the Victorian city of Christchurch and became the closest of friends. Pauline was sixteen and Juliet only a few months younger. It was an unexpected friendship, as their families had little in common: Pauline's parents were working-class (her father ran a fish-and-chip shop), while Juliet's were wealthier and well traveled, from England, her father the rector of the local university. But the girls had something that drew them together: They'd both been sickly children—Pauline with osteomyelitis (which left her with a limp) and Juliet with pneumonia (which would lead to tuberculosis)—and that brought with it a peculiar kind of isolation. Excused from gym class, the pair spent that period walking through the yard holding hands; they spoke almost exclusively to each other. The headmistress took Juliet's mother aside to express her concern that the girls might be growing too close—but Hilda Hulme did not want to interfere.

From this closeness the two built a wholly immersive imaginative life. They bonded through regular sleepovers at Juliet's house, and the swapping of chapters of the baroque novels they were writing, packed with tales of doomed romance and adventure. Pauline was stocky and boyish, with short black hair and a scar running down one leg; Juliet's hair had blond highlights, and she was taller and slimmer and wore well-tailored clothes. Pauline, who shuffled when she walked, was often ready to lash out; Juliet carried herself with the elegance and easy confidence of an aristocrat. They called each other by secret pet names based on their fiction (Pauline was "Gina" and Juliet "Deborah"). They dreamed of running away together to America, where their work would be published to great acclaim and adapted for film. They rode their bikes far into the countryside, took off their jackets and shoes and socks, and danced until they were exhausted. Some late nights, Pauline would sneak away and ride her bike to Juliet's house, where Juliet would slip out through a balcony. They would steal a bottle of her parents' wine and drink it somewhere out on the grounds, or ride Juliet's horse through the dark woods.

On a bright June afternoon in 1954, Pauline and Juliet took a walk through a local park with Pauline's mother—the place was vast (about 200 acres), with a few hiking paths cleared between the young pines and outcroppings of volcanic rock. When they'd gotten far enough away from any other visitors, Juliet provided a distraction—a pretty pink stone she planted on the ground—and as Honorah Parker bent down to take a look, Pauline removed a piece of brick she'd hidden in her bag, wrapped in a school stocking, and brought it down on her mother's head. The woman collapsed to the ground, and the girls took turns bludgeoning her—about forty-five blows to the head, her glasses knocked from her face, her dentures expelled from her mouth—until she was dead.

According to Pauline's journals, in the year leading up to the murder Pauline and Juliet had created their own religion, unimpressed by Christianity and inspired by elements in their lives both secular and sacred. They'd drawn on the Hollywood movies at their local theater for their coterie of "saints" (Mario Lanza, Orson Welles, Mel Ferrer), erected a "temple" (dedicated to the Archangel Raphael and to Pan) in a secluded corner of Juliet's backyard, and marked their personal holidays with elaborate, choreographed rituals. They believed they could have visions at will—visions of a "4th World" (also called "Paradise" or "Paradisa"), a holier realm inhabited by only the most transcendent of artists, a plane of existence far above that of Pauline's father, with his fish-and-chips shop, or her undereducated mother. With enough practice, each would soon be able to read the other's mind. Each made the other singular and perfect.

What eventually drove Pauline and Juliet to kill Pauline's mother was the fear of being torn apart: Juliet's parents, who were separating, wanted Juliet to stay with her father's sister in Johannesburg while they prepared to return to England; Honorah had refused to allow Pauline to go along. If this were to happen, the world they'd built together—over so many day-dreamy afternoons and secret nights out among the trees—would collapse. The girls could not permit that.

In April of 1954, Pauline wrote: "Anger against mother boiled up inside me. It is she who is one of the main obstacles in my path. Suddenly a means of ridding myself of the obstacle occurred to me." And then in June, a series of entries:

> We practically finished our books today and our main like for the day was to moider mother. This notion is not a new one, but this time it is a definite plan which we intend to carry out. We have worked it all out and are both thrilled with the idea. Naturally we feel a trifle nervous but the anticipation is great.
>
> We discussed our plans for moidering mother and made them a little clearer. Peculiarly enough I have no qualms of conscience (or is it peculiar we are so mad?).
>
> I feel very keyed up as though I were planning a surprise party. So next time I write in this diary Mother will be dead. How odd yet how pleasing.

And early on the morning of June 22, on a page of her journal labeled, in curling letters, "The Day of the Happy Event": "I am writing a little of this up on the morning before the death. I felt very excited and 'The night before Christmas-ish' last night. ... I am about to rise!"

FOR FIVE MONTHS before the stabbing, Morgan and Anissa discussed how they would kill their friend. They learned to speak in their own private code: "cracker" meant "knife"; "the itch" was the need to kill Bella; their final destination, the Nicolet Forest, was "up north" or "the camping trip."

Like those girls in Christchurch, they were drawn to each other out of loneliness. Each saw the other as an affirmation of her uniqueness; they shared a hidden, ritualized world. But Morgan and Anissa's private universe was spun not from the matinee idols and historical novels of the early twentieth century but from the online fictions of our own time. They had devoted themselves to an internet Bogeyman.

Like a fairy-tale monster, Slender Man emerged through a series of obscure clues, never fully visible. He first appeared online, in the summer of 2009, in two vague images that were quickly passed around horror and fantasy fan forums. In the first, dated 1983, a horde of young teenagers streams out of a wooded area toward the camera, while behind them looms a tall and pale spectral figure with its hand outstretched. The image is coupled with a message: "We didn't want to go, we didn't want to kill them, but its persistent silence and outstretched arms horrified and comforted us at the same time ..." In the second photo, dated 1986, we see a playground full of little girls, all about six or seven years old. In the foreground, one pauses to face the camera, smiling, as she climbs a slide; in the background, in the shade of a cluster of trees, others gather around a tall figure in a dark suit. If you look closely, you can make out wavy arms or tentacles emanating from its back. A label states that the photo is notable for being taken on the day on which "fourteen children vanished," and as a record of "what is referred to as 'The Slender Man.'" Making this all the more meta-real, these photos were presented as "documents": The 1986 image bears a watermark from "City of Stirling Libraries"; the photographers, respectively, are listed as "presumed dead" and "missing."

These images were created by a thirty-year-old elementary-school teacher (Eric Knudsen, who goes by the name "Victor Surge") in one of the collections of forums on the website Something Awful. Surge decided to take part in a new thread called "Create Paranormal Images." The game was to alter existing photographs using Photoshop and then post them on other paranormal forums in an attempt to pass them off as the real thing. The monster was deliberately vague, his story almost completely open-ended—and so the internet rushed in to make of him what it wanted. Bloggers and vloggers and forum members wrote intricate false confessionals of encounters with Slender Man, and posted altered photographs and elaborate video series all predicated on the assumption that "Slender" was a real entity and a real threat.

Over the next several years, the monster spread at an exponential rate, mainly through alternative-reality games—online texts and videos created by fans feeding off the narratives of other users in real time, creating a "networked narrative" that blurs the lines between reality and fiction. And as the story spread, it quickly lost its point of origin, becoming instead the creative nexus, for hundreds of thousands of users, of a dark, sprawling, real-time fairy tale. A sort of 4th World.

All that users knew at first was that Slender had the appearance of a lean man in a black suit, and there his humanoid features ended. He is unnaturally tall—sometimes as tall as twelve feet—and where his face would be is only blanched, featureless skin, stretched taut as a sausage casing, with shallow indentations in place of eyes and mouth. Occasionally, when he shows himself, a ring of long, grasping black tentacles, like supple branches, emerges from his back. Slender Man's motives are unclear, but he is associated with sudden disappearance and death. And he has a pronounced appetite for children. Like a gothic Pied Piper, he calls the children out and leads them away from their world, never to be seen again. And when he allows them to stay in their suburban homes, he infects them with the desire to kill, and the longing to be initiated into his darkest, innermost circle.

Slender Man, his fans have decided, has a peculiar attachment to the woods. Any woods, anywhere. Elaborate Photoshopped images populate the internet—of Slender lurking in the trees at the edges of suburban backyards, or appearing in the background of snapshots taken by unsuspecting hikers. Scores of YouTube clips show twentysomethings running through the woods, chased by Slender Man (who sometimes even makes an appearance, in a bad suit, on stilts, with a white stocking over his head). And then there are the "archival" photos, of historical Slender Man sightings around the world. One of the most arresting images shows Slender standing among the massive pines of a half-felled forest behind children in what might be nineteenth-century dress: It could be an early photo of Appalachia, or perhaps the Black Forest (some believe the monster first emerged long ago in Germany, the birthplace of some of our darkest folk tales).

For Slender's hundreds of thousands of online devotees he was a trip, a monster they were crowdsourcing in real time. His many, many fans and cocreators were mostly college-age guys, or guys in their early twenties—people with a lot of time to devote to the unreal. But because the internet is so wide open, and because there were so many avenues leading to Slender—from video games like Minecraft (where Anissa Weier first discovered him) to alternate-reality games, entire YouTube channels, and fan-fiction forums—there was no way to control who was exposed to this new monster and what they made of him. Morgan and Anissa, among the youngest members of the Slenderverse, were quickly consumed by the swirling, open-ended storyline. They latched onto him as a source of private ritual, the linchpin in the occult universe they were building together.

From the beginning, their friendship was forged by a kind of urgency. Anissa, in particular, suffered from bullying after recently transferring to their school (a fact she kept from her parents) and needed this months-old bond with Morgan to last. (Morgan would later claim that she'd gone ahead with the stabbing to keep Anissa "happy": "It's, um, hard enough to make friends, I don't want to lose them over something like this.") Their bond was only heightened by the alternate reality they inhabited together.

The Slender Man phenomenon actually feeds on the divide between young people's reality and that of adults: He exists, he *grows*, in the gap between adolescents' intuitive sense of the truth—their willingness to embrace the Mysteries—and the cool logic of their parents and teachers. "It should also be noted that children have been able to see [Slender] when no other adults in the vicinity could," reads one fan site. "Confiding these stories to their parents [is] met with the usual parental admonition: overactive imaginations."

The girls told each other they could see Slender and hear Slender, and in her notebooks Morgan drew the image of the faceless man again and again.

In Salem, Massachusetts, in 1692, a dark story spun by a cadre of teenage girls had radical real-world consequences. Their false accusations were as fantastic as any folk tale—a form that had become popular in Europe earlier that century—and as starkly good versus evil as the biblical drama that their harsh Puritan community thrived upon.

The "afflicted girls" of Salem—Abigail Williams and ten others—charged their neighbors with consorting with the Devil, and of tempting them to do the same. Abigail Hobbs, then fourteen, openly rebelled against her stepmother and claimed to wander the woods at night. She told everyone who would listen that she had no fear and nothing could harm her—she'd made a pact with Satan! Most outrageous of all, she said that she'd taken part in a gathering of nine witches during which they'd consumed an unholy sacrament. "I will speak the truth," she told the crowd when called into court. "I have been very wicked."

As the Slender Man legend evolved, the shadowy figure operated more like the Satan of Puritan times. Posters claimed that anyone who learned about Slender was in danger of becoming obsessed with him through a kind of mind control; increasingly, he killed through others—humans known as his "proxies," his "husks," his "agents." He took possession of them, and they did his bidding.

The fairy-tale concept of evil lurking in the woods may be as old as the idea of Satan himself. And all of them—children's monsters, Slender Man, the Devil—are kept alive by the stories we tell one another. Abigail Williams claimed to have a vision of elderly Rebecca Nurse offering her "the Devil's book"; in church, she cried out that she saw another of the village women perched high in the rafters, suckling a canary; she spotted malicious little men walking the streets of town recruiting new witches. Pauline Parker and Juliet Hulme's visions were more mystical and ethereal. Two months before the murder, over Easter vacation, Pauline stayed with Juliet and her family at the beach, and the pair had their first shared revelation. On Good Friday, out for a walk before sunrise, they saw what Pauline described as a "queer formation of clouds," "a gateway" into the 4th World. They suddenly realized that they had "an extra part of our brain which can appreciate the 4th World. ... [W]e may use the key and look into that beautiful world which we have been lucky enough to be allowed to know of."

As for Morgan and Anissa, in Waukesha, they, too, shared visions they claimed were tangible, hyper-realistic. Like the adults posting on Slender Man forums, the girls told each other that they were able to see "Slendy"—but with a vivid reality that set them apart from any healthy adult fan. According to Anissa, after she first told Morgan about the monster, Morgan claimed she'd spotted him when she was five, in a wooded area near her family's house. Anissa told Morgan that she'd seen him twice, in trees outside the window of the bus they shared to school.

When a detective questions Anissa shortly after her arrest, she asks, "So back in December or January, Morgan told you, 'Hey, we should be proxies,' basically?"

ANISSA: Yeah.

DETECTIVE: And you said what?

ANISSA: I said, "Okay, how do we do that?" And she said, "We have to kill Bella."

DETECTIVE: Okay. [Pause.] And do you know *why* she said that?

ANISSA: Because we had to supposedly prove ourselves worthy to Slender.

DETECTIVE: And what did you think of this?

ANISSA: I was surprised—but also kind of excited, 'cause I wanted proof that he existed. Because there are a bunch of skeptics out there saying that he didn't exist, and then there are a bunch of photos online and sources online saying that they *did* see him. ... So I decided to go along, to tag along, to prove skeptics wrong.

DETECTIVE: So did you think that you actually had to kill someone to do it?

ANISSA: Yeah.

DETECTIVE: Like, for real?

ANISSA: Mm-hmm.

About an hour into the interrogation, the detective asks Anissa, "When Morgan said to you, 'If we don't do this for Slender, our families and loved ones will be killed,' do you honestly believe that?" Anissa, crying, answers in an astonished-kid voice: "Well, *yeah*." More specifically, she believes that Slender Man "can easily kill my whole family in three seconds." Just hours earlier, during their long trek to the Nicolet Forest, the girls had announced each time they'd caught a glimpse of him along the way—in the suburban woods, among the trees by the highway. They could hear the rustling of him following close by.

MORGAN GEYSER'S DRAWINGS of Slender Man veer from stark, repetitive images evoking a phantom—a page covered in his symbol ("X"), a blank face with Xs for eyes—to the increasingly particular. In one pencil sketch, a girl with kitty-cat ears and tail lies on the ground, eyes closed, a skull floating above her head; looming over her is another humanoid kitty-girl, who looks straight at the viewer, a scythe in one hand. The speech bubble above her head reads: I LOVE KILLING PEOPLE! And in the most elaborate image, a slim, bald, and faceless figure towers over a row of children; enormous, octopoid tentacles emerge from his back, like long black fingers. Above this Slender-creature's head is written a message, as if to the artist herself: YOU ARE STRANGE CHILD ... IT WILL BE OF MY USE.

In that inscription, an adolescent girl, channeling the voice of a monster, exiles herself—she is "strange" and warped—only to accept herself again. The monster tells her, *Here in the Slenderverse, your strangeness is unique; your loneliness has a purpose; I am calling you to your destiny.* Just as in the 4th World, Pauline and Juliet's weirdness, their "madness," gives them psychic powers and untouchable brilliance. By some Brothers Grimm logic, a dark trial, a call to murder, becomes the girls' only prospect. On ten separate occasions in her interrogation, Morgan calls the stabbing "necessary."

In another sketch, a longhaired kid in a bloody sweatshirt looks as if she has thrown her arms around the neck of Slender Man, who embraces her in return. She is crying; his reddened cheeks are either bloodied or blushing. The two appear to be close, intimate; they are, perhaps, comforting each other. Here the meaning of that earlier inscription—HE STILL SEES YOU—seems to change. As if following the plotline of a teen romance, perhaps Slender's message has become, instead, I SEE WHO YOU REALLY ARE. Slender Man has inspired reams of online fan fiction, some of it romantic or even erotic, about teenage girls involved with the monster. Titles include "My Dear Slenderman," "Into the Darkness," "Love Is All I Want," "To Love a Monster," "I Slept with Slender Man," and "Slenderman's Loving Arms." A few of these stories have some 150,000 reads.

The occult is *orphic,* a word meant to evoke Orpheus and his dark romance. An ancient Greek myth tells of how, after the death of the musician's wife, he followed her into the underworld—only to fail at his one chance to bring her back to life. To build a private, occult world with someone is to travel with them into the dark—and the danger inherent in that is, inevitably, erotic.

Months before her mother's murder, Pauline Parker was sent to see a doctor at the suggestion of Juliet Hulme's father: He was concerned that his daughter's friend might be a lesbian. At their trial, there was much speculation about a possible sexual relationship between the two—a romance perhaps born out of their shared writings and nighttime escapades in the garden. Even putting aside the possibility of a lesbian romance, any sexuality for an unmarried woman, never mind a girl, was liability enough in the 1950s. When the case went to trial, the Crown prosecutor asked his witnesses leading questions about "orgies" and "sexual passion."

And what of the girls of Salem, and what they claimed to have seen of the dark? Abigail Williams was made notorious by Arthur Miller's 1953 play *The Crucible* (which premiered, incidentally, the same year Pauline and Juliet met); she became the lead harpy, the great finger-pointer, a seventeen-year-old girl capable of sending men and women to their deaths, embittered by her affair with local farmer John Proctor. But, in reality, Abigail was only eleven in 1692, and Proctor was sixty. Miller made large assumptions about what shaped her; he spun her story into one of young, female sexuality as a corrupting force. In Miller's play, she has suddenly come into the sexuality of an adult, but with an adolescent's inability to control her impulses. A new darkness—a dark eroticism and sexual envy—infuses his character's thoughts, has lured her out into the woods, out past the borders of good society, in search of a hex. And when she levels her accusations, her conviction is as compelling, as unassailable, as that of a child.

At the same time, in both Christchurch and Waukesha, the attacks were striking in their childishness. In spite of the girls' months of secret talks and journaling and to-do lists, when carried out, the attacks were stupid and clumsy; they had no idea what they were doing. Some of the details they had thought through were fairy-tale specific: Juliet's idea to distract Honorah Parker with a pink gemstone she placed on the park path (Parker stooped down to examine it before Pauline struck); Anissa's idea to lead Bella into the woods through the offer of a game of hide-and-seek. Think of the fact that Morgan and Anissa could still lure their friend into the woods through such a simple game; the bursts of energy with which that game is played; and Bella "hiding" from people she should truly have hidden from. Picture her attackers out there in the suburban woods, playing in high spirits—and then turning to another game, a dare, passing the knife back and forth between themselves until Anissa gives an order clear enough to bring their play to an end. That morning, Morgan brought the knife with her in the way that she might have brought a wand to a *Harry Potter* movie screening. And perhaps she believed that she *could* perform magic with a toy—but that idea brought with it no real-world consequences. Playing with a knife, of course, did.

Their childish incomprehension of the gravity of violence, and the callousness that comes with that, is painfully evident in the girls' interviews while in custody. When Anissa describes her nervousness as they approached the playground that morning, the detective asks what she was most nervous about. She answers, "Seeing a dead person. 'Cause the last time I saw a dead person it was at a funeral and it was my uncle." When asked what Morgan was upset about in the park, Anissa says, "Killing. She had never done that before. She'd stabbed apples before—with, like, chopsticks—but she'd never actually cut a flesh wound into somebody."

Pauline and Juliet continued to behave like immature girls, unaware of what was at stake, even after their arrest. When Pauline was taken into custody alone—at first, police believed Juliet was not directly involved—she didn't want to break her habit of journaling, and so she wrote a new entry, stating that she'd managed to pull off the "moider" and was "taking the blame for everything." (A detective on the case quickly seized it as evidence.) Once both girls were at the station, sharing a cell, they were placed on suicide watch—but they spent their first night (a police officer would later report) gossiping in their bunk beds, unconcerned about their new environment. During the trial, about a dozen foreign publications were represented in the courtroom, with most British newspapers printing a half-column daily, often on their front page—rare attention for a New Zealand case. In a courtroom packed with spectators, Pauline and Juliet were out of sync with the tone of the proceedings. Seated together in the dock, they appeared relaxed and indifferent, often whispering excitedly to each other and smiling. One journalist described their attitude throughout as one of "contemptuous amusement."

Then there is the physical fact of just how young all four of these girls were at the time of their crimes, Morgan and Anissa in particular—something driven home by their regular images in the press. After three and a half years in custody, Morgan's and Anissa's faces are recognizable. Their booking photos, published as a single splitscreen image, are iconic: These suspects have the round cheeks and unfashionable eyeglasses of children. Photos from their first hearings show the two in dark blue jail uniforms, their handcuffed wrists locked to shackles around their waists; at the same time, they are petite (the size of twelve-year-olds) and flat-chested. By their 2016 hearings, both girls, photographed in an array of cotton day dresses, have clearly entered puberty, with developed breasts; their bodies are transforming into those of young women right in front of us, their adolescence taking place in captivity. Anissa's hair, once cut just below her chin, now falls a few inches below her shoulders. Here it is made visible: the uneasy border between "child" and "adult," between the softness of girlhood, still visible in their baby fat, and the latent sexual threat of early womanhood, newly visible. Did the changes in their bodies increase the chance of them paying a greater price for their crime?

WISCONSIN LAW ALLOWS for anyone age ten or above to be tried as an adult for a violent crime. This ratchets the stakes up much, much higher: Both Morgan and Anissa were initially charged with first-degree intentional homicide, facing up to forty-five years in prison (they both pled not guilty for reason of mental illness or defect). If the judge had allowed both their cases to be moved to juvenile court, they would have remained in a juvenile facility, set for release at eighteen.

In the earliest days of this country, American jurisprudence followed the doctrine of *malitia supplet aetatem*—or, as translated, "malice supplies the age." Following the example of English common law, a child of seven or older who understood the difference between right and wrong—as if these were simple, stable concepts—could be held fully accountable. He could even be eligible for the death penalty. As *Blackstone's Commentaries* summed it up, in the 1760s, "one lad of eleven years old may have as much cunning as another of fourteen." It was not until more than a century after the founding of the United States, in 1899, that a juvenile court system was established. Industrialization had made clearer the need to protect children as a separate class—or, in Jane Adams's words, to create a court that would ideally play the role of the "kind and just parent."

But the biggest shift in juvenile justice has been our evolving understanding of the adolescent brain. Neuroscience research has shown that the prefrontal cortex is not fully developed until twenty-five years old, impairing a person's impulse control. There is also the lack of emotional development: The Supreme Court has described adolescence as "a time of immaturity, irresponsibility, impetuousness, and recklessness." As recently as 2005, the court outlawed the execution of minors as "cruel and unusual punishment," in a case in which the American Medical Association and the American Psychological Association filed briefs on new research into adolescent brain development. The same ruling leaned heavily on a 2002 case that prohibited the execution of individuals with intellectual disabilities: Because juveniles are immature, "their irresponsible conduct is not as morally reprehensible as that of an adult." The Supreme Court was not arguing that adolescence is a kind of mental disability, but perhaps that both share symptoms in common—vulnerability, instability, a skewed or heightened worldview—that render their actions harder to judge.

One of the earliest entries into the Grimms' original collection—one that would never make it into the later, popular edition—is a story called "How Some Children Played at Slaughtering." Like all the Grimms' folk tales, it is short and terse, and it goes something like this: In a small city in the Netherlands, a group of children are playing, and they decide that one should be the "butcher," one the "assistant," two the "cooks," and another, finally, the "pig." Armed with a knife, the little butcher pushes the pig to the ground and slits his throat, while the assistant kneels down with a bowl to catch the blood, to use in "making sausages."

The kids are discovered by an adult, and the butcher-boy is taken before the city council. But the council doesn't know what to do, "for they realized it had all been part of a children's game." And so the chief judge decides to perform a test: He takes an apple in one hand and a gold coin in the other and holds them out to the boy; he tells him to pick one.

The boy chooses the apple—laughing as he does, because in his mind, he's gotten the better deal. Still operating by a child's logic, he cannot be convicted of the crime. The judge sets him free.

IN THE MONTHS BEFORE Bella's stabbing in 2014, Morgan Geyser, nearly twelve, was both entering into adolescence (she had just gotten her period) and descending into mental illness.

After her initial five-hour interview came to an end, Morgan, still without her parents, in clothes and slippers provided by the Waukesha police, was placed in the Washington County Jail for juveniles. Anissa was there, too, but they were not allowed to interact. Morgan could have no visitors other than her parents, who were required to sit on the other side of a glass divider; only after a few months into her stay was she permitted to touch or hold them, and even then only twice a month. Over the summer, she became, as her mother, Angie, described her, "floridly psychotic." She continued to have conversations with Slender Man, as well as characters from the *Harry Potter* series (at one point, she claimed that Severus Snape kept her up until 3 a.m.); she saw unicorns; she treated the ants in her cell like pets.

In the fall of that year, Morgan was moved to the Winnebago Mental Health Institute for a few months of twenty-four-hour observation, to determine if she had a chance of being competent enough to stand trial. There, she was given a psychological evaluation that concluded that she suffers from early-onset schizophrenia—very rare for someone so young. Her state-appointed doctor learned that Morgan, since the age of three, had been experiencing "vivid dreams which she wished she could change"; and in the third grade, she began "seeing images pop up on the wall in different colors." She believed she could see ghosts and feel their embrace. At a hearing in December 2014, the judge found Morgan capable of standing trial and ordered her back to Winnebago for treatment—but the facility could no longer take her, now that she had been deemed "competent." Her parents asked for her $500,000 bail to be reduced to a signature bond so that she could be moved to a group home for girls with mental and emotional issues, but the request was denied because the home was not considered secure enough.

By late 2015, Morgan Geyser, diagnosed with schizophrenia, was still not being treated for her disease. She'd become attached to her visions and feared losing them, her only companions in her isolation. Alongside her "friends," she wandered through the forest of her thoughts.

CARL JUNG TOOK LONG WALKS through the sprawling Black Forest as a teenager, during which he improvised his own strain of Pagan mysticism, communing with the trees. He spoke of that same wilderness in a lecture in 1935, as the opening setting of the fifteenth-century romance *Hypnerotomachia Poliphili*: The novella begins, "At length my ignorant sleepes, brought me into a thick wood," and then descends, as Jung describes it, "into the underworld of the psyche." Jung said that forests, as dream imagery, were "symbols for secret depths where unknown beings live." (His mentor, Sigmund Freud, wrote of his own method of analysis as a walk through "a dark forest.") In Jung's *Liber Novus* (also known as *The Red Book*), completed around 1930, he wrote of the nature of the human imagination: "Thoughts are natural events that you do not possess, and whose meaning you only imperfectly recognize. ... [T]houghts grow in me like a forest, populated by different animals."

Morgan's hallucinations—magical characters speaking to her, imaginary friends, lifted from the pages of books or the internet—are grounded in something more specific: her genetic inheritance. Her father, Matt, began his lifelong struggle with schizophrenia at fourteen years old (he receives government assistance due to his illness). In a recent documentary, *Beware the Slenderman*, he talks about his coping mechanisms for living with schizophrenia: He runs numbers in his head and tries to "put up static" to block out his visual and auditory hallucinations. Matt and his wife, Angie, decided early on to delay sharing the fact of Matt's illness with their daughter until she grew older—why make her fearful of a genetically inherited disease that she might never have to face? She'd shown no clear warning signs.

In the film, Matt Geyser describes a life in which the boundaries between the real and the unreal are painfully blurred and an intellectual understanding of the difference is not enough to protect you. If, earlier on, he had decided to share his burden with Morgan, this is the picture he might have drawn for her: "Right now there's, like, patterns of, like, light and, like, geometric shapes that's like, always racing—like *always*, like *right now*. Everything seems normal to me 'cause this is my everything; this is how I've always seen things." But the more threatening hallucinations—including, he says, a "glaring demon-devil"—are more complicated. "You can, like, see it, and, like, you *know* it's not real. But it totally doesn't matter because you're, like, terrified of it," he says, becoming emotional. "I *know* the devil's not in the backseat, but—*the devil is in the backseat.* You know?"

In January 2016, after nineteen months without treatment, Morgan was finally committed to a state mental hospital and put on antipsychotics. By spring, her attorney claimed that her hallucinations were receding and her condition was improving rapidly. But in May of that year, after two years of incarceration, Morgan attempted to cut her arm with a broken pencil and was placed on suicide watch.

Late this September, Morgan accepted a plea bargain, agreeing to be placed in a mental institution indefinitely and thus avoiding the possibility of prison. Just weeks earlier, Anissa had also accepted a deal, pleading guilty to the lesser charge of attempted second-degree homicide. A jury recommended she be sent to a mental hospital for at least three years.

THE JOINT TRIAL of Pauline Parker and Juliet Hulme also hinged on the question of their mental health. Were the girls delusional? Clinically paranoid? Or had they been completely aware of the consequences of their actions and chosen to go ahead with their plan regardless? The defense argued that the girls had been swept up in a *folie à deux*, or "madness between two"—a rarely cited, now-questionable diagnosis of a psychosis developed by two individuals socially isolated together. The crime was too sensational and the defense too exotic for the jury to be persuaded. They deliberated for a little over two hours before finding the girls guilty.

Juliet got the worst of it. She was sent to Mt. Eden prison in Auckland, notorious for its infestation of rats and its damp, cold cells (particularly bad for an inmate who'd recently suffered from TB). There Juliet slept on a straw mattress and had one small window she could not see out of; the bathrooms had no doors, and sanitary napkins were made from strips of cloth. She split her time between prison work (scrubbing floors, making uniforms in the sewing room) and writing material the superintendent called "sexy stuff." She gorged herself on poetry: Byron, Shelley, Tennyson, Omar Khayyám. She taught herself Italian—she dreamed of making a living as either a writer or a singer of Italian opera—and she bragged in a letter that she and Pauline were exquisite singers. She also bragged about her studies, even her talent in knitting—she bragged incessantly. In a letter to a friend, Juliet's father worried that she was "still up in the clouds ... completely removed and occupied with herself and her grandiose ideas about poetry and writing." Five months after the crime, Juliet was "still much the same as she was immediately after the event. She feels that she is right and others are wrong." She remained unbowed, still immersed in literature and a vision of the great artist she could become. These were "delusions" she was not willing to let go of.

In spite of the harsh conditions of Juliet's incarceration, the girls' sentences were ultimately lenient. After five and a half years, both were released by order of the executive council, and each was able to start her life over under an alias.

Juliet Hulme, now Anne Perry, moved to England; using the shorthand she learned in prison, she got a job as a secretary. But she hadn't lost sight of her and Pauline's plan to one day move to California. When she was turned down for a visa (her criminal history was hard to overlook), she began working as a stewardess for an airline that often flew to the United States. One day, upon arriving in Los Angeles, she disembarked and never got back on the plane. She rented a lousy apartment, took on odd jobs, and wrote regularly. By her thirties, back in England, she'd launched a career as a crime novelist. She has since published more than fifty novels, selling over 25 million books worldwide.

In one of her earlier novels, the lead murder suspects seem inspired by Pauline and Juliet: a slightly androgynous suffragette and the taller, radiant, protective woman with whom she lives. They are brilliant and fearless; the suffragette's partner is exalted as having "a dreamer's face, the face of one who would follow her vision and die for it." In a later book, the detective-protagonist seems to speak for the unconventional mores of the author herself when he states that "to care for any person or issue enough to sacrifice greatly for it was the surest sign of being wholly alive. What a waste of the essence of a man that he should never give enough of himself to any cause, that he should always hear the passive, cowardly voice uppermost which counts the cost and puts caution first. One would grow old with the power of one's soul untested. ... "

The next chapter of Pauline's life was not marked by such bravado. She became Hilary Nathan and eventually moved to a small village in South East England. There she purchased a farmworker's cottage and stables, and taught mentally disabled children at a nearby school; she attended daily mass at the local Catholic church. After retiring, she gave riding lessons at her home. When her identity and location were revealed in the press in 1997, Pauline, then fifty-nine, quickly sold her property and disappeared.

She left behind an elaborate mural, on the wall of her bedroom, that the buyers believed she had painted herself—a collection of scenes that are part fairy-tale illustration, part religious allegory. Near the bottom, there is an image of a girl with dark, wavy hair (like her own) diving underwater to grasp an icon of the Virgin Mary; in another, the same girl—as a winged angel, naked and ragged—is locked in a birdcage. At the mural's peak, a beautiful blonde (a girl who resembles Juliet) sits astride a Pegasus—glowing, exuberant, arms outstretched. And the blonde appears again, on horseback, seemingly about to take flight, as the Pauline figure tries to bridle the animal.

On display in these images is both the narcissism of adolescence and the remorse of adulthood, the penance of a woman who has resolved herself to receive the sacrament every single day. And what bridges these two elements is an image at the mural's center: the Pauline girl seated, head bowed, under a dying tree against a dying landscape. The occult language of nature—those late nights in the garden, those dark plans in the woods—had nothing left to give her. It had lost its pagan power.

A POWERFUL NARCISSISM is in full view during the interrogation of Anissa Weier. After being arrested for the stabbing of Bella Leutner, the first question Anissa asks the detective is not about her friend's condition (that would not happen until two and a half hours later) but about how far she and Morgan had walked that day—"'Cause I'm not usually very athletic and I just wanna know." She seems very impressed by the challenges they'd faced on their long walk after leaving Bella, harping on the distance, the threat of heat exhaustion and mosquitoes, going without an allergy pill all day ("Is it bad?"), and the limited snacks (the granola bar she'd packed was "disgusting"; the Kudos bar was much better). She recounts with incredible precision everything she and Morgan ate that day, including free treats at a furniture store (a glass of lemonade and two cookies each). Near the end of her interview, she seems about to share a revelation with the detective:

ANISSA: I just realized something.
DETECTIVE: What's that?
ANISSA: If I don't go to school on Monday, that'll be the first day that I miss of school.

Anissa was later diagnosed with a "shared delusional belief"—a condition that faded the longer she was separated from Morgan. Her parents had gotten divorced just the year before and, along with the bullying at her new school, she'd been upset, unmoored—but otherwise mentally stable. While it is fairly easy, based on the video footage, to believe that something is wrong with Morgan—she is detached, spaced-out—it seems quite clear that Anissa is not ill. She appears more frightened than Morgan, more in touch with the reality of the situation, crying occasionally throughout. She doesn't read as flighty; she doesn't speak in a distant, spooky voice; she seems upset, but grounded. She answers questions with the eagerness and precision of a girl who wants to be the best student in class. And this is precisely why it's so upsetting to watch footage of the following exchange, about the immediate aftermath of the stabbing:

DETECTIVE: So [Bella] was screaming?
ANISSA: Mm-hmm. And then, um, afterwards, to try to keep her quiet, I said, "Sit down, lay down, stop screaming—you'll lose blood slower." And she tried complaining that she couldn't breathe and that she couldn't see.

DETECTIVE: So she started screaming, "I hate you, I trusted you"?

ANISSA: Mm-hmm.

DETECTIVE: She got up?

ANISSA: Yeah. She got up and tried to walk towards the street. ... It led to the other side of Big Ben Road.

DETECTIVE: So she tried to walk towards the street and what happened?

ANISSA: And then she collapsed and said that she couldn't see and she couldn't breathe and also that she couldn't walk. And so then Morgan and I kind of directed her *away* from the road and said that home was *this* way—and we were going deeper into the forest area.

DETECTIVE: So she said—she fell down and said she couldn't breathe or see.

ANISSA: Mm-hmm. Or walk.

DETECTIVE: Or walk. And you had told her to—

ANISSA: To "lay down and be quiet—you'll lose blood slower." And that we're going to get help.

DETECTIVE: But you really weren't going to get her help, right?

ANISSA: Mm, no.

At this point in the interview, Anissa is wrapped in a large wool blanket. The detective handed it to her because the space is chilly. Perhaps she was trying to gain Anissa's confidence, or perhaps it was simply instinctive, offering comfort to a young girl being held in a concrete room. Anissa has been crying—but whether this is from genuine remorse or a kid's fear of getting into trouble is anyone's guess. The look on her face does not tell us enough. And now the detective reads it back to her, the story of two girls who led their friend into the woods.

CHAPTER 3 QUESTIONS AND DISCUSSION TOPICS

1. How does culture define not only the context of a crime but also the public mindset about "acceptable violence"?
2. Which side of the nature versus nurture argument do you find more compelling to explain violent and/or criminal behavior, and why?
3. Why would children with a low IQ suffer greater risk of criminality and/or becoming repeat offenders once in the juvenile justice system?
4. Explain what the "maturity gap" is in the theory of crime.
5. Why do some prescribed intervention programs end up making juvenile offenders' situations worse rather than helping restore stability?
6. What is the Slender Man Phenomenon, and how did it originate and evolve on the internet?
7. Consider the adolescent girls who made accusations of witchcraft against their neighbors in the late-seventeenth-century Salem Witch Trials, leading to twenty executions. While modern society and sensibilities might consider the Salem girls' accusations outrageous and false, perhaps made for personal revenge or other "understandable" reasons to the contemporary mind, try to explain the cultural and psychological environment (i.e., from a psychological anthropology perspective) *as it was then* to explain the believability of their accusations.
8. Compare Juliet Hume and Pauline Parker's murder of Pauline's mother in 1954 to the Morgan Geyser and Anissa Weier's attempted murder of their friend, Bella Leutner, in 2014. *What are some of the similarities that characterize the perpetrators in both cases regarding why they committed and how they justified their crimes?*

Image Credit

Fig. 3.1: Screenshot from "The Bad Seed," https://www.youtube.com/watch?v=fZt7gtFiVJk. Copyright © 1956 by Warner Bros. Entertainment Inc.

Chapter 4

Forensic Methods for the Who, What, and Where

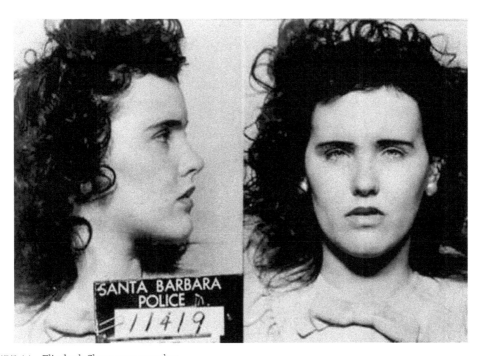

FIGURE 4.1   Elizabeth Short, 1943 mugshot.

INTRODUCTION TO CHAPTER 4

Homicide investigations follow an established protocol of crime scene documentation and evidence collection in order to preserve any forensic evidence and prevent contamination. One of the main reasons pieces of evidence are determined inadmissible in court is a failure to follow proper procedures in its handling. There is a ticking clock at every crime scene to gather evidence before it is lost to external elements (weather, animals, human interference, temperature, and decomposition) and becomes compromised. Cordoning off a crime scene as soon as possible and regulating who may enter the perimeter is crucial to all the procedures that follow.

But human error and lack of preventative measures to protect these small but critical clues have been the undoing of crime scene analysis in the past and continue to be an issue today. One high-profile example is the Elizabeth Short, aka "Black Dahlia," case of 1947. Short was a twenty-two-year-old (see Figure 4.1) who relocated to Los Angeles in hopes of becoming an actress. She ran aground of minor offenses in her youth, such as getting arrested in 1943 for underage drinking. Four years later she would indeed become famous, but not as she had intended. Short's naked body was found bisected in half at the waist and left in the Leimert Park area of Los Angeles by a passerby on January 15, 1947. It was obvious Short was killed elsewhere and her body deposited in this public place so that it would be found. The gruesome condition of her remains and facial mutilations became front-page news, guaranteeing the case a place in crime scene history forever.

What is less known to the public is how the crime scene was hopelessly trampled on from the start by passersby as well as journalists and numerous police officers, who came to the scene after hearing the shocking report on their radios (Reppeto, 2018). Furthermore, in the 1940s the police department in Los Angeles was lax in its privacy measures and allowed journalists and other interested civilians to sit at officers' and investigators' desks, often getting access to files and fieldnotes left unsecured. Police officers often had a symbiotic relationship with reporters such that shared information and informants helped further the investigative needs of both. Of course, journalists made full use of that information for their stories. But while journalists could follow leads that developed from this information, consistency in sharing those leads with the police department was sometimes problematic. The Black Dahlia case suffered several dead ends, red herrings, and individuals over the years who claimed to have identified the murderer—and to date, the case remains officially open and unsolved. Elizabeth Short was not a high-profile person before she became a victim; she was not from a wealthy family—much to the contrary. The crime scene where her body was found was a lost opportunity to obtain clues on the person who left her there. It became instead a cultural flashpoint of intersecting and competing interests that no one thought to protect for the sake of the case.

Trace evidence, which includes materials such as hair, fibers, fingerprints, dust, and microscopic material, is easily transferred from one surface to another, accidentally and without notice, by individuals, animals, and other elements that facilitate movement. Edmond Locard (1877–1966) was a French criminologist and forensic science pioneer who was the first to establish this principle of material transference. The Locard Exchange Principle is still observed in evidence collection and analysis today (Gardner & Bevel, 2009).

Compromised trace evidence can be the cause of misleading results or lost opportunities if the individual collecting the evidence lacks the proper skill or awareness. The first forensic unit with access to a crime scene is typically the trace evidence technician(s), as this is the most fragile form of evidence and has priority to be properly collected for preservation.

The murder of JonBenét Ramsey is another example of a case that suffered due to procedural failures. JonBenét was a six-year-old child beauty pageant queen from Boulder, Colorado. She was reported missing/kidnapped by her parents at 5:52 a.m. on December 26, 1996, after her mother allegedly found a ransom note on the stairs. Her body was eventually discovered later the same day in the basement wine cellar of her own home by her father. Mr. Ramsey hopelessly contaminated the crime scene and undermined potentially critical evidence that could have identified her killer when he removed a blanket from the body and then brought his daughter's remains upstairs. Police had earlier conducted a search of the house, and there is no explanation as to why or how they could have missed this room. During the intervening hours, friends and family and numerous police officers had open access in and about the house. Some of the Ramseys' friends cleaned up the kitchen and living room areas thinking they were helping during this stressful and emotional time but potentially removed or destroyed evidence in the process. Like the Elizabeth Short case, the Ramsey case has never been solved.

Besides trace evidence and other forms of evidence collection for indoor and outdoor contexts, the methodology for scientific documentation of a crime scene itself is crucial for interpretation and reconstruction of events at a site. Proper documentation and analysis aid law enforcement in identifying unknown victims and offenders and offer clues to their behaviors in and around the crime scene, which may ultimately lead to identifying them.

Interpreting evidence of behaviors is a critical skill archaeologists use to reconstruct movement and sequencing at archaeological sites. Outdoor crime scenes are a particular challenge to law enforcement, and their goals are somewhat similar to those of a field archaeologist. It is a little-known fact that outdoor crime scene documentation protocols borrow heavily from the guiding principles of field archaeology. Forensic archaeologists have special skill sets: excavation using scientific methods of measurement, soil assessment, mapping, using grids to note locations of artifacts to aid analysis and timeline calculations, assessment of the condition of any human remains within a burial or exposed to the elements, and consideration of scavenger behaviors and environmental elements that may have interacted with the artifacts or remains over time. In addition to mapping and other crime scene documentation, knowledge of how human beings as well as animals navigate a landscape have proven to be invaluable aids in profiling offenders. The social sciences, understanding the nature of movement (human or animal), and spatial analysis (profiling people and landscapes, or geographic profiling), have become important tools to law enforcement.

All of these components are present in modern outdoor crime scenes. It is not surprising that crime scene technology incorporates some of these very skill sets to ensure a scientific record of an outdoor crime scene or body dump site. For the sake of court, it is imperative that scientific reconstruction of a crime scene and its artifacts (including a body) can be made for the jury or investigators and the case does not rely on memory or officer notes alone. Ironically, many crime scene technicians are not aware of the origins of these archaeological protocols. Forensic archaeologists who have had additional training that accommodates evidence collection and preservation methods may also be called in to assist when a site is particularly complicated. The challenges of such a site are better addressed by specialists who have a wider array of archaeological/environmental expertise than a typical technician's training affords.

Historically, forensic archaeology played a role in interpretation of mass casualty sites from natural disasters, human error (mass transit), or human intention (terrorist bombings, military engagements, and coups). Often, the forensic archaeologists' skills are necessary to properly identify victims recovered from mass graves or traumatic event sites. Forensic archaeologists are much more regularly utilized, in addition to standard crime scene technicians, for outdoor crime scenes in the United Kingdom today than they are in the United States. This is a reflection of British law enforcement attitudes about forensic applications that are not as concerned with proprietorship as with getting as much information as special skill sets can procure.

Forensic archaeology is not to be confused with forensic anthropology. Forensic anthropology is the assessment of human skeletal remains for purposes of identification of the individual, establishing a timeline since death, and assisting the medical examiner in establishing a cause of death if the remains have been skeletonized. Forensic anthropologists can compile a biological profile of the individual based upon their skeletal remains. From those remains they can determine whether bone defects are from past injuries or injuries acquired at time of death. Forensic anthropologists can test for stable isotopes to analyze hair, bones, and teeth to find chemical elements in an isotope ratio that can identify the region where the individual grew up or spent significant time as a child. Isotopes are like signatures in the bones, and are acquired through an individual's diet, water, and the environment in which they live and remain.

Another method that aids in the identification of unknown remains or offenders is the field of forensic art. There are a number of digital, computer-generated programs that select basic shapes of different features to put together a quick image of an offender based upon a witness or a survivor's description. All these programs rely upon set algorithms, and so the face generated will lack the more subtle or unique aspects of a human face. Sometimes, a forensic artist is called upon to make manual adjustments to the digital image to "humanize" it further. The forensic artist is someone who has had specialized training in human

FIGURE 4.2   Photo of author (Sharon Moses) drawing forensic image.

facial anatomy and in constructing a facial image by hand. (See Figure 4.2.) While this may be more time consuming, often the image generated by an artist is more complete. The Federal Bureau of Investigation at Quantico still utilizes forensic artists as a point of preference over dependence upon purely digital/algorithm-based images.

The articles in this chapter draw upon interdisciplinary methods used to identify victims and offenders and document crime scenes. They include a discussion of the historical development of forensic science evidence (Shelton, 2012); a case study of a domestic homicide investigation (Steadman et al., 2009); a summary of geographic profiling (Andresen, 2020); and a discussion of the intersection between forensic science and anthropology (Moses, 2021).

Reading 4.1

Historical Development of Forensic Scientific Evidence

By Donald E. Shelton

THE HISTORY OF THE USE OF forensic science in criminal cases in the United States is well over a century old.[1] The search for scientific answers to age old human questions that gripped the western world in the 19th and 20th centuries was applied to many aspects of American society, including the criminal justice system. The courts allowed "experts" to give opinions about issues that had previously been left exclusively to the jury, primarily such as identification through fingerprints and details of death or injury through medical testimony. As the use and pursuit of science increased, there were corresponding increases in both areas of claimed expertise and the technological innovations that were used or developed to apply them.

Courts initially exhibited some reluctance to accept some of this claimed expertise as scientific, in handwriting analysis for example. However, courts eventually established a pattern of almost routine acceptance of expert witnesses offered by the prosecution as an aid to the jury in finding guilt. Courts required little or any scientific foundation to be laid by the prosecution for such testimony. In a distinctly non-scientific approach, the case law developed in application of the *Frye* doctrine which required only that such testimony be generally accepted. That standard is almost self perpetuating. As more courts admitted testimony from any particular forensic science field, other courts used those admissibility decisions to bolster the idea that the field became more "generally accepted." There was rarely any defense challenge to the empirical basis, or scientific reliability, of prosecution generated forensic science evidence.

The areas of claimed expertise offered in criminal cases by the government expanded, almost unquestioned by defense counsel or the courts. Prosecutors offered expert testimony based on the conclusions of criminal investigators, many of whom had little or no scientific training. In addition to fingerprints, courts allowed identification testimony (the "who" question) based on the experience and presumed expertise of witnesses in such areas as handwriting comparisons, microscopic hair comparisons, blood comparisons, and bite mark comparisons. The conclusion in such testimony was rarely couched in terms of probability. Not only was such testimony admitted, often these experts were allowed to testify that the claimed crime scene or related item—be it fingerprints, hair, writing, bite marks or whatever other residue investigators found—was a "match" for a similar item from the defendant and even that it was a unique match so that the defendant was the only person who could have generated the crime item.

Experts in other scientific areas were allowed to testify to conclusions about the origin of materials used in the commission of a crime (the "what" question) in order to tie those materials to similar items in the defendant's control. Comparison microscope examination was used as the basis for testimony that scene bullets and test bullets were fired from the same gun, or that a particular screwdriver or other tool was used to make the marks that were left at a scene, or even that the lead from a bullet at the scene came from the same batch of bullets connected to the defendant.

Still other investigators were allowed to give opinion testimony about the origins or mechanism of events at a crime scene (the "how" question). They gave opinions about such things as how a fire started based on pieces of the residue that had not been destroyed in a fire, or reconstruction of the details of how a wound was inflicted based on their observations of blood stain patterns at the scene or on the defendant.

The routine acceptance of forensic expert testimony expanded beyond areas of physical science or physical examination. Social science testimony, as distinct from physical evidence, was created and offered by the prosecutor to bolster the government's claim that an act of alleged sexual abuse had occurred. Psychologists, sociologists, social workers, and even counselors or police officers, were allowed by courts to give their opinion that the testimony, or other conduct, of a complainant were consistent with the testimony and behavior of other persons who had been abused in the manner similar to that described by the complainant. The clear purpose of that testimony, regardless of any instructional limitation given by the judge, was not only that the alleged abuse occurred but that the complainant was telling the truth about how it occurred. On the other end of that spectrum, however, courts were not allowing social scientists proffered by the defense to testify as to the unreliability of eyewitness testimony, either generally or under conditions similar to those that existed at the scene of an alleged crime.

Some forensic science and technology developments were created specifically for use in criminal justice investigation and adjudication. Firearm comparison, hair analysis, and tool mark comparison are good examples. Other forensic evidence originated in scientific and technical fields, particularly medicine, and later found often unexpected applications in the criminal justice arena. Blood typing and DNA are two obvious examples.

Fingerprint comparison was originally developed as a means of identification that was quickly adapted to criminal investigations and has been accepted as evidence in criminal prosecutions for over one hundred years.[2] Early visual analysis gave way to a range of techniques for finding and enhancing prints, and for locating comparison prints from a computerized database. Comparison of handwriting samples is one of the oldest types of forensic evidence. Although it was offered in courts even before the twentieth century, it was not widely accepted as scientific evidence until it became part of the cornerstone of the prosecution case in *State v. Hauptmann*,[3] the Lindbergh kidnapping case.

DNA profiling started as a method of determining paternity. The first use of DNA in a successful United States criminal prosecution was in *Andrews v. State*.[4] In *Andrews*, police matched DNA samples from semen to the defendant's blood in a rape case. The admission of DNA evidence in a criminal case was first approved by a state supreme court in *State v. Woodall*.[5] Subsequently, properly collected and analyzed DNA evidence has been routinely admitted. DNA test results are now admissible in virtually every jurisdiction. DNA matching has almost totally replaced blood typing for identification purposes and is probably the most important forensic science development in the twentieth century. Thirteen states have even adopted statutes authorizing admission of DNA evidence. DNA has become the "gold standard" of forensic scientific evidence and DNA typing is now universally recognized as the standard against which many other forensic individualization techniques are judged.

DNA testing has a remarkable ability, in the right circumstances, to provide conclusive exculpatory evidence after conviction when specimens were not tested at the time of trial. The postconviction power of DNA testing is attributable to the same characteristics of the technology that has made it so valuable during investigation and trial: the durability of DNA permits reliable testing years after the incident, and the polymorphism of DNA sequence systems greatly increases the probability of a conclusive exculpatory result. The highly publicized Innocence Project reports that, as of 2011, there have been 280 postconviction exonerations by DNA testing in the United States.[6]

While the emergence of forensic DNA evidence has proven to be a dramatically positive aspect of new breakthroughs in science and technology, one unanticipated effect is that those same new scientific analyses have cast doubt on some of the more traditional types of forensic scientific evidence that trial judges have long treated as reliable and generally accepted. New scientific methods have caused some to reassess the validity of such things as serology testing, comparative bullet lead analysis, bite mark identification, handwriting analysis, hair and fiber analysis, and tool mark and ballistics testimony. Postconviction DNA testing itself has resulted in proof of wrongful convictions that were based on seemingly reliable non-DNA forensic scientific evidence.[7] For example, twenty-two percent of the first two hundred postconviction DNA exonerations had been based on false hair or fiber comparisons, and almost forty percent had been based on serology evidence.[8] These exonerations are undisputable proof of the "documented ills" of other forms of scientific evidence, including perhaps such traditionally admitted forms of evidence as fingerprints. They have provided some of the impetus for the re-examination of those disciplines by the courts in light of new criteria for the performance of judges' roles as the "gatekeepers" of scientific evidence admissibility.

Endnotes

1. Generally, see William Tilstone, *Forensic Science: An Encyclopedia of History, Methods, and Techniques* (2006).
2. The landmark case in the United States is *People v. Jennings*, 252 Ill. 534, 96 N.E. 1077 (1911).
3. *State v. Hauptmann*, 180 A. 809 (N.J. 1935)
4. *Andrews v. State*, 533 So.2d 841(Fla. Dist. Ct. App. 1988)
5. *State v. Woodall*, 385 S.E.2d 253 (W. Va. 1989)
6. The Innocence Project, available online at www.innocenceproject.org (last visited November 26, 2011).
7. Findley, Keith A., *Innocents at Risk: Adversary Imbalance, Forensic Science, and the Search for Truth*, 38 Seton Hall L. Rev. 893 (2008), available online at http://ssrn.com/abstract=1144886 (last visited December 14, 2011).
8. Garrett, Brandon L., *Judging Innocence*, 108 Colum. L. Rev. 55, 81–83 (2008).

Bibliography and Table of Cases

Cases

Andrews v. State, 533 So.2d 841(Fla. Dist. Ct. App. 1988)

People v. Jennings, 252 Ill. 534, 96 N.E. 1077 (1911)

State v. Hauptmann, 180 A. 809 (N.J. 1935)

State v. Woodall, 385 S.E.2d 253 (W. Va. 1989)

Findley, Keith A., *Innocents at Risk: Adversary Imbalance, Forensic Science, and the Search for Truth*, 38 Seton Hall L. Rev. 893 (2008)

Garrett, Brandon L., *Judging Innocence*, 108 Columbia L. Rev. 55 (2008)

Tilstone, William, *Forensic Science: An Encyclopedia of History, Methods, and Techniques*, ABC-Clio Pub.: Santa Barbara, Cal. (2006)

Reading 4.2

Domestic Homicide Investigations: An Example from the United States

By Dawnie Wolfe Steadman, William Basler, Michael J. Hochrein, Dennis F. Klein, and Julia C. Goodin

T HE ROLE OF FORENSIC ANTHROPOLOGY IN domestic cases in the United States has expanded tremendously in the last two decades. In addition to working on traditional cases of personal identification of skeletal remains, forensic anthropologists routinely assist in missing person searches, apply forensic archaeological techniques at recovery scenes, estimate postmortem intervals, explain burning patterns of bone, and interpret trauma. Forensic pathologists also increasingly consult with forensic anthropologists in cases for which identity is known. For instance, forensic anthropologists assist in interpreting the direction of impact in carpedestrian accidents and detecting suites of healed and acute injuries in child abuse cases. Forensic anthropologists also must ensure that the methods they employ satisfy the current criteria for evidence admissibility in court.

This chapter provides a detailed report of a complex federal case illustrating the multidisciplinary nature of domestic homicide investigations that highlights the role of forensic anthropology. This case demonstrates the various forms of physical evidence that can be recovered from mass graves when standard archaeological procedures are correctly applied and underscores the critical need for cooperation between forensic pathologists and anthropologists in trauma analysis. Like many anthropological cases, the lengthy period between disappearance and recovery necessitated consistent investigative attention until critical information came to light.

In July of 1993, Lori Duncan,[1] her two little girls, Kandace and Amber, and her friend, Greg Nicholson, disappeared from Lori's home in Mason City, Iowa. Four months later, another man, Terry DeGeus, disappeared as well. The sole known connection between the cases was that both men had been involved in a drug distribution ring headed by Dustin Honken. Nicholson had recently agreed to cooperate with federal prosecutors and testify against Honken in an upcoming federal trial. Months and then years passed without any trace of the five missing persons. Although it became increasingly apparent to the federal authorities that the missing people were victims of foul play, it took over a decade for a team of investigators, prosecutors, and forensic scientists from a variety of federal, state, and local agencies to locate and recover the victims' bodies and bring to justice their murderers, Dustin Honken and his girlfriend and accomplice, Angela Johnson.

The Investigation

Dustin Honken was born and raised in northern Iowa. Though intellectually gifted, he was an academic underachiever. Upon graduation from high school, he attended a local community college and excelled in chemistry but eventually dropped out of school and moved to Arizona to live with his older brother. While in Arizona, Honken perfected a methamphetamine production method and began distributing this drug to two individuals in north Iowa, Greg Nicholson and Terry DeGeus, who, in turn, sold the methamphetamine to street level dealers. When one of Nicholson's customers was arrested, he agreed to cooperate with the police, and Nicholson was arrested. Nicholson was also given the opportunity to cooperate with the police, which led to Honken's arrest during March of 1993.

Honken was charged in federal court for distribution of methamphetamine and, during the pretrial proceedings, learned that Nicholson had been responsible for his arrest. On July 8, 1993, Honken negotiated a plea agreement and was scheduled to plead guilty on July 30. He was released from jail in the interim. Before his arrest, Honken had become romantically involved with Angela Johnson, the exgirlfriend of Terry DeGeus. Johnson was a high school dropout with a history of drug abuse and an assortment of occupations. Near the time of Honken's release, Angela Johnson purchased a Tec-9, a semiautomatic 9-mm handgun, from an area pawnshop. Investigators would later locate witnesses who described efforts by Honken and Johnson to learn the whereabouts of Greg Nicholson. A few days before Nicholson's disappearance, Honken was directed to the home of Lori Duncan.

Following his release, Greg Nicholson had lived at a variety of locations around Mason City, Iowa. In early July, a friend had introduced him to one of her coworkers, Lori Duncan. Lori was a divorced mother who worked at a factory to support herself and her two daughters, Kandace, age 10, and Amber, who was 6 years old. Nicholson moved into the Duncan home in mid-July. All four members of the household were last observed by relatives, friends, and neighbors on Sunday, July 25, 1993.

On Monday morning, July 26, Lori Duncan uncharacteristically failed to report to work. Later that day a welfare check at Lori's home turned up only a note indicating that Lori had to leave on short notice but would be in contact soon. Nicholson, Lori, Kandi, and Amber were never seen alive again. Just four days later, at his scheduled court appearance on July 30, 1993, Honken informed the federal prosecutor that he no longer intended to plead guilty and told the prosecutor that the case against him was "not as good as you think it is."

With Nicholson unavailable and his whereabouts unknown, the case against Honken was in jeopardy. The government attempted to resurrect its case by pursuing information regarding Terry DeGeus, Honken's other drug distributor. On October 27, 1993, Angela Johnson was subpoenaed to testify before the grand jury and was questioned about DeGeus's drug business and his involvement with Honken. A few days later, on November 5, Johnson left a telephone message for Terry DeGeus telling him to meet her that evening in Mason City. After leaving for that meeting, DeGeus was never seen alive again.

Because Nicholson and DeGeus could not be located, all charges against Honken were dismissed in September of 1995. However, Honken was arrested again during the early spring of 1996 for assembling a methamphetamine laboratory in Mason City. Honken was released from jail pending trial, this time wearing an ankle bracelet that allowed authorities to monitor his whereabouts. Honken's best friend was also arrested and investigators pressured him to tell them about Honken's drug activities. He cooperated with the authorities in a plea arrangement. Honken's friend told the police that Honken was trying to learn how to electronically defeat the ankle device and that his intentions were to kill the current witnesses against him, including police, informants, and laboratory personnel. He also stated that, although Honken never told him so directly, Honken had hinted that he had killed the people who were missing since 1993. Finally, Honken's friend told investigators that he had helped Honken cut up, melt, and discard the remnants of a gun during the winter of 1993–1994. Although the friend was unfamiliar with firearms, he drew a sketch that closely resembled the profile of a Tec-9, the model that had been purchased by Angela Johnson.

Honken's pretrial bond was revoked in light of this new information, and he was incarcerated until his trial. However, Honken apparently believed he could continue to escape justice by killing witnesses. While awaiting trial in jail in 1996, Honken unsuccessfully solicited the murder of his best friend, who had betrayed him. Years later, this conspiracy would be added to the murder charges arising from the 1993 disappearances.

Although the investigation into the disappearances in 1993 had continued, it was reenergized in 1996 with the new information supplied by Honken's best friend. The investigation now focused on both Honken and Johnson as the persons responsible. Finding the bodies became even more crucial, yet there were few reliable leads, and investigators hit several dead ends. For instance, one investigative theory was that DeGeus, who had worked at his father's excavation/demolition business at the time of his disappearance, may have participated in the killings of Nicholson, Duncan, and her two daughters and that the bodies may have been buried at the site where DeGeus was working at the time. It was further theorized that DeGeus may have later been killed to ensure his silence. Following this theory, the investigators found the site where DeGeus was working on July 26, 1993, a farm field where buildings had been knocked down and buried. Investigators examined the site utilizing ground-penetrating radar and cadaver-trained search dogs, but no human remains were found.

The investigation continued without significant progress until 1999. Honken had finally pled guilty to the 1996 federal drug charges and was serving a 20-year sentence in a Colorado prison. In the summer of 1999, the first of several prisoners contacted federal authorities in Iowa to provide information that Honken was bragging to fellow inmates that he had "killed his rats." Honken shared details of the killings to at least one inmate that would ultimately be corroborated by forensic scientists.

In November 1999, prosecutors began presenting evidence to the grand jury in pursuit of murder indictments against Honken and Johnson. One of the persons subpoenaed was Angela Johnson's best friend during 1993. Though this woman had been interviewed and summoned to the grand jury several times, she always claimed that she had no information about the disappearances. During the summer of 2000, she was interviewed yet again and finally admitted that Angela Johnson had confessed to assisting Honken with the kidnapping and eventual murders of Nicholson, Duncan, and the two young girls. Specifically, Johnson had obtained entry to the Duncan home by posing as a lost saleslady and then used a handgun to control the victims until Honken arrived. They bound the adults then transported all four victims to a wooded area in the country. Johnson related to her friend that Honken took Greg Nicholson and Lori Duncan a distance from the car before shooting and killing them both. He then returned to the car, where Johnson was holding the two frightened girls. Honken executed each with a bullet to the head. All four were buried in a grave. Johnson further told her friend that Nicholson was killed so that he could not testify against Honken, and the others had been murdered because they were potential witnesses to Nicholson's abduction. Johnson's friend further disclosed that, on a separate occasion, Johnson had confessed that she and Honken had murdered Terry DeGeus. On the day DeGeus disappeared, Johnson told her that she had called DeGeus and asked him to meet her in Mason City, which he did. Johnson then took DeGeus to a remote location where Honken was waiting. Honken killed DeGeus with a gun and an aluminum baseball bat and buried him in a hand-dug grave.

Unfortunately, Johnson did not disclose the location of either grave to her friend. Nevertheless, with this information the case against Johnson was now stronger than the case against Honken, since rules of evidence based on the 6th Amendment Right to Confrontation would prevent using Johnson's confession against Honken. Thus, changing the focus of the investigation, and despite the fact that the bodies of the five murder victims had still not been recovered, authorities sought and obtained an indictment of Angela Johnson on five counts of murder. On the seventh anniversary of the Nicholson-Duncan disappearances, Angela Johnson was arrested and transported to the Benton County jail to await trial.

The Benton County jail is a relatively small facility, housing both male and female prisoners in separate cells on the same floor. Prisoners are able to communicate with one another by talking through the walls and passing notes, often using books on the jail's book cart. Using these methods, Johnson was befriended by a male inmate who, though currently serving a life sentence in another state for conspiring to import heroin into the United States, was temporarily in Iowa to testify in another case. He told Johnson that he knew a prisoner at the federal prison in Leavenworth, Kansas, who was serving a life sentence and had no hope of ever being released. He told her that he thought he could convince this federal prisoner to admit to committing the five murders, which would set Johnson free and she could then sue the federal government for false arrest. The only problem with this plan, he explained, is that the prisoner would need something to prove his credibility to the authorities, such as maps of where the bodies had been buried. Johnson eventually provided two maps to her jailhouse friend, detailing where the bodies could be found and information about the bodies themselves. In hopes of exchanging this information for potential leniency in his own case, the inmate turned the maps over to federal authorities.

Recovery of a Mass Grave

Johnson's two hand-drawn maps identified street names and other landmarks. Iowa detectives quickly located two areas near Mason City, which, according to the maps, should contain the clandestine graves. Iowa authorities then contacted the St. Louis, Missouri, FBI Evidence Response Team (ERT) for forensic assistance. Additional assistance was requested of Omaha Division's FBI ERT and the ERT Unit (ERTU) based out of the FBI Laboratory in Quantico, Virginia. After securing federal search warrants that authorized examination of two possible burial sites, the ERT began its site investigations on October 11, 2000. The first scene was an abandoned farmstead and adjacent corn field along Killdeer Avenue in Cerro Gordo County. Soil coring and probing limited further subsurface searching to an area approximately 10 m x 50 m along the actively cultivated corn field. A cadaver dog and handler were unable to locate buried or surface-scattered remains. However, geophysical prospecting in the form of ground-penetrating radar identified so many subterranean anomalies as to make the technique ineffective. The ERT selected what appeared to be the most promising area among the numerous anomalies and dug a 1 x 1 m test pit. However, the excavation revealed only the approximately 30-year-old burial of a calf, a large segment of metal rail, and other debris buried 63 cm (24.8 in) below the surface. Following a day of test excavations and sampling, the ERT decided to complete a site map of the farmstead and preliminary surveys for future searches that would entail removal of the upper levels of the cornfield plow zone using heavy equipment.

This work proved crucial: investigators would return to this site a month later and find the remains of Terry DeGeus.

The following morning the ERT continued mapping the Killdeer Avenue site while other investigators began to search the second potential site, located on Lark Avenue. Here, certain landmarks were found that appeared consistent with one of Angela Johnson's jail house maps. Searchers were drawn to two vehicle tires beneath a bush in the area of Lark Avenue and a railroad right of way. They understood from Johnson's description that tires were placed over or near the grave. Again, a cadaver dog failed to alert to the area. Ground-penetrating radar indicated the existence of an anomaly below ground surface. Confirmation of possible buried remains was first received when a small piece of bone was found in the upper 20 cm of a soil core sample. This sample prompted more intrusive testing of the spot.

The excavation began by digging a small, controlled test pit, or "window," in what was thought to be the center of the anomaly as delineated by ground-penetrating radar. That small (40 cm x 35 cm x 30 cm) (16 x 14 x 12 in), rectangular pit revealed commingled animal and human bones. Above and among the clavicles of an adult human were what would later be identified as the bones of an opossum (*Didelphis virginiana*) and short-tailed shrew (*Blarina brevicauda*). If this was a mass grave of murder victims, the commingling of nonhuman remains at the top of the grave was initially puzzling. However, subsequent excavation revealed an infilled burrow, or "krotovina," which extended from the area of the opossum and shrew bones toward and through the eastern edge of the grave. What originally appeared as the intentional burial of road-kill, or a family pet, on top of human victims was demonstrated through archaeological excavation, geological characteristics, and zoological consultation to be the natural wintering and death of an opossum inside another rodent's abandoned chamber. A less controlled excavation and documentation of the remains and associated geotaphonomic evidence of bioturbation could have resulted in an incorrect or inconclusive explanation for the coexistence of the nonhuman and human occupants of the grave.

The creation of the initial excavation window, beyond offering the first confirmation of buried human remains, established a starting point for full excavation. It also offered an idea of how to orient the mapping system that would be used to record those excavations and their finds in three dimensions. A grid system of 1 x 1 m stringed units was established at ground surface over the interpreted size and orientation of the grave. After the existing surface was defoliated and its contours and cultural debris were mapped in relation to the three-dimensional grid system, excavation proceeded by expanding the initial excavation window across the exposed human remains toward the original edges of the grave feature. This expansion involved carefully slicing, in effect thin-sectioning, the fill from above the remains, keeping a vertical wall or profile of fill in front of the excavator throughout

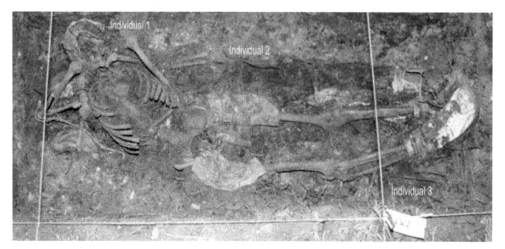

FIGURE 4.2.1   Full excavation to the top of Individual 1 resulting in the partial exposure of Individuals 2 and 3 (photograph Lavone Tienken, used with permission of M. Hochrein).

the process. As a result, evidence encountered in the excavated vertical profiles could be photographed and mapped *in situ* preserving their contexts in relation to the human remains and other features of the general scene. To preserve potential geotaphonomic tool marks, and to better clean the excavation, a vacuum was carefully used to clean loosened fill. All excavated fill was screened through a minimum ¼-in hardware cloth to recover smaller evidence possibly overlooked in the excavation. Screening was critical in that a decision was made to collect the skeletal remains of each victim's hands and unclothed feet en masse rather than detail each phalange or carpal/tarsal. Although this technique did reduce excavation time in a situation in which multiple victims were interred, its downside was that some hand bones became commingled between victims, and a small number were not recovered.

After 24 hours of continuous excavation Individual 1, the uppermost skeleton in the grave, was completely exposed. Individual 1 was lying supine and slightly curved at the waist on top of Individual 2 (Figures 4.2.1 and 4.2.2). The wrists were bound by a clothesline-type ligature. Duct tape was wrapped around the eyes and nasal regions of the individual. A green synthetic fabric sock protruded from the mouth. Stitching around the torso indicated this individual was interred while wearing a natural fiber shirt or undershirt. Remnants of jeans or denim type pants included only the pocket linings, stitching, zipper, and some rivets. Behind the right hip was a billfold found to contain a driver's license bearing information for Gregory Nicholson. The right foot of the individual bore a white athletic sock and athletic shoe, and the left foot was covered only by a white athletic sock (Hochrein 2000: 57–58).

A large root that had grown over the femora of Individual 1 was later examined by a University of Missouri botanist. The dendrochronological conclusions were that a minimum of four growing seasons had passed in order for the root to grow to its collected size

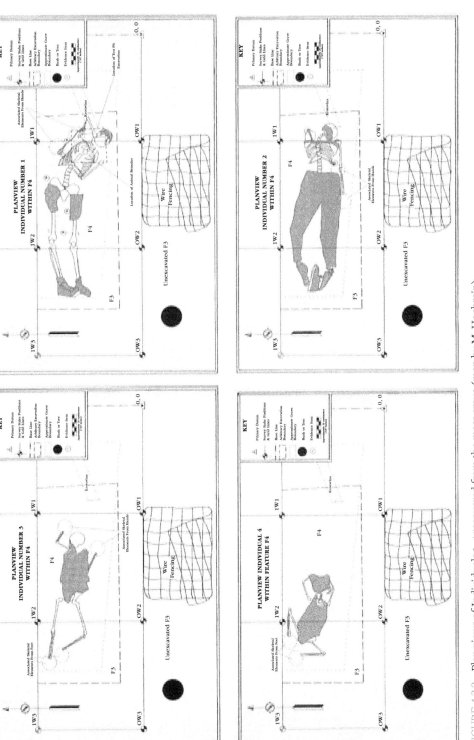

FIGURE 4.2.2   Plan views of Individuals 1–4 recovered from the mass grave (map by M. Hochrein).

from the bush located on the south side of the grave. This did not contradict the purported timing of the victims' disappearances and supposed deaths approximately 7 years before. Bioturbation and root activity effectively sewed the remains of Individual 1 to the fill and to portions of Individual 2, extending the excavation time. Below the plow, or root, zone, subsequent victims were less affected and more easily extracted from the grave.

Individual 2 was found immediately below Individual 1 at depths between 40 cm (15.7 in) and 65 cm (25.6 in), and there was no stratigraphic evidence of fill or detritus between the skeletal remains. The skeleton was face down with clothesline-type ligatures around the left wrist and both ankles. As with Individual 1, duct tape was wrapped around the head, and a green synthetic fiber sock protruded from the mouth. Deteriorated segments of cloth and stitching indicated a shirt-type garment was worn at the time of disposal. Beneath the remnants of that garment was an intact brassiere. Additionally, this victim appeared to wear dark-colored sweat pants and white athletic socks. One athletic shoe was found between the feet (Hochrein 2000: 58).

As with Individuals 1 and 2, the lack of stratigraphy between Individuals 2, 3, and 4 indicated all were buried contemporaneously. Individual 3 was found immediately below Individual 2 at depths between 40 and 70 cm (15.7 and 27.6 in). The articulated remains were situated face down. Clothing associated with Individual Number 3 included a dress-like garment and apparent underpants, or panties. At depths between 50 and 77 cm (19.7 and 30.3 in), the remains of the smaller of the two juvenile victims were encountered directly beneath those of Individual Number 3. The articulated remains of the fourth victim lay supine. Most of the torso lay under and between the legs of Individual Number 3, and the legs were flexed into a frog or squat-like position. A shirt-type garment was pulled up and over the head, thus trapping the hands in the garment sleeves above the head. Other clothing associated with Individual Number 4 included a single piece, multicolored synthetic fiber swimsuit covering the torso.

Following 36 hours of excavation, mapping, and photography, all the human remains were removed from their secret interment. Documentation of the geotaphonomic record continued, however; as the grave was measured, a metal detector was used to search for additional evidence, and the grave walls were examined for evidence of possible tool marks. No additional ballistic evidence was recovered from the grave fill or beyond the grave walls. Although no tool marks were identified, clues of the grave's construction were reflected in its dimensions and microstratigraphy above the remains of Individual 1. The horizontal dimensions of the grave seemed just large enough to accommodate Individual 1, the tallest of the victims. All four victims were deposited in a grave that had a maximum depth of 77 cm (2.5 feet). The stratigraphy above Individual 1 consisted of individual lenses of soil consistent with the amounts of soil held in each shovel-full of backfill. Given these geotaphonomic characteristics, the conclusion was reached that this grave was excavated and filled using one or more hand shovels rather than heavy equipment.

Anthropological Analysis
Methodology
The autopsies of the first four victims were conducted jointly by the forensic pathologist and anthropologist. Each set of remains was placed on a gurney to be unwrapped, washed, and analyzed separately. The protocol was the same for all individuals and included an inventory of the bones and teeth present, a description of all clothing, ligatures, and personal effects, radiography, development of a biological profile, description and interpretation of perimortem and postmortem trauma, and photographic documentation. Soil from the clothing and pelvic and cranial cavities were carefully screened for additional physical evidence, such as projectiles. There was commingling of bones, principally of the subadults, at the bottom of the grave.

These were reassociated with the youngest two victims based on size and development. The biological profiles were consistent with the missing individuals, and the identifications of the adults were ultimately confirmed by dental analysis and that of the subadults by mitochondrial DNA (mtDNA). Thus, the importance of the anthropological analysis rested on the interpretation of perimortem trauma.

It was quickly evident that all four individuals suffered gunshot trauma. Typically, when a bullet penetrates a bone at or about a 90° angle it produces a beveled, circular defect that is widest away from the weapon. In other words, beveling occurs on the internal surface of a bone in an entrance wound and on the external surface for an exit wound (DiMaio 1999; Smith, Berryman, and Lahren 1987). These physical characteristics allow reconstruction of the trajectory of the bullet as it passed through the bone. If a projectile strikes the bone tangentially, then the bullet may graze the bone and produce a keyhole-shaped defect. The circular, internally beveled portion represents the entrance wound, whereas the adjacent triangular portion, surrounded by external beveling, is created when all or part of the bullet exits (Dixon 1982). Thus, the triangular portion points to the direction of fire.

In any case of violent death, blunt trauma to the skeleton must also be a concern for the anthropologist. However, since the bodies were buried for over 7 years, it is possible that fractures occurred after death and decomposition via bioturbation, surface pressures, and excavation. Thus, it is necessary to distinguish perimortem and postmortem fracture patterns. In general, perimortem fracture margins will be the same color as the surrounding bone because they have gone through the same postmortem processes. In this case, the bones were dark brown, the color of the soil, and so recent fresh postmortem fractures were easy to discern because the margins were much lighter in color than the surrounding bone. In addition, perimortem long-bone fractures may splinter and have adherent fragments with jagged edges, whereas dry bone is more brittle and will shatter into fragments of similar size (Maples 1986; Sauer 1998).

Analysis of the Victims

The skeleton of Individual 1, found at the top of the grave, was nearly complete and well preserved. Bindings of the face and appendages were observed as described above (Figure 4.2.3). The individual was estimated to be a 30–40 year-old male of European descent who stood between 67 and 73 inches (175–183 cm). Antemortem pathology included spinal arthritis, a healed fracture of the right second metatarsal, and antemortem tooth loss. Dental records confirmed these were the remains of Greg Nicholson, who was 34 years old at the time of his disappearance.

A circular defect was located on the left occipital, immediately behind the left mastoid process. The internal beveling indicated this defect was a gunshot entrance wound and was accompanied by fractures that radiated through the basicranium, face, and left side of the skull. A bullet was located in the posterior nasal aperture, and there was no exit wound. The trajectory of the gunshot was therefore back to front and slightly left to right. Another gunshot wound was observed on the right 5th rib near the vertebral end. Beveling characteristics

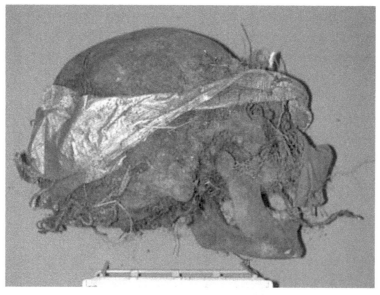

FIGURE 4.2.3   Skull of Individual 1, Greg Nicholson, with duct tape and a child's sock over the face (photograph permission of D. W. Steadman).

indicated a back to front trajectory. Finally, multiple perimortem fractures of the neural arch of the 4th cervical vertebra suggested direct trauma and/or severe rotation of the neck.

Individual 2 was buried immediately below Individual 1 in the mass grave and was similarly bound. The remains were of a 30–40 year-old female of European descent with a stature of 61–67 inches (159–167 cm). The spine and left shoulder exhibited osteoarthritis, and there were multiple dental restorations and some antemortem tooth loss. The remains were identified via dental records as those of Lori Duncan, who was 31 years old when she disappeared.

Of all of the victims in the grave, Lori suffered the greatest amount of perimortem skeletal trauma. A large defect above the left orbit had extensive external beveling, indicating a gunshot exit wound. The shape was irregular, since it abutted a preexisting fracture radiating from the other side of the skull (Figure 4.2.4), but appeared to be an example of an exit keyhole wound (Dixon 1984). Both the circular and triangular portions exhibited external beveling and there was little internal beveling. A semicircular defect in the fractured greater wing of the right sphenoid was suspected to be the entrance wound, although this area of bone is too thin to demonstrate beveling (Quatrehomme and İşcan 1999). If this was the entrance wound, then the trajectory of the bullet was right to left and slightly upward. The facial skeleton was extremely fragmented and detached, as was the right side of the skull. There was also gunshot trauma of the proximal left ulna and at least two ribs. Though the trajectory of the bullet could not be determined for the ulna, one of the ribs demonstrated clear beveling that indicates a back to front bullet path. The findings suggested that there

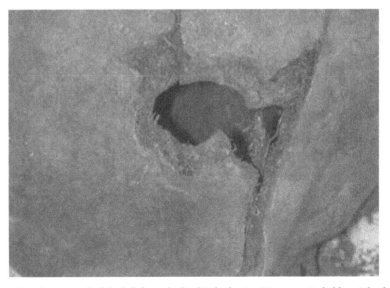

FIGURE 4.2.4   Gunshot wound of the left frontal of Individual 2, Lori Duncan. Probable exit keyhole wound (photograph permission of D. W. Steadman).

was a minimum of two gunshots, one to the head and one to the thorax. This is a conservative estimate, since it cannot be ruled out that the two rib wounds resulted from the same projectile and that the ulna could have been wounded by the same bullet that hit either the thorax or skull. Finally, the left 4th metacarpal and right ilium exhibit perimortem fractures due to blunt trauma.

Individual 3 was buried just below the adults and is the older of the two subadults. Sex cannot be estimated reliably for subadults because the pelvic and cranial characteristics do not diverge until after puberty. Based on the dental and long-bone development, age was estimated to be between 8 and 11 years. The skeleton did not exhibit antemortem pathology.

A gunshot entrance wound was present on the right superior occipital bone immediately below the Lambdoid suture and approximately 1.7 cm to the right of midline (Figure 4.2.5). Fractures radiated from the defect onto the right frontal, basicranium and left and right parietals. No distinct exit wound was identified, but the bullet likely exited through the upper facial region near the midline as evidenced by the jagged margins around areas of missing bone in the superior nasal aperture and left maxillo-orbital region. The facial bones were traumatically separated. The findings were consistent with a gunshot wound to the back of the head.

The last victim, Individual 4, was placed in the grave first and was the youngest. Based on dental and epiphyseal development, the age was estimated to be between 5 and 7 years.

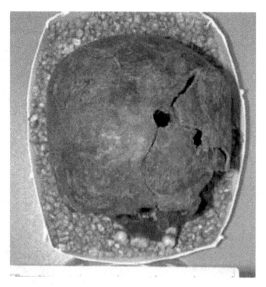

FIGURE 4.2.5   Gunshot entrance wound on the occipital of Individual 3, Kandace Duncan (photograph permission of D. W. Steadman).

Sex was not estimated, and there were no skeletal pathologies. A gunshot entrance wound was on the superior occipital bone just right of Lambda, very similar in location to that of Individual 3. Fractures radiated from the defect onto the right side of the skull and the basicranium. Part of the right temporal and sphenoid was detached from the skull, and the facial bones were too fragmentary to reconstruct.

The bullet likely exited the face near the midline, as evidenced by the jagged margins of the fractured superior nasal aperture. As with Individual 3, the trajectory of the gunshot was back to front.

Lori Duncan's children lacked dental records, so mitochondrial DNA (mtDNA) was sampled from the bones of Individuals 3 and 4 and compared to mtDNA of Lori Duncan's mother, who was still living. Unlike nuclear DNA, which is contributed by both parents, mtDNA is inherited only from the mother. In addition, mtDNA has a much lower statistical specificity than does nuclear DNA, since all maternally related individuals have identical mtDNA. Thus, confirming identifications in this case relied on multiple modalities. The mtDNA of both subadults were identical to each other and to Lori's mother, and the biological profiles were consistent with the missing girls. In addition, the clothing was identified by Lori's mother, and Lori's children were known to disappear at the same time as Lori. Through these means, 10-year-old Kandace and 6-year-old Amber Duncan were positively identified.

Although it is not possible for the anthropologist or pathologist to reconstruct which victim was killed first, it is clear that the Amber and Kandi were each shot in the back of the head, and the adults suffered multiple gunshot wounds as well as blunt trauma. The two children were placed in the grave first, followed by the two adults. The bullet recovered from Nicholson's skull, the only projectile recovered from the grave site, was too badly damaged to yield significant class information.

The Search for Terry DeGeus

Following the identification of the first four victims, investigators turned their attention to finding the body of Terry DeGeus. By November of 2000, the Killdeer Avenue site that had previously been searched by the ERT without success was now more accessible because the corn had been harvested. Using heavy equipment, investigators gradually removed thin layers of topsoil until they observed an area of soil that differed in color. When a boot was brought to the surface by heavy machinery, hand excavation of the grave began. The grave revealed the skeletonized remains of an adult buried face down with the legs bent such that the feet were above the buttocks. This matched the description on Johnson's map on which she had written: "The 1 is buried on his knees like he would make me be when I would beg for my life (face down)." The skeleton was clad in a hooded sweatshirt that covered the head, a jean jacket, metal accoutrements of pants, underwear with a handwritten name of "DeGeus, Terry" on the band, a leather belt with a Harley Davidson buckle, socks and leather work boots. Several personal effects were also recovered from the grave, including a pack of cigarettes, money, a cigarette lighter, nail clippers, and a watch.

The anthropologist employed the same protocol as before to derive the biological profile and to interpret perimortem injuries. The remains were those of a 30–40-year-old male of European descent who stood between 65 and 71 in (170 and 178 cm) tall. Antemortem pathologies included osteoarthritis of the spine, a healed fracture of the left acromion process, and a well-healed fracture of the left fibula. The remains were positively identified as those of Terry DeGeus, aged 34 years, by comparison of antemortem and postmortem dental X rays.

The skeleton exhibited extensive perimortem trauma. The skull was highly fragmentary, and much of the anterior frontal bone and right inferolateral vault were missing, each area exhibiting multiple radiating fractures. Green staining, consistent with oxidizing copper, was noted on the internal aspect of the right temporal fragments. The location and distribution of the stains suggested perimortem fragmentation of the temporal bone, after which some bone fragments were in contact with metal during decomposition. A copper jacket was found inside the sweatshirt hood that covered the skull. A semicircular defect was present on the greater wing of the right sphenoid. As this is a naturally thin area of bone, beveling characteristics were not present. The bullet likely entered the right side of the skull and exited the left frontal.

A gunshot wound of the third thoracic vertebra was evidenced by bone loss of the anterior centrum and copper staining. Further, radiographs revealed metallic fragments embedded in the margins of the wound. The left proximal humerus also exhibited gunshot trauma and fragments of bone and metal remained embedded in the medullary cavity. The trajectory of these wounds could not be determined. There was also a gunshot wound on the iliac crest of the left ilium. Beveling indicated a back to front and slightly right to left trajectory. A minimum of three bullets penetrated this individual—the skull, thorax, and pelvis. The gunshot to the humerus could have been coincident with the skull or thorax trauma. Perimortem fractures of the dentition indicated Terry DeGeus also suffered blunt trauma.

The Prosecutions of Honken and Johnson

With the discovery and successful identification and analysis of perimortem trauma of all five missing persons, criminal proceedings could move forward against Dustin Honken and Angela Johnson. The investigation of the murders was over 10 years old, and hundreds of witnesses and informants had been interviewed. Prosecutors waded through scores of boxes of evidence and records to decide who to subpoena to testify in court. The prosecution sought to demonstrate that Dustin Honken masterminded the efforts to eliminate DeGeus and Nicholson so they could not testify against him on the earlier drug charges. The Duncan family was simply collateral damage.

On August 30, 2001, Dustin Honken, now 33 years old, was charged with five counts of federal witness tampering murder, five counts of drug conspiracy murder, five counts of continuing criminal enterprise murder, one count of soliciting murder of a witness, and one count of conspiracy to tamper with and solicit the murder of a witness. Honken was tried in the United States District Court for the Northern District of Iowa. In addition to informants, several forensic expert witnesses testified. The maps drawn by Angela Johnson that led investigators to the graves were introduced into evidence, and an FBI ERT specialist testified as to the location and recovery of the remains. Two forensic pathologists from the Office of the Iowa State Medical Examiner testified that the cause of death was gunshot trauma and the manner of death was homicide for each individual. In the United States, only forensic pathologists are legally empowered to determine manner of death (homicide, suicide, accidental, natural, or undetermined). Next, the forensic anthropologist provided lengthy testimony on the perimortem trauma suffered by each individual. Finally, a firearms expert testified that spent bullets recovered from DeGeus had class characteristics consistent with having been fired from a Tec-9.

Following a lengthy defense, the jury received the case. After deliberating for 17 hours over three days, the jury returned guilty verdicts on all counts. After a penalty proceeding that lasted several days, the same jury sentenced Dustin Honken to life in prison for the counts relating to the murders of the three adults and sentenced him to death for the murders of Kandi and Amber Duncan. The trial, including the penalty phase and deliberations, lasted 11 weeks.

The trial of Angela Johnson began in the same courtroom approximately five months later. She faced five counts of drug conspiracy murder and five counts of continuing criminal enterprise murder. The forensic experts again presented their evidence. A different jury found Angela Johnson guilty as charged on all counts. After a short penalty phase proceeding, the jury sentenced Johnson to life in prison for the two counts relating to the murder of Greg Nicholson and imposed a penalty of death in connection with the counts relating to each of the other four murder victims. Johnson's trial took 10 weeks.

These cases were remarkable in several respects, not the least of which was the application of the death penalty in the state of Iowa. Though Iowa does not have the death penalty, the death penalty could be applied because these proceedings were in federal court. Although prosecution of a federal death penalty case in a non-death-penalty state is not unprecedented, it is rare. Some local controversy was generated by the fact that for the first (and second) time in more than 40 years a jury of Iowans was called on to deliberate in a death penalty case. In addition, Angela Johnson achieved the dubious distinction of being the first woman in America to receive a federal death sentence since the early 1950s, when Ethel Rosenberg resided on death row.

Conclusion

This case exemplifies the multidisciplinary cooperation required for murder investigations. Dogged perseverance on the part of the investigators kept this from becoming another missing persons "cold case." It must be noted that our discussion has focused on only a small portion of the total forensic effort; there are many other important facets of the investigation not described here, including firearms, document, DNA, and fingerprint analyses.

This case also demonstrates how archaeology, properly applied in concert with other forensic specialties, can be used as a tool for reconstructing the events of a crime rather than merely collecting evidence from a scene. The archaeological excavation of the Lark Avenue grave site demonstrated the amount of contextual information that can be gleaned beyond the victims' skeletons. In this case, plant activity offered chronological information about the victims' interments. The recorded remnants of each victim's clothing, such as a bathing suit, suggested the time of year the murders took place. Geological evidence explained the presence of nonhuman animal activity within the grave. Zoology helped to distinguish the natural versus intentional placement of nonhuman animal remains. Finally, stratigraphic evidence and three-dimensional mapping of each victim's position within the grave helped to clarify and confirm perimortem activity and to compare that with witness and subject statements.

Perhaps the most salient effect of applying archaeology at this crime scene was the manner in which it allowed for the recreation of the scene for juries in Dustin Honken's and Angela Johnson's federal trials. They could better imagine the horrors of that night in 1993 in seeing how the children were thrown into the grave, their hands so close to their mother's. The jury could reflect on the last moments of Greg Nicholson and Lori Duncan lives—each bound with duct tape around their faces and the children's socks in their mouths. Similarly, the detailed anthropological description of the perimortem injuries, especially of the little girls, created a great deal of tension and sympathy in the courtroom. Although juries have come to expect much forensic fanfare (the so-called CSI effect), careful investigation and analysis allow investigators to accurately and respectfully tell the story of each victim without sensationalism.

Endnote

1. The authors received permission to use real names of the defendants and victims by the U.S. Attorney General's office, since the trials of those charged for the murders detailed in this case study are complete. All information provided at the trial by the authors is in the public record via trial transcripts. The authors chose not to use the names of various informants.

References

DiMaio, V. 1999. *Gunshot Wounds: Practical Aspects of Firearms, Ballistics and Forensic Techniques* (2nd ed.). Boca Raton, FL: CRC Press.

Dixon, D. 1982. Keyhole lesions in gunshot wounds of the skull and direction of fire. *Journal of Forensic Sciences* 27(3): 555–566.

———. 1984. Exit keyhole lesion and direction of fire in a gunshot wound of the skull. *Journal of Forensic Sciences* 29(1): 336–339.

Hochrein, M. J. 2000. Federal Bureau of Investigation Evidence Response Team Crime Scene Investigation, Killdeer Avenue and Lark Avenue Sites, Cerro Gordo County, Iowa, October 11–13, 2000. Unpublished manuscript.

Maples, W. R. 1986. Trauma analysis by the forensic anthropologist, in K. J. Reichs (ed.), *Forensic Osteology: Advances in the Identification of Human Remains*, pp. 218–228. Springfield, IL: Charles C. Thomas.

Quatrehomme, G., and İşcan, M. Y. 1999. Characteristics of gunshot wounds in the skull. *Journal of Forensic Sciences* 44(3): 568–576.

Sauer, N. 1998. The timing of injuries and manner of death: Distinguishing among antemortem, perimortem and postmortem trauma, in K. J. Reichs (ed.), *Forensic Osteology: Advances in the Identification of Human Remains* (2nd ed.), pp. 321–332. Springfield, IL: Charles C. Thomas.

Smith, O. C., Berryman, H., and Lahren, C. 1987. Cranial fracture patterns and estimate of direction from low velocity gunshot wounds. *Journal of Forensic Sciences* 32(5): 1416–1421.

Reading 4.3

Geographic Profiling

By Martin K. Andresen

Introduction

Geographic profiling was pioneered by Professor D. Kim Rossmo, currently at Texas State University, San Marcos, and is a technique used by police to prioritize suspect lists in a criminal investigation. Geographic profiling uses the locations of a connected series of criminal events to determine the offender's "anchor point"—most often the offender's residence, but it may also be a work place, school, hangout, or friend's residence. Because this technique uses a connected series of criminal events, the most common uses of geographic profiling are in the investigation of serial murder, rape, arson, burglary, or robbery. Though the discussion that follows will focus on serial offending for simplicity, it should be noted that geographic profiling can also be used for non-serial criminal events that involve multiple locations. For example, the series of criminal events may be connected as the locations of where an offender stole a vehicle, robbed a convenience store, robbed a liquor store, and then abandoned the vehicle. Geographic profiling has proven to and continues to be a useful method for understanding the nature of serial offenders from an academic perspective, partially because it allows for the classification of different offender types. But geographic profiling has also proven to be an instructive tool for the practice of investigative policing.

From a theoretical perspective, geographic profiling is rooted in the geometry of crime. However, geographic profiling also takes routine activities and rational choice into account because it considers where an offender may travel to and assumes that offenders are rational because otherwise their actions could not be predicted. Probably the most critical aspect of the geometry of crime necessary to understand geographic profiling are the concepts of the buffer offenders will "place" around their home and distance decay. Both of these concepts ... show how offenders are expected to travel some distance from their residence (anchor point), but not too far; they only travel as far as necessary. As discussed [previously], the buffer zone around the home is an attempt by the offender to hide the location of their residence or other anchor point, but is also a product of the geometry of space such that there are fewer criminal event opportunities close to any offender's home (or any single point in space).

In this chapter, geographic profiling will be explained in the context of what it is and how it is done. This is important to understand because geographic profiling has a specific function within investigative policing; most notably, it does not solve crimes. Once we have covered geographic profiling in the context of criminology, we will move into how geographic profiling has been applied in the fields of counter-insurgency, counter-terrorism, biology/zoology, and epidemiology. This is a fascinating literature that shows how good research in the social sciences can inform research in the so-called hard sciences. These new applications of geographic profiling show the strength of this method for understanding predatory species, more generally than human predators, but will also have a feedback effect on criminological research. A better understanding of the predatory behaviors of other species may help us to better understand the predatory behaviors of humans. We conclude with a brief discussion of the future of geographic profiling along these lines, and others.

Geographic Profiling: What It Is and How It Is Done

As stated previously, geographic profiling is a criminal investigation technique with the purpose of trying to determine where the offender lives (Rossmo, 2000). Geographic profiling, on its own, cannot solve crimes, but it can aid in this process because it is able to help sort through the (often) massive amount of information that police must sort through in major investigations. One of the best analogies I have come across to describe geographic profiling comes from the television show *Numbers*. In the pilot episode, geographic profiling was used to help identify a serial criminal. The FBI were trying to figure out who the serial offender was and a mathematician (a brother of a FBI agent) said he could help them figure out where the serial offender lived. Because of the nature of television shows the FBI agent was very puzzled and did not see how they could figure out where the serial offender lived when they could not even figure out where the next target was going to be victimized. The mathematician used the analogy of a water sprinkler that operated in a circle. He stated that it would be impossible to predict the next location of where a drop of water would land because there were too many variables to consider: the order of the droplets leaving the sprinkler, wind direction and velocity, evaporation rates, and so on. However, if you know the pattern of where previous water droplets have landed you will be able to make a very precise estimate of where the sprinkler is located. This is what geographic profiling does. But this is not a simple task. There are a number of steps that must be undertaken when geographic profiling is used as an investigative technique.

The first and extremely important step is to determine that a serial offender is behind the crimes of interest. This step is extremely important because geographic profiling is useful in identifying the most probable location of the offender's residence. Consequently, there can only be one offender to identify; if there are multiple offenders involved, geographic profiling will focus on the most prominent offender's residence under the assumption that location decisions for the crimes are based on their awareness space. Needless to say, geographic profiling begins at the original investigation stage that determines which offences, if any, are connected. This is called a linkage analysis or a comparative case analysis and must be done before a geographic profiling case can be considered. As outlined by D. Kim Rossmo (2006, 2014), this process involves identifying the similarities and differences between the different criminal events with the need to have more of the former than the latter. This is done through the use of physical evidence, offender descriptions, or crime scene behavior (Rossmo, 2000).

Once it has been determined that a serial offender is at work, geographic profiling may be brought in as a criminal investigation tool. This involves a mathematical representation of the spatial pattern of the crime sites. The locations of the linked crimes are entered into software that uses the Criminal Geographic Targeting (CGT) computer algorithm. This CGT computer algorithm is then used to generate jeopardy surfaces that are three-dimensional probability surfaces identifying the most probable locations of the offender's residence. This is done using several different considerations, a number of which we have discussed in the previous theoretical chapters (namely Chapters 3 and 4, routine activity theory and the geometry of crime), which may be classified as activity nodes, pathways, crime generators, and crime attractors. These considerations may include: crime locations, offender type, the target backcloth, the street network, bus stops and transit stations, physical and psychological boundaries (edges), zoning and land use, neighborhood demographics, the routine activities of the victims, displacement (media coverage and/or uniformed police presence can cause spatial displacement of subsequent criminal events in the crime series that the CGT computer algorithm can account for because our behavior is predictable), and the hunting style/pattern of offenders.

The hunting style of serial offenders is based on research published by D. Kim Rossmo in 1997, based on serial murder cases. The hunting style is a typology that describes the methods by which the serial offender searches for and attacks their victims. Rossmo identified four methods that serial offenders use to search for victims: hunter, poacher, troller, and trapper. Hunters leave their home residence and search for victims within their awareness space, poachers begin their victim search from an anchor point other than their home residence, sometimes travelling outside of their home municipality, trollers are opportunistic serial offenders who simply encounter victims throughout the course of their routine activities, and trappers lure victims into their home or some other location in order to better control the victim. There are three methods of attack identified by D. Kim Rossmo: raptor, stalker, and ambusher. Raptors attack their victims very shortly after the first encounter, stalkers will wait for the best opportunity to attack, and the ambusher attacks in locations where the serial offender has a high degree of control. There are various combinations of these victim identification and attack methods that lead to even more combinations of when, how, and where the serial offender will encounter/identify the victim, attack the victim, commit the primary criminal event (rape, murder, sexual murder, etc.), and release the victim or dispose of the body. Each one of these steps could have a different location (Rossmo, 2000).

From all this information, the CGT computer algorithm generates the geographic profile (jeopardy surface). The output of the CGT computer algorithm is a 40,000-pixel grid ... that represents the output. Figure 4.3.1 shows two geographic profile images, one two-dimensional (geo-profile) and one three-dimensional (jeopardy surface)—white shows a high degree of probability for finding the serial offender's home residence in Figure 4.3.1a and the peaks in Figure 4.3.1b show the same information in three dimensions. D. Kim Rossmo has described this output as representing a volcano with a caldera (Rossmo, 2014).

This geographic profile can then be used within the criminal investigation process through a number of strategies, generally classified as suspect-based and area-based. Suspect-based strategies include, but are not limited to: searching or prioritizing police records; court records; sex offender registries; and government databases regarding parole, probation, mental health, schools, current and past property ownership, various vehicle registrations, and credit information. Area-based strategies can include directing police patrols or surveillance to particular areas, or prioritizing individuals based on particular locations (Rossmo, 2006, 2014).

It should be clear from this brief discussion of the process of geographic profiling that it is no simple task. Performing geographic profiling requires a geographic information system because of the spatial data used in the calculation of the jeopardy surface, a database management system, and visualization capabilities to view the resulting jeopardy surface and potentially have it interact with other spatial information. The first commercial application for performing geographic profiling was *Rigel*, developed in 1995 by D. Kim Rossmo while he was studying at Simon Fraser University—D. Kim Rossmo developed the original software himself in 1991. *Rigel* is the most widely used geographic profiling software in law enforcement and common in academic circles, with two other software packages available (*CrimeStat* and *Dragnet*) that are primarily used for academic research. Needless to say, in order to be proficient in this application of geographic profiling, and its related software, training in both the theory of environmental criminology and the practice of geographic profiling are necessary.

One final consideration on the technical side of geographic profiling is worthy of discussion at this point: how well does geographic profiling perform? There are two methods that have been used to determine how well a geographic profile performs: error distance and the hit score percentage. The error distance is a measurement of the distance between the absolute peak of the jeopardy surface and the actual location of the serial offender's home

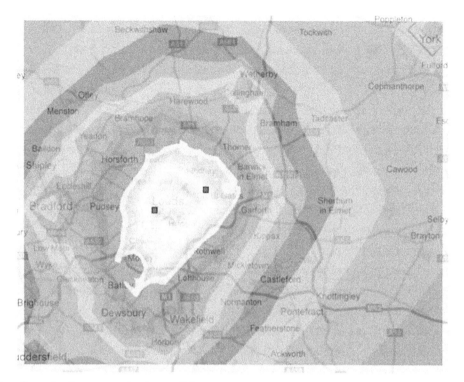

a) Two-dimensional representation (geoprofile)

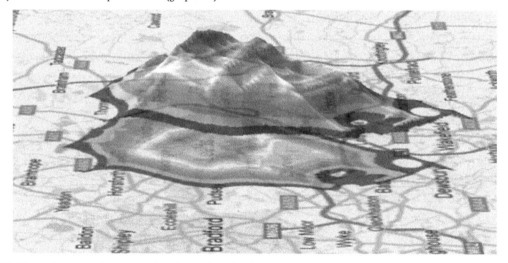

b) Three-dimensional representation (jeopardy surface)

FIGURE 4.3.1   Geographic profile.

Source: Images courtesy of Professor D. Kim Rossmo

residence: the greater the distance, the greater the error. Though this may initially appear to be a reasonable method of assessing geographic profiling, it is not particularly instructive because it does not evaluate geographic profiling based on what it is supposed to do. Recall from the previous discussion that geographic profiling does not directly solve serial crimes. Geographic profiling is a criminal investigation tool to help in the process of filtering through the potentially huge amount of information law enforcement officials have to process. Fundamentally, error distance assumes that the primary goal of geographic profiling is to solve the serial criminal events because the criterion it uses is the distance between the peak of the jeopardy profile (the greatest probability of the offender's home residence location) and the actual location of the serial offender's home residence. This is a problematic evaluation criterion because geographic profiling is not used to simply investigate a single address located within the entire jeopardy surface. D. Kim Rossmo (2011) puts forth a much more appropriate evaluative measure for geographic profiling, the hit score percentage. The hit score percentage is the ratio of the geographic size of the area that must be searched (from the highest probability grid cell to the lowest probability grid cell) before the serial offender's home residence is located relative to the entire hunting area. For example, if all of the serial criminal events occurred within a 10 square kilometer area and the serial criminal offender is located within the first square kilometer of the jeopardy surface the hit score percentage would be 10 percent. However, in research on the evaluation of geographic profiles based on actual police operational performance in various police agencies, D. Kim Rossmo (2011) reported an average hit score percentage of 5 percent and a median hit score percentage of 3 percent. In other words, 95–97 percent of the total hunting areas did not have to be searched, a considerable time and resources savings for law enforcement agencies.

New Applications of Geographic Profiling

The use of geographic profiling in criminal investigations is indeed an important endeavor that must continue. However, there have also been some very interesting recent geographic profiling applications that have included: cellular telephone switch tower sites in kidnapping cases, the stores in which bomb components have been purchased, and a historical analysis of the locations of anti-Nazi propaganda postcards left in the streets of Berlin, Germany in the early 1940s (Rossmo, 2014). Additionally, there have been new applications of geographic profiling that have proven to be very instructive, but for different reasons: counter-insurgency, counter-terrorism, biology/zoology, and epidemiology (Rossmo, 2012). As argued in what follows, understanding these more recent applications of geographic profiling may be able to help develop new knowledge for the application of geographic profiling to criminal investigations.

Counter-terrorism and Geographic Profiling

The Central Intelligence Agency (2003, p. 1) in the United States defines terrorists as

> [t]hose who employ terrorism, regardless of their specific secular or religious objectives, strive to subvert the rule of law and effect change through violence and fear. These terrorists also share the misguided belief that killing, kidnapping, extorting, robbing, and wreaking havoc to terrorize people are legitimate forms of political action.

This is a serious threat to populations around the globe because these acts of terrorism occur in many countries, rich and poor alike. Despite the political economy issues surrounding the presence of terrorists and terrorism, any efforts to reduce these acts contributes to the betterment of society. Of course part of this effort should be removing, or at least reducing, the reasons for why terrorists exist in the first place, but this effort should also include addressing the problem we have today. As has been shown in some recent research, geographic profiling has proven to be instructive in this area. At this time, geographic profiling has been applied to: help military analysts identify the location of enemy military bases (Brown et al., 2005), identify the location of terrorist hideouts based on their attack locations (Bennell & Corey, 2007), and identify the targets of terrorist attacks (Rossmo & Harries, 2011).

Craig Bennell and Shevaun Corey published a book chapter in 2007 that investigated the possibility of applying geographic profiling to terrorists. In their research, they wished to know if geographic profiling could be instructive to locate the hideout of the primary terrorist orchestrating a set of terrorist attacks. In this sense, this application of geographic profiling is similar to the situation, mentioned previously, that if there are multiple terrorists involved, which is often the case, geographic profiling will focus on the most prominent terrorist's hideout under the assumption that location decisions for the terrorist attacks are based on their awareness space. Craig Bennell and Shevaun Corey noted that the assumptions for geographic profiling may not always be met in the context of terrorists and their attacks. Though terrorists do typically have multiple crime sites that can be linked to the same group (because they tend to take responsibility for the terrorist attacks for political reasons), it cannot be assumed that the terrorists are not commuting into the area where the attack is to take place or that the terrorist cannot move their anchor point—these authors also refer to an assumption regarding the uniform distribution of suitable targets, but this is not a concern for geographic profiling (Rossmo & Velarde, 2008). Despite the inability to always maintain that assumptions hold true, Craig Bennell and Shevaun Corey undertook their analysis (using *Dragnet*) to analyze the terrorist attacks of two groups, one in France and one in Greece. They found that geographic profiling did not work well for the terrorist attacks undertaken by the French group, Action Directe. For this terrorist group, the primary terrorist of concern had his anchor point (hideout) location in Portugal and committed the terrorist acts in France. Needless to say, the hit score percentage for this case study was 100 percent. The second terrorist group, Epanastatikos Laikos Agonas (ELA), was based in Greece and committed the analyzed terrorist attacks in Greece. In this particular case, the geographic profile proved to be useful.

The lesson to learn from this research was that geographic profiling is instructive for the application of identifying terrorist hideouts, but only if the hunting style is hunter—this hunting style is also referred to as a marauder. This is true for geographic profiling, in general. If the hunting style is poacher, also referred to as a commuter, geographic profiling will not prove to be instructive for identifying the location of a terrorist hideout. Again, the same applies to geographic profiling, in general. The difficulty in this context, or any context involving geographic profiling, is that it is very difficult to know if the principal person in the terrorist group is behaving like a marauder or a commuter. Though this is possible if there is *some* intelligence on the terrorist group, this may not be able to be known, *a priori*. Consequently, geographic profiling can be useful in the context of counter-terrorism to help find the location of terrorist hideouts but it must be remembered that the resulting geographic profile would only be applicable if and only if the principal/planning terrorist in the terrorist group is committing the terrorist attacks "close" to their hideout.

In another application of geographic profiling to counter-terrorism, D. Kim Rossmo and Keith Harries (2011) took a different approach. The study of terrorist activities has identified the existence of "terrorist cell sites". These terrorist cell sites may be meeting places, rented apartments, telephone calls, storage, cell houses, safe houses, and so on, which are used as part of the planning of a terrorist attack. As would be expected because of the spatial constraints we operate within through our everyday routine activities, there is a strong spatial component to these terrorist cell sites as well. Rossmo and Harries performed a geospatial analysis on terrorism data from Turkey (terrorist cell sites and their corresponding target sites) in order to obtain a better understanding of the spatial character of terrorist activities.

In an example of an assassination of a Turkish government minister, Rossmo and Harries showed that most of the terrorist cell site locations were approximately 1.5–5.5 kilometers (average distance approximately 4 kilometers) from the assassination site. This clearly showed that the terrorist cell sites were close but not too close to the terrorist target sites. In their analysis of a total of 38 terrorist attacks they found that there was a definite geospatial structure to the terrorist activities. For example, Rossmo and Harries found that terrorist cell sites were clustered and that the two distance distribution characteristics put forth in the geometry of crime (and the pattern theory of crime) were definitely present: a buffer zone and distance decay. This information could then be used to help identify, through prioritizing information, other related intelligence information: police reports, intelligence assessments, cellular telephone intercepts, suspects, suspicious purchases, and so on.

Overall, Rossmo and Harries found that "minor terrorism incidents" such as theft and graffiti could be explained using the pattern theory of crime, whereas "major terrorism incidents" such as assassinations and bombings could be explained using an inverted version of the pattern theory of crime. These terrorist cell sites could be used as crime locations in the creation of a standard geographic profile to then predict the most probable location of the terrorist attack itself. Essentially, these authors proposed an extremely novel approach to geographic profiling to "flip it on its head" and use geographic profiling as a target identification technique. This is an area of future research in geographic profiling.

Biology and Epidemiology

The application of geographic profiling to the various phenomena of terrorism is an important and an interesting extension of this criminal investigation technique. However, such an extension is still within the criminological realm. In another set of research, D. Kim Rossmo has teamed up with a group of biologists to study the applicability of geographic profiling to predatory behavior, more generally. This extension has been used to study the predatory behavior of bats, bumblebees, and sharks; it has also proven to be instructive in the context of infectious disease control and the control of invasive species.

Steven Le Comber and colleagues published a journal article in 2006 that investigated the applicability of geographic profiling to the foraging behavior of two species of bats in Scotland. 13 bats from each species (a total of 26 bats) were captured and tagged with a radio transmitter to track their movements. Based on the foraging activities of these tagged bats, Steven Le Comber and colleagues were able to locate the roosts for the bats much more efficiently than just performing a random search. One species of bat had a hit score percentage of 27 percent and the other species of bat had a hit score percentage of 7 percent, a significant improvement over a 50 percent hit score percentage for a random search. This analysis showed the utility of geographic profiling in analyzing the foraging patterns of the different species, specifically being able to show that the two different species of bats exhibited different patterns of foraging. The fact that the foraging patterns of two species of bats can be modeled in the same manner as serial criminals is interesting in and of itself, but this also means that geographic profiling can be used for ecological purposes. For example, if a species is protected or endangered, geographic profiling could be used to identify the roost, or nest, of the species and, potentially, identify its foraging grounds for the purposes of conservation and restricting various forms of development.

In a laboratory study of bumblebee foraging behavior Nigel Raine, Rossmo, and Le Comber (2009) were able to show that geographic profiling could be used to identify the likely locations for the nests of bumblebees, including the consideration of flower (target) densities. This is a particularly useful application because these authors note that it tends to be very difficult to locate the nesting sites of wild bees. And because of the declines in bumblebee populations across Europe and North America (Carvell et al., 2006) knowledge of these nesting sites may prove to be helpful. As such, the use of geographic profiling on this context is similar to the previous discussion, conservation.

In an extremely interesting application of geographic profiling, Martin, Rossmo, and Hammerschlag (2009) were able to use geographic profiling in order to discover that the spatial patterns of shark predation were not random. These authors were able to identify the search base (anchor point) for these sharks at Seal Island, False Bay, South Africa and understand the predatory strategies of these sharks considering factors such as prey detection, capture rates, and competition from other sharks. Perhaps most interesting, Martin and colleagues (2009) found that smaller (younger) sharks exhibited significantly greater areas for their prey search patterns than larger (older) sharks. There may be other factors at play that these authors recognize, but this does suggest that as sharks age they learn, or at least refine, their hunting strategies. Though on the surface this may not appear to be particular interesting in the context of criminal investigations, some recent research I have undertaken with Richard Frank and Marcus Felson indicates that this reduction in the area covered in search patterns may be a common pattern (Andresen, Frank, & Felson, 2014). In our research, we investigated the distance travelled to crime based on the age of the offender. We found that for most crime types there was an initial increase in the distance travelled to crime as offenders aged but this distance subsequently decreased, substantially in some cases. In the case of humans this is partially because younger offenders need to avoid the watchful eyes of their parents and/or guardians, but this will also occur because the younger offenders need to investigate bigger areas to see what is actually available. If this is the case, what may be occurring is that once the offenders learn about the opportunity surface and that they do not have to travel as far as they initially did when they were younger, distance is minimized in order to be efficient. This is conjecture at this stage, and based on calculating the distance travelled to criminal events, not the awareness spaces of offenders, but it is intriguing that the predatory behavior of the great white shark appears to be similar.

Geographic profiling has also proven to be very instructive in the field of public health. Steven Le Comber and colleagues published a journal article in 2011 that investigated the application of geographic profiling to infectious disease control. They began their research with a reanalysis of the classic epidemiological study of the 1854 London cholera outbreak. This outbreak was first analyzed by Dr. John Snow who identified the Broad Street pump as the source of the cholera outbreak, drawing water downstream from a sewage out pipe. The handle for this water pump was removed and the outbreak stopped. Steven Le Comber and colleagues analyzed the 321 disease sites and the 13 neighborhood water pumps using geographic profiling and found that the Broad Street pump ranked first, with a hit score percentage of 0.2 percent! Subsequently, the authors analyzed 139 disease case locations and 59 mosquitogenic water sources in Cairo, Egypt for malaria. Of the 59 mosquitogenic water sources, 7 tested positive for being sources of malaria. In the application of geographic profiling, the geoprofile ranked all of the mosquitogenic water sources according to their probability of being contaminated. The geoprofile ranked 6 of the 7 contaminated water sources in positions 1 through 6 and all of the 7 contaminated water sources had a hit score percentage of 2 percent. In a comparative analysis these authors found that geographic profiling outperformed other spatial analytic techniques commonly used in this research area. Needless to say, geographic profiling, at this early stage of application, has proven to be a useful tool in public health.

And lastly, geographic profiling has been applied to identifying the source locations for invasive species (Stevenson, Rossmo, Knell, & Le Comber, 2012). These authors analyzed 53 invasive species in Great Britain (flora and fauna) in a variety of habitats (man-made and natural). They found that in 52 of the 53 invasive species cases, geographic profiling outperformed more traditional spatial analytic techniques in this research area to identify the source populations of the invasive species, with an average hit score percentage of 2.6 percent. Moreover, the authors found that geographic profiling was able to identify the sources of the invasive species in the early stages of the invasions when controlling the invasion would be more likely to be effective.

Criminology to Biology/Epidemiology and Back Again

Despite the general interest of the newer applications of geographic profiling, and their direct implications for the safety and security of different human and animal populations, there is another significant implication of this more recent research. Though there are many serial criminal investigations that allow for more data to be available to refine the practice of geographic profiling, waiting for another set of serial homicides, for example, is not the most pleasant way of thinking of future data. If, and it does appear to be the case, the predatory behaviors of other animal species are similar to those of humans, this new research can be used to better understand the predatory behavior of humans. For example, if humans, similar to sharks off the South African coast, also reduce the size of their search area as they age, this information may be useful for the ranking of potential offenders in a criminal investigation; in such a situation, it may be possible to solve a serial criminal investigation sooner because of a better understanding of spatial predatory behavior, more generally. These, of course, are empirical questions that may be able to be answered with future research.

This is a very clear application of (environmental) criminological research that has been able to have an impact in fields outside of its original application. The very nature of environmental criminology is that ideas were "borrowed" from other disciplines such as geography and economics in order to provide a better understanding of criminological phenomena. The status of the field of environmental criminology is a testament to the success of this borrowing of ideas from other disciplines. Because of this success, these theories have developed within criminology such that the ideas are now more our own rather than simply co-opted ideas from elsewhere. But as this chapter on geographic profiling has made perfectly clear, the borrowing of ideas is now in the other direction. Geographic profiling is not only proving to be a useful tool in a number of applications, which will likely continue to grow, but also helping to develop models within those respective disciplines because of new and valuable information. And, because of this new insight into predatory behavior in a wide variety of species ranging from marine invertebrates to bumblebees to bats to trees to sharks, we may be in a better position to understand ourselves.

References

Andresen, M. A., Frank, R., & Felson, M. (2014). Age and the distance to crime. *Criminology & Criminal Justice*, 14(3), 314–333.

Bennell, C., & Corey, S. (2007). Geographic profiling of terrorist attacks. In R. N. Kocsis (Ed.), *Criminal profiling: International theory, research, and practice* (pp. 189–203). Totowa, NJ: Humana Press.

Brown, R. O., Rossmo, D. K., Sisak, T., Trahern, R., Jarret, J., & Hanson, J. (2005). *Geographic profiling military capabilities*. Final report submitted to the Topographic Engineering Center, Department of the Army, Fort Belvoir, VA.

Carvell, C., Roy, D. B., Smart, S. M., Pywell, R. F., Preston, C. D., & Goulson, D. (2006). Declines in forage availability for bumblebees at a national scale. *Biological Conservation*, 132(4), 481–489.

Central Intelligence Agency. (2003). *National strategy for combating terrorism*. Washington, DC: Central Intelligence Agency. Retrieved July 22, 2013, from www.cia.gov/news-information/cia-the-war-on-terrorism/Counter_Terrorism_Strategy.pdf

Le Comber, S. C., Nicholls, B., Rossmo, D. K., & Racey, P. A. (2006). Geographic profiling and animal foraging. *Journal of Theoretical Biology*, 240(2), 233–240.

Le Comber, S. C., Rossmo, D. K., Hassan, A. N., Fuller, D. O., & Beier, J. C. (2011). Geographic profiling as a novel spatial tool for targeting infectious disease control. *International Journal of Health Geographics*, 10(1), Article 35.

Martin, R. A., Rossmo, D. K., & Hammerschlag, N. (2009). Hunting patterns and geographic profiling of white shark predation. *Journal of Zoology*, 279(2), 111–118.

Raine, N. E., Rossmo, D. K., & Le Comber, S. C. (2009). Geographic profiling applied to testing models of bumble-bee foraging. *Journal of the Royal Society Interface*, 6(32), 307–319.

Rossmo, D. K. (1997). Geographic profiling. In J. L. Jackson & D. A. Bekerian (Eds.), *Offender profiling: Theory, research and practice* (pp. 159–175). Chichester, UK: John Wiley & Sons.

Rossmo, D. K. (2000). *Geographic profiling*. Boca Raton, FL: CRC Press.

Rossmo, D. K. (2006). Geographic profiling in cold case investigations. In R. Walton (Ed.), *Cold case homicides: Practical investigative techniques* (pp. 537–560). Boca Raton, FL: CRC Press.

Rossmo, D. K. (2011). Evaluating geographic profiling. *Crime Mapping: A Journal of Research and Practice*, 3(1), 42–65.

Rossmo, D. K. (2012). Recent developments in geographic profiling. *Policing: A Journal of Policy and Practice*, 6(2), 144–150.

Rossmo, D. K. (2014). Geographic profiling. In D. Weisburd & G. J. N. Bruinsma (Eds.), *Encyclopedia of criminology and criminal justice* (pp. 1934–1942). New York, NY: Springer-Verlag.

Rossmo, D. K., & Harries, K. D. (2011). The geospatial structure of terrorist cells. *Justice Quarterly*, 28(2), 221–248.

Rossmo, D. K., & Velarde, L. (2008). Geographic profiling analysis: Principles, methods, and applications. In S. Chainey & L. Tompson (Eds.), *Crime mapping case studies: Practice and research* (pp. 35–43). Chichester, UK: John Wiley & Sons.

Stevenson, M. D., Rossmo, D. K., Knell, R. J., & Le Comber, S. C. (2012). Geographic profiling as a novel spatial tool for targeting the control of invasive species. *Ecography*, 35(8), 704–715.

Reading 4.4

Forensic Art and Anthropology

By Sharon K. Moses

Abstract

Forensic artists must overcome ingrained ideas of what the human face "should" look like in order to learn how to draw it realistically. Ironically, those ingrained images and perceptions tucked away in our minds present the biggest obstacles to realism. As a teacher of a forensic art class in anthropology at Northern Arizona University, I encounter students of varying degrees of artistic ability and background. I do not require that students have pre-requisite courses in art before taking my course because I believe that any student can learn to draw faces more realistically if they apply some basic forensic art techniques used in composite sketching combined with an understanding of facial anatomy. This article is about teaching Northern Arizona University students forensic art drawing methods, but it is also about the lesser-known aspect of doing composite sketches, such as applying cultural understanding and sensitivity when interviewing traumatized witnesses and survivors of crime. The result is a very holistic approach to composite sketching rather than a purely technical one.

Key words: forensic art, facial anatomy, facial reconstruction, composite sketch, crime

A 6-Year-Old Child's Drawing of Herself, Her Brother, and Her Cat (Author's Personal Collection)

Sharon K. Moses, "Forensic Art and Anthropology," *Practicing Anthropology Journal*, vol. 43, no. 3, pp. 16–22. Copyright © 2021 by Society for Applied Anthropology. Reprinted with permission.

Introduction

Some people like to draw beautiful landscapes, animals, or portraits of loved ones. I draw criminals and unidentified dead people. Not that I have anything against drawing beautiful subjects—sometimes I even indulge in it myself. I just feel more compelled by a mystery and solving a "puzzle." Sketches that will aid law enforcement to catch a baddie or help identify someone to provide closure to families or help bring about justice is a pretty compelling incentive for me in my artwork.

My students at Northern Arizona University (NAU) are similarly compelled. Admittedly, we are a different breed of cat. Some are simply curious as to how forensic artists do their work when they take the class. Others have intentions to use these skills in future law enforcement related work. Movie portrayals and popular culture would have you believe we are, pencil and sketchbook in hand, ready to whip out a photo-perfect image based upon a 5-minute description. LOL. And in the digital age with software programs that can piece together a digital image—why are hand drawn images even necessary? Well, for starters, a computer algorithm is a pretty cold thing, and it will only print out what you program into it and select from a template of pre-determined features. While it is true that a computer image can be produced much quicker than a hand drawn effort, complaints about computer generated images include the resultant "generic" look. Images can be so open to interpretation that it could simultaneously be someone or anyone. Forensic artists are a bit more tuned in to the subtleties and can tweak a feature for the right eyebrow arch or capture something individualistic if a witness can only describe the feeling invoked rather than remember the feature itself. Let's see a software program do that! It is also a dirty secret that: (1) Many who work with digital software programs must still have an understanding of how to work the program properly and have an artist's understanding of proper proportion on a face—without it, a computer-generated image can look like the subject went too many rounds in the ring, Rocky style—"cut me Mick!" (2) It is instructive to know that the FBI still prefers to use forensic artists rather than rely completely on a digitally produced image. Together, the two methodologies can be employed for the best result (Wilkinson 2004).

When asked, the majority of us will draw people as stick figures with balloon-like heads, almond eyes and caterpillar eyelashes. These unprepared renderings stern from roots of human representation established in our pre-adolescent days. In adulthood, some of us might include a few flourishes to add a touch of "style" in the effort, but essentially the effort is based upon the same premise that we "know" what a face should have. Unless one has an avocation using realistic drawing or is on a path toward commercial art or other art-based fields that demand realism, most of us rely on those symbolic representations from childhood as "good enough" when pressed to produce a representation of a human being. Forensic art is a field that demands a level of realism but provides, sometimes literally, bare bones with which to work. We are tasked with drawing composite sketches based upon witnesses who may have had only a fleeting glimpse of a suspect. Surviving victims of a traumatic event may be easily triggered and, thus, make it difficult to navigate a conversation and acquire a workable description. Depending upon where we live, we may also need to understand multicultural populations, cultural and gender-restrictive behavior, and varied educational levels. All this influences how individuals identify themselves and the world they inhabit. Forensic artists who interview witnesses and survivors need to understand how to navigate those conversations without adding to their difficulty.

This article focusses on my students at Northern Arizona University and the process they undergo toward learning to draw realistic forensic sketches and how to apply anthropological principles in a real-world context. Statistically, the majority of those who take my Forensic Art Methods class are from anthropology, criminology/criminal justice, psychology, and biology fields. Among these students, a majority plan to pursue a career either in law enforcement or some form of forensic science. Nearly all of them enter the class with a viewpoint that they "can't really draw faces" but hope it will help them understand how better to approach it. Few believe they will come out on the other side with actual realistic-looking faces. I'm happy to say the majority are pleasantly surprised with what they can produce by the end of the course.

Where to Begin?

As with any university class, one must establish a benchmark before proceeding with new knowledge of a topic. In this case, students must understand why they draw a human face the way they do to avoid repeating entrenched mistakes. Of course, there is a certain amount of theoretical exploration about how the brain works to interpret images and an introduction to proper proportions and placement of features on a human face—typical fare for an art class. Understanding how to contrast light and shadow is vital to create the illusion of depth in a two-dimensional medium, and we cover this too, in relative detail, as it pertains to facial features. In addition to instructional lectures about looking for the negative spaces, highlights, and shadows rather than drawing shapes with hard outlines, I incorporate concepts about brain function and how we draw upon lived experiences and memory to render an object or person (Brady, Alvarez, and Störmer 2019; Fan et al. 2020; Manifold 2019). We discuss how the brain processes information daily, "seeing versus knowing," and begin by deconstructing some of those ingrained ideas about the human face. But students do not sign up for a forensic art class, or any art class for that matter, eager to do more reading than drawing. Striking a balance is key to gaining student attention and engagement.

To establish a benchmark of skill and for comparative purposes and to track progress, I have students draw a face of a person they have seen before but without referencing a picture while they make the drawing. Most students get a chuckle out of this first drawing effort because of its lack of sophistication. At the same time, it provides a goal for individualized improvement. I was the beneficiary of this strategy when I began my training as a forensic artist (Stuart Parks 2016; Taylor 2018). More than that, this forces the student to confront and appreciate what witnesses go through when asked to remember a face they may have only seen for a few seconds or minutes. Describing a face sufficiently to enable a forensic artist to draw a likeness is a source of more than general angst for an art assignment. To assist in identifying a perpetrator of a crime can be daunting. Some witnesses respond by simply declaring they "can't remember" enough to be helpful, and it is upon the forensic artist and the interview process to try to help the witness to remember—and surprisingly, many do—once provided with a "safe" and less pressurized environment to do so.

Artists' Boot Camp

This drawing was not done by a child but by an adult who had no formal artistic training or anatomical understanding of a face. This is a typical example of the way students will draw at the beginning of my forensic art class. It captures perfectly the ingrained, simplified, and symbolic representation of "knowing" what a human face should have—eyes, nose, mouth, ears, and a reliance on drawing in the shapes of those features with hard lines inside a circle or oval plane that stands for a facial shape.

An Impromptu Face Drawn by an Adult without Artistic Training or Background (Author's Personal Collection)

NAU Student, Josafat Landavazo - Drawing from Memory of a Face Seen Only a Few Minutes Using No Reference

Landavazo's Second Drawing of Same Face, after Several Weeks of Forensic Art Training and Using a Reference

Learning how to depict realism and getting students to detach from their symbolic and outlined shapes is a little like artists' boot camp. You must prohibit or restrict using hard lines, except in limited and specific instances, and teach students how to replace lines with blending (use of a blending stump and tortillons). Using the contrast of highlights and shadows against one another to imply lines instead of actually drawing them is key to realism. This is because the brain will process the information and fill in the lines that are implied, creating more depth. It is why we can see parts of pictures or look at:

a jmbled snetnce yet konw waht the wrods are sppusosed to say.

Our brain will pull from our information filters and fill in those blanks to provide a recognizable picture. Because we know English and the alphabet, a jumbled sentence like the one above can still be processed as our filters glean from established knowledge to mentally flip the letters back into proper order. The problem is that imagery filters (mostly symbolic) interfere with drawing realistically. We want to manually fill in spaces based upon what we believe we know instead of what we see. Following our filters before understanding the principles of realistic drawing causes our drawings to look cartoonish.

The Evolution of Skills and Use of References

Above is a benchmark drawing by student, Josafat Landavazo, on the first day in one of my Forensic Art Methods classes. This is a drawing of an individual whose picture the class was exposed to for only a few minutes on a slide show. They did not know ahead of time that they would be asked to draw this individual. When given the task, they were told to draw according to what they could remember of him. In absence of a reference, this forced students to pull from their imagery filters and incomplete memory. The second drawing is also by Landavazo several weeks later of the same individual. The difference is that students were now tasked with using the techniques they had acquired in the first four weeks of class and were allowed to use a photograph as a reference. Two principles were applied here: (1) the necessity of references when putting together a composite sketch and (2) without a reference of any kind, the brain's filters and symbolic memory will insert themselves because one cannot draw a representation in a void. Incomplete and inaccurate representations result.

When conducting the witness interview, it is considered a best practice to make sure your witness is not sitting directly across from you or in the line of vision of others in the room. Posters on the wall and other images of human beings should be avoided also. Instead, the witness should be provided a catalog of images (most forensic artists use a mugshot book designed with the purpose of highlighting different facial features). Otherwise, in absence of references, it is not unheard of for the witness to begin incorporating parts of the artist's face with whom they are working or features from others in the room or any other unintended references. Not all forensic artists believe in using references, however. Though considered controversial, there are some who prefer to obtain as much as possible from witness description alone. One such forensic artist is Jeanne Boylan.

1995 *Newsweek* Cover Showing J. Boylan's Forensic Sketch of Unabomber, Being Held by a Forensic Sketch Artist Who Drew a 1987 Version. Note the similarity between Boylan's sketch and the face of the previous sketch artist.

Boylan's approach is to spend as many hours as she can with witnesses to try to tap into small details that are all but forgotten. There is no denying that Boylan has vast experience, over 7,000 cases, and her composite sketches have proven successful time and again. On the following page is a now famous sketch of the Unabomber (Ted Kaczynski) that Boylan composed and was featured on the cover of Newsweek magazine on July 10, 1995. This is how the witness described the Unabomber, whom she only saw for a few minutes on a day she looked out an office window and witnessed a man as he was planting a bomb beneath a car (Getz 2017). However, in 1987, an earlier sketch/watercolor, pictured to the right, was also done by another artist based upon descriptions provided by the same witness. Note the uncanny resemblance to the previous sketch artist in the Boylan sketch. It has been speculated that the witness was describing, years later, a memory of the creation of the first composite session in 1987 and drew upon her memory of the sketch artist himself in lieu of any references to use and to compensate for a faded memory of the Unabomber.

The Sum of the Parts Equals the Whole

Forensic composite sketching is learning to follow a facial reference down to its details and using its highlights, grey tones, and shading almost akin to an exercise in cartography and following a road map. This is a major hurdle for most students. Below are examples of early efforts to draw eyes, nose, and lips using a reference but not yet "seeing" it.

Original 1987 Forensic Sketch/Watercolor by Unnamed Forensic Artist Pictured with *Newsweek*

Below are examples of youthful lips and an eye of an elderly person, drawn by NAU student, Kaci Stalcup, after instruction in how to use references properly, and following them closely to define the highlights, contrast, and shading rather than imposing one's own idea of what should be there. Outlining in hard lines was prohibited. By moving away from hard lines to define the shape of each feature, the images dramatize how depth and realism are created using contrasts where light and dark meet, instead allowing the perception of the brain fill in the lines implied.

Students were tasked with drawing a face and communicating the ethnicity of the individual. In this case, actor Viola Davis was the subject. Note the differences in rendering style but still communicating the resemblance and the ethnicity. No two forensic compositions will be exactly alike between artists, but they should still resonate with the viewer as identifiable. Rendering ancestry/ethnicity requires knowledge of cranio-facial structures and an ability to use gradations in portraying skin tones without losing the emphases on shadows and highlights for definition (Flood 2010). Subtle proportional differences in features must be mastered so the face maintains realistic integrity (Mancusi 2010).

Students were given a number of mugshots to create several composites of serial killers. Students did not know who they were drawing. Here [next page] is one of Ian Brady.

There are varying degrees of skill among students, but many fall on a spectrum of realism by the time they finish the course for composite sketching. Once the student has mastered drawing the individual features, they are then tasked with drawing a full composite, putting together disparate features to create a new face.

Untrained Sketches of an Eye, Nose, and Lips—Based upon No References and What the Brain "Knows" to Represent Them

NAU Student, Kaci Stalcup's Realistic Drawing of an Eye, Nose, and Lips after Two Weeks of Forensic Art Training and Using a Reference

NAU Student, Kristin McEwen's Drawing of Actor Viola Davis

NAU Student, Jennifer Gonzalez's Drawing of Actor Viola Davis

Mugshot Photo of UK 1960s Child Serial Killer, Ian Brady

NAU Student, Taylor Antone's Composite Drawing of Ian Brady

Students in my class use the standard catalogue of mugshot references for facial shape, hair, eyes, nose, and lips. From these, the student puts together a new face—hopefully one that bears a resemblance or has recognizable characteristics to identify the individual being drawn.

I was taught that every forensic artist has their own style and that no two artists' renderings of the same composite will look exactly the same. However, if they are based upon the same selected feature references, there should be a recognizable similarity between the composites to understand they are of the same person. Forensic composite sketches aim for as much realism as possible, but they are not intended to be portraits. This point is often misunderstood by the general public, who tend to judge the quality of a composite sketch based upon whether they'd want to hang it on a wall! Realism yes, exactness to a suspect as a measure of the forensic artist's talent—not so much. While some forensic artists, like Lois Gibson, Karen Taylor, Betty Pat Gatliff, and Carrie Stuart Parks, seem to have a knack for renderings that when apprehended, bear striking resemblance, sometimes even "near photographic" to the offender, these are not common. Law enforcement relies on a sketch that is general enough to resonate with someone in the public who sees it and recognizes enough from the features to call in a tip. Forensic artists are also taught not to get overly attached to their sketches as a reflection of their own idea of correctness. When the witness tells you they are satisfied with the rendering, you stop drawing. As much as you might want to adjust the nose (to what you think looks more appropriate) or other features, you cannot—"thems the rules." So, your sketch is only going to be as complete or accurate as your witness indicates it can be (Stuart Parks 2003, 2016; Taylor 2001, 2018).

The Witness Interview and Courtroom Relevance

As mentioned earlier in this article, students are also taught ways to properly interview potential witnesses. In this regard, anthropology and cultural understanding play a significant role when encountering people of different backgrounds, ages, and gender. In today's world, it has become painfully obvious that many of those entrusted with working with the public and in particular, traumatized victims or witnesses, need to learn more empathetic skills to get past a barrier of mistrust and tension.

A common reason for reluctance in witnesses to provide a description for a forensic artist is the misunderstanding that they might describe someone (inaccurately) causing law enforcement to fail or be responsible for an innocent person being arrested or worse, wrongly convicted. Part of the interview should always be to reassure the witness that any amount of a description is helpful, and that while forensic sketches are intended to be used as a tool that aids law enforcement in identifying a specific pool of suspects or eliminate certain suspects in the investigation and apprehension, it is not evidence in its own right. Composite sketches are *not admissible* as evidence in court because they are technically barred by the heresay rule (when a person has heard, seen, or said something out of court—this information cannot be cross-examined, such as unsubstantiated gossip) and cannot be used to prove guilt of the defendant. The only exception to this is when an identifying witness is suspected of perjury or unintended misidentification that can be proven. In this case, the composite sketch can be used to demonstrate the fabrication or inaccuracy.

Witnesses who are also victims require the forensic artist to tread lightly. Because a description is best acquired as soon after a criminal incident as possible, it is often difficult timing to interview someone who may have been a victim of rape or assault or witness to a brutal crime against someone else. In these cases, it is wise to put the witness in a quiet or relaxing environment removed from the pressure of authority figures. The interviewer should be dressed professionally, but casually, to promote a feeling of non-pressure. The forensic artist doing the interview should not be dressed in a uniform or present an authoritarian image. This can be intimidating. I often will request a neutral place for the interview, such as a private meeting/conference room in a library or school—away from the police department if possible. There is a word of caution, however. It is unwise to conduct an interview in one's own home—and if the witness insists on staying in their own home, you should ask for a police assistant to go with you but remain in a separate room. Sometimes, investigating officers will insist that the interview be conducted at the police department and to be present. If you do have to accommodate this limitation—absolutely avoid doing the interview in the confines of an interrogation room. They are not built for comfort and tend to emphasize a somber and rigid atmosphere. Request an office space or other quiet area where you will not be interrupted, and ask that the officer who wishes to be present (if you can't talk them out of it) to remain seated at the farther end of the room and to not ask any questions or participate in any other way than as observer.

Finally, besides being cognizant of words and utterances that can "trigger" a traumatized witness, sometimes the forensic artist must be familiar with local populations and diverse cultures. Allow silences to occur between sentences, questions and answers between yourself and the witness. Many times, if you interrupt or speak too soon to fill in the void of silence, this discourages the witness and interrupts their own pace. As a way into a conversation and to help the witness feel comfortable before getting down to questions, it is a good approach to have the witness talk about themselves a bit. You can slowly lead the conversation up to the day of the "incident"—what they were doing before it happened, etc. A witness will recount more when relaxed, feeling safe, and respected.

In today's world with the cultural and ethnic tensions that too frequently lead to misunderstandings, anger, and violence, it cannot be overemphasized that any career that requires interaction with others in the context of a legal issue needs to be tempered with more understanding and respect. Forensic artists are tasked with representing depictions of all manner of people, but they cannot allow personal biases or views to interfere with those representations. While the main topic in Forensic Art Methods is self-explanatory, I find that it needs to be based upon a foundation of respect, and this is a component that is taught alongside the artistic skill set.

Acknowledgements

I received my forensic art training from some of the best in the field: Carrie and Rick Stuart Parks, FBI trained and who now operate the largest forensic art institute in the United States, offering courses and certifications in all manner of forensic art, and Karen Taylor, a high profile forensic facial reconstructionist who worked many successful years in the FBI and was trained by Betty Pat Gatliff. Gatliff was known for establishing the foundation of forensic art and facial reconstruction as a field in the United States and who sadly passed in January 2020. In addition, Lois Gibson has inspired me over the years. To date, I have received 180 hours of forensic art training and credit these masterful teachers with teaching and inspiring me to contribute when I can to assist law enforcement and to teach others.

References Cited

Brady, Timothy F. George A. Alvarez, and Viola S. Störmer 2019 The Role of Meaning in Visual Memory: Face-Selective Brain Activity Predicts Memory for Ambiguous Face Stimuli. *Journal of Neuroscience* 39(6): 1100–1108.

Fan, Judith E., Jeffrey D. Wammes, Jordan B. Gunn, Daniel L. K. Yamins, Kenneth A. Norman and Nicholas B. Turk-Browne 2020 Relating Visual Production and Recognition of Objects in Human Visual Cortex. *Journal of Neuroscience* 40(8): 1710–1721.

Flood, Jan 2010 *Facial Reconstruction for Artists*. Springfield, MO: Windsong Books.

Getz, Dana 2017 The Unabomber Sketch Artist is Famous in Her Own Right. URL:<https://www.bustle.com/p/ who-was-the-unabomber-sketch- artist> (March 27, 2021).

Mancusi, Stephen 2010 *The Police Composite Sketch*. New York: Humana Press/Springer Science+Business Media.

Manifold, Marjorie Cohee 2019 Understanding and Instructing Older Students Who Cannot Draw Realistically. *Art Education* (Reston) 72(5): 19–24.

Stuart Parks, Carrie 2003 *Secrets to Drawing Realistic Faces*. Cincinnati, OH: North Light Books.

Stuart Parks, Carrie 2016 *Forensic Composite Art Training*, Highlands Ranch, CO.

Taylor, Karen 2001 *Forensic Art and Illustration*. New York: CRC Press.

Taylor, Karen 2018 *Understanding the Human Face, Forensic Art Training*, Scottsdale, AZ.

Wilkinson, Caroline 2004 *Forensic Facial Reconstruction*. New York: Cambridge University Press.

Statement for No Conflicts of Interest

The author declares no conflict of interest in the writing of this article or the subject matter.

1. How is it that forensic scientific evidence can sometimes be responsible for wrongful convictions?
2. What are some of the limitations forensic anthropologists face when assessing human remains?
3. Why would a forensic archaeologist be necessary if a forensic anthropologist is already present at an outdoor crime scene?
4. What is GPR (often used at archaeological sites), and what is it used for at a crime scene?
5. How is knowledge of plants and the environment useful in forensic analysis of an outdoor crime scene?
6. Why would forensic art not be considered "evidence" in court, even if it is effective in helping law enforcement to identify a suspect?
7. Briefly explain how geographic profiling is used to help law enforcement find an offender.
8. Why would sketches of a crime scene be necessary if photographs can be taken?

Image Credit

Fig. 4.1: Source: https://commons.wikimedia.org/wiki/File:Black_Dahlia_Mugshot.jpg.

Chapter 5

A Woman's Touch: When Women Kill

FIGURE 5.1 Elizabeth "Lizzie" Borden.

FIGURE 5.2 The Borden House, circa 1892.

INTRODUCTION TO CHAPTER 5

Elizabeth "Lizzie" Borden was accused of the axe murders of her father, Andrew, and step-mother, Abby, in Fall River, Massachusetts, on August 4, 1892. (See Figures 5.1 and 5.2.) A line in a children's rhyme is a testament to the enduring mythos and fascination of the gruesome unsolved murders:

> Lizzie Borden took an axe
> And gave her mother forty whacks

When she saw what she had done
She gave her father forty-one*

While Lizzie was technically acquitted of the murders at the time by an all-male jury, the court of public opinion left no doubt of her guilt. She was a social pariah after her trial but refused to leave Fall River. She bought a new house and lived out her life there. The general consensus among modern crime analysts is that it is highly likely Lizzie was indeed involved in the murders. The savagery of the crime brought national attention to the case, and some rallied around the stature and gender of the accused as "proof" that Lizzie did not commit the crimes (Miller, 2016). Despite the fact there was no evidence of anyone else present in the house when the murders were committed (besides the maid) and no one else was ever charged with the crime, Lizzie appears to have been acquitted largely based upon the social and cultural norms of the time, which insisted that a woman could not have perpetrated such a ghastly crime. There was sufficient circumstantial evidence: Lizzie and her stepmother were civil at best but tension between them was ongoing and known. She and her sister were beneficiaries of the vast inheritance from her father, equivalent to seven million dollars in today's currency. That is, as long as Mr. Borden died before changing his will to benefit his new wife. Yet, Lizzie's defense team made sure to dress her in feminine finery—lace and delicate patterns—to fit the image of an upper-class genteel woman in the courtroom. As Lizzie fulfilled her end of the social contract for appearance's sake, the all-male jury was willing to oblige and set her free.

Aileen Wuornos has been touted as the first female serial killer in the United States. (See Figure 5.3.) Of course, this is not true, but the nature of her murders performed with male-pattern violence (she killed strangers/clients with a gun after invitations to sex and left her victims' bodies in secluded areas), makes her case an uneasy "fit" within the criteria used to assess homicide offenders (Shipley & Arrigo, 2004). Wuornos was a prostitute who looked for clientele while hitchhiking along interstate highways, mostly in Florida, from 1989–1990. She murdered seven men, all of whom she claimed, in a failed self-defense plea, had tried to rape her or otherwise harm her. Her background story in the article by Downing (2013) makes the argument for the effects of childhood abuse and neglect (nurture) as the principal reasons that led her to commit homicide as an adult.

Most serial killers tend to be male, and so the bulk of research on this special category of killer is based upon a male-centered database. The result has been a list of assessment criteria that don't often fit female serial killers. A central point of contention is that female serial killers are seldom, if ever, motivated by sexual fantasies to commit their murders. They may

---

* Source: https://www.britannica.com/story/lizzie-borden-took-an-ax.

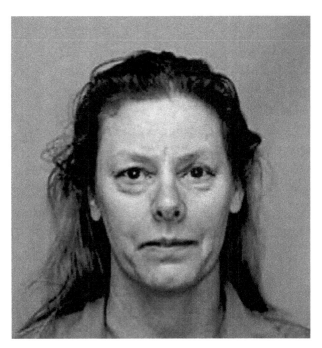

FIGURE 5.3　Mugshot of Aileen Wuornos, incarcerated in Florida State Prison in 1991.

enjoy killing and the feeling of power and dominance, and they may have sadistic traits like their male counterparts, but females generally don't experience sexual gratification when they kill (Douglas et al., 1995).

Female murderers (non-serial killers) kill for the same basic reasons most homicides are committed: greed, revenge, or jealousy. Female killers are also less likely to kill using violent means—their murders tend to be "quiet" in that they are typically within the home, a care facility, or some other familiar place where they work or spend a great deal of time. Most of their victims are known to them—they are friends, family, patients, or acquaintances. Their murders tend to look accidental or due to illness. Women prefer using methods like drowning, poisoning, pushing victims down precipices, or situations that suggest natural causes. When women kill without camouflaging their violence as something else, it is considered unusual.

There is research to suggest that women who partner with significant others (typically males) also change the dynamic at the homicide crime scenes in which they are accomplices. Some begin as secondary partners, subservient to the male, but some become the dominant partner over time. The Craigslist Team Killers demonstrate the need by the female, Miranda Barbour, to claim the role of leadership over her husband, Elytte, and insist she was a serial killer, even when there was no evidence to substantiate her claim. This is an interesting development and suggests an evolving perspective of power and status that a female would be willing to fabricate even if it had a potential to jeopardize her court case. Scott-Snyder (2019) discusses this case in greater detail.

In the 1980s, satanic cults were often blamed for traumatizing and indoctrinating offenders who claimed to have grown up in families that practiced devil worship and where child abuse and sexual abuse were rampant (Shewan, 2017). We see this storyline used in the Craigslist Team Killers' account. Often alleged survivors of satanic cults claimed traumatic events, brought out of repressed memories, that led them into a life of crime and/or mental and emotional problems. There were hints that there existed a nationwide network of satanists in the 1980s. Many popular books were written of alleged accounts by survivors of satanist families. Crime scenes where candles or scribblings interpreted as symbols were found were assumed to be associated with the occult by default. All of this came to be known as "satanic panic." But after nearly a decade of case studies, the Federal Bureau of Investigation concluded that no such network existed and much of the unsubstantiated claims were fabricated for attention or commercial reasons (Shewan, 2017).

This chapter introduces the concept of gender and how it informs public opinions about violent crime. The two readings illustrate changing attitudes about women accused or convicted of violent crime, whether serial crime or single offenses.

Reading 5.1

Serial Killing and the Dissident Woman: Aileen Wuornos

By Lisa Downing

WUORNOS: "Hey, by the way, I'm going down in history."
MOORE: "What a way to go down in history."
> —(Recorded telephone conversation between Aileen Wuornos and her partner
> Tyria Moore, 1991)

A raped woman got executed and was used for books and movies and shit.
> —(Aileen Wuornos in interview with Nick Broomfield, 2002)

I want the world to know I killed these men, as cold as ice. I've hated humans for a long time. I am a serial killer. I killed them in cold blood. Real nasty.
> —(Aileen Wuornos cited in Oliver Burkman, "Florida Executes Woman Serial
> Killer," *Guardian*, 10 October 2002)

IN THIS CHAPTER, I EXPLORE WAYS in which the available discourses of the exceptional murdering subject that have been sketched out so far in this book are a particularly problematic fit in the case of Aileen "Lee" Wuornos (1956–2002), a lesbian, prostitute, and victim of sexual abuse, who killed seven men in Florida between 1989 and 1990.[1] I examine how the label of "serial killer" was debated with regard to Wuornos, and how it was at times rejected; at times adopted as a badge of agency and of selfhood by Wuornos herself who continually sought, like those around her, to make sense of herself through her crimes. Her discourse alternated, as seen in the chapter epigraphs, between assertions that her killings were acts of self-defense and statements that interpret them as a proud bid for recognition via the evocation of the "cold-blooded" serial killer.

Wuornos was frequently described in the media as "the first female text-book case of a serial killer," after the pronouncement of an FBI spokesperson to this effect.[2] In fact, it may well have been the *method of killing* used by Wuornos that earned her this label. Commenting on the FBI's description of Wuornos, Candice Skrapec writes: "This is patently false, unless one uses a definition of a female serial killer as a female who kills a number of people over time using 'male' methods of killing."[3] As Skrapec points out,[4] there had, in fact, been numerous female multiple killers prior to Wuornos (women allegedly representing 10–17 percent of all known serial murderers).[5] Wuornos's crimes, then, are unusual because they defy the norms established for the way in which members of the sexes murder. They certainly fail to match up with Robert Ressler's observed pattern for specifically female homicides: "When there is violence involving women, it's usually in the home, with husbands and boyfriends. It's a close in, personal crime."[6] The difficulty in defining Aileen Wuornos, then, seems to lie in the fact that the modus operandi of her multiple murders was problematically "masculine": she killed alone; she killed strangers, in public spaces, using a gun (rather than the "feminine" methods of poison or smothering); and her habit of hitchhiking as a means of soliciting clients for paid sex was interpreted as a predatory method of hunting for victims.[7] The perception that Wuornos killed "like a man"[8] was additionally doubtless reinforced by the factors of her lesbianism and her aggressive, hostile, "unfeminine" attitude in court. In her feminist study of prostitute-killer Peter Sutcliffe, Nicole Ward Jouve writes: "Why is it that no women go about murdering 'punters,' convinced they're on a God-given mission to rid the city of its litter? It's not just that the case is never reversed: we can't even imagine it being reversed."[9] In some ways, then, Aileen Wuornos did the unthinkable; she brought about this reversal, allegedly taking revenge on physically abusive "punters" by shooting them dead, and professed a continuing belief that she would go to Heaven while those who condemned her to multiple death sentences would rot in Hell.[10]

Aileen's contradictory self-presentation is complicated by the ways in which the commercially viable myth of the extraordinary "first female serial killer" was utilized by her friends, including her lover Tyria Moore; her "adopted mother," born-again Christian Arlene Pralle; and her lawyer-turned-agent, Steven Glazer, in order to market her story and her persona. (This is the central thesis of Nick Broomfield's 1993 documentary, *Aileen Wuornos: The Selling of a Serial Killer.*) The very marketable Wuornos has certainly been extensively represented on celluloid: Broomfield went on to release a second documentary, *Aileen: Life and Death of a Serial Killer*, in 2003, after Wuornos's execution. She has also been the subject of several narrative films, including the made-for-TV *Overkill: The Aileen Wuornos Story* (Peter Levin, 1992). This film was controversial, as the rights to her story were sold to the production company by Tyria Moore in conjunction with members of the arresting police force (leading to the officers' dismissal from service).[11] Additionally, the award-winning *Monster* (Patty Jenkins, 2003) saw Aileen played by highly paid, glamorous Hollywood actress Charlize Theron, transformed by makeup and prosthetic teeth to resemble the real-life killer, and who reportedly studied Broomfield's documentaries between takes to aid the widely commented-upon verisimilitude of her performance. The commercial mine that was the persona and story of Aileen Wuornos also resulted in numerous true-crime books on the case, the first of which was Michael Reynolds's unsympathetic and often misogynistic *Dead Ends* (1992). These also include Christopher Berry-Dee's *Monster: My True Story*, a biographical work allegedly coauthored with Wuornos, but which disingenuously passes itself off as Aileen's "true" story on the tenuous grounds that transcriptions of her trial testimonies and of recorded conversations are inserted between the chapters in bold uppercase type. Finally, she has, like Dennis Nilsen, been the subject of avant-garde queer artworks that resist the mainstreaming of the killer's story, such as Millie Wilson's 1994 installation *Not a Serial Killer* and Tammy Rae Carland's video *Lady Outlaws and Faggot Wannabes* (1995). Both works critique the media's overexposure and exploitation of Wuornos.[12]

As the titles of both Jenkins's biopic and Berry-Dee's book suggest (though the film is rather sympathetic to its fictionalized Aileen, whereas the book is not), Wuornos was portrayed primarily as a "monstrous" figure, that construction which Foucault tells us was one of the discourses that went to make up the modern subject of criminality and assure its "othering" from the norm.[13] Patty Jenkins has commented in a documentary made for the release of the 2006 DVD box set of *Monster* and the Broomfield films that she wanted to show how "some people don't have a choice but to become a monster."[14] While Jenkins seems to have approached the subject matter of *Monster* sensitively, it has been noted that coverage of the film's success did not focus much on the real-life plight of Aileen herself. Kyra Pearson comments that "in her acceptance speeches for three separate best actress awards for portraying Wuornos in the film, Charlize Theron never acknowledged Wuornos, nor did she use these occasions to raise awareness of violence sex workers commonly face."[15] Nick Broomfield has also expressed the sentiment that "on the night of the Oscars there was very little discussion about Aileen. ... It made me rather angry."[16] The real-life figure behind Theron's role was made to disappear as attention was—in typical Hollywood fashion—entirely brought to bear on the audacious uglification of Theron for her role (the temporary making monstrous of an exemplum of ideal femininity). Fascination with Theron's transformation thereby overshadowed the story that Jenkins wished to tell: how society made of Aileen Wuornos a monster (see figs. 5 and 6).

Wuornos's identity as a "monster" is constructed with reference to her divergence from cultural norms (or ideals) of class-bound and heterosexual femininity, not only in her lifestyle as prostitute and lesbian, but also—as we have seen—in having killed in a "masculine" way. Although 100 years after Lombroso's account of the criminal woman, the extent to which violence, lesbianism, and prostitution, as three forms of dissident female behavior, intersect to produce the figure of the inappropriately "masculine" woman is visible in portrayals of Wuornos. It is instructive to compare the othered representation of lesbian killer Wuornos with representations of gay male murderer Nilsen, who, while also subject to homophobic discursive treatment, as we have seen, is more closely aligned in creative

FIGURE 5.1.1　Charlize Theron as Aileen Wuornos in *Monster* (Patty Jenkins, 2003).

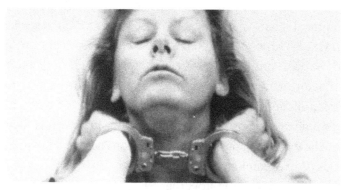

FIGURE 5.1.2　Iconic image of Aileen Wuornos in court, attempting to push back her hair while cuffed. *Aileen: Life and Death of a Serial Killer* (Nick Broomfield and Joan Churchill, 2003).

(if not true-crime or mass media) texts with the nineteenth-century Romantic figure of the artist-murderer that he too cites in his own writings. Wuornos, on the other hand, is relegated the role of serial-killing monster, an improperly gendered peg in the cultural slot marked "sex-beast."

In what follows, I will explore the range of responses to this "rare specimen."[17] As Helen Birch has written, many media discourses about Wuornos assume that she was "self-conscious about what being a serial killer means; in other words, murdering men was her way of courting celebrity."[18] Other sources insist that Wuornos was a troubled, traumatized survivor of past abuse, and/or mentally ill. By reading feminist defenses of Wuornos that claim she is inaccurately described by the label "serial killer" and more accurately served by that of "victim," alongside the vilifying and misogynistic media reports of her crimes, sentence, and execution, I will assess what is really at stake in claiming that Wuornos, a socially disenfranchised woman, used the availability of the archetypal figure of the exceptional-killer-as-celebrity to stake a claim to fame/infamy. I will pay attention to how signifiers of economic deprivation and mental illness intersect with discourses of gender and sexuality in rendering representations of Wuornos exceptional as a killer and monstrous as a woman. In a second section, I will argue that Wuornos's acts and self-presentation need to be considered not only within the dichotomy of the feminist framework of victimhood and the media presentation of serial-killing criminality, but also as acts of radical dissent in and of themselves, intelligible alongside a consideration of radical feminist Valerie Solanas's attempted murder of Andy Warhol in 1968 as a political statement. In such a reading, Wuornos would be a reactive social agent not a passive, defensive victim. Finally, I will argue that the presence of this seldom-articulated, discursively underrepresented figure of a "radical feminist serial killer" nevertheless haunted the Wuornos case and may be responsible for the particularly harsh sentencing and treatment meted out to Aileen. The North American criminal justice system has been argued to be generally more lenient in sentencing women than in sentencing men, but *considerably* more punitive in cases of violent female homicides than in those of their male counterparts, especially when the murdering woman can be seen to flout blatantly other cultural expectations of femininity.[19]

Reading the Violent Woman—Monster, Victim, or Mad Woman?

Criminologists Elizabeth Comack and Salena Brickey have recently argued that "efforts to make sense of the Violent Woman" tend to do so according to three related, but distinct, categories: those of "the bad," "the mad," and "the victim."[20] These three (simplistic) constructions for attempting to reduce nonstereotypical female behavior to the comprehensible are the primary conflicting ways in which Aileen's behavior has been debated and explained.

As David Schmid has asserted, true-crime books, along with lowbrow media, tend to focus on the most sensationalist aspects of a crime and the most stereotypical myths of the murderer, in order to ensure an avid readership.[21] Additionally, their commonly conservative view of gender norms and defense of a right-wing social order tend toward the production of a straightforward moral tale (often in tandem with a hypocritical focus on tantalizing details of the lurid or sexual aspects of a case). Accordingly, and as we would expect, it is here that we find some of the most virulent expressions of misogyny and monstrous othering directed at Wuornos. In an interesting article, Megan Sweeney comments on the, perhaps unexpected, fact that true crime is a popular genre of reading material with incarcerated prisoners, especially women. This perhaps helps us to understand one means by which subjects who will go on to be criminals, or who are already criminals, might self-construct using the vilifying (yet also sometimes mythologizing and therefore aggrandizing) discourses found in these books.[22] Sweeney likewise views this phenomenon through a Foucauldian lens as "self-disciplining" and as a mechanism by which the female criminal is encouraged to adopt "a normalizing gaze that compels her to confess to her character weaknesses."[23] Sweeney makes mention of Michael Reynolds's *Dead Ends*, commenting that it "elides any mention of Wuornos's myriad and profound experiences of social injury, including years of sexual abuse, rape, and homelessness."[24] She further comments that an incarcerated woman she interviewed, whom she calls "Audrey," had read *Dead Ends* and contested strongly Reynolds's account of Wuornos as "a villain that was just out with a gun slingin' it around like a cowboy, just shootin' people for no reason,"[25] as that was not consistent with "Audrey's" own experiences of committing crimes as a woman. This demonstrates that the reading of true crime can promote, for the female reader, the production of reverse-discourse and a questioning of the normative moral perspective presented therein, as a counterweight to the self-loathing identification to which it may also lead.

This counter-reading depends on an empathy with the criminalized female perspective and, as is amply evidenced, most of the true-crime and mass media discourse produced about Wuornos (as was seen in the case of Hindley) is from a mainstream, establishment (masculine) perspective and presumably targeted at a readership from a similar demographic. In this, it says more about male expectations of women in general and female criminals in particular than about female experience, as "Audrey's" comments illustrate. Indeed, in an interview with Broomfield in his 1993 documentary, *Dead Ends* author Reynolds expresses blatantly judgmental and misogynist views about Aileen and, by extension, sex workers. He tells Broomfield that Aileen was lazy throughout her life. She didn't apply herself as a prostitute *or* as a criminal. She didn't even make the effort to wear makeup to attract her "punters."[26] Christopher Berry-Dee's fraudulently subtitled *Monster: My True Story* is similarly biased in its perspective. About her childhood abuse, Berry-Dee writes: "We ... know that Lee was having full sex from around the age of nine. *We cannot even think that she was some kind of 'slut' at that age, as so many observers feel content to believe.*"[27] That he uses the phrase "having sex," rather than "being raped," to apply to a nine-year-old girl is as telling as the implication that "slut" would be a perfectly reasonable label to apply to an older girl or woman. Similarly, describing Wuornos's time as a prostitute and killer, he writes, "The true nature of Lee's psychopathic personality was ... unleashed ... in a car *with a vulnerable man at some lonely place.*"[28] That Berry-Dee can twist the gendered power dynamic such that the male "john" appears as the default vulnerable party in any encounter between a man paying for sex and a prostitute—an encounter that, moreover, takes place in the former's car—is again telling. The (perceived) facts of

Wuornos's exceptional case provide an alibi for gleeful distortion of the statistical reality of gendered violence in the case of prostitutes.[29]

Such examples of garden-variety misogyny aside, Berry-Dee soon gets into his stride of vilifying Wuornos as an exceptional woman, worse even than those other sluts and nonmurderous predatory hookers for whom he so casually reveals contempt. He writes: "Sometimes society and circumstance throw up a female killer who, because of her crimes and, indeed, because she is a woman, stuns and sickens us all. Lee Wuornos was that very rare specimen."[30] The "sickening" rare specimen is soon named "monster" by Berry-Dee. This comes in the context of Lee's perceived relinquishment of a façade of remorse and desire for forgiveness. "She [originally] wanted to 'make it good with God' before she died," Berry-Dee writes. However, "this would soon change as the months passed inexorably by during which Aileen Wuornos would metamorphose into *the true monster that she really was*."[31] This exemplifies the mechanism with which we are by now familiar: in the construction of the murdering subject, the true essence of evil is always understood to have been hiding beneath the façade of normality, waiting to emerge. Finally, Aileen's turning her back on both God and her lover are read as signs of her egotism and increasing obsession with fame:

> She had been allowed newspapers and she avidly poured [*sic*] over the notoriety she was now receiving from the world's media. Her emotions, which had originally centered around Tyria, started to take a back seat. Religion and turning to God was way back in the past. She was becoming a celebrity—a person of some import and, for the first time in her life, she felt she had at least achieved something of value.[32]

What is not admitted of in this condemnation is the fact that Tyria had betrayed her, both by taking part in a recorded telephone call in which she entrapped Aileen into incriminating herself at the behest of the police, and in mercilessly selling her story to the highest bidder. As Nick Broomfield points out, while Aileen Wuornos's persona is not immediately easy to sympathize with, the pathos of her position lies in the fact that everyone she had trusted in her life ultimately betrayed her.[33]

The recourse to the "monster" figure and the meaning of the repeated ascription to Aileen of the "serial killer" label in the media and true-crime may be explained by the fact that these discourses obviate the necessity to look for deeper explanations of motive—and therefore for the possibility of mitigation or moral complexity. "Monster" is the ontological essence of otherness, inexplicable by its very nature. And, as I hypothesized in the introduction to this book, that ascribed quality of the serial killer's crimes that consists in randomness and motivelessness carries on a tradition of belief in a subject who is in no way like the rest of us, who is capable of an *acte gratuit*. It ensures one-dimensionality and removes from us the responsibility even to *try* to understand. Feminist critics of criminology Lynda Hart and Belinda Morrissey concur. Hart points out that inserting Wuornos's murders into the serial killer narrative casts them as enigmatic and inexplicable,[34] while Morrissey theorizes that, in the guise of "monster" and "serial killer," Aileen "no longer challenges because she now has more in common with a celluloid or literary icon than with flesh and blood women who harbour legitimate grievances."[35]

Lynda Hart's position perhaps best exemplifies the feminist defense of Wuornos. It focuses on the institutional violence and exploitation she suffered and shores up Wuornos's own original defense that she was an abused prostitute defending herself from violent clients who raped and injured, or attempted to rape and injure, her. Indeed, Hart's *Fatal Women* is dedicated "to Aileen Wuornos" and "to all the women who have been vilified, pathologized, and murdered for defending themselves by whatever means necessary." This casts Wuornos very far from the serial killer mold, and in the discourse of victim, despite her obvious capacity for violence (exemplified by the fact that she shot her first victim repeatedly, leading to the sound bite "overkill" being used in relation to her crimes and becoming the title of her first biopic). Comack and Brickey further clarify the systemic nature of the need for female self-defense asserted by Hart: "The Violent Woman of feminist discourse ... emerged as the 'Victimized Woman.' Her violence was not of her own making but a response to her 'victim' status under conditions of patriarchy."[36]

However, this (feminist) view of self-defense and victimhood is slightly different from the one that was used in court by Aileen's attorney. The case for the defense too relied on Wuornos's status as victim, but focused principally on the facts of the extensive sexual abuse and neglect she had suffered as a child:

> Her early life ... included her abandonment at three months of age. Her father, in prison for sexually abusing a young girl, committed suicide when Wuornos was seven. She was raised by an alcoholic grandfather who sadistically beat her. Wuornos began life on the streets at 15 and was raped at least five times before she was 18 years old. Her life of drinking, drugs, and abuse eventually led to prostitution.[37]

According to Morrissey, this focus on the past abuse she suffered risks taking attention away from the idea that she really was defending herself against harmful attacks by her clients at the time of the crimes. It makes her instead into a damaged, traumatized woman and suggests the idea that she could have been projecting the abuse of the past onto her "clients" in the present. Morrissey sums up: "Aileen Wuornos was at the mercy of either inhuman lusts or of previous abuse; at no time did her story of reasonable self-defense receive anything but scant consideration."[38] And, moreover, the focus on the past abuse perversely contributed to confirming the "serial killer" diagnosis, "since a disturbed childhood is a feature of many serial killers."[39] What was obviously not taken into account is the extent to which abuse in childhood is rather likely to have a different adult outcome for women than for men, owing to the former group being socialized to internalize trauma and the latter to externalize it as self-assertion and aggression.

Moreover, where in the case of male serial killers who murder female sex workers, the victims' biographies and occupations are often evoked by defense counsels in the service of victim-blaming,[40] in the Wuornos case, the victims were elevated to saintly status, despite the first victim's (Mallory's) prior 10-year sentence for attempted rape, a fact that was not revealed to the jury during Wuornos's original trial. Wuornos's sex, sexuality, and class are doubtless responsible for the reversal that operates in her case. Claudia Card writes:

> Those who have come to be known as serial killers in the past have been rela-tively powerful or privileged men who preyed upon women, especially powerless women (such as the prostitutes murdered by Jack the Ripper, or college stu-dents murdered by Ted Bundy), or upon relatively powerless men (such as the young gay men of color murdered by Jeffrey Dahmer). Aileen Wuornos has never been socially powerful or privileged, and those she killed were white, heterosexual, middle-class men who would easily have had social protection for doing to her what she said they would have done had she not defended herself.[41]

Indeed, as Pearson has pointed out, the dubbing of Wuornos in the press as "Damsel of Death" is designed to suggest proximity to the idea of a "damsel in distress": the hitchhiking Wuornos, by the roadside, armed with a hard-luck story. In this narrative, her johns/vic-tims can be elevated from punters to chivalrous gentlemen who would never normally have thought of paying a prostitute and were merely helping out a woman apparently in trouble.[42] Contrast Mallory's wife's genteel and gender-conforming description of her husband, the convicted attempted rapist: "He was so sweet ... if he saw a woman in distress, he would stop and help her"[43] with Aileen Wuornos's vitriolic testimonial: "Mallory ... was a mean moth-erfucker. ... He starts to get violent. The son of a bitch. He's holding me down. He's going to try and rape me. ... I shot him."[44] Wuornos's account sounds callous, yet it has a direct-ness; it is stripped of any social niceties and reveals the very bones of her truth. Wuornos is, however, damned by her class-marked vernacular, her anger, and her "unladylike" use of profanities here, as when she snarls at the judge following her first death sentence: "I hope your wife and kids get raped in the ass."[45] Juxtaposing Wuornos's social-sexual dissidence with the perceived respectable, middle-class, family-oriented heterosexual maleness of her victims (including a former police chief), the court and the media worked, as Schmid puts it, to "demonize [Wuornos's] lesbianism" while "exonerat[ing] her victims."[46] In response to Wuornos's outburst following her sentencing, the judge remorselessly retorted "may God have mercy on your corpse." Unlike male sentenced killers, Wuornos is presumably not even assumed to have a soul.[47]

The stark socioeconomic disenfranchisement of Aileen Wuornos combined with her appearance as a "masculine" lesbian served to dehumanize the female killer who robbed the lives of "family men" and threatened middle-class standards in the eyes of a gender-normative America reared on family values. In Carland's video, *Lady Outlaws and Faggot Wannabes*, Carland's voice-over, heard against a backdrop of footage of Wuornos speaking in court and in police custody, emphasizes the markers of working-class poverty and butch mannerisms that drew the media's attention to her:

> Every time she swears, swaggers or snarls they take a picture. Her skin is evidence. The way it hangs on her thick bones like gravity prematurely got the best of her. Too much sun and cheap soap. Never enough protection. Her hands are evidence. Hands that have trailed the bodies of women—looking for the place that makes breath halt. ... The chain that hangs from her belt loop is evidence. Low and on the left.[48]

Yet Aileen's erratic speech and behavior in court were not only considered rude and gender nonconformist. They hinted at a mental disturbance. She had a diagnosis of borderline personality disorder, but was considered technically sane. (A personality disorder, as distinct from a psychosis, is less likely to qualify for an adjudication of legal insanity, as those diagnosed as suffering from the former are felt to be able to understand the "nature and quality" of the act they commit.)[49]

The question mark around Wuornos's sanity (the "mad" as distinct from "bad" discourse) intersects with arguments about her status as a victim, and therefore was subject to the same suspicion from those determined to condemn her as evil. Despite the multiple abuses she had suffered in childhood and adulthood, despite visible symptoms of posttraumatic stress disorder and personality disorder, the court could find no compassion for Aileen Wuornos. Even Berry-Dee who, as we have seen, is far from being Wuornos's biggest champion, hints at the spite inherent in the multiple death sentence verdict, stating that, despite hearing expert psychiatric testimonies that Aileen was mentally ill, "the jurors neither forgot nor forgave the woman they had come to know during the trial."[50]

Nick Broomfield believed as early as 1992 that Aileen was telling the truth about the violent assault by Mallory and that his attack, and her initial defensive killing of him, prompted a mental breakdown that led to the other murders. By the time of Wuornos's execution, some 10 years after her first trial, the signs of a troubled, fragmented person had strongly increased, such that indications of delusion and dissociation consistent with what is called psychosis were present. Broomfield was anxious for Aileen to appeal her sentence on the grounds of self-defense and diminished responsibility one final time. The footage he recorded of a conversation with her the day before her execution shows a Wuornos no longer interested in proclaiming self-defense, but possessed of a delusional conviction that the police had "set her up" to become a serial killer. She claimed that officials knew that she had killed Mallory from the beginning, as her DNA was all over the crime scene, and that they had left her at large in order both to "clean up the streets" and to birth a sensational serial killer whose story would make them money. Moreover, her belief that the authorities were sending sonic-waves into her cell to penetrate and control her thoughts suggests a degree of paranoia hardly consistent with the fact that, a day prior to the taping of this conversation, she was considered in an interview with a psychiatrist to be sane enough to be executed. What is worthy of note, however, is that Aileen's fantasy that the police "created" her as a serial killer has a grain of truth, if not *literally*, as a premeditated ruse, then certainly on the level of the workings of discursive construction and commercial entrepreneurship. Aileen was indeed set up, constructed, made subject, and sold as serial killer, but retroactively—not prior to—her crimes. Her delusion lies only in assuming intention before the fact on the part of the authorities.

Aileen's relationship to her common categorization as either monster or victim is a schizoid one that mirrors the division within the society in which she was tried. At times echoing the feminist line of self defense, at other times adopting the serial killer label, Aileen plays with various discourses, but the only one she never takes up is that which engages with the possibility of her own madness. In 1992, Aileen claimed, lucidly and logically, to Nick Broomfield that she was not a classic serial killer, and that counting the number of crimes committed is a red herring when trying to understand her case. Each killing had been a case of self-defense, she states, and a principle—the right to defend oneself from harm—should count for more than the number of times one has had to do so. "It's not about a number, but about a principle," she repeatedly tells Broomfield.[51] By the time of the 2002 interview, when Aileen was depressed, obviously delusional, and ready to die, Broomfield commented in an interview made for the 2006 DVD box set release of the film that "she very much acted the part of the serial killer," proclaiming: "I killed those seven men in cold blood. I'm coming clean. There was no self-defense."[52] The press picked up on such statements, made repeatedly in Wuornos's petitions to have her death sentence hastened by the state of Florida. "I am a serial killer. I would kill again," she is reported as saying in the *Advocate*.[53] And, in the *Chicago Sun-Times*: "I just flat robbed [and] killed them, and there was a lot of hatred behind everything."[54]

David Schmid comments on such stark proclamations by Aileen that "Wuornos's almost parodically vicious assertion of her extreme, inhuman deviance represents her attempt to seize control of the narratives about her."[55]

It is possible that Aileen had merely grown sick of her life on death row and, desperately seeking release via execution, concurred with the identity that others so clearly expected of her. It is also possible, however, that her proud boasts had a rebellious function and that she was genuinely trying to articulate a type of agency and subjectivity that are not identical in meaning with those of the male "serial killer," the profile by which she was being understood. As Pearson has argued, for profilers, media, and judiciary "the process of making her intelligible as a female serial killer depended on labeling her male and masculine."[56] Yet what if Aileen's specific kind of serial-killing monstrosity lay in personifying the threat of the man-hating, castrating, feminist lesbian that, as was amply seen in the course of her trials and media coverage, is patriarchal America's disavowed bogeywoman?

The Female "Serial Killer" as Radical Feminist Terrorist?

In addition to the three explanatory categories applied to Aileen's subjectivity and crimes discussed in the previous section: feminine evil (the supposition implied in the superstitious and gender-conservative true-crime narrative); the instinct for self-defense (argued by feminist commentators and by Nick Broomfield); and insanity (a further mitigating factor in Aileen's defense for Broomfield, confirmed by psychiatric defense witnesses at the original trial), David Schmid suggests a fourth possibility that deserves further investigation: that of political resistance. He writes: "Being honest about Wournos's status as a violent woman and locating Wuornos's murders within a tradition of resistance to violence against women open up a consideration of her murders as a political act, as an act of protest."[57] Moreover, Seltzer has suggested that it makes sense to think of serial killing more generally "as a sort of subpolitical class protest,"[58] an idea that makes particular sense in the cases of female murderers Myra Hindley and Aileen Wuornos, both alienated in different ways from the intersecting economic, cultural, and gendered classes to which they belonged.

That Wuornos was killing as a more or less conscious gesture of defiance of the patriarchy is corroborated by some of the statements she has made, such as the following cited in Reynolds: "I feel like a hero. 'Cause I've done some good. I'm a killer of rapists."[59] Patty Jenkins's biopic also suggests, at moments, this reading of Wuornos, especially in one striking sequence of dialogue between Lee (Theron) and "Selby" (Ricci). (Interestingly, this powerful scene is abridged in the released version and appears in full only in the "extras" of the 2006 DVD box set.) Lee's speech is as follows:

> People kill each other every day and for what? For politics. For religion. And they're heroes. No. There's a lot of shit I can't do any more. But killing's not one of them. And letting those fucking bastards out there go and rape somebody else isn't either. … There's a whole world of people out there killing and raping, Selby. But I am the only one killing them. … Look at me, Sel. You know me. You do. Do you think I could do it otherwise? I'm not a bad person. I'm a real good person.[60]

The notion of a "real good person" who removes rapists and killers from the streets before they can attack women transforms Aileen from mad/sad victim into a feminist avenger, uncannily answering Ward Jouve's question about the existence of the murderous prostitute cleansing the streets of aggressive "punters" in revolt against systemic male violence.

Like Valerie Solanas, author of the *SCUM Manifesto* ("Society for Cutting Up Men"), Wuornos at times casts herself as responding to violent men in the only language they understand. Killing, violence, and rape are their currency—and Wuornos obliges by becoming proficient in that language. When Valerie Solanas writes that "the male likes death—it excites him sexually and, already dead inside, he wants to die,"[61] and then attempts to deliver annihilation to men, she follows a joined-up logic that appears (within the system of that logic) expedient rather than cruel, since, according to her, men will in any case ultimately self-destruct. Like Aileen Wuornos, Valerie Solanas had been a prostitute. Like Valerie Solanas, Wuornos wrote and spoke in angry, exclamatory tones. Like Aileen Wuornos, who "killed like a man," Solanas raised her gun and shot Andy Warhol.

However, following her crime, Solanas was recognized as an activist by fellow feminists who rallied to her defense. Florynce Kennedy, a radical feminist lawyer, declared Solanas "one of the most important spokeswomen of the feminist movement," and Ti-Grace Atkinson named her the "first outstanding champion of women's rights."[62] For reasons that, we might hypothesize, are related to class, cultural capital, and education (Solanas having had status within the bohemian subculture she inhabited in the 1960s that Aileen certainly lacked), Wuornos's crimes were not received in this spirit by feminists. In an article in 1994, Richard Greiner actually dubbed Wuornos "feminism's first serial killer," stating in his title that "Feminists Should Gloat over Their Serial Killer."[63] Yet feminists very definitely did not gloat, champion, or even defend Wuornos's acts *in these terms*. Pearson has pointed out the lack of concerted support on the part of sex workers', lesbians', and women's rights groups for Wuornos:

> [While] the Coalition to Free Aileen Wuornos displayed a banner encouraging participants at the 1993 March on Washington for lesbian and gay rights to "Support Dykes who Fight Back," some members of the Lesbian Avengers in New York presumably hesitated to advocate for Wuornos, believing either that she was not a lesbian or that "there were women more worthy of the group's support."[64]

Those few that rose to champion her from a feminist standpoint, then, did so only on the grounds that she was a victim of abuse and rape acting in self-defense: a victim of the patriarchy not a voluble, violent, and agentic opponent of it. It is as if there is an unwillingness on the part of many feminist groups to accept women's capacity for violence, which is an odd political contradiction as one might expect that feminism would oppose the essentialist gender stereotyping which holds that women are gentle and peaceful while men are naturally violent. Skrapec has stated that this is a deeply ingrained belief of Western culture, which may explain why even most feminists might have trouble deconstructing it: "The public is at once fearful of and fascinated by the individual who lives by his or her own rules. The notion so violates the idea of femaleness, tied to her traditional nurturing role, that *a woman is denied her identity as a multiple murderer.*"[65]

It is in recognition of the general lack of willingness to see her on her own terms, perhaps, that Wuornos's defiant insistence both on being recognized as a victim of male violence *and* seen as a "serial killer" begins to make sense. The subjectifying discourse of "radical lesbian feminist serial killer," which might be closer to the subject position she would have wished to occupy in the public eye, is not a culturally available one, despite Greiner's acerbic coining of a similar label. Where the (male) serial killer is an unlikely hero, a bad boy celebrity, the feminist warrior is not even articulable. Even Valerie Solanas, for all her cult status and following, was similarly considered mentally ill, and her acts provoked no major feminist uprising. Avital Ronell states that Solanas "was not meant to have disciples or spawn a new breed of revolutionaries. ... She had no followers. She offered the uniquely American dead-end-one-warrior-revolution spinning on its own determined axis."[66]

Yet there is evidence to suggest that the figure of the murderous radical feminist lesbian *is* a specter haunting both Aileen's discourse and that of her culture, as seen in the following anecdote recounted to Reynolds by Tyria, about an evening when Aileen and Tyria were watching *Roseanne*:

Roseanne was a hoot. She was doing this routine about serial killers, about how they were always men who were psychos; but if one of them turned out to be a woman, everybody would just call her a man-hater, and Lee has just burst out "that's me she's talking about."[67]

A different way of looking at the much-touted accusation of the misogynist stereotype of the "man-hating lesbian" in the case of Wuornos might, in fact, be to consider it as a proudly adopted identity and form of political subjectivity, in the face of few alternatives. Yet here, in the *Roseanne* example, the putative threatening figure is neutralized as a sick joke rather than accorded the reverence meted out to the male serial killer.

Women's anger, as we have seen, is not permitted in mainstream discourse. Wuornos's anger has, in the discourses observed in the first section, been supplanted with madness or with victimhood, even by her would-be defenders, or obfuscated with metaphysical notions of evil by those who wish to put her beyond the reach of sympathy or human understanding. Much less can the notion that women might enjoy the violence they commit be countenanced. Schmid writes:

> In order to demonstrate that Wuornos was not an "ordinary" female multiple murderer ... but something much more dangerous and threatening, a female serial murderer, true-crime accounts of the case must demonstrate that Wuornos not only killed the seven men but enjoyed doing so.[68]

Where the patriarchal view reads evidence that Lee may have enjoyed killing men as proof of her monstrous evil, a feminist reading may hold it up as evidence of her *humanness*. Why on earth would it be that male killers might derive some sort of satisfaction from committing a violent act against a hated figure, but no woman ever would? If the role of "serial-killing woman" were to become, even theoretically, one of empowerment and resistance for women in patriarchy, it becomes clear why there would be a strong investment in silencing that interpretation. It becomes clear too what is at stake in the strategy of *turning the female serial killer into a man*, following philosopher Jeffner Allen's assertion that "a woman is not violent, and if violent, a female is not a woman."[69] Just as feminist ideas about the meaningful genderedness of the predominantly male serial-killing phenomenon, such as Jane Caputi's argument that it is "sexually political murder ... functional phallic terrorism,"[70] are dismissed in favor of the idea of the serial killer as "random" and "motiveless," so Wuornos must be an anomaly, a monster rather than a symptom. The stakes are high when it comes to maintaining that serial killing be understood as an individual aberration rather than an inevitable product of culture. For society to accept otherwise would mean acknowledging the very existence of patriarchy.

"Victim feminism" alone may be no more politically useful or accurate in accounting for Lee's crimes than misogynistic accounts of her as "evil whore and callous thief."[71] Following Schmid's lead, I think it behooves us to "be honest about Wuornos's status as a violent woman." This involves refusing to interpret the exceptional female figure who kills as a cipher of "randomness," of nihilistic meaninglessness, as is implied in the actions of the subject labeled the "serial killer" (that label so contested in relation to Wuornos), and seeing her, in the wake of Valerie Solanas perhaps, as a "dead-end-one-warrior-revolution" without the education or opportunity to articulate a political position that she nevertheless embodied and enacted.

Backlash: Punishing the Violent Woman

Even if Wuornos did not explicitly articulate her subject position as that of a "feminist terrorist," the threat offered by the specter of this figure was nevertheless evidently felt in the speculations surrounding her figure and case. Broomfield comments in a voice-over at the beginning of the 2003 documentary that "the idea of a woman killing men, a manhating lesbian prostitute who tarnished the reputation of all her victims, brought Aileen Wuornos a special kind of hatred." And Miriam Basilio has commented that Wuornos's killings may be obliquely linked to a backlash against the gains of feminism at the end of the last century and the beginning of this one: "The use of Wuornos to redefine the category of criminal deviance known as the serial killer to include women occurs at a time when women's greater social mobility is causing anxiety in conservative sectors of American society."[72] In light of the fearful, conservative attitudes that, as I have been exploring, were elicited by the case of Aileen Wuornos, it is perhaps not surprising that her sentencing was so harsh and that appeals for the overturning of her multiple death sentences unsuccessful. As Broomfield has pointed out, Aileen was clearly made to pay for having committed violent crimes while female, since more sadistic male serial killers have been treated with greater clemency: "Even Ted Bundy was offered life imprisonment. This was never offered to Aileen Wuornos. At the time I met her she had three death sentences."[73]

Aileen's sentencing was, statistically, unusual. As Renée Heberle writes in 1999 (so prior to Aileen's death, but not to her sentencing), "only 533 women have been among the 19,161 confirmed executions since 1632, and only three women have been among the 437 offenders executed since 1973."[74] However, she goes on to explain that

> some women convicted of capital murder are more likely to land on death row
> than others not because their crimes are worse, as defined by statutory law,

but because they do not enact a properly feminine gender identity. Subject to a social order that requires a certain complementary, dualistic gendered economy, the women on death row are those marked as monstrous, as beyond the pale of not just human but, particularly, feminine behavior.[75]

As has been demonstrated throughout this chapter, this is obviously especially pertinent to the case of Wuornos. Yet, unsurprisingly, the fact that there is a particularly punitive attitude to gender nonconforming women (as well as to socioeconomically disenfranchised individuals and people of color) in operation in death-sentencing is disavowed in juridical discourse. Justice Kogan, writing to support the upholding of Aileen's death sentence by the Florida Supreme Court, states:

> Some might characterize trials such as Wuornos' as social awareness cases, because Wuornos herself unquestionably has been victimized throughout her life. I am aware that some sentiment has arisen to portray Wuornos in this light. Nevertheless, "social awareness" does not dispose of the strictly legal issues, beyond which this Court must be absolutely blind. Whether Wuornos were male or female, the facts remain that the State's theory of this case is sufficiently supported by the record.[76]

Kogan's insistence on justice's gender-blindness and desperate attempt to play down the extraordinarily relevant factor of the intersection of Wuornos's sex, gender, and behavior in determining the treatment she received in custody, in media representations, and in sentencing are supreme examples of patriarchy-denial. Wuornos has to be killed it seems because otherwise, as Heberle points out, Kogan might have had to admit that Wuornos's actions were "a rational response to the concrete knowledge available to her about the world and about men."[77]

The idea that Wuornos not only was a killer who, like Myra Hindley, was "monstrous" by dint of flouting the dictates of "natural" femininity, but also offered the fantasy figure of a "radical lesbian feminist serial killer" may have been instrumental, at least at the level of American society's collective unconscious, in ensuring the vengeful death of Aileen Wuornos. However, instead of acknowledging this possibility, most discourses emphasize Wuornos's similarity to a male serial killer, since the male serial killer is a lone wolf, a random exceptional individual who strikes at will and whose exceptionality keeps his acts safely meaningless. The very idea that Wuornos's crimes *may mean something*—that she may be a prophet of female revolt, a member of a dissatisfied class—provokes too much anxiety to be borne. As Claudia Card has put it, with reference to Wuornos's sentencing: "The message to other women is clear: violent women are abnormal, criminal, and *will not be tolerated*."[78]

Endnotes

1. The victims were Richard Mallory (whose prior conviction for attempted rape was suppressed in the evidence presented at Wuornos's trial), David Spears, Charles Carskaddon, Peter Siems, Troy Burress, Charles "Dick" Humphreys (a retired chief of police), and Walter Jeno Antonio (a police reservist).

2. See: Michael Reynolds, *Dead Ends* (New York: Warner Books, 1992), p. 238.

3. Candice Skrapec, "The Female Serial Killer: An Evolving Criminality," in *Moving Targets: Women, Murder and Representation*, ed. Helen Birch (London: Virago Press, 1993), 241–268, pp. 266–267.

4. Ibid., p. 266.

5. Eric Hickey, *Serial Murderers and Their Victims* (Pacific Grove, CA: Brooks/Cole, 1991), p. 107.

6. Cited in Kyra Pearson, "The Trouble with Aileen Wuornos, Feminism's 'First Serial Killer,'" *Communication and Critical/Cultural Studies*, 4, 3, 2007, 256–275, p. 259.

7. "Once labeled a serial killer, Wuornos was transformed into a predator whose hitch-hiking is read as an act of enticing innocent and good-hearted men who think they are stopping for a 'Damsel in Distress' stranded on the highway, when, as *Time* put it, they meet the 'Damsel of Death.'" Schmid, *Natural Born Celebrities*, p. 261.

8. Reynolds, *Dead Ends*, p. 232.

9. Ward Jouve, *Streetcleaner*, p. 34. See also: Cameron and Frazer, *Lust to Kill*: "This book began from a simple observation: there has never been a female Peter Sutcliffe," p. 1.

10. Footage in Nick Broomfield and Joan Churchill, *Aileen: Life and Death of a Serial Killer* (2003), 3 Disc Limited Edition, including Patty Jenkins's *Monster* and Nick Broomfield's documentaries, Metrodome, 2006.

11. Miriam Basilio, "Corporal Evidence: Representations of Aileen Wuornos," "We're Here: Gay and Lesbian Presence in Art and Art History," Special Issue of *Art Journal*, 55, 4, 1996, pp. 56–61, p. 56.

12. See: ibid.

13. David Schmid tells us that "ironically, when Wuornos was first contacted, shortly after her arrest, by a Hollywood producer interested in making a film about her, Wuornos pleaded with the producer to 'please don't make me a Monster.'" Schmid, *Natural Born Celebrities*, p. 241.

14. Patty Jenkins speaking in "*Monster*: The Vision and the Journey," DVD extras, 3 Disc Limited Edition, Metrodome, 2006.

15. Pearson, "The Trouble with Aileen Wuornos," p. 260. Pearson adds: "This public distancing from Wuornos is striking in light of Oscar-night acceptance speeches by Julia Roberts and Hilary Swank for their respective portrayals of legal assistant

turned activist Erin Brochovich [*sic*] and transgendered youth Brandon Teena a few years before," p. 260.

16. Broomfield speaking in "The Making of a Monster," DVD extras, 3 Disc Limited Edition, Metrodome, 2006.

17. Aileen Wuornos with Christopher Berry-Dee, *Monster: My True Story* (London: John Blake, 2004), p. 78.

18. Birch, "Introduction," in *Moving Targets*, 1–6, p. 6.

19. See: Vivien Miller, " 'The Last Vestige of Institutionalized Sexism'? Paternalism, Equal Rights and the Death Penalty in Twentieth and Twenty-First Century Sunbelt America: The Case for Florida," *Journal of American Studies*, 38, 3, 2004, 391–424; Kathryn Ann Farr, "Defeminizing and Dehumanizing Female Murderers: Depictions of Lesbians on Death Row," *Women and Criminal Justice*, 11, 1, 2000, 52–53; and Renée Heberle, "Disciplining Gender; Or, Are Women Getting Away with Murder?," *Signs: Journal of Women in Culture and Society*, 24, 4, 1999, 1103–1112.

20. Elizabeth Comack and Salena Brickey, "Constituting the Violence of Criminalized Women," *Canadian Journal of Criminology and Criminal Justice*, 49, 1, January 2007, 1–36, p. 3.

21. Schmid, *Natural Born Criminals*, p. 13.

22. Megan Sweeney, "Living to Read True Crime: Theorizations from Prison," *Discourse*, 25, 1&2, Winter & Spring 2003, 55–80.

23. Ibid., p. 69.

24. Ibid., p. 68.

25. Ibid.

26. Broomfield, *Aileen Wuornos: The Selling of a Serial Killer* (1993), 3 Disc Limited Edition, including Patty Jenkins's *Monster* and Nick Broomfield's documentaries, Metrodome, 2006.

27. Wuornos with Berry-Dee, *Monster*, p. 229. My italics.

28. Ibid., p. 196. My italics.

29. Claudia Card writes: "Evelina Giobbe, president of a support group for ex-prostitutes, confirmed the credibility of Aileen Wuornos's plea for self-defense in an interview with Geraldo Rivera, saying, 'Women in prostitution are commonly sexually assaulted, raped, battered, and robbed by customers. Aileen's fears are not unfounded. Close to 2,000 men a year used her in prostitution. So to say three to six a day, that seven of them may have assaulted her fits with the stats that are in there. Abstracted from that context, seven men may sound like a lot; in context, it sounds like probably a fraction of those who threatened the life of Aileen Wuornos.'" Cited in Card, "Review of Lynda Hart, *Fatal Women: Lesbian Sexuality and the Mark of Aggression* (London and

New York: Routledge, 1994)," *Journal of the History of Sexuality*, 6, 1, July 1995, 150–152, p. 151. And David Schmid adds: "The law enforcement perspective on Wuornos exhibits not only a failure to understand the situation that Wuornos claimed she was in, but also an inability or unwillingness to appreciate that a woman's assessment of the degree of danger in a particular situation may be very different from that of a man." Schmid, *Natural Born Celebrities*, p. 235.

30. Wuornos with Berry-Dee, *Monster*, p. 78.

31. Ibid., p. 188. My italics.

32. Ibid., p. 196.

33. Broomfield and Churchill, *Life and Death of a Serial Killer*. Ken Mentor in his review of Broomfield's *Selling of a Serial Killer* makes this point too: "Wuornos, although not necessarily a sympathetic character, has been exploited by nearly everyone associated with her case, and in fact, her entire life." "Review: Nick Broomfield, *Aileen Wuornos: The Selling of a Serial Killer*," *Teaching Sociology*, 26, 1, January 1998, 89–90, p. 90.

34. Hart, *Fatal Women*, p. 137.

35. Morrissey, *When Women Kill*, p. 39.

36. Comack and Brickey, "Constituting the Violence of Criminalized Women," p. 8.

37. Mentor, "Review of Broomfield," p. 90.

38. Morrissey, *When Women Kill*, p. 39.

39. Pearson, "The Trouble with Aileen Wuornos," p. 265.

40. Cameron and Frazer cite the following, from cataloguers of murder Morris and Blom-Cooper, as a typical example of this reprehensible discursive trend: "Some women may *contribute to their own deaths* by running the risks *associated with prostitution*, of which violent death is *an occupational hazard*. ... The prostitute, whose client is unknown to her, may be murdered *simply* because she represents a readily accessible sexual object to her killer, to whom anonymity in his victim may be important. More commonly, prostitutes are the only women *prepared to cooperate* in the sado-masochistic perversions which form, for the killer, an integral part of the homicidal drive." Terence Morris and Louis Blom-Cooper, *A Calendar of Murder* (London: Michael Joseph, 1964), pp. 276, 323. Cited in *Lust to Kill*, p. 31. Cameron and Frazer's italics.

41. Card, "Review of Hart," p. 151.

42. Pearson, "The Trouble with Aileen Wuornos," p. 262.

43. Cited in ibid.

44. Wuornos with Berry-Dee, *Monster*, p. viii.

45. Footage in Broomfield, *Selling of a Serial Killer*.

46. Schmid, *Natural Born Celebrities*, p. 232.

47. Footage in Broomfield, *Selling of a Serial Killer*.

48. Cited in Basilio, "Corporal Evidence," p. 60.

49. See: Flora Rheta Schreiber, *The Shoemaker: The Anatomy of a Psychotic* (New York: Signet, 1984), esp. p. 367, for the distinctions between psychiatric insanity and legal insanity, and between personality disorders and psychoses. Schreiber's book is an attempt to prove that multiple murderer and rapist Joseph Kallinger was suffering from a severe paranoid schizophrenia that directly led to his crimes, and that he required incarceration and treatment in a psychiatric hospital, rather than detention in a prison. (Kallinger was originally adjudged to be suffering from a personality disorder and therefore convicted as sane and sent to prison, where he killed an inmate following a psychotic hallucination in which an imaginary presence allegedly appeared and told him to do so.)

50. Wuornos with Berry-Dee, *Monster*, pp. 201–202.

51. In Broomfield, *Selling of a Serial Killer*.

52. Broomfield, "Introduction to *Life and Death of a Serial Killer*," DVD extras, 3 Disc Limited Edition, Metrodome, 2006.

53. "Florida Serial Killer Wants Death Penalty," *Advocate*, 3 July 2001. Cited in Pearson, "The Trouble with Aileen Wuornos," p. 268.

54. "Woman Serial Killer Wants to Die," *Chicago Sun-Times*, 20 July 2001, 3. Cited in Pearson, "The Trouble with Aileen Wuornos," p. 268.

55. Schmid, *Natural Born Celebrities*, p. 240.

56. Pearson, "The Trouble with Aileen Wuornos," p. 258.

57. Schmid, *Natural Born Celebrities*, p. 234.

58. Seltzer, *Serial Killers*, p. 135.

59. Reynolds, *Dead Ends*, p. 236.

60. The dialogue of *Monster* is heavily based on Wuornos's 12-year prison correspondence with a lifelong friend to which she agreed to allow Jenkins full access hours before her execution.

61. Valerie Solanas, *SCUM Manifesto* (London: Verso, 2004), p. 66.

62. Both cited in Avital Ronell, "Deviant Payback: The Aims of Valerie Solanas," introduction to Solanas, *SCUM Manifesto*, 1–31, p. 10.

63. Richard Greiner, "Feminists Should Gloat over Their Serial Killer," *Human Events*, 25 March 1994, p. 15. Cited in Pearson, "The Trouble with Aileen Wuornos," p. 257. (Pearson takes Greiner's sound bite as the title of her article, but does not expand upon the implications of this idea.)

64. Karena Rahall, "Aileen Wuornos's Last Resort," *Assaults on Convention: Essays on Lesbian Transgressors*, ed. Nicola Godwin, Belinda Hollows, and Sheridan Nye (London: Cassell, 1996), p. 115. Cited in Pearson, "The Trouble with Aileen Wuornos," p. 257.

65. Skrapec, "The Female Serial Killer," p. 263. My italics.
66. Ronell, "Deviant Payback," p. 9.
67. Reynolds, *Dead Ends*, p. 95.
68. Schmid, *Natural Born Celebrities*, pp. 235–236.
69. Jeffner Allen, *Lesbian Philosophy* (Palo Alto, CA: Institute of Lesbian Studies, 1986), p. 38.
70. Caputi, *Age of Sex Crime*, p. 2.
71. Morrissey, *When Women Kill*, p. 9.
72. Basilio, "Corporal Evidence," p. 60.
73. Broomfield, voice-over in *Life and Death of a Serial Killer*.
74. Heberle, "Disciplining Gender," p. 1103.
75. Ibid., p. 1106.
76. Florida Supreme Court, 644 So.2d 1000 (1994), Justice Kogan concurring.
77. Heberle, "Disciplining Gender," p. 1110.
78. Card, "Review of Hart," p. 152. My italics.

Reading 5.2

Team Killers: The Craigslist Killer

By Stephanie Scott-Snyder

The Craigslist Killer

In the early morning hours of November 12, 2013, residents of Sunbury, Pennsylvania, discovered the body of 42-year-old Troy LaFerrera in an alleyway behind a neighborhood home. He had been strangled and stabbed multiple times.

Within days, newlyweds Miranda (age 19) and Elytte Barbour (age 22) were arrested for the murder. According to statements ascribed to Miranda, she and her husband of only 3 weeks had plotted to kill together—for the sheer thrill of it. To put their plan into action, the twosome had placed a personal ad on Craigslist promising female "companionship" in exchange for money. Miranda claimed that she and Elytte intended to use these ads as ethical tests to protect young girls from would-be sexual predators by murdering the men who answered them; LaFerrera responded.

On the night of the murder, Miranda lured LaFerrera into the front seat of her car before telling him that she'd lied about her age in the online ad and was really only 16. She later told police that this was an ethical barometer of sorts; when LaFerrera wanted to proceed with the sexual encounter, he sealed his own fate. As LaFerrera began to slide his hand up Miranda's thigh, she asked, "Did you see the stars tonight?" The seemingly benign and almost flirtatious question was actually a prearranged signal between Miranda and Elytte, who was hiding beneath a blanket in the back seat. Upon hearing that, Elytte was to blitz LaFerrera from behind, wrap a cord around his neck, and strangle him. However, when Elytte didn't respond quickly enough, Miranda grabbed the knife she'd hidden in the driver's side door pocket and stabbed him. Elytte eventually joined in and ultimately choked LaFerrera to death.

After they'd disposed of the body, the couple bought cleaning supplies with which to wipe down their vehicle. They then went to a strip club to celebrate the emotional and physical high they felt following their kill. The homicide commemorated their 3-week wedding anniversary (Lysiak, 2014).

In a statement to police, Miranda, who quickly became dubbed the Pennsylvania Craigslist Killer, disclosed that LaFerrera was not her first victim. She claimed to have slaughtered dozens more in a 6-year-long satanic killing spree spanning multiple states. She had reportedly joined a cult at the age of 13 and warned police that they wouldn't find a trail of buried corpses, but rather would only "find body parts" (Murphy, 2014). Regarding her claims of serial murder, Miranda's family expressed doubt and characterized her as a manipulative liar. To date, there has been no evidence to corroborate any of the cult murders for which Miranda claimed responsibility (Lysiak, 2014).

Miranda is currently serving life for the brutal slaying of LaFerrera. She pled guilty to second-degree murder, a plea bargain that ensured the death penalty was taken off the table at sentencing. She has no regrets, and maintains that she loves her husband, and believes that her victim deserved to die. She has told authorities, "If I were to be released, I would do this again" (Draznin, Candiotti, & Welch, 2014).

Perhaps even more jarring than her apparent lack of empathy is the fact that Miranda Barbour stated during a jailhouse interview, "I knew we were going to do this since the day we met" (Murphy, 2014). This statement begs the question, "How does one know whether a potential mate is primed for murder?" Certainly first-date conversation doesn't consist of "What do you like to do for fun? I enjoy killing people." How then, do killer couples come together? At what point do they cross the threshold from learning one another's boundaries to becoming co-conspirators? What are the dynamics underlying their attraction?

Serial Killing Teams

Psychologically speaking, Miranda and Elytte Barbour were on the path to becoming a serial killer couple. Although in the nascent stages of their homicidal career at the time of their apprehension, their intent was never to commit only one murder. They cast a wide net, as evidenced by their use of the Internet to lure potential victims. Additionally, their motive was akin to that of the mission-oriented serial killer who seeks to rid the world of a particular type of individual, in this case, sexual predators.

Serial murder is estimated to comprise less than 1% of all homicides annually (Federal Bureau of Investigation [FBI], 2005), with 13% of such crimes being committed by teams. Of these, 56% involve two killers, while the remaining 44% involve three or more offenders working in tandem. Male–male pairs account for the largest proportion of two-person killing teams (30%), and male–female duos rank second, comprising 25% of such partnerships (Newton, 2008).

When women commit serial murder, they are more likely to do so as part of a team than they are to act alone. In fact, some analyses indicate that close to one-third of all female serial killers have never committed a solo homicide and have killed only within the context of a team's endeavors. A female team killer is defined as a woman who kills or partakes in the systematic murder of multiple victims in conjunction with one or more accomplices. A

TABLE 5.2.1   A Comparison of Serial Killing Teams and the Women Who Join Them

Male–Female Teams	All-Female Teams	Family Teams
One male and one female	Exclusively women (two or more)	Three or more persons of both sexes; not necessarily biologically related
Active period of 1 year	Active for 1 to 2 years	Active for 1 year or less
Sexual relationship between members	Sometimes involve sexual relationships; various motives (profit, crime, compassion, etc.)	Nonsexual relationships; members share a love of murder and mayhem or a compulsion to kill
Serial sexual homicide, maintained by the synergy of the pair's own sexual relationship	Target victims who are old, young, vulnerable, or otherwise incapacitated	Teams may go on crime sprees involving multiple felonies, commit serial sexual homicide, or both
Crimes involve sexual torture	MO mimics that of a solo female serial killer (poison, suffocation)	Kills are extremely violent
Various motives for female partner (transfer of sadism, psychopathy, domestic abuse)		Women involved tend to be young, submissive, and loyal to the group leader

Source: Adapted from Kelleher and Kelleher (1998).

woman is classified as a team killer, even if she does not physically commit the murders herself, as long as she participates in the homicidal activities of the team (Kelleher & Kelleher, 1998). For example, if she lures or restrains individuals who are then killed by her partner(s), she is considered to be a team killer.

Kelleher and Kelleher (1998) have distinguished three types of killing teams involving female serial killers (FSKs): (1) male–female teams, (2) all-female teams, and (3) family teams (Table 5.2.1). A team's overarching characteristics are determined by a host of factors, including the individual activities of the dominant team member, the number of participants, the group's gender makeup, and the relationship among team members. Given these differences, it stands to reason that each type of team enacts its crimes in a slightly different fashion.

Male–Female Teams

The male–female team is the most common of the three serial killing units, especially in the United States. It is composed of one male and one female who are usually sexually involved with one another. Serial sexual homicide is their primary criminal activity. The male partner is often a sexual predator and serial killer in his own right, while the female partner is easily dominated and manipulated by him; in a sense, she may be characterized as one of his victims. That said, there are also cases in which the female is an active and engaged killer who exhibits a level of sexual psychopathy that rivals that of her male counterpart (Kelleher & Kelleher, 1998).

The team's focus on serial sexual murder is maintained by the synergy of their ongoing sexual relationship with one another in addition to their pathological obsession with sexual domination and control; in other words, they are aroused by their murders. Such teams commit horrifically brutal crimes, commonly torturing their victims before killing them. They tend to target children and adolescents, and their offenses often garner a great deal of media attention before they are caught (Kelleher & Kelleher, 1998).

One of the key features of sexually driven serial homicide is the element of fantasy. As the male partner is often the dominant team member, it is typically his sadistic fantasies that become the blueprint for the team's activities. These deviant thoughts are the manifestation of years of his maladaptive response to adverse emotions such as fear, anxiety, and powerlessness, resulting from an abusive or otherwise traumatic past (Morton & Hilts, 2008). In other words, eroticizing violence is his escape from negative emotionality.

When women kill with a male partner, their motives often become commingled with those of their accomplice. In some cases, these women may be both vulnerable due to their own abuser history as well as impressionable. They may therefore be coerced or easily influenced by their male partner to sexualize violence. However, because many of them are significantly younger than their male counterparts and have had no trouble with the law prior to meeting their accomplice, it seems logical to assume that they are actually victims of sadistic, manipulative men under whose spell they've fallen. However, this conclusion fails to recognize the fact that women such as Charlene Gallego, who murdered 10 victims in Sacramento, California, alongside her husband, and Karla Homolka, who, along with her partner Paul Bernardo, was responsible for the deaths of at least three teenage girls in Canada, quickly transformed into fully participating partners in crime; they not only recruited victims, but became complicit in torture and sexual assault and in some cases acted out their own violent fantasies. Therefore, one school of thought is that these women may have *always* had the potential to act out their rage and despair on others. The question, however, is whether they would have if they had never met their (male) partners (Johnston, 2012b).

Male–Female Dynamics

Serial killer couples forge an intense and nearly instantaneous connection and exhibit complex relational dynamics. It would be remiss not to discuss the application of attachment theory within this context given its relevance to the interactional styles, criminal patterns, and developmental trajectories of not just serial killer couples, but serial sexual homicide offenders in general. Attachment during one's formative years, whether secure or insecure, impacts many critical facets of adult life, including agential capacity (or the person's concept thereof), approach to trauma, self-image, response to impulsivity, ability to build trust, and, of course, the pattern and health of future relationships. Thus, it seems particularly apropos to examine attachment with respect to the bonds that the partners entrenched in serial killer couples form with one another.

Healthy relationships are established over time, with each person sharing increasingly more personal details about themselves; this lays the foundation for trust and emotional intimacy. In the rapid and sexual unions created by male–female serial killer teammates, the partners become too familiar too fast; they fail to respect or recognize both physical and emotional boundaries and offer too much personal information upfront, often expecting (or demanding) the same in return; these couples also frequently engage in sexual activity almost immediately upon meeting. As the male is usually the dominant team member, it is not uncommon for him to coerce the often dependent or vulnerable female into entering the relationship full-throttle. The female partner commonly loses her individual identity in lieu of her status as a member of the killing team.

Research reveals that romantic partners involved in these twosomes share some analogous traits; rather than developing a stable bond built on trust and respect, these commonalities prime them to forge a compelling, if combustible, kinship built on emotional instability, deviance, and maladjustment. For example, in addition to disrupted attachment, many such partners (both male and female) experienced horrific childhood trauma, including physical abuse, neglect, exposure to criminal sexual behavior, and parental mental illness. Together, these factors laid the foundation for their dysfunctional adult relationships. For instance, serial killer Debra Brown was severely abused by her father, who reportedly suffered from psychiatric issues. Debra's boyfriend-accomplice Alton Coleman, was neglected by his mother, who was a prostitute and frequently had sex with johns in front of him. Similarly, serial killer spouses Rose and Fred West were both raised in families where incest and deviant sexuality ran rampant (Johnston, 2012b).

It is not uncommon for both teammates to romanticize their relationship as well as their crimes. However, while the male is often the psychopathic and/or sadistic leader, the female, who is his follower and the facilitator of his crimes, may in fact participate because doing so transfers some of his sadistic tendencies onto a target *other than herself*. By the same token, some women join in the killing because it is their way of usurping some of their partner's strength, thus affording them a brief feeling of control in an otherwise chaotic situation.

Several notorious female serial killers have cited this notion of the transfer of sadism as fundamental to their crimes and have cast themselves as reluctant accomplices in the crimes of their abusive male partners. They have publicly spoken of fearing for their lives, of having been controlled, and of having to choose between saving themselves or killing someone else. While no one truly knows how they would respond if forced to choose between killing or being killed, it is difficult to reconcile such killers' presentation of themselves as victims with the facts of their cases.

As previously mentioned, women such as Karla Homolka and Charlene Gallego were not unwilling participants or even passives ones. Rather, they demonstrated extreme cruelty of their own accord, often when their male partners weren't present. They suggested new ways to abduct victims and even sought the best camera angles to creatively capture their rape-murders on film. As incongruent with "feminine nature" as these facts are, when the collective histories of spouses of sexual sadists are examined, domestic violence is a common thread. These women are often abused by their spouses and come to regard them with a combination of love and fear, which leaves the criminal justice system struggling to determine whether they should be treated as victims or accomplices once caught (Johnston, 2012e).

The period of homicidal activity for a male–female team tends to be relatively short (approximately 1 year), in part because these teams are often poorly organized. Additionally, due to the vicious and very public nature of their kills, they do not remain at large for long. Because the crimes perpetrated by these pairs are undertaken in a cooperative way, the level of criminal organization largely depends on each individual team member's capacity for organization as well as the degree of collaboration between the two. In some cases, the murders become opportunistic, reckless, and disorganized, leading to quicker apprehension. In others, however, well-organized male–female teams have been able to remain at large for several years (Kelleher & Kelleher, 1998).

Karla Homolka and Paul Bernardo

"[Karla Homolka] remains something of a diagnostic mystery. Despite her ability to present herself very well, there is a moral vacuity in her which is difficult, if not impossible, to explain."

—Dr. Angus McDonald (Kilty & Frigon, 2016)

Karla Homolka was arrested on February 19, 1993, after she and her husband Paul Bernardo raped and murdered three teenage girls in Ontario, Canada. The couple's first victim was Karla's younger sister Tammy.

When Karla was 17, she met 23-year-old Paul Bernardo. Within 2 months, the couple was engaged. Paul began spending much of his time with the Homolka family and soon developed an obsession with 15-year-old Tammy Homolka. He would peep through her window and sneak into her room to masturbate while she slept. Karla helped him by breaking the blinds in her sister's room so that he could get a better look.

In December of 1990, Bernardo convinced Karla to offer him Tammy's virginity as a Christmas present, as he was disappointed that he was not Karla's first sexual partner. With her parents asleep in the upstairs bedroom, Karla drugged her sister. She and Bernardo then stripped Tammy and proceeded to videotape themselves sexually assaulting her while she was unconscious. During the course of the attack, Tammy choked to death on her own vomit. Tammy's death was officially ruled accidental.

Six months later, on the morning of June 15, 1991, the couple took their second victim. Bernardo was driving through Burlington, Vermont, halfway between Toronto and St. Catharines, when he came upon 14-year-old Leslie Mahaffy. She was locked out of her house after having missed her curfew. He led her to his car where he forced her into the back seat and blindfolded her.

Once home, Karla and Bernardo proceeded to videotape themselves torturing and raping Leslie over the course of the next several hours. When the recordings were presented at Bernardo's trial, he could be heard threatening Leslie, telling her that her behavior would determine whether she lived. As the tapes progressed, the sexual torture escalated and Leslie cried out in pain. Bernardo could be seen sodomizing her with her hands bound with twine.

According to Bernardo's testimony, the day after the video was taken, Karla administered a fatal dose of Halcion to Leslie. However, Karla claimed that it was Bernardo who killed Leslie by means of strangulation. Whichever the case, the couple subsequently dismembered the body and put each piece into a different cement block before disposing of them in nearby Lake Gibson.

Nearly a year later, Karla and Bernardo claimed a third victim, Kristen French. On the afternoon before Good Friday, the couple was actively cruising for victims in the vicinity of Holy Cross Secondary School when they came upon the 15-year-old walking home. They pulled into the parking lot of a nearby church and Karla got out of the car, pretending to need directions; Bernardo then grabbed Kristen from behind. Once he'd forced her into the car, Karla restrained Kristen.

During the course of the 3-day Easter holiday, Karla and Bernardo recorded themselves torturing, raping, and sodomizing Kristen. They forced her to drink toxic amounts of alcohol and to be sexually submissive to Bernardo. Unlike Leslie, Kristen was never blindfolded, so one might assume that they always intended to kill her.

Kristen was murdered on Easter Sunday, 1992. Again, however, Karla and Bernardo's stories about the specifics of her death were in conflict. Bernardo reported that Karla had beaten Kristen after she'd tried to escape and then ultimately strangled her with a noose that she'd secured to a hope chest. He noted that immediately afterward, Karla had gone to fix her hair for Easter dinner. Karla, on the other hand, later testified that it was Bernardo who strangled Kristen. She indicated that he did so while she watched. That evening, the couple ate Easter dinner with Karla's family; they dumped Kristen's nude body in a ditch the next day.

Karla and Bernardo were arrested in 1993. In 1995, Bernardo was convicted of the murders of Leslie Mahaffy and Kristen French. He was sentenced to life in prison with a dangerous offender designation, the maximum penalty permitted under Canadian law. Throughout the course of the investigation, Karla told detectives that Bernardo had abused her and that she'd been a reluctant accomplice to the murders. As a result, the prosecution agreed to make a deal; Karla pled guilty to the reduced charge of manslaughter in exchange for serving a 12-year custodial sentence.

After the plea bargain had been accepted, graphic and unambiguous videotapes of the crimes surfaced, proving that Karla was a far more active participant than she'd led the court to believe. According to Bernardo's attorney, the tapes revealed Karla sexually assaulting *four* victims, engaging in sexual activity with a female prostitute in Atlantic City, New Jersey, and drugging an unconscious victim. As a result, the Canadian Press dubbed the deal she'd made with prosecutors the "Deal with the Devil."

Before being sent to prison, Karla was evaluated by a plethora of psychologists, psychiatrists, and court officials, and one thing struck them all—how radically different she presented herself to each audience. Research reveals that the masks worn by psychopathic female serial killers are a means of manipulating others to achieve the outcome that best suits them at any given moment. Thus, various emotional and psychological presentations are displayed in different settings and to different individuals, as such offenders' motivations are opportunistic in nature (Perri & Lichtenwald, 2008, 2010). In fact, according to an interview with Karla's former friend and colleague Wendy Lutczyn, she now believes that Karla is a psychopath, and not an abused woman as she had once claimed (Cairns & Fenlon, 2005).

As a result of the plea bargain, the central tenet of which was her assertion of having been abused at the hands of Bernardo, Karla was released from prison in 2005. Karla clearly played the gender card masterfully and relied on social and cultural scripts about the victimization of women and women's incapacity for heinous violence to minimize her culpability. Her psychopathic personality fostered her ability to manipulate not only the court system but the general public; she presented herself as a victim of gender violence, which, in turn, *forced* her to victimize other females. However, it is imperative to note that since Karla's release from prison she has led a relatively normal life. She is married and has children of her own. Can her previous serial violence therefore be characterized as a sort of dormant trait brought out by the dynamics of her relationship with Paul Bernardo? In other words, does the fact that she has lived without recidivating (something that is unlikely for both serial offenders and criminal psychopaths) highlight the impact or strength of her (specific) male partner's influence? Had she never met Paul Bernardo, would Karla Homolka have realized her own homicidal fantasies? These questions emphasize some of the enigmatic differences between FSKs who work alone and those who partner with a male romantic partner.

Thrill Kills

Most people can at least rationalize the act of killing under duress from an abusive partner or can even understand the sexualization of violence as a maladaptive coping response to trauma. But what about killing for the sheer excitement of it? Dr. Joni Johnston (2014) tested three hypotheses for how murder teams form when two people kill for sport:

- A dominant, murder-minded individual coerces a good-hearted person.
- A dominant individual convinces someone who seems to be a good person, but who harbors murderous tendencies.
- Two homicidal yet cowardly people come together; their dysfunctional relationship gives them the courage to act on their dark fantasies.

Although these scenarios can be applied to both opposite-sex and same-sex couples, gender implications are embedded in the social dynamic. As the male partner is often the leader in a male–female team, the gender inequity and inherent power imbalance that is part of the larger cultural narrative is reflected in these pairs when a female kills (another female!) at the behest of her male partner.

Dr. Johnston's research did not support the concept that morally upright individuals are corrupted by partners with murderous intent. However, she did find striking examples of weak-minded dependent persons who were extremely malleable; their dominant partners were able to quickly and easily transform them into whatever they wanted—and needed—them to be. Myra Hindley is one such exemplar.

Myra Hindley and Ian Brady

Myra Hindley was a mousy, unremarkable woman, with a seemingly low chance of becoming a serial killer—until she met Ian Brady. Myra quickly became sexually intoxicated by Brady's commanding presence, and he knew it. Brady repeatedly tested Myra's loyalty, roping her further and further into his aberrant ruses.

Myra became adept at luring victims, many of whom she knew, and many of whom may not have fallen prey to the pair had she not been the one to entice them into the couple's car. Having a woman present changed their perception of the situation and ultimately their perception of their own safety, and Brady knew that, too. The victims felt safe with Myra; they trusted her.

Between July of 1963 and October of 1965, the couple sexually assaulted and brutally murdered five victims ranging in age from 10 to 17. They then buried the bodies on Saddleworth

Moore in Britain. After she was apprehended, Myra admitted that despite knowing right from wrong and never having had a violent urge of her own, she not only willingly participated in the killings, but she also came to enjoy them.

As with Myra and Brady, thrill-kill duos typically have one member who drives the murder. However, this doesn't mean that the other partner is idle. Most of these teams consist of a dominant person who partners with an equally enthusiastic accomplice or someone who, due to an absence of intestinal fortitude or a substantial lack in their own character, is easy to bring on board (Johnston, 2014).

All-Female Killing Teams

All-female killing teams are the second largest group of team killers that involve FSKs. That said, these teams are exceptionally rare, even by the standards of obscurity set forth by the phenomenon of the FSK. As the name indicates, these units are made up of two or more women who work in tandem to commit serial murder. While the majority of such teams typically have only two members, there may be multiple perpetrators who are jointly active in the perpetration of the crimes. Similar to their male–female counterparts, these teams typically have one dominant member who orchestrates the killings and one or more submissive members who are easily manipulated and/or controlled. In such scenarios, the dominant woman may take on the role of active killer, or she may step back and assume the responsibility of primary organizer without ever committing an actual murder. Regardless of the particular dynamics and modus operandi, these teams are surprisingly prolific and often target victims who are very old, very young, vulnerable, or otherwise incapacitated (Kelleher & Kelleher, 1998).

In some cases, a sexual relationship exists between (or among) team members. However, exclusively female teams also form for a multitude of other reasons. Unlike male–female teams, which are principally driven by sexual sadism, the murders of all-female killing teams are spurred by a wide variety of underlying reasons, which may encompass an array of motivational categories, such as profit, crime, or angel of death (Kelleher & Kelleher, 1998).

The average age of the women involved in exclusively female killing teams is higher than that of female members of male–female teams. The typical member of an all-female killing team makes her first kill in her mid-20s. Moreover, female killing teams remain active for approximately 2 years before they are apprehended or the murders otherwise cease; this is an active period twice as long as that of the average male–female killing duo (Kelleher & Kelleher, 1998). There are other dissimilarities as well. Whereas the murders committed by the typical male–female serial killing team involve a variety of weapons or killing styles and are commonly gruesome, the murders committed by female killing teams tend to mirror those committed by solo FSKs. Therefore, "tidier" tactics such as poison and suffocation are the preferred methods.

Amelia Sach and Annie Walters

The first known case of a female killing team occurred in England just after the turn of the 20th century. Amelia Sach and Annie Walters established a private residence in London, from which they offered lodging and adoption services to unwed pregnant women. Playing on the stereotypes of the time, they advertised their services in newspapers, promising young women confidential assistance with guaranteed anonymity devoid of record keeping—pain and stigma-free relinquishment of their babies. They soon had a healthy clientele.

When expectant mothers—of which there was a steady stream—entered the establishment, they were charged a fee. After they gave birth, Amelia would take the baby from them, and then hand the child over to Annie. Annie, who lacked the capacity to plan such an operation, had no difficulty following her dominant partner's instructions; she dutifully murdered the babies using chlorodyne before disposing of their tiny bodies in the Thames. Amelia would then return to the mothers and say that the baby had been adopted, offering no further details due to confidentiality restrictions. She would then demand further payment to cover miscellaneous expenses. The two women were arrested for their "baby farming" operation, which they'd undertaken solely for profit; they were ultimately sentenced to death.

The Murder District

A decade following the execution of Amelia Sach and Annie Walters, another female killing team was active in Europe, this time in Nagyrev, Hungary. This team, headed by Mrs. Julia Fazekas, was composed of several black widows. The group became known as "The Angel Makers" and is estimated to have killed approximately 50 men.

In Hungary at the time, the family of a teenage bride was tasked with choosing her future husband, and the girl had no choice but to accept her family's selection. Divorce was not socially acceptable, even in cases of an alcoholic or abusive husband. During World War I, able-bodied men were sent to war to fight on behalf of Austria-Hungary, and rural Nagyrev was designated as a holding camp for Allied POWs. The POWs were afforded limited freedom to move about the village, giving them the ability to interact with many of the young women in town—many of whom were glad to be temporarily rid of the husbands who'd been forced on them by their families. Thus, many women began sexual relationships with one or more of the foreign prisoners. However, when their husbands returned, they forbade these affairs and wanted things to return to their prewar status quo.

Mrs. Fazekas, the town midwife, presented a solution: eliminate the problematic husbands. She persuaded the unhappy wives to dispatch their husbands with arsenic made by boiling flypaper and skimming off the poisonous residue. As more and more women came forward with the same problem, Fazekas organized a murderous group that targeted husbands and later problematic parents and other bothersome relatives for the women of Nagyrev. Nagyrev eventually became known as the Murder District.

The network of black widows was shut down when one of the targets survived the dose of arsenic slipped into his red wine by a woman with whom he had only a passing acquaintance. His story launched an investigation into several women in the town, one of whom confessed to having poisoned seven victims under the direction of Mrs. Fazekas. When authorities went to arrest Mrs. Fazekas, she committed suicide before she could be placed under arrest.

Alpine Manor and Lainz General Hospital

In more recent years, two cases of serial murder committed by female teams have attracted media attention due to their extreme viciousness. Both cases occurred in the 1980s and involved the murder of patients in medical facilities, one at a large general hospital and the other at a nursing home. In both instances, a single dominant individual controlled the actions of the team and made life-or-death decisions about the patients under their care. The pathological need for control played a vital role in these killings.

In 1986, Catherine May Wood was the timid 24-year-old nursing aid supervisor at Alpine Manor Nursing Home in Walker, Michigan. By all accounts, she was depressed; she was dangerously overweight (reaching 450 pounds at her heaviest point) and had recently ended her 7-year marriage. That same year, Gwendolyn Graham moved to Michigan and was hired at Alpine Manor. Although Catherine was her supervisor, it was Gwendolyn who took the lead in their personal relationship, which developed quickly.

Gwendolyn was a staunch and demanding woman who exacted control over Catherine. Their relationship brought new meaning to Catherine's life, and she began to diet and take pride in her appearance. The two began a sexual relationship, which included casual sex with other women. Gwendolyn had a penchant for extreme sex, so their encounters often involved rough play and choking behaviors. As Catherine was intent on pleasing her new partner, she remained compliant.

It was in October of 1986 that Gwendolyn first approached Catherine with the idea of committing murder as a way of intensifying their sexual stimulation. At first, Catherine dismissed the comment as a nefarious joke. However, the couple took their first life within 3 months of that conversation (Kelleher & Kelleher, 1998).

Gwendolyn's initial plan was to select six victims whose first letters of their last names would spell out M-U-R-D-E-R. However, the scheme proved too elaborate, as she hadn't anticipated the tenacity of several of the would-be victims. She shifted gears and began targeting only the frailest patients. Between January and April of 1987, the pair attacked a total of 10 nursing home residents, resulting in the deaths of five. Each time, their MO was the same:

Catherine was the lookout while Gwendolyn smothered the victims with a damp washcloth. On some occasions, the duo had sex immediately following their kill, as a way of reliving and often heightening the perverse thrill. Akin to many male–female teams, Gwendolyn and Catherine's crimes were sexually motivated, as their sole purpose was to increase the couple's level of arousal; murder became an integral and climactic part of their sexual discourse.

Unlike the Alpine Manor murders, the slayings at Lainz General Hospital in Vienna, Austria, did not involve a sexual relationship among the killers. This all-female killing team involved four perpetrators, who acted under the leadership of Waltraud Wagner between 1983 and 1989. Waltraud recruited other nurses to help her dispatch patients whom she found irritating. In short order, the team had its killing routine down to a science—administering a morphine overdose or pinching the patient's nostrils closed and forcing water into their mouth until they drowned. The team ultimately confessed to 49 murders after they were overheard bragging about their latest kill at a local tavern (Newton, 2006).

Family Killing Teams

The third category of serial homicide teams in which women play an integral part is the family killing team, which is composed of three or more individuals of both sexes. The members may be related by blood or affinity, or they may be unrelated persons who have come together to form a family-like unit for the sole purpose of conducting criminal activities. Typically, the dominant member of such teams is a male (Kelleher & Kelleher, 1998).

Family serial killing teams share many common characteristics with male–female teams. For instance, family teams may engage in crime sprees or commit serial sexual homicide or both. These teams can range from highly organized to very disorganized. However, regardless of their ability to coordinate their murders, family teams tend to be extremely violent and their crimes very public. Therefore, their period of murderous activity is often relatively short, about a year. The female team members are typically young and submissive, similar to the female members of the male–female teams (Kelleher & Kelleher, 1998).

When these teams are composed of individuals primarily drawn together by their mutual attraction to murder and mayhem, the team predictably engages in an extended crime spree that includes a host of felonies, not just murder. For example, the notorious Karpis–Barker gang, led by Ma Barker, was motivated primarily by profit, not murder, and their crimes included extortion, theft, and armed robbery (Kelleher & Kelleher, 1998).

However, in cases of (often not biologically related) family teams where the common denominator among members is the compulsion to kill, the sheer purpose of forming the team is to commit serial murder. In these cases, the killers will be controlled by an often charismatic figurehead who is a committed and sometimes experienced serial killer in his or her own right; while this person will direct the murders, he or she may or may not actively participate in the family's homicidal ventures. The leader, who is typically an aggressive or abusive male, demands extreme loyalty from the other members of the team. Such teams are exceedingly rare and fall within the scope of cult activity, with the Manson clan offering a notorious example.

Conclusion

Women who commit serial homicide with a partner or partners tend to exhibit a universal set of characteristics: (1) an average age between 20 and 25 at the time of their first kill; (2) a total number of known victims ranging between 9 and 15; and (3) an active period that lasts from 1 to 2 years (Kelleher & Kelleher, 1998).

The three types of serial killing teams in which FSKs become involved are male–female teams, all-female teams, and family teams. While the idea of women participating in any type of overt violence, let alone serial murder, is in conflict with gender conventions, it is the dynamics inherent to the male–female killing teams that most clearly highlight the explicit gender commentary germane to the operation of these partnerships. In such instances, some women initially become involved in the killing duo as a means of escaping domestic abuse by the male partner, while others lack strong character and demonstrate dependent personality features, making them likely to give in to their dominant partner's attempts to mold them despite the fact that they know the difference between right and wrong. Still, other women have a need for power and control and/or a penchant for or fascination with murder, live a rich fantasy life in which violence and sexuality are fused, or display psychopathic tendencies. The murders committed by male–female teams are almost always sexually motivated and thus often increase the intensity of the couple's own sexual chemistry.

When women form all-female killing teams, their motives vary widely, ranging from profit to compassion, and their methods are reflective of those of solo FSKs (e.g., poison and suffocation). Comparatively, women who become members of family killing teams seem to have more in common with women in male–female partnerships due to the gender inequity resulting from the (usually) male domination of both teams. Whatever the specific combination of internal and external events that leads a woman to participate, whether passively or actively, in the serial elimination of others, it is a rare occurrence by any standard and one that is continually viewed by society as in violation of gender norms.

References

Cairns, A., & Fenlon, B. (2005, June 1). Ex-pal: Karla psychopath—wants her jailed for life. *Toronto Sun*. Retrieved from http://canadiancrc.com/Newspaper_Articles/Toronto_Sun_Ex-pal_Karla_jailed_for_life_01JUN05.aspx

Draznin, H., Candiotti, S., & Welch, C. (2014, February 18). Woman accused in Craigslist slaying tells newspaper: I've killed lots of others. *CNN*. Retrieved from http://www.cnn.com/2014/02/16/justice/craigslist-thrill-killing-confession/index.html

Federal Bureau of Investigation (FBI). (2005). *Serial murder: Multidisciplinary perspectives for investigators*. Washington, DC: Behavioral Analysis Unit, National Center for the Analysis of Violent Crime.

Johnston, J. E. (2012b). Fatal attraction: The chemistry between serial killer couples [blog post]. *Human Equation*. Retrieved from https://www.psychologytoday.com/blog/the-human-equation/201210/fatal-attraction

Johnston, J. E. (2012e). Serial killer couples: Understanding the wife [blog post]. *Human Equation*. Retrieved from https://www.psychologytoday.com/blog/the-human-equation/201209/serial-killer-couples

Johnston, J. E. (2014). Partners in crime: Peer pressure, dysfunctional relationships, and murder [blog post]. *Human Equation*. Retrieved from https://www.psychologytoday.com/blog/the-human-equation/201401/partners-in-crime

Kelleher, M. D., & Kelleher, C. L. (1998). *Murder most rare: The female serial killer*. New York, NY: Dell.

Kilty, J. M., & Frigon, S. (2016). *The enigma of a violent woman: A critical examination of the case of Karla Homolka*. New York, NY: Routledge.

Lysiak, M. (2014, April 28). Exclusive: Craigslist Killer Miranda Barbour tells how and why she killed. *Newsweek*. Retrieved from http://www.newsweek.com/2014/05/09/exclusive-craigslist-killer-miranda-barbour-tells-how-and-why-she-killed-248670.html

Morton, R.J., & Hilts, M.A. (Eds.). (2008). *Serial murder: Multi-disciplinary perspectives for investigators*. Quantico, VA: Federal Bureau of Investigation.

Murphy, D. (2014, March 30). 'Craigslist Killer' Miranda Barbour claims two men survived death trap. *Daily News*. Retrieved from http://www.nydailynews.com/news/national/craigslist-killer-miranda-barbour-claims-men-survived-death-trap-article-1.1739570

Newton, M. (2006). *Hunting humans: An encyclopedia of modern serial killers* (2nd ed.). New York, NY: Facts on File, Inc.

Newton, M. (2008). *Criminal investigations: Serial killers*. New York, NY: Chelsea House.

1. What are some of the differences between the way most women murder their victims and the way men kill?
2. Why are women serial killers so difficult to categorize by the system currently in place, and how have cultural notions of gender impacted this issue?
3. What was the initial justification for the murder perpetrated by the Craigslist Team Killers, and what does the need for this justification imply about the offenders?
4. What role did Miranda Barbour's husband play in the murder, and why do you think he went along with it?
5. What are the arguments for environmental factors behind the Aileen Wuornos case?
6. Miranda Barbour was only nineteen years old at the time of her arrest, making her birth year 1994, while satanic panic stories of "satanic families" were popular in the 1980s and faded by the 1990s. Why do you think she used this debunked storyline to explain her behavior?
7. What evidence is there that Aileen Wuornos suffered from personality disorders?
8. Why do you think some profilers are reluctant to categorize Wuornos as a serial killer?

Image Credits

Chapter 6

Will the Real Serial Killer Please Stand Up?

Popular Culture, Murderabilia, and Commercialization of Homicidal Violence

FIGURE 6.1   Photo of actor Anthony Hopkins as Hannibal Lecter.

FIGURE 6.2   Display of Dexter action figure on his boat at the 2011 Comic Con.

INTRODUCTION TO CHAPTER 6

It is no understatement to say that crime scene investigation and true crime shows are moneymaking entertainment. The original *CSI* (Crime Scene Investigation) television series, which made its debut in 2000, quickly became a number-one draw as the *most-watched television show in the world*. It won that title for five years, receiving the prestigious International Television Audience Award for a drama series. It spawned a franchise with spinoffs such as CSI Miami, Manhattan, and Washington, DC. Then came the *NCIS* (Naval Criminal Investigative Service) dramas and all their spinoffs.

The *Law and Order* drama series dealing with the justice system began in 1990, ten years prior to *CSI* and all of its descendants, and has been broadcast for twenty-one years and counting. Although the show did not tend to explore actual crime scene investigation and analysis, instead focusing on the crime and resulting courtroom drama, it demonstrated a growing niche of public interest. By 2020, there were nineteen active/renewed crime scene or police procedural shows broadcast in the United States (Porter, 2020).

But lest we forget, the concept of good guys versus bad guys has been a popular theme in film and since television entered the households and lives of the American public. From the 1940s through the 1950s, film noir highlighted a certain cynicism that had crept in during the post–World War era. Society had suffered a disillusionment about humankind and the willingness of some to exploit and harm others for personal gain and power. Fate usually dished out just deserts to offenders in the end, but people inevitably got hurt along the way. From the late 1950s through 1960s, the TV Western reigned supreme with shows like *Gunsmoke*, *Wagon Train*, *The Rifleman*, and *Bonanza*, to name a few. These captured the idea of civilization and law over chaos and injustice and held the number-one spot in serial entertainment. These shows also promoted 1950s values about family, loyalty, and right and wrong, and championed ideas about taking matters into one's own hands when the law was not around to do the job. Concepts of masculinity and leadership, the role of gender and who was "worthy" of mercy, forgiveness, or leniency that were applauded then would be challenged and called into question in today's world. The daily promotion of these ideologies would have affected viewers, children and adult alike, in reaffirming or influencing beliefs and value systems.

By the late 1960s to 1970s, the "anti-hero" was born: the flawed individual who was not necessarily a nice guy but had a set of values that were unconventional yet understandable. This individual was not a hero in the traditional sense of the word but was someone who reliably followed their inner compass within *their* definition of right and wrong. The anti-hero was not always in tune with society, and the character often blurred the line between being a good guy or a bad guy. Films like *Bonnie and Clyde*, *The Godfather* and its sequels, *Dirty Harry*, *Taxi Driver*, and *Dog Day Afternoon* are examples of this shift.

The idea of what constituted acceptable violence and by whom also evolved. A separation between children's and adult viewing grew as the entertainment industry entered into a social experiment in response to antiwar and antiviolence sentiments.

Major theatrical and award-winning releases also evolved over time. Examples of early crime films include *Night of the Hunter* (1955), wherein actor Robert Mitchum played a serial killer masquerading as a preacher in the popular Western format of the time; and Alfred Hitchcock's *Psycho* (1960), which delved into the psychology of the disturbed mind of character Norman Bates. The latter film was inspired in part by the real-life case of Ed Gein, who dug up corpses and murdered two women. Ed Gein again served as inspiration for Buffalo Bill in *Silence of the Lambs*, and "I ate his liver with fava beans and a nice chianti" became a hallmark quote of a new psycho-antihero, Hannibal Lecter.

Popular entertainment frequently crosses the line from reality into fiction, if it recognizes a line at all. Commercialization of violence, murder, and serial killers in particular are a low-risk investment for the entertainment industry; after all, they wouldn't pursue those productions if the public had no taste for them. But do fictional portrayals do justice to depicting what a serial killer's thought process truly is and what behaviors they are likely to engage in (or not)? Are truth and realism sacrificed on the altar of profit and Nielsen ratings? The answer seems to be a resounding *yes*.

Characters like fictional Dexter Morgan (from the TV series *Dexter*), the serial killer who has a "code" and only kills those who deserve it, and Hannibal Lecter (from the films *Manhunter* and *Silence of the Lambs*, based on books by Thomas Harris, and the *Hannibal* TV series) who has a penchant for preying on and eating the unforgivably "rude," socially reprehensible, and corrupt as his character evolves and his popularity surges. (See Figures 6.1 and 6.2.) The latest incarnation of *Dexter: New Blood* (2021) on Showtime depicts another evolution of Dexter Morgan as he breaches his own code of ethics, with interesting outcomes.

Commercialization of murder and violence is not limited to television and movies, video games, or music—one can find popular action figures, mugs, t-shirts, and a multitude of other merchandise in the collectibles market as well. This is a market, however, that has faced legal and ethical challenges by those who feel the wrong people may benefit or that heinous crimes are romanticized.

Murderabilia is defined as any object that has value because of its connection to a murderer (a personal possession, clothing, artwork, a written document, a family photo, etc.), to the murderer's crime scene, or to another notorious criminal event. There are arguments pro and con about the legitimacy of murderabilia and the right to sell or collect it. Does facilitating murderabilia sales (as a seller or buyer) promote rewarding the wrong people, show disrespect for victims? Or does preventing its sale step on the right of self-expression? The first reading by Devlin (2010), provides a case study of the ethics of murderabilia—the public archiving of the papers of Ted Kaczynski.

Domestic violence has been an ongoing problem in society and shows no sign of abating in the United States. About 25 percent of women have at some time in their lives been victims of domestic violence; about one in five murder victims were killed by their intimate partners (NRCDV, 2022). This latter statistic includes male victims of domestic abuse; though male victims are significantly less common than women victims, it is still significant to consider them as part of the widespread problem of physical abuse in American households and the level of "acceptability" of violence our culture tolerates. The reading by Liebler et al. (2016) considers how domestic violence is depicted in popular culture, and its resulting public perception.

Reading 6.1

The Ethics of Archiving "Murderabilia": The Papers of Ted Kaczynski

By Nora Devlin

Abstract

This essay examines the ethical implications of the 1997 accession of the papers of Theodore Kaczynski by the Labadie Collection at the University of Michigan. The author seeks to analyze the actions of Assistant Curator Julie Herrada. Ethical issues such as sensitivity to the community, the archivist's duty in dealing with controversial collections, and the idea of "reactive advocacy" are discussed. Third party privacy rights and the archivist's ethical dilemmas in dealing with donors and restrictions are also analyzed. Ultimately, this essay shows that the case of the Kaczynski papers is extremely useful in highlighting some of the ethical issues that archivists deal with on a smaller scale every day.

T**O COLLECT ONLY THE PLEASANT, THE** democratic, the pleasing records that document our past—the aspects of American life that make us all proud—would be so simple. However, this is not life—nor should it be—and these types of records do not give a complete picture of our culture and our history. These were the thoughts of Julie Herrada, the then Assistant Curator of the Labadie Collection at the University of Michigan, when she wrote to Ted Kaczynski in 1997 requesting all of his personal writings and materials that he had in his possession. The papers that Kaczynski eventually sent to Herrada were housed in the Labadie Collection, an archive that had long made it its mission to document the radical and social protest movements in American history, acquiring materials on antiwar, transgender, anarchist, and alternative sexuality movements (none of which would be considered mainstream). Concerns over controversial acquisitions, media interference, third-party privacy rights, and donor requests all played a significant part in Herrada's experience, and add an invaluable dimension as a case study to any further discussion of such issues.

The University of Michigan and the Ted Kaczynski Papers, 1997–1999

Ted Kaczynski was arrested in 1996 on charges of being the notorious "Unabomber" for two decades. During his violent campaign he mailed bombs to individuals involved in fields related to science, genetic engineering, forestry, airlines, and universities. Before his arrest in 1996, three people were killed and twenty-four were injured (Herrada, 2003–2004, p. 35). Kaczynski was captured in 1996, and after a long trial, pleaded guilty on January 22, 1998. He was sentenced to four life sentences plus 30 years in prison (D. Johnson, 1998). Kaczynski later tried to withdraw his guilty plea, arguing that he was coerced into the plea agreement, but his appeal was denied (Egelko, 2001).

So how did Julie Herrada come to acquire the unusual collection of correspondence that Kaczynski had in his jail cell in Colorado? Soon after Kaczynski's arrest, Herrada saw the potential for scholarly research that his radical writings might hold. In 1997 she wrote to Kaczynski's attorney and basically asked for *all* his writings (Dodge, 2005). At the time she contacted him, Kaczynski was part of a media frenzy. His writings and crimes had garnered the public's continuing, morbid fascination. Herrada pointed out in an interview for *Library Journal* that her job involved keeping track of events followed in the radical press and collecting new materials accordingly (*Library Journal*, 2002). Noting the increasing interest of the radical and anarchist press in his writings, she indicated that she could not ignore the opportunity.

Four months after writing to Kaczynski's attorney (Judy Clarke), she received word that he was interested and wanted information on the library and its mission. Soon after, Kaczynski sent all the correspondence that he had written and received since his arrest (Herrada, 2003–2004, p. 38). After that, papers started arriving every 6 to 8 weeks (K. Johnson, 2001). Kaczynski sent the correspondence before any deed of gift was signed—he was only allowed to keep a small portion of letters in his cell, and fearing their destruction, sent them to Herrada (Herrada, 2003–2004, p. 38).

The first ethical issue in this acquisition was the validity of the acquisition itself. Herrada's accession of this collection was directly in line with the Society of American Archivists' Code of Ethics' statements on collecting policies (as it existed at the time). According to Section III of the Code (Collecting Policies), "acquisitions should be made in accordance with a written policy statement ... and consistent with the mission of the archives" (The Society of American Archivists, 1992, Section III). The collection must be within the collecting scope, and not acquired for any other reason. While Kaczynski was obviously a well-known and controversial figure, it was not his fame or the potential media attention that the institution would garner that interested Herrada. Rather, as Herrada consistently points out, it was never his crimes that interested her in his writings: "I was interested in the papers not because he killed people. It was his writing on social protest" (K. Johnson, 2001).

Archivists have an ethical responsibility to document the past as defined by their collecting scope. They should not let their own personal condemnation of an individual's actions influence their recognition of a historically valuable or pertinent collection. No argument can be made that these materials did not fit within the Labadie Collection's scope. After all, it is considered to be one of the most comprehensive collections of anarchist and radical history in the world (Herrada, 2003–2004, p. 36). Many social radicals view Kaczynski's ideas as a smaller part of a larger radical movement called "green anarchism," an anti-technology theory and movement. His theories and actions were widely discussed among radicals and anarchists (Herrada, 2003–2004, pp. 35–37). The controversial nature of such an acquisition makes the justification of its "fit" all the more necessary, with a collecting policy being crucial for justifying acquisition (Metzmeier, 1997, p. 30).

Controversy, the Media, and the Role of the Archivist

Not many archivists are thrown into the middle of media storms. Herrada experienced firsthand the challenges presented to an archival institution after acquiring a controversial, contemporary collection. Archivists usually respond to hostility concerning controversial acquisitions with arguments of the importance of documenting *all* of society or providing access to scholars or both. Herrada is no exception: "I don't condone [his] behavior, but I feel I have a responsibility to researchers in the future so they have access to that kind of material. ... I think people have a right to know there are dissenting views. I can't make the judgment whether or not to provide access to controversial or unpopular ideas" (*Library Journal*, 2002).

The scenario was more complicated than this, however, as Herrada soon discovered. Controversial acquisitions are inherently infused with a variety of ethical concerns. Some parallels can be made to other such acquisitions, most notably the accession of KKK materials at the Clarke Historical Library at Central Michigan University. Frank Boles discusses his experience with this acquisition in the 1990s. He was presented with a similar situation of media interest, issues of sensitivity, and an unexpected need to explain to society not only the worth of such an acquisition, but the significance of archives in general (Boles, 1994). Just as one prosecutor argued that Kaczynski's materials shouldn't be considered of value, as he was "nothing but a serial murderer" (Archivalia, 2007), critics of the CHL accession argued that the KKK materials were irrelevant, because their creators were "just a bunch of bigots" (Boles, 1994, p. 54). The general public often does not understand an archives' reason for collecting materials from individuals considered evil, seeing such acquisitions as a legitimization of their practices (Boles, 1994, p. 54). What is the archivist's ethical responsibility in responding to such criticisms? The University of Michigan had very little precedent for dealing with the controversy and media attention that came about with the accession of high profile collections, so Herrada was left to use her instincts and her repository's mission statement (Herrada, 2003–2004).

One important ethical necessity is to respond to the criticism with an appropriate mixture of sensitivity and explanation—and a clarification that documenting such histories is not to legitimate or condone them, but to record them with the same equality as any other historical event in the United States. The issue of sensitivity to the community is acute in Herrada's case because of its contemporary nature. Some of the victims of Kaczynski's attacks still lived in the Ann Arbor area. The accession had the potential to make the library appear insensitive to the recent tragedies (Herrada, 2003–2004, p. 39). Herrada's acquisition garnered national and local criticism. While very few individuals took personal offense, they misunderstood her reasons for the accession and resented the additional attention it provided Kaczynski. Victims, family of victims, attorneys involved in his prosecution, and even media personalities felt that the preservation of his materials would increase his celebrity status—which was absolutely true (Blumberg, 2005). Many argued that the coverage surrounding this collection held the potential to re-victimize his victims. One media personality said that the University of Michigan was "glorifying" him (Herrada, 2003–2004, p. 43). This is an ethical dilemma unavoidable in the acquisition of living, notorious figures, and due to the lack of any guidance in the SAA's Code of Ethics, must be dealt with on a case-by-case basis—usually through collaboration with colleagues and knowledge gained by experience.

Sensitivity is crucial, but should not interfere with the archival mission. As one archivist comments, "being sensitive to such feelings should not preclude professional responsibility to fairness, objectivity, and intellectual freedom, all fostered through collecting comprehensive, well-rounded collections" (Lamoree, 1995, p. 150). Archivists have the ethical responsibility to protect their collections from political or outside pressure. Their mission statement and collecting policy must be considered first and foremost, well ahead of the media or other individuals' attempts to interfere with such objectives (Hurley, 2005).

Herrada responded by emphasizing the significance of documenting all of society and the fact that the collection fell squarely within their collecting scope (Herrada, 2003–2004, pp. 43–45). More than ever, outreach was crucial in educating the public about the ethical responsibility of the archivist to "preserve the record, however odious" (Adkins, 2007). What emerged from this situation was the realization that the general public really had no idea why an archive would want records associated with such evil. Claims of historical value often do not satisfy people, and the public generally shows little interest in trying to understand the reasons for such acquisitions (Boles, 1994, pp. 58–59). This is a significant problem in the archival community, one that requires advocacy and education; Boles asserts that "unless a substantial minority of the general population understand and appreciate the need for archives ... to possess controversial material, the archivist's ability to collect such material will be compromised" (Boles, 1994, pp. 58–59).

Reactive Advocacy

Herrada notes her fear of the loss of unpopular records, stating "institutions documenting local history should be collecting materials relevant to their communities, especially if they are controversial. These materials may otherwise be destroyed out of shame, embarrassment, fear or misunderstanding" (Herrada, 2003–2004, p. 43). Herrada's acquisition presented the unique opportunity for "reactive archival advocacy." Much has been discussed in archival literature about promoting an archive's functions in society, or showcasing particular collections or exhibits; but what about taking a controversial situation rife with negative publicity, and using it to educate the public on the significance and function of archives? This education could provide the platform for a successful acquisition, and the presence of future collections of a similar nature (Boles, 1994, pp. 59–64). Herrada even believes that situations like what she faced, while tense and potentially dangerous, increase awareness of archives; so "a little controversy" is not always a bad thing (Herrada, 2003–2004, p. 45). Such opportunities provide a good platform for advocating for archival significance.

Creating an argument that the general public believes and appreciates is the greatest challenge and allows a potentially negative situation to be turned into a positive one. But how to handle potential reactive advocacy is not always clear-cut—and whatever route is chosen has the potential to cause further chaos. First, neutrality should be emphasized (Lamoree, 1995, p. 150). The accessioning of this collection had nothing to do with Kaczynski's crimes, but rather with his radical theories. Herrada acknowledged his evil, but she did not assert that she wanted to document this evil for any type of accountability. The Labadie Collection strictly documents radical movements, and that is why Kaczynski's papers are housed there. In some ways, this may have been less satisfactory to the public. It was a current tragedy, and looking objectively at intellectual contributions of a serial murderer is difficult for the public, and nearly impossible for victims. An archivist must show the ethical necessity of documenting controversial, sometimes evil figures in society by pointing to the risk of, as Herrada states, "whitewashing social history" (Herrada, 2003–2004, p. 45). Otherwise controversial figures may suffer the same fate that minorities and other victims of "hidden histories" have suffered in the past—voicelessness in records, and subsequent lack of historical documentation.

The media provides an interesting sidelight in this narrative. Newspapers obviously focus on the headlines that will sell their stories (Goerler, 1999). When they got wind of this collection, it was not Kaczynski's radical writings or correspondence they were interested in, but the fact that the University of Michigan was giving research credit to the writings of a serial killer. They could not look past this fact and understand Herrada's motives for accessioning the collection. Despite the fact that the media was unhelpful in this situation—in fact, Herrada found them unprofessional and distrusted their motives—many archives can use them to their advantage (Herrada, 2003–2004, p. 42).

The SAA's Code of Ethics, in any of its variations then and now, does not specifically address the issues of controversial collections, media involvement in archives, or public advocacy. However its references to the functions and uses of archives, as well as their relationships with donors, the public, and responsibilities for documenting society, speak volumes (The Society of American Archivists, 2008 and 1992). Herrada and her colleagues might have considered utilizing the code in response to criticism after the acquisition. One of the purposes of the code in existence then was "to educate people who have some contact with archives, such as donors of material, dealers, researchers, and administrators" (The Society of American Archivists, 1992, Section I). When the public learns that such a code exists, and that it informs decisions based on "moral and legal responsibilities" and not simply to increase an institution's fame and prestige (The Society of American Archivists, 1992, I), it can begin to trust and understand actions that before were unfathomable. Herrada was following both her own mission statement and the Code of Ethics urging archivists to "make available documentary materials of long-term value that have lasting value to the organization or public that the archivist serves" (The Society of American Archivists, 1992, Section II). The code is (and was) useful to the public in that it gives an explanation of the basic functions of archives—which provides an understanding of how they sometimes accept unpopular acquisitions.

One last ethical issue specific to controversial acquisitions is the archivist's treatment of donors. Herrada did not condone Kaczynski's actions, and obviously recognizes the pain he had caused to numerous individuals. However, Kaczynski had the ethical right to obtain (just as Herrada had the ethical responsibility to give) fair treatment. The Code of Ethics states that archivists have the responsibility to inform donors about processes and procedures regarding use and restrictions, as well as to follow all agreements made (The Society of American Archivists, 1992, Sections IV and VIII). Herrada characterized the correspondence between archivist and donor in this situation as "candid, explanatory, direct and unambiguous" (Herrada, 2003–2004, p. 38). She emphasizes that she treated him the same way she would treat any other donor. Although there is not a lot of discussion on the treatment of controversial donors, the Code of Ethics and common sense recommends equitable dealing (Herrada, 2003–2004). This professionalism and fairness is evident in all of the procedures Herrada had to subsequently implement (discussed below). Even though Kaczynski was a convicted serial killer, his wishes and restrictions had to be enforced the same as any other donor's. In other words, Herrada had the ethical imperative to make sure that he understood the implications of his donation just as any other donor would (Greene, 1993, pp. 36–37).

Third Party Privacy and Donor Restrictions

Kaczynski had no interest in maintaining his own privacy in the collection he donated to the University of Michigan. The collection held nothing concerning his criminal activity, or contained any defamatory information not already known to the public. Kaczynski is an interesting case in this way; although he was a "celebrity" and perhaps most vulnerable to further invasion in his privacy as the most easily identifiable person in the collection (Hodson, 1991, p. 115), it was not his own confidentiality he was concerned about. Rather, he feared for the collection's misuse and the third-party privacy issues that went along with it (Herrada, 2003–2004, p. 38).

It took a long time to reach a deed of gift agreement, because Kaczynski was extremely apprehensive about possible exploitation by the media and invasion of his correspondents' privacy. He tried to impose unreasonable access and time restrictions on the collection. A deed of gift was finally signed on July 10, 1999, but getting there was not easy. Kaczynski wanted to restrict his collection to use only by "serious scholars," with the intent of keeping out journalists. The Deed of Gift Policy for the University of Michigan did not allow for donors to pick and choose those who could access their materials. Equal access was required, and discrimination not allowed (Herrada, 2003–2004, pp. 38–39). "Selective access" should not be condoned no matter how much a donor insists—it is an issue that should never be conceded to by the archive (Hodson, 2004, p. 198). The SAA Code of Ethics asserts that "reservation for exclusive use" should be avoided when possible (The Society of American Archivists, 1992, Section VIII).

Herrada had to look at his request from an ethical standpoint—granting use to some individuals, and denying it to others based solely on arbitrary feelings of the donor interferes with individuals' freedom of access to public collections. Although Kaczynski's fears may have been well founded, he sought to grant access based on "personal, political … or other biases or prejudices" (Hodson, 1991, p. 109). The Code of Ethics emphasizes the fact that restrictions had to be applied equitably, without discrimination (The Society of American Archivists, 1992, Section VIII).

Once such matters were made clear to Kaczynski, his next attempt was to restrict the collection until 2020 (with the exception of those letters that were unsigned or from the media). Although the Code of Ethics and the university's policy did not specifically prohibit it, the Labadie Collection usually tries to dissuade donors from imposing unreasonable restrictions. Herrada claimed that Kaczynski "tested their boundaries" in this respect, and although her institution's policy did not stipulate particular lengths that are unreasonable (or reasonable), she felt ethically obligated not to close the collection unless she understood his reasoning (Herrada, 2003–2004, pp. 38–39). So why was Kaczynski so set on imposing long restrictions and choosing who could view his materials? His relationship with the media was strained. He distrusted their motives, and hated their involvement in his trial (Herrada, 2003–2004, pp. 38–39).

Herrada was able to cite the guidelines present in the Code of Ethics in her dealings with Kaczynski. Section IV states that "archivists [should] discourage unreasonable restrictions on access or use, but may accept, as a condition of acquisition clearly stated restrictions ... and may occasionally suggest such restrictions to protect privacy" (The Society of American Archivists, 1992, Section IV). Herrada considered both the Code of Ethics, and Kaczynski's own concerns. She found the ethical standards on which she based her decisions (both the SAA's Code and the University of Michigan's policies) very helpful in her dealings with Kaczynski—despite the fact that the SAA in particular offered arguably ambiguous guidelines to apply on a case-by-case basis. The code was perhaps most helpful in her conveyance of her reasoning to Kaczynski (Herrada, 2003–2004, pp. 39–41). As was noted, the Code of Ethics is in existence not only to guide archivists in their daily decisions, but to inform the public on the role, rules, and policies that archives should be governed by (The Society of American Archivists, 1992, Section II).

Much has been written on the archives of celebrities, and how the ethical concerns of privacy differ for them. However, when considering the case of a celebrity's papers, it is the third parties present in their materials that are usually the biggest concern. Often archivists consider the "celebrity" to be the best source for deciding whose privacy in the collection should be protected (Hodson, 2004, pp. 195–197). Although there are legal issues in the invasion of privacy of third parties, it was the ethical rights that Herrada was concerned with. Celebrities (such as Kaczynski) have very few reasonable privacy rights. However, those people with whom Kaczynski corresponded, whether or not they retain a legal right to privacy, had the ethical right to maintain a reasonable degree of confidentiality as enabled by the archivist. This being said, deciding upon a course of protection of privacy (or merely determining what might be embarrassing to individuals) was no easy task. However, it was reasonably clear to Herrada that those who corresponded with a serial murderer might not want their identity revealed to the media (Behrnd-Klodt, 2005, p. 59). In this case, Kaczynski's own insistence to protect their privacy, combined with the common sense that most individuals would not want such correspondence revealed, made the decision somewhat easier (Hodson, 1991, p. 111).

At first, Kaczynski outlined a scenario in which a classification system based on access levels was created. This was not acceptable to Herrada, so she decided that she would have to review the correspondence to determine the necessary restrictions (Herrada, 2003–2004, p. 39). After the deed of gift was signed, and she began to process the letters, Herrada realized that Kaczynski's concerns were valid. The letters were extremely personal. She points out that "coupled with the media's attraction to the story, [she] sensed a dangerous mixture" (Herrada, 2003–2004, p. 40). More than 700 people wrote to him from everywhere—about everything. The most mundane to the most intimate stories and events were relayed. Some wrote about philosophy or the environment (topics he was associated with), while others wrote about depression or their family. Herrada notes that the variation in correspondents was staggering: "housewives, academics, teenagers, grandmothers, secretaries, anarchists, journalists, scientists, survivalists, writers, artists, mental health professionals, college students, teachers, and environmental activists, in addition to many women who were interested in initiating romantic involvement" (Herrada, 2003–2004, p. 40). Some signed their letters, others did not. But regardless, these individuals had no idea where their correspondence had found its final resting place. Herrada recounts the difficult decision: "the people never imagined their letters would end up in the archives of a public institution. This is what I was grappling with. I even lost sleep over it. ... I was now in the difficult position of being responsible for people's privacy, at the same time making a professional pledge not only to care for these materials but to make them available to the public" (Herrada, 2003–2004, pp. 40–41).

Herrada was dealing with the traditional struggle of access versus privacy. One of the most difficult ethical decisions archivists deal with is maintaining this balance (Schwarz, 2005, p. 82). Herrada found herself, "an advocate and a protector of both sides of a complex and sensitive issue" (Gaudette, 2004, pp. 21–25). And, although the Code of Ethics acknowledges that access to materials is important, it also recognizes that some of the material may be sensitive, and that the privacy of the creators and those who were the subject of the materials needs to be respected (The Society of American Archivists, 1992, Sections VII and VIII). The Code emphasizes the sensitivity of materials dealing with third parties: "archivists respect the privacy of individuals who created, or are the subjects of, documentary materials ... especially those who had no voice in the disposition of the materials" (The Society of American Archivists, 1992, Section VII).

The revision made to the code in 1992 reflected changing ideas about the necessity of privacy in archival collections, and an increased concern that archivists should pay close attention to the rights of third parties. The archival community used to prioritize access to research materials above all else. This began to change in the 1990s, as archivists were encouraged to balance this priority with third party privacy rights. The ethical code's guidelines on the subject were ambiguous at best, and difficult to apply in a standardized way. Many archivists have to come up with "creative solutions" ("Ethical Perspectives," 2005, p. 62–64). In other words, archivists and manuscript curators have to use the Code of Ethics, along with their institutions' policies, to "weigh the need for openness and the need to respect privacy rights to determine whether the release of records or information from records would constitute an invasion of privacy" (The Society of American Archivists, 1992, Section VII).

Herrada's first instinct was to close the collection for a long time. She recognized the problem in revealing the correspondents' identities, noting that she had never before in her career dealt with a contemporary collection so diverse and personal (Herrada, 2003–2004, p. 41). Time restrictions on blind donors in correspondence collections are common, useful, and often very easy to implement (Hodson, 1991, pp. 108–109). Although they discussed the idea of closing the collection until the time of all the correspondents' deaths, this would have been unfeasible (since some of them were extremely young) and could have violated the non-closure policy. In considering the situation, Herrada looked at the potential research value of indicating the correspondents' names, and realized that revealing their names would have only been valuable to the media, not researchers, and thus had the potential to seriously damage the authors for no ethical purpose (Herrada, 2003–2004, p. 41). Ultimately, it was decided to black out the authors' names and any identifying information on all individuals except for famous persons, media figures, or Kaczynski himself (Herrada, 2003–2004, pp. 41–42). Although some archivists suggest analyzing whether specific people would be embarrassed by the content of the information, the number of correspondents coupled with the difficulty in tracking them down (and the compounded messiness this might have caused) would have made this too difficult or tedious a feat (Hodson, 1991, p. 116). Rather, Herrada had to assume that most people thrown in the limelight for corresponding with a serial killer would be embarrassed.

The issue of respecting individual privacy is inextricably intertwined with the public's trust in the archival community. The conscious decision to sacrifice individuals' privacy for the goal of research or documenting a subject thoroughly compromises, as Heather MacNeil points out, the public's faith in the "integrity of the institution" (quoted in Gaudette, 2004, pp. 28–29). Actions such as these knowingly exploit the privacy of people who have no idea that their letters are in a public place (Gaudette, 2004, pp. 28–29). One advantage that Herrada had was a good working relationship with Kaczynski. When donors have an active role in making decisions regarding restrictions and privacy, "they may feel less threatened by it" (Greene, 1993, p. 36). Working with the donor's requests and respecting his or her wishes is usually considered the most ethical approach to protecting the privacy of third parties. Although Herrada used her own judgment to determine what type of privacy measures to take, completely ignoring the donor's wishes and administering one's own personal judgment calls can create an ethically messy situation. Because there were no hard and fast rules (and still are not) to govern the issues of access and privacy, often the donor is best suited to making such decisions (Greene, 1993, pp. 36–38). Additionally, respecting donor wishes follows the Code of Ethics' direction to always "observe faithfully all agreements" made with them (The Society of American Archivists, 1992, Section IV).

The Effect of the Kaczynski Acquisition
on the Wider Archival Community

From this acquisition, Herrada gained experience in collecting controversial acquisitions, becoming somewhat of an expert on the topic, as well as a proponent for it. She urges that an institution that documents local history should be collecting records that fall within its scope, "*especially* if they are controversial" (Herrada, 2003–2004, p. 43). She recognizes their potential destruction in the face of the public's misunderstanding of their historical value, and urges archivists to look at the situation from an ethical standpoint: "If we, as keepers of history, collect and protect only what is appealing, socially acceptable, or politically correct, we are hardly doing our jobs. ... We might be appalled and bewildered by some of the events of our era, but we have the resources, the social values, the context, and the perspective to thoroughly document them" (Herrada, 2003–2004, p. 44). A comparison was actually made between the collecting of materials related to underrepresented groups (like minorities) and those related to controversial or unpopular figures. Both involve the necessity of utilizing proper ethics.

Herrada has received inquiries from other institutions facing similar situations, including a collection of Timothy McVeigh's fan mail and materials related to the Branch Davidians. Both of the contacts involved in these collections had comparable concerns to those she experienced with the Kaczynski papers. If nothing else, the contacts she has received since then from archivists dealing with similar situations shows an increased awareness in the archival (if not the general) community. People recognize the validity of accessioning the controversial collections of unpopular figures, and are utilizing her experience with the Kaczynski papers to deal with issues specific to their situations (Herrada, 2003–2004, pp. 44–45).

Many view controversial acquisitions (especially of current figures) as complicated and not worthy of archivists' time and attention. Avoidance of such situations by archivists is common (Lamoree, 1995, pp. 149–150). Many seem to forget their ethical duty to be fair and professional in documentation and collection selections, simply because they are afraid of the negative publicity that may occur. One valid response to negative publicity is to argue for the documentation of evil in the face of the world forgetting it (Lamoree, 1995, p. 149–150). Herrada did not use this approach. It was not his "evil" she wished to document, but merely his radical writings. She utilized the necessary neutrality and highlighted the collection's historical significance without compromising her own or her institution's values. It was crucial that Herrada not appear to be sympathizing with Kaczynski or acting as a proponent of his ideas by accepting his collection, but merely documenting his contribution to the radical history of the United States. Again, reactive advocacy is key here.

Herrada's essay, although not overly cited in scholarly archival articles since its appearance, has definitely not been ignored. It has been the subject of student papers (Bodemer, 2005) and course readings assigned for understanding collection development and privacy rights and restrictions (Dominican University Graduate School of Library and Information Science, 2006). Her article has been frequently cited in the "zine" or "zinebrarianship" movement of late (in which Herrada herself is involved)—likely because of the Labadie Collection's contents, and its active collecting of these types of publications (Herrada, 1995).

Herrada's case study provides a platform for discussing third-party privacy rights in public and private manuscript collections. Her paper was included in the 2002 Privacy and Confidentiality Roundtable session on third-party privacy rights alongside other examples such as privacy rights in gay and lesbian archives and those of famous figures (The Society of American Archivists, 2007). Her experience has the potential to be utilized further. It is a unique case involving a controversial collection and figure, and extremely complicated privacy and ethical issues.

Impact and Aftermath at the Labadie Collection

Kaczynski's correspondence covers a diverse range of subjects, including philosophy, technology, and even mundane, everyday topics such as gardening. It holds great potential for a variety of scholarly research topics. And Herrada was right in projecting future use of the collection—scholars (and not just the media) were interested. A variety of professionals including lawyers, authors, and political theorists came to find meaning and research value in the collection (K. Johnson, 2001). The collection has been utilized by a wide array of individuals for diverse purposes, from students studying handwriting analysis to filmmakers and professors (J. Herrada, personal communication, March 16, 2009). Not surprisingly, because of the contemporary nature of the collection, and Kaczynski's recent trial, access to the material was demanded almost immediately. Although the initial requests to view the materials were from the media, researchers and scholars came later (Herrada, 2003–2004, p. 42).

When questioned about the type of impact this acquisition has had on the Labadie Collection in general, Herrada claims that it has challenged the institution in positive ways. It has forced them to think more acutely about the inherently complex privacy issues in high-profile acquisitions. Additionally, it has clarified and solidified their institution's mission to document the radical history in the United States, and "facilitate scholarly research ... [to] enhance the educational process." Herrada also notes, although no other collections have been as controversial, it has helped to educate the staff about the processes and ethical issues unusual in such collections, and how they must be individually handled (J. Herrada, personal communication, March 16, 2009).

This essay urges all archivists and manuscript curators to consider the various elements in the case. Controversy, advocacy, sensitivity to the community, media involvement, donor restrictions and third party privacy issues all played a part in complicating an already difficult situation. The material of unpopular contemporary figures provides a unique platform for showcasing and emphasizing many of the ethical dilemmas archives face to a smaller degree every day. Frank Boles argues, "in a democratic society archivists must educate the population to and advocate the need for the fullest application of the profession's collective documentary mission. Unless this advocacy and education occur, archivists' ability to perform the profession's documentary mission will erode in areas surrounded by public controversy" (Boles, 1994, p. 59). It is through defending acquisitions like the Kaczynski Papers that a more representative documentation of society will take place.

References

Adkins, E. 2007 (January 28). Preserve the Record, However Odious. *New York Times*. Retrieved April 8, 2009, from <http://query.nytimes.com/gst/fullpage.html?res=9901E0D9173FF93BA15752C0A9619C8B63>.

Archivalia. 2007. US: Unabomber's Papers. Retrieved March 16, 2009, from <http://archiv.twoday.net/stories/3697137>.

Behrnd-Klodt, M. L. 2005. The Tort Right of Privacy: What It Means for Archivists ... and for Third Parties. In Menzi L. Behrnd-Klodt and Peter J. Wosh (eds.), *Privacy and Confidentiality Perspectives: Archivists and Archival Records* (pp. 53–60). Chicago: Society of American Archivists.

Behrnd-Klodt, M. L. and P. J. Wosh. 2005. Ethical Perspectives. In Menzi L. Behrnd-Klodt and Peter J. Wosh (eds.), *Privacy and Confidentiality Perspectives: Archivists & Archival Records* (pp. 61–66). Chicago: Society of American Archivists.

Blumberg, P. 2005 (June 17). Unabomber Papers Puzzle Panel: Prosecutors Can't Explain Why They Won't Release His Documents. *San Francisco Daily Journal*. Retrieved April 8, 2009, from <http://www.cooley.com/files/tbl_s5SiteRepository/FileUpload21/481/SFDJ-ProBonoJun2005.pdf>.

Bodemer, B. *Article Critique: "Letters to the Unabomber: A Case Study and Some Reflections."* Retrieved March 20, 2009, from <http://www2.hawaii.edu/~wertheim/652BodemerHerrada.pdf>.

Boles, F. 1994. "Just a Bunch of Bigots": A Case Study in the Acquisition of Controversial Material. *Archival Issues*, 19(1), 53–65.

Dodge, C. 2005 (July/August). The New Monastic Librarians. *Utne Reader*. Retrieved from <http://www.utne.com/2005-07-01/the-new-monastic-librarians.aspx>.

Dominican University Graduate School of Library and Information Science. (2006). *LIS 775: Archival Administration and Services.* Retrieved March 31, 2009, from <https://sremote.pitt.edu/faculty/ adjunct/dbicknese/lis775/,DanaInfo=domin.dom.edu+index.htm>.

Egelko, B. 2001 (August 18). U.S. Appeals Court Rules Kaczynski Guilty Plea Stands. *SFGate.com.* Retrieved March 10, 2009, from <http://www.sfgate.com/cgi-bin/article.cgi?f=/c/a/2001/08/18/ MN66102.DTL&type=printable>.

Gaudette, M. 2003–2004. Playing Fair with the Right to Privacy. *Archival Issues*, 28(1), 21–34.

Goerler, R. E. 1999. Archives in Controversy: The Press, the Documentaries, and the Byrd Archives. *American Archivist*, 62(2), 307–324.

Greene, M. A. 1993. Moderation in Everything, Access in Nothing?: Opinions About Access Restrictions on Private Papers. *Archival Issues* 18 (1), 31–41.

Herrada, J. 1995. Zines in Libraries: A Culture Preserved. *Serials Review* (2), 79–88. doi:10.1016/0098-7913(95)90033-0.

Herrada, J. 2003–2004. Letters to the Unabomber: A Case Study and Some Reflections. *Archival Issues*, 28(1), 35–46.

Hodson, S. 1991. Private Lives: Confidentiality in Manuscripts Collections. *Rare Books and Manuscripts Librarianship*, 6(2), 108–118.

Hodson, S. 2004 (Fall/Winter). In Secret Kept, In Silence Sealed: Privacy in the Papers of Authors and Celebrities. *American Archivist*, 67(2), 194–211.

Hurley, C. 2005. Role of Archives in Protecting the Record from Political Pressure. In Margaret Procter, Michael Cook and Caroline Williams (eds.), *Political Pressure and the Archival Record* (pp. 151–171). Chicago: Society of American Archivists.

Johnson, D. 1998 (May 5). Judge Sentences Confessed Bomber to Four Life Terms. *The New York Times.* Retrieved April 1, 2009, from <http://query.nytimes.com/gst/fullpage. html?res=9A07E7DD1631F936A35756C0A96E958260>.

Johnson, K. 2001 (June 19). Library Offers Unabomber's Papers. *Nation.* Retrieved April 3, 2009, from <http://www.usatoday.com/news/nation/2001-02-19-unabomber.htm>.

Lamoree, K. M. 1995. Documenting the Difficult or Collecting the Controversial. *Archival Issues* 20 (2), 149–153.

Library Journal. 2002 (March 15). Julie Herrada: Labadie Collection, University of Michigan: Archiving Alternatives. *Library Journal.* Retrieved April 8, 2009, from <http://www.libraryjournal.com/ article/CA200618.html>.

MacNeil, H. 1990. Defining the Limits of Freedom of Inquiry: The Ethics of Disclosing Personal Information Held in Archives. *Archivaria*, 138–144.

Metzmeier, K. X. 1997. The Ethics of Disclosure: The Case of the Brown and Williamson Cigarette Papers. *Provenance*, 15, 27–36.

Schwarz, J. 2005. The Archivist's Balancing Act: Helping Researchers While Protecting Individual Privacy. In Menzi L. Behrnd-Klodt and Peter J. Wosh (eds.). *Privacy and Confidentiality Perspectives: Archivists and Archival Records* (pp. 82–92). Chicago: Society of American Archivists.

The Society of American Archivists. 1992. *Code of Ethics for Archivists and Commentary, 1992*. Retrieved March 1, 2009, from Center for the Study of Ethics in the Professions at IIT, <http://ethics.iit.edu/codes/coe/soc.amer.archivists.1992.html>.

The Society of American Archivists. 2007. *2002–2003 Annual Report: Privacy and Confidentiality Roundtable*. Retrieved March 1, 2009, from <https://sremote.pitt.edu/saagroups/privacy/,DanaInfo=www.archivists.org,SSL+pc2003.asp>.

The Society of American Archivists. 2008. *Code of Ethics for Archivists, 2008*. Retrieved March 1, 2009, from Center for the Study of Ethics in the Professions at IIT, <http://www.archivists.org/governance/handbook/app_ethics.asp>.

Reading 6.2

Domestic Violence as Entertainment: Gender, Role Congruity and Reality Television

By Carol M. Liebler, Azeta Hatef, and Greg Munno

T HE PURPOSE OF THIS STUDY WAS to examine how young adults react to televised domestic violence in reality TV, with particular attention to how gender factors into perceptions of acceptability. Domestic violence is defined here as behavior used to control another person that may be physical or emotional, and includes physical harm or name calling. It may occur regardless of class, race, marital status, sexual orientation or living arrangements, and in both public and private spaces.

Domestic violence in the United States is a significant public health concern, with 54 million Americans reporting they have been a victim of domestic violence (No More, 2013) and nearly 25% of women and 14% of men experiencing severe physical violence by an intimate partner (NISVS, 2010). Perpetrators of domestic violence are most likely to be male and 18–35 years old, and victims are most likely female, with increased risk to young women (Klein, 2009). In June of 2013 the World Health Organization released a report highlighting violence against women "as a global health problem of epidemic proportions" (www.who.int, 2013).

Popular culture's daily diet of aggression, including domestic violence, may contribute to this epidemic. If such aggression goes unchallenged in music or television content, it becomes more acceptable, even normalized. In fact, mediated narratives of domestic violence hold messages of tolerance for men and of blame for women (Nettleton, 2011), and such content is disseminated into a cultural space in which domestic violence is rarely discussed interpersonally (No More, 2013).

There is little question that the television landscape is filled with aggression of all types, a phenomenon that has been documented for many years. This study focuses on reality television, a genre that has increased in popularity over the past decade (Nielsen, 2011), and one that has particular potential to resonate with viewers. Reality TV captures "real" people engaging in "real" activities, and viewers are therefore more likely to relate to characters and to imitate behavior (Coyne, Robinson & Nelson, 2010). Indeed, one gratification obtained from reality TV viewing is personal utility (Barton, 2009). And although there is evidence that there is less physical aggression in reality TV than in television dramas, there is more relational aggression than in other program genres, that is, behavior harming a relationship or social environment (Coyne, Robinson & Nelson, 2010). Such aggression is likely to be portrayed as justified and lacking consequences (Smith, Nathanson & Wilson, 2002), which makes it more likely to stimulate aggressive acts (Anderson, Berkowtiz, Donnerstein, Huesmann, Johnson, Linz, Malmuth & Wartella, 2003). Other research indicates that affinity for the programming increases with perceived realism (Papacharissi & Mendelson, 2007).

The programs applied in this study, *Jersey Shore*, *Real World*, and *Teen Mom*, all center on relationships and often on romance. Viewing romantically oriented programs is related to idealized perceptions of relationships (Eggermont, 2004) and is a predictor of sexually-oriented conversations among girls and of boys' perceptions of peers' sexual experience (Vandenbosch & Eggermont, 2011). In fact, viewers consider romance to be a salient characteristic of reality television (Nabi, 2007). Such findings make the incidence of domestic violence in such programming all the more worthy of attention since viewers may be tuning in specifically to watch relationships, Furthermore, reality television is filled with stereotypical gender roles (e.g., Edwards, 2004), with past studies indicating that its gendered content leads to cultivation among young viewers (e.g., Signorielli & Kahlenberg, 2001; Signorielli, 1989). Indeed, many young women believe regular viewing of reality television normalizes fighting in a romantic relationship (www.girlscouts.org), and college women who are heavy television viewers are more likely to accept rape myths (Kahlor & Morrison, 2007). No academic research, however, has examined televised domestic violence in relation to audience perceptions.

Views of Domestic Violence

People generally agree that physical acts such as punching or forced sex constitute domestic violence, although less agreement is found for forms of verbal aggression or behaviors such as stalking (Carlson & Worden, 2005). As the present study focuses on perceived acceptability of televised domestic violence, it is important to examine research on the public's tolerance of it.

Generally, there is emphasis on the female's role in instigating or being somewhat deserving/responsible for the violence toward her, the public places blame elsewhere than on the perpetrator, such as on "personality characteristics or defects and alcohol abuse" (Worden & Carlson, 2005, p. 1221). Worden and Carlson note a very troubling finding in that people underestimate the difficulties of getting out of a toxic relationship. The level of emotional dependence and fear of further harm are not considered and the victim is to blame for her or his situation. Although the public may blame the victim, research shows that there is an understanding that domestic violence is diffused throughout the population. A survey administered in the state of California to assess the perceptions of domestic violence found an overwhelming number of respondents believed that anyone could be a victim of domestic violence regardless of their gender, age, race or socio-economic background. Further, respondents believe that children who are exposed to violent behavior in a domestic relationship are more likely to develop anger problems and have mental health issues. The effects of domestic violence on friends and family were also surveyed and the results show that two-thirds of Californians say they have a friend or family member who has been in a domestic violence relationship (Blue Shield, 2012). Aligning with the Center for Disease Control's national survey (2010), a third of women and a fourth of men experience some form of domestic violence and the likelihood of knowing a victim or abuser may be high. Domestic violence is not discriminatory towards age, race, gender or economic background as shown by the research.

Role Congruity and Gender

Role Congruity theory specifies that members of groups are evaluated more positively when they conform to what is socially or culturally expected of that group. When it comes to gender, women and men are situated in specific roles, and these roles, while frequently stereotypical carry expectations. Therefore, women and men's behaviors are viewed through the lens of what is perceived as normative for their gender, or in other words, they are judged whether they fit into a traditional feminine or masculine binary.

Eagly (1987), who first conceptualized role congruity theory, discussed normative assessments of women and men in relation to aggressive behaviors, consistent with the type of content evaluated in the present study. According to Eagly, aggression as a social behavior

Real World

is categorized as more relevant to role behavior among men than women, with men more likely to be viewed as aggressive, competitive and tough. Similarly Gunter, Harrison and Wykes (2003) reported that men and women interpret violence in relationships differently. Men are more likely to support aggressive behavior in various situations and overall women find violence in relationships more serious than men. However men and women alike find violent behavior from a woman more acceptable. These judgments can be explained by the different ways that men and women think of violence. Women typically use aggression to express their emotions whereas men use it to control a situation.

Some domestic violence researchers suggest that women tend to use violence as a factor in conflict whereas men use it as a means to control someone else, specifically their significant other in a domestic relationship. Therefore, the types of violence carried out by men and women are very different. Women's violence, "is far less injurious and less likely to be motivated by attempts to dominate or terrorize their partners" (Kimmel, 2002, p. 1356). There is some evidence that reported cases of physical aggression from women are equal to that of men, yet cases where injuries are reported are much higher among women (Archer, 2000, p. 651). Aggression from women may seem more acceptable because it is not threatening, i.e., it does not typically lead to injury. Yet, aggressive behavior from a woman may be viewed as unacceptable because she is behaving outside of her gender role. Traditionally, aggressive behavior for women is in the form of indirect or relational aggression, i.e., "spreading malicious gossip, socially excluding others from the group, destroying another's property, and displacing aggression on objects" (Gunter, Harrison & Wykes, 2003, p. 134). In contrast, it may be more acceptable for a man to behave violently and more physically as it is within his gender role. The socialization of aggression and violence makes it acceptable for men to behave more aggressively than women, thereby reinforcing traditional binaries of masculinity and femininity.

Teen Mom

Aligning with gender-role stereotypes, men are viewed as more threatening than women, even when the woman is the perpetrator. This idea is supported by the claim that men are more likely to injure their victim than women are. Thus, people are more accepting/tolerant of violent behavior between gay and lesbian partners or relationships where the woman is the perpetrator because they are thought of as less threatening (Seelau & Seelau, 2005). Yet although people may find a male perpetrator in a male-female relationship is the most serious, his aggressiveness has been normalized as a trait of masculine behavior. Consistent with this line of inquiry, and particularly germane to the present study, is Carlsen and Worden's (2005) analysis of perceptions of domestic violence. They found that respondents were more likely to label behaviors as domestic violence and to find the behavior unlawful if the perpetrator was male: "This so-called double standard may simply reflect unspoken assumptions about men's greater potential for inflicting injuries, projections about likely police reactions to these briefly described incidents, or internalization of public education and media images of DV as a crime committed by men against women" (p. 1214).

In the present context, role congruity theory provides a framework to examine viewers' possible application of binaries to television content, and to explore the degree to which behaviors are perceived as more or less acceptable depending on how they align with normative gender roles. Based on the above literature, this study examines the following questions.

RQ1: How acceptable do male and female viewers find domestic violence in reality TV?
RQ2: How does the gender of the aggressor and victim affect perceived acceptability?

Method

This study employed a focus group method with a volunteer convenience sample. Participants were recruited through undergraduate classes with an incentive of a $25 gift card raffle per session. Data were collected in eight sessions at a mid-sized northeastern university. Of the eight sessions, six were mixed in gender and two sessions were divided by gender (one session all female and one all male) because of the social constructionist nature of focus groups and the possible influence of status (Hollander, 2004). Sessions were approximately 75 minutes in length and averaged 10 participants per session. They included completing pre and post-viewing questionnaires, rating an edited 24-minute video of content from three reality TV programs, and focus group discussions. Each participant was assigned a number to facilitate data collection and help maintain anonymity. The Institutional Review Board approved the protocol.

Pre-viewing questionnaire. Sessions began with the collection of basic demographic and television viewing habits of each participant. Participants were also asked how frequently (never, occasionally, frequently, always) they watch Teen Mom, Jersey Shore and Real World.

Video stimulus and rating. Participants viewed the 24-minute video and used a perception analyzer system to rate in real time, moment-to-moment, how much they personally approved of the content they were viewing. Approval was based on how acceptable the participant found the content based on their personal evaluation and judgment of acceptable behavior. The dials ranged from 1–100, with 50 as the neutral point. A rating of "1" indicated that the participant found the video content completely unacceptable whereas "100" meant that the participant found the video content completely acceptable. The edited video provided clips of episodes from three programs (Jersey Shore, Teen Mom, The Real World) and included scenes of both aggressive and non-aggressive behaviors so as not to prime participants to the focus the study. These scenes included aggression between significant others, housemates and/or friends. The three programs are primetime shows on the MTV network, and were selected for the popularity and high viewership among young adults. Season four of Teen Mom averaged 2.38 million viewers, Jersey Shore averaged 3.13 viewers in its sixth season and The Real World averaged 1.39 million viewers in 2011 during the San Diego season, the season used in this study (Bibel, 2012; German, 2011).

Post-viewing questionnaire. The video-rating part of the session was followed with a post-viewing questionnaire in which participants were asked to rate on a Likert scale (1 strongly disagree to a 5 strongly agree) their attitudes toward and personal experiences with aggression. For example, "the material viewed in this video is reflective of real life situations," "sometimes raising your voice in an argument is necessary," and "an argument with a friend/ significant other has resulted in me raising my voice/engaging in a physical altercation."

Focus group discussion. Each viewing was followed by a videotaped discussion that probed why the participants responded to the content in the ways they did. After monitoring participant reactions to the video, the moderator asked specific questions about scenes that received either relatively positive or negative responses in each session.

Analysis. Participants were exposed to 14 scenes of relational aggression, rating those scenes on a 100-point scale for discussion and analysis purposes, the different types of aggression in the edited video were categorized as either verbal (swearing, threatening or using hostile language towards another person) or physical aggression (engaging in a physical alteration with another person). In some cases, the scene included both forms of aggression.

Violence was further categorized into four categories girl on girl, girl on guy, guy on guy and guy on girl. These categorizations described the aggression and victim of the violent behavior, i.e., girl on guy means the female cast member was the perpetrator and the victim was a man.

The perception analyzer data were downloaded and analyzed with SPSS, as were the quantitative measures from the two questionnaires. All focus group discussions were videotaped and transcribed. Transcripts were uploaded to the online program DeDoose and coded for relevancy by question and other emergent themes. The excerpts below were taken verbatim from the transcripts, that is, they were not edited for grammar or wordiness.

Results

A total of 80 undergraduate (61 female, 19 male) students participated in the study. Of these, 52 (65%) classified themselves as white, 9 (11.3%) as Asian or Asian American, 7 (8.8%) as Black, 5 (6.3%) as Hawaiian/Pacific Islander, 4 (5.0%) as Mixed Race and 3 (3.8%) as Other. Most participants (96.3%) fell between the ages of 18–20. Participants reported watching Jersey Shore (68.8%) more frequently than the Real World (40%) or Teen Mom (30%).

Generally, participants did not find the domestic violence on the three shows very acceptable, but the degree of acceptability varied. Overall, participants found verbal aggression more palatable than physical aggression. Men rated the aggression depicted, be it verbal or physical, as more acceptable than women did, and many of those differences were significant (details below). Moreover, the gender of the aggressor and victim seemed to matter as did the context of the aggression. Some of these aggressive acts were between housemates or friends, whereas others were between significant others.

Men rated the composite violence measures for each individual show as more acceptable than women did (on the 100 point scale with 1 being completely unacceptable), although only for Teen Mom were those differences significant, men = 41.06, women = 29.02, 12.86 $p < .05$. Men also rated the composite scores for all the violent scenes (M = 35.19) as more acceptable than women (M = 28.27), but this difference was not statistically significant. For the verbal only scenes, men averaged a 42.97 acceptability rating, and women a 35.90; this result approached significance at $p < .06$.

Overall, participants found it more acceptable for men than women to engage in physical aggression. Of the 14 scenes of aggression shown to participants, eight depicted physical violence. Within those, men were the aggressors in five scenes, women in three. Participants gave the scenes featuring male physical aggression an average rating of 32.76, which is on the negative end of the scale, but nonetheless significantly more acceptable than the average 26.94 rating they gave women aggressors, $t = 4.88$, $p < .001$.

Of the 14 scenes, six featured women aggressors, with three scenes in which they limited their aggression to verbal attacks, and three who also engaged in physical attacks. On average, viewers rated the verbal attacks by women (M = 39.87) as significantly more acceptable than physical attacks by women (M = 26.94), $t = 9.489$, $p < .001$.

The aggression found most acceptable was verbal aggression of a woman toward a man in Teen Mom (M = 62.67). Least acceptable, again from Teen Mom, was a scene of physical violence between two women (M = 15.65).

Men rated the aggression shown within each segment as more acceptable than women. Men gave instances of girl-on-girl aggression an average rating of 33.48, while woman gave such scenes a 24.08 mean rating, t = 2.25, p < .05. For girl-on-guy violence the difference between men (M = 45.84) and women (M = 35.68) was also significant, t = 24.54, p < .05. Women rated guy-on-girl violence (M = 28.22) lower than men (M = 37.23) did, and the pattern held for scenes of guy-on-guy violence, with men giving such scenes a 40.19 mean rating and women a 37.81. These differences were not significant.

The finding that male participants found the content more acceptable than female participants reflects their own lives and experiences. Questionnaire items queried the extent to which participants found it necessary to resort to physical aggression or to raising their voice (1 = strongly disagree, 5 = strongly agree). Male participants (M = 2.16) were significantly more likely than women (M = 1.43) to perceive the need to "get physical" in a confrontation (t = 3.36, p < .001) and to have gotten physical with a friend (t = 5.07, p < .001). They were not, however, significantly more likely to report having gotten physical with a significant other, although the t statistic approached significance. Notably, both men and women reported having raised their voice to a significant other. [I]n every instance men had higher means than women, whether referring to physical or verbal aggression.

The focus group discussion provided insight into the circumstances under which our participants tolerated televised domestic violence. Some criticized the violence and found it unacceptable but others focused on blaming the victim.

To start, many male participants rationalized the violence. Take for example the following excerpt from the all male group, in relation to a scene in Jersey Shore in which Jenni is pushed by her boyfriend, Roger:

P2: Well when he was like I knew it was you the whole time 'cause the whole time she was like thinking like 'oh he didn't think it was me so it's okay,' but then he was like 'I knew it was you.'

M: Right.

P2: And he pushed her.

MOD: Right.

P4: When you're in the process of fighting someone, you're not really like seeing anybody else, you're just seeing the person. So, she's trying to come in between—I mean first of all, that's not her place because he's huge compared to her.

MOD: Uh huh.

P4: Like if he sees her yeah, it's not like 'oh my god that's my girlfriend I have to stop,' like he was kind of like 'get out of the way because I need to get the guy'.

MOD: Uh huh.

P4: So it kind of like—I see how you know, it looks bad because he pushed his girlfriend and she like broke her foot but at the same time they're both big guys like you shouldn't get in the middle of that.

P10: I agree that girls should stay out of a guy's fight.

In other words, these male viewers blamed Jenni for getting pushed, not her boyfriend for having pushed her. But they were not alone in this view. More than one female viewer agreed with them, as exemplified here: "She should have just stayed out of it. Like, it wasn't her fight, like, it wasn't her battle, she should've just stepped back."

On the other hand, many female participants were disconcerted at the implication that Jenni was to blame. One young women referenced a scene in which Roger's friends are discussing the incident "um and then you saw like the other guys eating lunch or something ... and they were saying like oh yeah like women should never get involved, like it's her fault for like trying to get in the middle of things like so like justifying, that it was okay for him to like push her because she was out of like her place."

Several other participants were troubled that Jenni ultimately blames herself for getting hurt and explicitly tells Roger "It's not your fault you didn't recognize me." One young woman put it this way "I think it's bad too like, she like kind a like, she like, felt bad about it almost. She felt bad that he pushed her you know. She was like she was like, yeah I totally think it's fine that he pushed me essentially, is what she was saying ... and uh she wasn't even mad about the fact that like he was like, yeah I should yeah I did mean to push you."

The Teen Mom clip, in which Janelle fights with her roommate and is also pushed roughly into a car by her boyfriend, Kieffer, elicited strong reactions from our participants. Both the most and least acceptable scenes were from this show, and over all, men found the aggression in this show significantly more acceptable than the women did but they too were at times uncomfortable. For example, here is an exchange between male participants that touches on both girl-on-girl and guy-on-girl violence.

P3: I thought the catfight was cool.

MOD: The catfight was cool?

P3: I don't mind. In a movie, like, if, it were like an actual movie like in Batman, I thought that, like, whatever, I forgot whatever her name was [pause] Catwoman, I thought that was pretty cool watching like a chick just kick ass.

P1: I mean I just thought it was a little more like, it was like mellow and controlled. I guess the girl fight, like, it was kind of just like okay with that. Whereas when the guy and her started fighting, it was like it wasn't like I was nervous but I was just, like, he's gonna hit her of course, there it goes like, okay, like, American culture.

MOD: Because, because

P5: Like he threw her in the car and, like, pushed her.

P1: That was like a little more threatening, I think, than the two girls.

A number of participants, both male and female, found the violent scenes funny, or at least, the content was not something to be taken seriously:

P3(F): I think it's all, like just funny how stupid it is, like how ridiculous it is like when they were fighting in Teen Mom, I was like dying.

P2(F): Um I think it's, like, I think everything's really funny but I think Jenelle was, like, completely crazy and stupid.

And from a different session:

P12(M): Uh it was the girl that, like, uh who had a horrible voice from Teen Mom, just, like, kept going back to her boyfriend.

MOD: Jenelle?

P12(M): Oh she's the worst.

[Laughter]

P12(M): If I met her I wouldn't, I wouldn't be able to handle myself. She was like a child … well technically she is a teen mom but you know.

[Laughter]

P11(F): I just like didn't like how they have babies at that age.

Across these programs, however, many female participants expressed concern over what they saw as an endorsement for the domestic violence they viewed and were concerned that reality programming normalizes such aggression. Said one young woman: " ... my least favorite part was in, like, Teen Mom when she, like, went back to him. That just made me so upset, like, inside." Others spoke at more length:

> um I don't like the whole domestic violence thing either 'cause I feel it's like the image that that's normal behavior that you should just be ... that if your boyfriend or that your girlfriend hits you or you hit your boyfriend that that's acceptable behaviors and you can just hug and make up in five minutes like you said. 'Cause I really don't think that that should happen. I don't think that that's normal at all so if any of my boyfriends ever hit one of my friends, like, it would not just be okay like that.
>
> Right after seeing them make up like nothing happened and how, like, the girl from Teen Mom and Jenni from uh Jersey Shore how the day after they're, like, hugging them, saying they love them. What is that? That message telling young girls like just, like people taking something away from the show is like saying 'oh look the guy pushed them, abused them in some way' and you know the day after they're fine.

Consistently, it was the women viewers who highlighted the possible effects of this type of content. But it is noteworthy that many of them expressed sentiments that were indicative of third person effect (e.g., Leone, Chapman Peek & Bissell, 2006; Scharrer, 2002; Hoffner, et al., 2001). That is, they pointed to possible effects of the content they had viewed, but always in terms of effects on others, not themselves. In particular, these young women perceived viewers younger than themselves as more vulnerable to negative effects. For example:

> I just don't think that it has anything like—there is no positive value whatsoever to society, like, like a person, like, throwing things on the ground, like, shattering like glass, like that's not in any shape, way, shape or form like positive. Like, god forbid, like, a little kid sees it in, like, passing and, like, tries to do the same thing, like, that's not good.
>
> So that, those kinds of patterns I think subconsciously you know if you're in a loving relationship where the girls think, like 'oh yeah it was a mistake, they were intoxicated' take them back the next day, like, I just think that message, that overall message just ... just like how things like Rihanna and public— publically now dating Chris Brown and her fans like young girls like that. Like, I just think that has a lot—that has a big effect on young girls.

Discussion

This study has examined how young adults respond to televised domestic violence, and specifically, how acceptable they find reality television portrayals of both verbal and physical aggression for both men and women. Our findings indicate that consistent with role congruity theory, level of acceptability varies contextually and with gender.

The scenes shown to our participants were illustrative of the complexity surrounding what is considered domestic violence, and where, when and how it takes place. Our participants made clear distinctions in their assessments of the various victims and aggressors, and the types of violence shown.

First off, the gender of the aggressor and victim mattered. The perception analyzer data reveal for all participants an order of acceptability: guy-guy, girl-guy, guy-girl, girl-girl. The type of aggression affected acceptability also, with verbal aggression deemed less problematic than physical aggression, although this was less true for male aggressors. These findings align with role congruity theory in that it is socially expected for men to behave more aggressively than women: "boys will be boys." Therefore, participants may be been more inclined to positively evaluate aggressive behavior from men as it conforms to what is socially and culturally expected of them. In contrast, participants may have rated aggressive behavior between two women the least acceptable because it deviates from the social script for feminine behavior, although the focus group data did indicate an element of male gazing, in which our male participants enjoyed watching, in the words of one of them, "a cat fight." A woman aggressing against a man was likely perceived as less threatening (Seelau & Seelau, 2005) and therefore more acceptable.

The gender of the participant factored in as well, with data, both quantitative and qualitative, indicating that male participants found the aggression more acceptable than female participants. This finding, coupled with those above, is characteristic of the culture of hypermasculinity in which men are socialized into and expected to perform aggressively and even violently, including callousness about women and sex (Jhally, 2013; Scharrer, 2005).

Interestingly, although our participants did not score scenes of domestic violence as highly acceptable, neither did their ratings come in at the bottom of the scale. All of the scenes were found acceptable to at least a minimal degree with some ratings surprisingly high. Notably, acceptability was even more manifest in the focus group discussions, especially in the all-male group moderated by a man.

The focus group discussion revealed a tendency for at least some of our participants to blame the victim, especially when the victim was female. This finding is illustrative of the larger cultural narrative whereby women victims are blamed for transgressions against them (Friedman & Johnston, 2013; Meyers, 2004; Berns, 2001). Friedman & Johnston (2013, p. 180) argue that in news content, blame is often focused on the individual not on the broader "societal or cultural values that produce the violence." The same was true of our focus group participants who were considerably more likely to blame an individual character than the broader social context. Moreover, the content itself did little to advance an understanding of the causes and consequences of abusive relationships.

Although considerable effort was made to recruit an even number of men and women for our study, women responded in greater numbers to our incentive. Perhaps the topic simply appealed to women more than men; regardless, the small sample size for the male participants constrained our quantitative analyses. Another possible limitation of our study was social desirability. Although the perception analyzer system is a relatively unobtrusive measure, survey questionnaires and focus group discussions are not. It is possible that our participants responded in a "politically corrective" fashion, rather than share their true feelings and experiences about domestic violence, although we felt that the focus group sessions stratified by gender helped to minimize this concern. Finally, the scenes in our edited tape were largely heteronormative. Although the Real World excerpts included a gay character, the violence shown was between roommates, not lovers. We suggest future research incorporate more and varied scenes of domestic violence across genre types.

Jersey Shore, Real World and Teen Mom do not include warnings about domestic violence in their content. Yet this genre of reality programming glamorizes dramatic behavior such as yelling, hitting and kicking, all for the purposes of entertainment as viewers become voyeurs of troubled relationships. A notice from The National Domestic Violence Hotline precedes scenes with blatant physical aggression, and although such mobilizing information may be helpful, it is hardly sufficient when flashed on the screen too briefly for viewers to fully process the message. Our findings indicate that the programs tap into and reinforce a culture of hyper-masculinity and victim blaming, leaving some viewers troubled but others laughing.

References

Anderson, C. A., Berkowitz, L., Donnerstein, E., Huesmann, L. R., Johnson, J., Linz, D., Malamuth, N., Wartella, E. (2003). The influence of media violence on youth. *Psychological Science in the Public Interest*: 4(3): 81–110.

Archer, J. (2000). Sex differences in aggression between heterosexual partners: a meta-analytic review. *Psychological Bulletin*, 126 (5), 651.

Barton, K. M. (2009). Reality television programming and diverging gratifications: The influence of content on gratifications obtained. *Journal of Broadcasting & Electronic Media*, 53(3): 460–476.

Berns, N. (2001). Degendering the problem and gendering the blame: Political discourse on women and violence. *Gender and Society*, 15(2): 262–281.

Bibel, S. (2012). MTV brings the original 'Teen Mom' cast back for two emotional specials in October. Retrieved from http://tvbythenumbers.zap2it.com/2012/09/19/mtv-brings-the-original- teen-mom-cast-back-for-two-emotional-specials-in- october/149252/

Bibel, S. (2012). MTV bids farewell to 'Jersey Shore' with a seven day marathon. Retrieved from http://tvbythenumbers.zap2it.com/2012/12/11/mtv-bids-farewell-to-jersey-shore-with-a-seven-day-marathon/161254/

Blue Shield of California Foundation. (2012). Groundbreaking New Poll Finds Adults In California Believe Domestic Violence Can Happen to Anyone; Educating Youth on Domestic Violence is Key to Preventing and Reducing it. Retrieved from http://www.blueshieldcafoundation.org/sites/default/files/publications/ downloadable/Blue_Shield_Domestic_Violence_256- A_Public_Memo_10-12_Final.pdf

Carlson, B. E. & Worden, A.P. (2005). Attitudes and beliefs about domestic violence: Results of a public opinion survey. *Journal of Interpersonal Violence*, 20(10), 1197–1218.

Coyne, S. M., Robinson, S. I., & Nelson, D. A. (2010). Does reality backbite? Physical, verbal, and relational aggression in reality television programs. *Journal of Broadcasting & Electronic Media*, 54(2), 282–298.

Creative Communications Group. (2009). Domestic violence should not happen to anybody ... Ever ... Period! Retrieved from http://www.domesticviolence.org/definition/

Dovidio, J., Hewstone, M., Glick, P. & Esses, V. (Eds.). (2010). *The SAGE handbook of prejudice, stereotyping and discrimination*. Thousand Oaks, CA: SAGE Publications.

Eagly, A. (1987). *Sex differences in social behavior*. Hillsdale, NJ: Lawrence Erlbaum Associates.

Edwards, L. H. (2004). 'What a girl wants': Gender norming on reality game shows. *Feminist Media Studies*, 4(2), 226–228.

Eggermont, S. (2004). Television viewing, perceived similarity, and adolescents' expectations of a romantic partner. *Journal of Broadcasting and Electronic Media*, 48(2): 244–265.

Friedman, B. & Johnston, A. (2013). Blame narratives: News discourses of sex trafficking. *Media disparity: A gender battleground* (C. Armstrong, ed.): 177–190. Lanham: Lexington Books.

Gerbner, G., Gross, L., Morgan, M., & Signorielli, N. (1982). Charting the mainstream: Television's contributions to political orientations. *Journal of Communication*, 32(2), 100–127.

Girl Scout Research Institute. (2011). Real to me: Girls and reality TV. Retrieved from http://www.girlscouts.org/research/pdf/real_to_me_factsheet.pdf

Gorman, B. (2011). MTV invades the sunny beaches of San Diego when 'The Real World' premieres with a new season on Wednesday, September 28. Retrieved from http://tvbythenumbers.zap2it.com/2011/09/15/mtv-invades-the-sunny-beaches-of-san-diego-when-"the-real-world"-premieres-with-a-new-season-on-wednesday-september-28/103877/

Hoffner, C., Plotkin, R. S., Buchanan, M., Anderson, J. D., Kamigaki, S. K., Hubbs, L. A., Kowalczyk, L., Silberg, S., & Pastorek, A. (2001). The Third-Person effect in perceptions of the influence of television violence. *Journal of Communication*, 51(2), 283–299.

Hollander, J.A. (2004), The social contexts of focus groups. *Journal of Contemporary Ethnography*. 33(5), 502–637.

Jhally, S. (Producer), & Earp, J. (Director). (2013). *Tough Guise 2: Violence, Manhood and American Culture*. United States: A Media Education Foundation Production.

Kahlor, L. A., & Morrison, D. (2007). Television viewing and rape myth acceptance among college women. *Sex Roles*, 56 (11/12), 729–739.

Kimmel, M. S. (2002). "Gender Symmetry" in Domestic Violence: A Substantive and Methodological Research Review. *Violence against Women*, 8(11), 1332–1363.

Klein, A.R. (2009). Practical implications of current domestic violence research: For law enforcement, prosecutors and judges. Washington, DC: U.S. Department of Justice.

Leone, R., Chapman Peek, W. & Bissell, K. L. (2006). Reality television and third-person perception. *Journal of Broadcasting & Electronic Media*, 50(2): 253–269.

Meyers, M. (2004). African American women and violence: gender, race and class in news. *Critical Studies in Media Communication*, 21(2): 95–118.

Nabi, R. L. (2007). Determining dimensions of reality: A cognitive mapping of reality TV programs. *Journal of Broadcasting & Electronic Media*, 51, 371—389.

National center for injury prevention and control: Division of violence prevention. (2010). Intimate partner violence in the United States. Retrieved from http://www.cdc.gov/violenceprevention/pdf/cdc_nisvs_ipv_report_2013_vl7_single_a.pdf

Nettleton, P. H. (2011). Domestic violence in men's and women's magazines: Women are guilty of choosing the wrong men, men are not guilty of hitting women. *Women's Studies in Communication*, 4:139–160.

Nielsen (2011, Sept. 21). 10 years of primetime: The rise of reality and sports programming. Retrieved from http://www.nielsen.com/us/en/newswire/20U/10-years-of-primetime-the-rise-of-reality-and-sports-programming.html

No More (2013, Sept. 26). Study finds sexual and domestic violence widespread, largely undiscussed. Retrieved from http:// nomore.org/cbs-news-study-finds-sexual-and-domestic-violence-widespread-largely-undiscussed/

Papacharissi, Z. & Mendelson, A.L. (2007). An exploratory study of reality appeal: Uses and gratifications of reality TV shows. *Journal of Broadcasting & Electronic Media*, 51(2): 355–370.

Scharrer, E. (2005). Hypermasculinity, aggression, and television violence: An experiment. *Media Psychology*, 7(4), 353–376.

Scharrer, E. (2002). Third-Person Perception and Television Violence: The Role of Out-Group Stereotyping in Perceptions of Susceptibility to Effects. *Communication Research*, 29(6), 681–704.

Seelau, S. M., & Seelau, E. P. (2005). Gender-role stereotypes and perceptions of heterosexual, gay and lesbian domestic violence. *Journal of Family Violence*, 20(6), 363–371.

Signorielli, N. (1989). Television and conceptions about sex roles: Maintaining conventionality and the status quo. *Sex Roles*, 21(5/6), 337–356.

Signorielli, N. & Kahlenberg S. (2001). "Television's World of Work in the Nineties." *Journal of Broadcasting & Electronic Media* 45.1: 4–22.

Smith, S. L., Nathanson, A. L, & Wilson, B. J. (2002). Prime time television: Assessing violence during the most popular viewing hours. *Journal of Communication*, 52(1), 84–111.

Vanderbosch, L. & Eggermont, S. (2011). Temptation Island, The Bachelor, Joe Millionaire: A prospective cohort study on the role of romantically themed reality television in adolescents' sexual development. *Journal of Broadcasting & Electronic Media*, 55:4, 563–580.

World Health Organization. (2013). WHO report highlights violence against women as a 'global health problem of epidemic proportion.' Retrieved from http://www.who.int/mediacentre/news/releases/2013/violence_against_women_20130620/en/

1. How do popular culture and media entertainment affect our perceptions of serial killers and violent crime?
2. Name some specific incorrect portrayals of serial killer traits given to popular fictional serial killer characters.
3. Despite the public shootings and mass casualties we suffer in society, why do you think the violence not only continues but appears to be growing?
4. What do you think about the controversy surrounding the sale of murderabilia? Should it be allowed or made illegal? Why do you feel that way?
5. Does murderabilia serve a purpose beyond monetary benefit or personal possession?
6. How might popular reality shows promote aggression toward women?
7. What is "role incongruity," and how does this affect the way people view violence?
8. Under what circumstances does our society "blame the victim"?

Image Credits

References

Chicago Tribune. (2006). Evolving science challenges old arson convictions. http://www.chicagotribune.com

Criminal Legal News. (2022). The pseudoscientific practice of blood spatter analysis. www.criminallegalnews.org

Cullen, D. (2009). *Columbine*. Twelve Books Publishing, Hachette Book Group.

DiBiase, T. A. (2015). *No-body homicide cases: A practical guide to investigating, prosecuting, and winning cases when the Victim is missing*. CRC Press, Taylor and Francis Group.

"DNA exonerations in the United States (1989–2020)." (2020). Research Resources, Innocence Project. https://innocenceproject.org/dna-exonerations-in-the-united-states/

Douglas, J., Burgess, A., & Ressler, R. (1995). *Sexual homicide: Patterns and motives*. The Free Press.

Finnis, A. (2021, March 11). What happened to James Bulger? The harrowing story of the boy murdered by Jon Venables and Robert Thompson. *I News UK*. https://inews.co.uk/news/uk/james-bulger-what-happened-death-murder-killers-jon-venables-robert-thompson-907387

Gardner, R. M., & Bevel, T. (2009). *Practical crime scene analysis and reconstruction*. CRC Press, Taylor and Francis Group.

Hunt, P. (2016). *First estimates of judicial costs of specific crimes, from homicide to theft*. Researcher Spotlight, RAND Corporation Media Resources, Office of Media Relations.

Kotlowitz, A. (1999, April 18). A bad seed? *New York Times*. https://www.nytimes.com/1999/04/18/books/a-bad-seed.html

Leonard, K. (2013, December 18). Murderabilia: When does a fascination with crime go too far? *U.S. News and World Report*. https://www.usnews.com/news/articles/2013/12/18/murderabilia-when-does-a-fascination-with-crime-go-too-far

Lowrey, A. (2010, October 21). True crime costs. *Slate*. https://slate.com/culture/2010/10/does-every-murder-in-the-united-states-really-cost-society-17-million.html

Miller, S. (2016). *The Borden murders: Lizzie Borden and the trial of the century*. Schwartz and Wade, Penguin Random House Canada.

National Academy of Sciences. (2004). News release, FBI-commissioned study on bullet lead analysis. Archives.fbi.gov/archives/news

National Resource Center on Domestic Violence (NRCDV). (2022). The scope of the problem: Partner homicide statistics. https://vawnet.org/sc/scope-problem-intimate-partner-homicide-statistics

"Overturning wrongful convictions involving misapplied forensics." (n.d.). Innocence Project. https://innocenceproject.org/overturning-wrongful-convictions-involving-flawed-forensics/

Porter, R. (2020, June 20). TV long view: How much network TV depends on cop shows. *The Hollywood Reporter*. https://www.hollywoodreporter.com/tv/tv-news/heres-how-network-tv-depends-cop-shows-1299504/

Reppetto, T. A. (2018). The Black Dahlia Murder and Parker's police. In *American detective: Behind the scenes of famous criminal investigations* (pp. 184–199). Potomac Books.

Rumbelow, D. (2013). *The complete Jack the Ripper*. Revised & updated ed. Virgin Books.

Sereny, G. (1999). *Cries unheard: Why children kill: The story of Mary Bell*. Metropolitan Books.

Shewan, D. (2015, September 8; updated 2017, June 14). Conviction of things not seen: The uniquely American myth of satanic cults. *Pacific Standard Magazine*. https://psmag.com/social-justice/make-a-cross-with-your-fingers-its-the-satanic-panic

Shipley, S. L., & Arrigo, B. A. (2004). *The female homicide offender: Serial murder and the case of Aileen Wuornos*. Pearson Prentice Hall.

Teurfs, K. (2021). Freckle-faced killer Eric Smith, now 42, freed on parole, says he's engaged. *48 Hours, CBS News*. https://www.cbsnews.com/news/eric-smith-murderer-parole-derrick-robie/

Williams, M. E. (2019, July 7). Who's your daddy? The twisty history of paternity testing. *Salon*. https://www.salon.com/2019/07/07/whos-your-daddy-the-twisty-history-of-paternity-testing/

Printed in the USA
CPSIA information can be obtained
at www.ICGtesting.com
LVHW060525060923
757313LV00020B/84